JEALOUSY

Theory, Research, and Clinical Strategies

JEALOUSY

Theory, Research, and Clinical Strategies

GREGORY L. WHITE
University of California at Santa Cruz

PAUL E. MULLEN
University of Otago School of Medicine

Foreword by
Philip Shaver

THE GUILFORD PRESS
New York   London

© 1989 The Guilford Press
A Division of Guilford Publications, Inc.
72 Spring Street, New York, NY 10012

Printed in the United States of America

This book is printed on acid-free paper.

Last digit is print number: 9 8 7 6 5 4 3 2 1

Library of Congress Cataloging-in-Publication Data

White, Gregory L.
   Jealousy: theory, research, and clinical strategies / Gregory L.
White, Paul E. Mullen.
      p.   cm.
   Includes bibliographies and index.
   ISBN 0-89862-385-5
   1. Jealousy.   2. Love.   3. Psychotherapy.   I. Mullen, Paul E.
II. Title.
   [DNLM: 1. Affective Disorders.   2. Affective Symptoms.
3. Jealousy.   BF 575.J4 W584j]
BF575.J4W48   1989
152.4—dc20
DNLM/DLC
for Library of Congress   89-7534
                                                                    CIP

Foreword

Academic psychology has changed in recent decades. Twenty-five years ago, under the influence of behaviorism and Western individualism, psychology was characterized by the study of lone white rats (or solitary pigeons) poised in front of high-tech Skinnerian food dispensers or scurrying through avenues of artificial mazes. Psychologists unwittingly created visual metaphors of Western society's notion of happiness: physically healthy, carefree individuals, working hard (and all alone) in a clean, temperature-controlled environment, having access to food—or, even better, direct stimulation of the brain's pleasure centers. (The mazes were somewhat reminiscent of big city streets and sidewalks, along which gray-clad organization men rushed to clutch the levers of capitalism.) In recent years psychologists have become more interested in human beings—interdependent creatures with complex ideas and goals, strong feelings, and deep attachments to lovers, friends, and family.

Between these swings of the intellectual pendulum, Western societies, perhaps especially the United States, experimented with an extreme form of individualism in which people "did their own thing," moved freely from place to place, changed partners and friends, abandoned children (at least emotionally), and tried to suppress feelings of attachment, guilt, and jealousy. (Odd as it seems, every form of attachment, except to oneself, was considered passé.)

Now, along comes this scholarly book—a thoughtful, provocative, and gracefully written work—dealing with one of Western society's temporarily denigrated feelings: *jealousy*. Far from being expunged, jealousy—along with love, loneliness, caring, and sympathy—is as prevalent and insistent as ever. It still shocks and frightens us with pangs of need, vulnerability, and dependence; still motivates constructive communication about wishes, boundaries, and rights; still shows us, often in instructive ways, how capable we are of love, panic, and rage. Unfortunately, jealousy also leads, in too many instances, to wrenching anguish, paranoiac fantasies, desperately hostile tirades, and acts of violence (including murder). This happens when jealousy grows too intense, mingles with psychopathology, touches on nerves rubbed raw in childhood or past relationships, or overpowers previously adequate but never maximally stress-tested coping techniques. We can acknowledge jealousy, rather than suppress it, yet still seek help in understanding and controlling it.

The study of jealousy is part of contemporary psychology's fascination with human emotions and close relationships. To Greg White and Paul Mullen's credit, they have distilled the best theoretical and empirical work on jealousy and organized it into a framework composed of two influential theories: Lazarus's cognitive theory of emotion, stress, and coping; and Kelley's interdependence theory of close relationships. Lazarus's theory is typical (because it is the prototype) of contemporary appraisal theories of emotion. Kelley's theory, developed in conjunction with other premier emotion and close relationship researchers, influences all contemporary studies of relationship formation, maintenance, and dissolution. Placing jealousy within these conceptual frames makes it sensible, points to new research possibilities, and assists the development of the emotions-and-relationships field.

The clinical sections of the book are equally impressive: deep without being obscure, remarkably thorough in historical scholarship, forward-looking, and supremely useful. It's no exaggeration to say that *Jealousy* is a landmark work, one that transcends disciplinary and theoretical boundaries. All future investigators of the topic will gladly consult this book, and find no need to go beyond it for an accurate portrayal of the previous literature.

I, like the many other clinicians and researchers who will read this book, am in debt to White and Mullen. It is a pleasure to be working, not alone in a mindless, sterile box, but in a cooperative, vibrant field in which the fruits of others' intellectual labor can be so richly shared.

Philip Shaver
State University of New York at Buffalo

Preface

We hope that this book provides a comprehensive and integrative approach to the understanding and treatment of romantic jealousy. We have drawn from both our academic perspectives and clinical experiences to provide researchers, clinicians, students, and the sophisticated lay audience with material that is useful for both practical and theoretical concerns.

Although personal, theoretical, and pragmatic considerations may encourage the individual reader to understand jealousy better, we think that there are more systemic forces that generate contemporary interest in jealousy. Social and economic changes commencing with the industrial revolution have had, and continue to have, profound impacts on the nature of romantic relationships and marriage in societies around the world. Especially in the West, the problems of the nuclear family are held accountable for all manner of breakdown in the ability of society to provide stability and socialization for its young. At the same time, the great majority of Westerners continue to embrace the romantic ideal of an idealized, happy couple whose relationship is unique and self-sustaining. Attempts to define alternatives to traditional marriage are no less affected by the historical changes in social and economic conditions and by mythologies of idealized and fulfilling intimate relationships.

Romantic jealousy is a phenomenon deeply involved in both the ongoing restructuring of the modern family and in the mythology of romantic love. Jealousy appears to be a concern for so many contemporary relationships because social change and romantic myth have combined to greatly restrict interdependence and self-definition to the romantic/marital relationship. The partners of the nuclear couple need each other to a very great extent, both in the economic sense of helping each other through mundane existence and in the existential sense of providing a definition of self that has meaning beyond the mundane. The extended family is gone, and stable friendship networks are threatened by mobility and the necessities of work. Intimacy and lasting interdependence with workmates is often severely constrained by organizational structures, customs, and roles. And, aside from mythologies of the patriarchy, by and large organized religion provides no more answer to the problems of the romantic and marital relationship than do the numerous utopian groups of our age.

As we illustrate in this book, jealousy can be thought of as a reaction to threats to the interdependencies and self-definitions that generate and are generated by the nuclear romantic relationship. If, as we believe, we live in an era in which the nuclear relationship is a primary arena for interdependence and self-definition, then jealousy and its resolution would be particularly problematic in our time; and so it appears to be. Various writers and artists have portrayed the problem of jealousy from a number of perspectives.

We have attempted to review theory and research from the perspectives of four systems: the biological, the personal, the interpersonal, and the cultural. We have taken the tack of developing a general model and then using it as an aid in reviewing the literature on jealousy related to the four systems. We hope that our attempts to integrate diverse literatures will aid the reader who is attempting to understand the multi-system unity of jealous phenomena.

Acknowledgments

We would like to thank the many colleagues who have helped us shape and refine our thinking about jealousy over the years. Our thanks to John Werry of the University of Auckland School of Medicine for bringing us together. For G. W., Harold Kelley and Barry Collins provided intellectual and moral support early on. Other helpful and encouraging colleagues from academic and clinical settings have included Sally Armentrout, Art Aron, Elaine Aron, Eliot Aronson, Robert Bringle, Robert Brown, Bram Buunk, Gordon Clanton, Susan Czajkowski, Judith Dubignon, India Fleming, Faith Fuller, Harold Gerard, Steve Gordon, Alan Gross, Ralph Hupka, David Less, Jay Mann, Christina Maslach, James Miller, Ron Miller, Judson Mills, Lou Moffett, Barbara Mullens-Moorman, Margaret O'Brien, Lauren Oliver, Michael Passer, Letitia Ann Peplau, Ayala Pines, John Raeburn, Karen Rook, Abdul Aziz Said, Peter Salovey, Judith Schwartz, Harold Sigall, Julian Silverman, Valerie Simmons, M. Brewster Smith, Kenwyn Smith, Sheldon Starr, Robert Tannenbaum, Terri Thames, Ralph Turner, and Leroy Wells.

We would like to acknowledge our debt to our clients and patients over the years who have struggled with jealousy and who have enlisted our aid in that struggle. We hope that our work in some way will translate into the relief of psychological pain and the growth of individuals and relationships.

We are much indebted to Denise Reynolds and Mary-Anne Jensen who have assisted in typing and otherwise preparing the manuscript. Jean Park provided invaluable assistance with the references. Mr. Seymour Weingarten, Editor-in-Chief of Guilford, has been very helpful in bringing this book to completion and in tolerating our reticence to meet deadlines. We also appreciate the able assistance of our editor at Guilford Publications, Ms. Sarah Kennedy, in transforming the manuscript into book form. We also wish to express our gratitude for the comments of anonymous reviewers of earlier versions of our work.

Our wives, Therese Helbick, Ph.D., also a clinical psychologist, and Elizabeth Mullen have contributed their own constructive comments as well as emotional support for our efforts. Our children have in their own way contributed to our understanding of sibling jealousy, and we appreciate their tolerance of our project. Finally, we would like to thank each other for adapting to the style and viewpoints of the other and for staying with a project that initially spanned the country of New Zealand and wound up as an exercise in trans-Pacific communication.

Contents

1

Introduction

O, beware, my lord, of jealousy!
It is the green-ey'd monster, which doth mock
The meat it feeds on.
                    Shakespeare, *Othello*, act III, scene iii

He that is not jealous, is not in love.
                    St. Augustine, *Confessions*

. . . for love is as strong as death,
jealousy is cruel as the grave.
                    Song of Solomon 8:6

Jealousy is an old and recurring theme in human relationships. Dilemmas of jealousy are captured in myth, drama, comedy, biography, literature, dance, sculpture, and painting, as well as in the popular press and graffiti. These dilemmas are frequently acted out in everyday life as well as in therapy. In our own culture, it is clear that jealousy is a common and often painful experience. Jealousy also appears to be universal. Although cultures differ in the frequency and forms of their jealousy, there are no reports of jealousy-free societies.

In this book we concentrate on romantic jealousy. Romantic jealousy is neither an emotion nor merely a state of mind, still less a way of behaving. Rather, we believe it is more useful to think of jealousy as particular patterns of emotions, thoughts, and actions that emerge in particular social and psychological situations. These patterns may induce the label of jealousy and in turn may be affected by the act of adopting the label. Jealousy is not a thing, but a complex process that is both interpersonal and intrapersonal. This basic as-

1

sumption, we hope, not only yields better theory, but also promotes more flexible clinical approaches.

Despite (or perhaps because of) a rich history of commentary on jealousy, the empirical study of jealousy is in its infancy. Only in recent years have there been sustained attempts to study normal or pathological jealousy (Bringle & Buunk, 1985; Clanton, 1981; Mullen & Maack, 1985; White, 1981b; White & Helbick, 1988). We are still at the early stages of the expected debates concerning conceptualization, measurement, and causes of jealousy.

In addition to the conceptual and research challenge posed by jealousy, it is obvious that a good deal more is at stake than scientific curiosity. Jealous people kill others. As we discuss in more detail later, it has been estimated that up to 20% of all murders involve a jealous lover. One refuge for battered wives reported that about two-thirds of those at the shelter attributed their husbands' repeated assaults to excessive and unwarranted jealousy (Gayford, 1979). Another survey of 150 battered women found that most had jealous and sexually threatened husbands (Roy, 1977). Yet another reported that jealousy was the major reason for women's violence toward their romantic partners (Stets & Pirog-Good, 1987).

In a nationwide survey of marriage counselors, jealousy was cited as *the* or *a* major focus of counseling for about one-third of all client couples under 50 (White & Devine, in press). Another survey of 641 marriage guidance clients indicated that 15% presented with female jealousy and 15% presented with male jealousy as the problem for resolution (Krupinski, Marshall, & Yule, 1970). Surveys of college students reveal that about half have had at least one romantic relationship breakup over jealousy-related issues, and that about 10% of both men and women report jealousy as a recurring theme in their romantic relationships (White, 1988). A nationwide survey of readers of *Psychology Today* showed that romantic jealousy was a common and perplexing problem (Salovey & Rodin, 1985).

Against this background of scientific interest and human need, it is distressing to find that comparatively little research has been conducted on jealousy. For example, we can find no outcome studies on therapeutic treatments for jealousy, fewer than 10 research articles on sibling jealousy, and fewer than 60 research articles on normal romantic jealousy spanning several decades of research.

We can think of at least four reasons for this state of affairs. First, unlike many topics in social science, jealousy transparently seems a multisystem phenomenon involving personality, relationship, culture, and perhaps biology. This realization works against the development of simple formulations. Second, it is only rather recently that norms proscribing empirical, nonclinical research on topics related to romantic and sexual relationships have substantially weakened, both within the general public and within the scientific community. Third, jealousy may be so common and "explanations" for it may be widely shared among Westerners that it may seem that there is little to explain that isn't "obvious." If "everyone knows" what jealousy is, the focus may be on its clinical remediation rather than on underlying causation.

Finally, jealousy poses serious questions about psychological "normality" and "abnormality" that vex laypersons, clinicians, and researchers alike. Jealousy motivates normal people to think, feel, and behave in ways that seem quite out of character. Like love, jealousy may seem like temporary insanity; unlike love, jealousy is hardly enjoyable. Differentiating between "normal" and "pathological" jealousy makes for conceptual and research issues that plague similar attempts to differentiate between "normal" and "disordered" personalities (Millon, 1981).

SCOPE OF THE BOOK

We have several purposes in mind for this volume. First, we hope to present a conceptual model of jealousy that provides a framework for ordering past research. Second, we review literature from diverse sources and fields that contributes to our understanding of jealousy. Third, we hope to illuminate areas in which future basic and clinical research is needed. Fourth, we hope to provide clinicians with material that will allow them to improve treatment of those who are jealous, including those who are "pathologically" jealous. Finally, we hope to contribute to the broader understanding of romantic relationships and of "abnormal" psychological states.

As may be apparent from these purposes, we have written the book to be helpful to students, clinicians, and researchers alike. We assume that most readers will have some background in theory from social/personality psychology, clinical psychology, or psychiatry. We try to be as explicit as possible about material taken from various literatures, avoiding jargon where possible and adapting (or bending) the language of other authors into our theoretical model.

At the outset, we would like to draw attention to the relatively sparse research base on romantic jealousy, whether normal or pathological. Where possible, we draw on research to buttress our model of jealousy. As is typical of a developing field, much of this research is not published, but has been reported at conventions and conferences and has been shared among other researchers, and is (we hope) winding its way through the journal production mills. This raises problems of how much we should describe unpublished research and how much confidence we should put in it. We generally try to describe unpublished research in a bit more detail, but give more weight to published research. Some jealousy data are reported as incidental findings in research focused on other topics. Often, we draw on clinical experience or case history literatures to provide suggestive evidence.

The plan of the book is as follows. In Chapter 2 we present our formal definition of jealousy and outline a process-oriented model of causes and consequences of it. This model is embedded within the cognitive–transactional theory of stress and coping developed by Richard Lazarus and his colleagues (Lazarus & Folkman, 1984). We also adopt a metatheoretical model about how to conceptualize aspects of close relationships (Kelley et al., 1983). Our model of romantic jealousy provides a structure for subsequent reviews of previous literatures. That is, we try to be explicit in how we think the existing literature is related to elements of our model, and we try to suggest areas for future research, based on our reading of gaps between the existing literature and our model.

The next four chapters are reviews of and commentaries on four different literatures. Each is concerned with a different level of analysis from the others. Chapter 3 presents and critiques the sociobiological approach to jealousy. Chapter 4 discusses personality approaches to jealousy, with a primary focus on psychodynamic formulations, sibling rivalry, and trait research outcomes. Chapter 5 surveys the ways in which relationship characteristics and dynamics may contribute to jealousy, and it reviews gender differences concerning different aspects of jealousy. Chapter 6 covers cultural and social factors affecting jealousy. We also discuss important conceptual issues that we think are useful, not only for those interested in the cultural level of analysis, but also for therapists who seek to recognize the impact of culture on clinical presentation and treatment.

In the final three chapters, we move from a research focus to a more directly clinical concern. Chapter 7 discusses differential diagnoses of pathological jealousy, with special attention to the frequent observation that psychologically healthy individuals may behave in quite abnormal ways when jealous. We try to tease out differences between pathological states that may be manifested as unreasonable jealousy and pathological states that may result from the twists and turns of normal jealousy. Both are differentiated from jealousy that is symptomatic of grosser disorders such as dementia. Chapter 8 is concerned with violence, a not infrequent outcome of both pathological and normal jealousy. Chapter 9 surveys the literature on treatment for normal and pathological jealousy, and concludes with a set of recommendations for the therapist who works with jealous people or jealous relationships. Although we believe that this chapter stands on its own and will benefit therapists by itself, we hope that the other chapters will provide those who treat jealous persons with a set of concepts and findings that will increase their therapeutic effectiveness.

We also present a methodological appendix for the benefit of those interested in the content and technical details of jealousy measures discussed throughout the book.

PROBLEMS IN CONCEPTUALIZING JEALOUSY

Before we turn our attention to our particular model in Chapter 2, we would like to draw attention to some preliminary concerns with conceptualizing and defining jealousy. These concerns are partly epistemological and partly related to a desire to make clear at the outset the assumptions that underlie our treatment of jealousy.

As we have said, our focus is on the jealousy that can occur in romantic and sexual relationships. We acknowledge that people can believe themselves to be in romantic relationships without behaving sexually, and that people who have sex together may not be romantically involved. For purposes of discussion, however, we use the term "romantic relationship" in the broad sense of suggesting either romantic or sexual feelings and behaviors.

Jealousy and envy are sometimes confused in research and theory, because the word "jealous" can be used to connote envy, as in "He is jealous of Tom's new car" (Smith, Kim, & Parrott, 1988). We scrupulously reserve the word "envy" for such situations. Although we do discuss envy as an emotion that may be found among the jealous, we prefer not to dwell, as others have, on definitional battles distinguishing the two (Salovey & Rodin, 1984, 1986; Smith et al., 1988; Spielman, 1971). This is in line with our general assumption that jealousy cannot be rigidly defined in any of its particulars.

Definition and Reification

Reification is a serious problem in scientific research, particularly at present in the social sciences (Gergen & Davis, 1985; Gould, 1981;

Quine, 1960; Watzlawick, Beavin, & Jackson, 1967; Wittgenstein, 1963). To mistake a useful concept for material reality can lead to errors in conceptualization, measurement, and utilization of knowledge. To avoid this problem, we use the term "jealousy" as a concept referring to patterns of events, not to the events themselves. As will be elaborated later, we do not define jealousy as an emotion, thought, or behavior. We hope in doing so to avoid fruitless debates about what *the* structure of jealousy is. For example, is it a simple or complex emotion (cf. Hupka, 1984)? If it is a complex emotion, what are its invariant component emotions? Or is jealousy a desire to act in a certain way (e.g., to exact revenge), or perhaps a cluster of invariant behaviors that occur when a person is jealous?

Related to the problem of reification is the problem of localization of the phenomenon. For example, we would (ideally) not study poverty merely by studying poor people. Poverty can be observed in people, but it can also be observed in dwellings, archives, economic indicators, and attitudes that may be held by the nonpoor. Likewise, we may say that a person is jealous without necessarily localizing jealousy within the person. We could say, "She is demonstrating feelings, thoughts, and behaviors that within her experience, romantic relationship, and culture would be labeled by herself or others as jealousy." For convenience, however, we say, "She is jealous." But if we forget the convenience and localize jealousy within the person, we may lose the richer understanding of the ways in which the person, situation, relationship, and culture combine to produce jealousy.

One common solution to this problem is to ascribe thing-like properties to the concept so that measurement can proceed, and then to explore patterns of correlates of the product of measurement (item, scale, fact, etc.). For example, jealousy may be defined as a cluster of four emotions (say, anger, grief, envy, and surprise). A scale assessing these can be constructed and a total score developed to indicate the extent of "jealousy." Then, based on theory or hunch, we measure other variables and see whether they correlate with our jealousy scale. Clearly, the resulting set of correlates depends very much on the definition and resulting measurement of jealousy. As we lose track of the original measurement, the danger increases of assuming that some *thing* called "jealousy" exists and is related to other things we have measured.

In this book, we attempt another solution to the problems of reification and localization. As described later in Chapter 2, we define jealousy as particular patterns of thoughts, feelings, and behaviors that can be observed when self-esteem and/or the romantic relationship is threatened in particular circumstances. There is no one pattern or set of circumstances that will invariably hold across different personal histories, relationship dynamics, or cultures. We propose, then, to define and study jealousy as a pattern, not as a thing with materialistic attributes.

Our *scientific* definition should not be confused with *naive* definitions or labels. As social scientists, we want to describe and predict patterns of reactions that *we* will label jealousy. Whether or not the average person labels the same patterns as jealousy or not is a separate issue. Ultimately, however, a complete theory of jealousy should be concerned with the phenomenology of the meaning of "jealousy" as a label culturally appropriate to describe certain events.

Hupka (1981) comes close to our position when he states that jealousy as a term identifies the "particular situation or predicament in which the jealous individual finds himself or herself" (p. 314), rather than any particular set of emotions. The *situation* labeled romantic jealousy, according to Hupka, "is a cognitive, psychological, and social phenomenon. It is a state of mind based on ideas of how individuals should act with respect to each other, on cultural norms and personal motives" (1981, p. 316). Hupka's position (and ours) reflects a social-phenomenological approach in which concepts such as romantic jealousy represent a class of internal processes. These processes include interpreting and constructing meaning in a situation. This construction of meaning contributes to the development of particular emotions and behaviors (Averill, 1982; Garfinkel & Sacks, 1970; Gergen & Davis, 1985).

The Role of Theory in Definition

We accept the argument that one's theoretical or metatheoretical perspective strongly affects the development of definitions of concepts or phenomena that the theory is trying to explain. The most extreme and classic example of this is radical behaviorism (Skinner, 1938), which denied the existence of internal processes such as cognition and hence could only account for their existence in behavioral terms. Another classic example is the definition of "defense mechanism" as a method to reduce anxiety resulting from unconscious conflicts. The term "defense" is predicated on the theoretical supposition of an internal war.

Hence, it is sometimes difficult to separate definition from the causal theory underlying it. For example, to call jealousy a reaction to a threat to self-esteem implies that one accepts the causal reality of the self-concept. We see only two ways out of this difficulty. One is to remain as descriptive as possible, referring only to observable phenomena. We might define jealousy then as "verbalizations of feelings of disgust and anger with one's romantic partner." This is the route of radical behaviorism, which has led to a dead end (Bandura, 1976; Lazarus, 1977). The other possibility is to embrace the difficulty and to be explicit about our underlying theoretical positions from the start. We favor this tack, and do not adopt the pretense that we are offering a perspective on jealousy that is somehow free of our theoretical biases. However, we have attempted to come to grips with a variety of theoretical and research traditions in developing our model. We hope that this has kept us from the worst excesses of our own biases.

OTHER JEALOUSIES

There is very little research on other jealousies besides romantic jealousy. Most of the other work on jealousy is about sibling rivalry (Banks & Kahn, 1982; Dunn, 1983, 1984; Dunn & Kendrick, 1982; Griffin & De La Torre, 1983; Lamb & Sutton-Smith, 1982), and many of the sibling rivalry results are reported as secondary findings in a larger research project on sibling relationships in general. It is possible to think of a great many other situations that might also be called jealousy. These include jealousy of one friend when another attends to a new relationship; jealousy between parents and grandparents over the relationships they have with the children/grandchildren; professional jealousy among coworkers; father jealousy over breastfeeding (Waletzky, 1979); and so on.

Because of the lack of research and of space limitations, we do not present an explicit analysis of other jealousies in this book. However, we think that our general approach will be helpful in understanding and researching these other jealousies. As with romantic jealousy, we suppose that it will be useful to (1) conceptualize other jealousies as patterns of thoughts, feelings, and behaviors that (2) result when self-esteem or the relationship is threatened or lost because of (3) the perceived relationship (actual or potential) between the partner (parent, child, organization) and a rival (child, sibling, coworker). We hope that our model of romantic jealousy can be rather easily adapted to other jealousies in its general form and processes, though not in the content specific to romantic jealousy.

2

A Model of Romantic Jealousy

In this chapter we present our conceptual definition of romantic jealousy. We provide theoretical support for our approach and contrast it with previous concepts of jealousy. We then move on from our definition to a process-oriented model of jealousy. This model is in part guided by the metatheoretical analysis of close relationships of Kelley et al. (1983), which emphasizes the difference between descriptive and causal analyses of relationships. Our model also incorporates elements of Lazarus's influential cognitive–transactional theory of stress and coping (Lazarus & Folkman, 1984). We explicitly link concepts provided by Kelley et al. and Lazarus to our definition and model of jealousy.

We then use our model to review and critique previous jealousy research. In part, we do this to demonstrate how our model can be useful in suggesting whether previous research extends our knowledge of jealousy or confuses it. Throughout the book, we continue to use our model for the twin purposes of organization and analysis of previous research and theory.

A DEFINITION OF ROMANTIC JEALOUSY

Romantic jealousy is a complex of thoughts, emotions, and actions that follows loss of or threat to self-esteem and/or the existence or quality of the romantic relationship. The perceived loss or threat is generated by the perception of a real or potential romantic attraction between one's partner and a (perhaps imaginary) rival.

This definition has several important features:

1. Jealousy is a *complex* of thoughts, emotions, and actions. The term "complex" is used in a descriptive sense to refer to a whole made

9

up of interrelated parts; we do not mean "complex" in its psychodynamic sense (e.g., "mother complex," "Electra complex," etc.).

2. There are two psychological situations (internalized representations of the experienced world and the person's relation to it; see
Lewin, 1936; Murray, 1938; Sullivan, 1953) that trigger the complex.
These are the loss of or threat to self-esteem and loss of or threat to
the romantic relationship. Neither of these is held to be primary.
Different thoughts, emotions, and actions may make up the complex
if the loss or threat is primarily to self rather than if it is primarily to
the relationship. (In subsequent discussion, we use the term "threat"
to discuss triggers of the jealousy complex, but at all times the
possibility of loss in addition to threat is implied.)

3. These two psychological situations are themselves a result of
the perception of a real or potential rival relationship, which makes
the situations inherently social as well. Even if the rival is an illusion,
the jealous person acts as if a third person is involved. Hence the
jealousy complex is likely to be affected by the jealous person's
appraisal of the relationships among self, partner, and rival.

4. The perception of the rival relationship may be accurate, as
when a jilted lover is confronted with the beloved's actually starting
a new relationship, or it may be imaginary. The actions and feelings
of the jealous may appear quite rational or at least normative, given
the premise of an actual (or potential) rival, even if this premise is
quite irrational or unwarranted.

5. The perception of the potential for a rival relationship to
develop is included, as well as the perception of an actual, existing
rival relationship. This is important because jealousy is frequently
based on the anticipation of a rival relationship's forming.

6. The definition handles the problem of unrequited love in two
ways. In situations where no romantic relationship exists between
the jealous person and the loved one, the threat may be primarily to
self-esteem. Or the jealous person may imagine that a romantic
relationship actually exists, regardless of how unlikely this may seem
to an observer. Threat to this perceived relationship may then be
inferred from rivals.

7. A rival relationship may threaten or damage qualities of the
primary relationship without necessarily threatening or actually
ending the relationship. Trust may diminish; emotional support may
be disrupted; or there may be a loss of a sense of uniqueness or
specialness about the relationship (Constantine, 1986; Simmel,
1950). Emotions and attempts to cope may be quite peculiar to the
qualities that are perceived as threatened when the whole relationship is not at risk.

8. The term "romantic" (e.g., "romantic relationship") itself points to a variety of relationships that involve blends of different kinds of love (e.g., passionate love, companionate love) (Hendrick & Hendrick, 1983; Sternberg, 1986). The way in which jealousy develops and is played out may be radically affected by the blend that characterizes the particular relationship at hand.

Implications of Conceptualizing Jealousy as a Complex

We have said that jealousy is a complex of emotions, thoughts, and behaviors that follows two prototypical psychological situations. We assume that the complex is somewhat stable over time and hence can be characterized as a pattern. Of course, the jealous person may exhibit different patterns over time, or may alternate between or among different patterns. This possibility suggests that there is no one pattern of emotions, thoughts, and behaviors that *is* jealousy. Many jealousy complexes are possible.

Attending to the patterned aspect of jealous thoughts, behaviors, and emotions is important for three reasons: sensitivity to labeling processes; research efficacy; and understanding of self-maintaining systems aspects of the complex.

Pattern Labeling

Effects of Labeling Processes. There are discrepancies between jealous individuals and others, including social scientists and therapists, about which experiences should be labeled as jealousy. For example, people may label themselves as jealous if they get angry about the situation, but not if they are afraid or embarrassed (see Buunk, Bringle, & Arends, 1984). Their romantic partners may label them as jealous if they are angry, afraid, or depressed, but not if they are sexually aroused by the situation. Social scientists like ourselves construct theoretical definitions and then label as jealousy whatever conforms to those definitions.

It would be a mistake to confuse the actors' definitions with those of social scientists. Just because jealous people may label themselves as jealous only if they get angry, this does not mean that "jealousy" does not involve other emotions. Jealousy as a *social science construct* does involve emotions other than anger if a jealousy theory predicts them and research supports the theory.

For purposes of theory development and clinical intervention, it is useful to understand the processes that lead jealous individuals, their partners, and other involved observers to label some reactions

as "jealous." Labeling oneself as jealous is part of the jealousy complex, as labeling is a consequence of threat to self or the relationship.
The labeling process is particularly interesting, because it is likely
that how one reacts to jealousy-inducing situations affects how one
labels oneself, and that how one labels oneself affects subsequent
reactions (Berger & Luckmann, 1966; Bush, Bush, & Jennings, 1988;
Schutz, 1932/1967). This reciprocal influence of label and other
reactions is especially apparent when we consider the role of culture
in providing labels.

Pattern Labeling and Culture. Unless the pattern of emotions,
thoughts, and behaviors roughly conforms to cultural expectations
of what jealousy is, neither the person nor (nonscientific?) observers
will label the person as jealous. For example, consider the following
interaction: A male visitor to a friend's home asks whether he may
sleep with his friend's wife that night. The husband smiles, feels
happy, and eagerly agrees to the arrangement. In fact, he goes out of
his way to afford his friend and wife privacy by putting out the lamp.
In the morning he is genuinely pleased to hear that his friend and
wife got along so well.

From our Western perspective, we might assume that the husband is really jealous and then search for the hidden causes of why he
acts as he does. This is because the pattern of his emotions, thoughts,
and actions does not fit our pattern for jealousy, even though the situation is so transparently a situation that should induce jealousy (we
think). However, within the husband's own culture of the Ammassalik
Eskimo, the situation poses no threat to self-esteem or relationship
(and may actually enhance his communal esteem). But if the husband
were to find his wife and friend copulating without the lamp ritual, it
would not be unusual for him to kill the friend (Mirsky, 1937b).

The point is that the pattern of the husband's behavior is not
consistent with our own cultural expectations of what a jealous person
may be thinking, feeling, and doing. We must assume either that he is
massively denying or lying, or that he is not in fact jealous. It is
because the match between expected patterns and actual patterned
responses is likely to be crucial in labeling oneself or others as jealous
that we emphasize the patterned nature of the jealousy complex.

Above, we have suggested that labels and other reactions are
reciprocally linked. At the cultural level, normative patterns are
likely to be internalized and to serve as scripts shaping the particular
reactions once threat or loss from a rival relationship is perceived
(Berger & Luckmann, 1966; Boucher, 1979; Schank & Abelson, 1977;
Walster & Walster, 1977). It is likely that one aspect of such scripts
consists of stereotypes about what a jealous person does when first

threatened (e.g., he or she gets angry, but not depressed). Hence, normative expectations about how the jealous should feel, think, and behave influence not only the labeling of the jealous, but to some extent the form of the jealousy complex.

A major criticism we have of previous jealousy research, especially studies in which factor analysis is used to "identify" underlying dimensions of jealousy, is that researchers have relied upon their own cultural definitions of jealousy to write items assessing jealous thoughts, feelings, and behaviors (White, 1984). An analogous process can occur in clinical settings when therapists assume that their own subcultural definition of a jealous pattern applies to their clients. In both cases, the discrepancy between observers (researchers, therapists) and observed (subjects, patients) in the assumed pattern of jealousy may be more informative of cultural differences than of individual personality dynamics of the observed.

Promoting Empirical Advance

A second reason for conceptualizing the jealousy complex as a patterned reaction is for the purpose of scientific investigation. We are interested in explaining consistencies, in phenomena that exhibit regularity, or in pattern. One way of thinking of scientific advance is through competition among theories that attempt to show a pattern to phenomena that seem irregular or "random" or inexplicable from the point of view of less complete theories (Popper, 1965, pp. 240–244). By starting with the assumption of pattern among emotions, thoughts, and behavior, we hope to promote theory development that at its outset is more comprehensive than the development of theories dealing with just jealous behavior or just jealous feeling or just jealous thought. It is more useful to link hypothetical causal factors to identified patterns than to proceed piecemeal by linking causes to isolated elements of patterns. Conceptualizing patterns as the dependent variable may inhibit overtheorizing about the ways in which the behaviors, thoughts, and feelings of the jealous are related.

It should be possible to identify different patterns of emotions, thoughts, and behaviors, and then eventually to explain the factors that lead to the development, maintenance, and decay of such patterns. For example, when studying large samples of jealous people, we may find that thoughts about personal inferiority, feelings of sadness and despair, and demands on the beloved for commitment are intercorrelated. Another cluster of reactions may consist of thoughts of revenge and comparison to the rival, feelings of anger and rage, and behaviors intended to damage the rival relationship.

These two clusters or patterns are among many that may be found. Researchers of causes of these clusters or patterns may eventually discover that the first pattern becomes predominant through the joint action of high dependence on the partner, an attitude that true love is rare, and a relative lack of interpersonal skills. The second pattern may be more likely when there is a rigid sex-role orientation, relatively less dependence on the relationship than the partner has, and high satisfaction with the primary relationship.

Although these patterns and their causes are speculative, the point is that by assessing patterns as well as their elements, we may achieve a richer and more coherent theoretical understanding of jealousy.

System Properties of Jealousy Complexes

A jealousy complex can evolve its own self-sustaining dynamic, much as systems are said to sustain themselves (up to a point) in spite of changes in the surrounding causal context. For example, the body maintains a rather narrow range of chemical composition of the blood, in spite of great fluctuations in diet, drug ingestion, and ambient temperature (Miller, 1978). Organizational structures may remain relatively constant, even though the personalities operating in them change (Katz & Kahn, 1978).

If research is directed at finding patterns of reactions, then it becomes easier to identify sets of jealous reactions that remain relatively stable, even though their original causal context changes. Pattern stability in the face of such change is evidence for self-sustaining systems (Hoffman, 1981; Kuhn, 1974; Miller, 1978).

As a jealousy example, consider the relationships among the thought that one is inferior to a romantic rival, feelings of depression, and coping strategies of denial alternating with demands for commitment from the beloved. This particular jealousy complex may maintain itself in the following way: The perception of inferiority may increase depression as the jealous person anticipates the loss of the relationship. Subsequent demands for commitment by the depressed partner may be vague, inept, or half-hearted, leading to rejection or ambivalence from the beloved. This is coped with by denial or downgrading of the extent to which the relationship is threatened. This denial inhibits changing aspects of the self or the relationship thought to be unsatisfactory to the beloved. Future information suggesting that a rival relationship is deepening may then be (realistically?) attributed to a rival's superior qualities. This attribution stabilizes or deepens depression, at which point the cycle repeats itself.

This example is speculative, in large part because research jealousy has neglected identifying patterns of responses to threat or loss. However, our assumption that patterns of jealous thoughts, emotions, and behavior may have self-sustaining properties leads us to adopt a systems point of view in thinking about jealousy.

Some Applications of Systems Thinking

There is a paradox in our approach so far. Our definition focuses on patterns of thoughts, emotions, and actions exhibited by the jealous person, but we have maintained that by focusing on the person we may overlook the fact that he or she is embedded within relationships and a culture. We cope with this problem by adopting a systems theory point of view. Emotions, actions, and thoughts are components of a system called the person (not to be confused with a parallel system called the body). The person is a subsystem of more complex systems of relationships among persons, including the romantic relationship and the jealousy triangle. Relationships themselves are subsystems of even more complex orderings, which may include family, work, friendship networks, and so forth up to culture (Bertalanffy, 1968; Kuhn, 1974; Miller, 1978).

One useful idea from systems theory is that any system simultaneously exhibits stability (homeostasis) and change (morphogenesis). Sources of stability or change can come from within the system itself or from other systems. For example, the relatively stable pattern of relationships among thoughts, feelings, and behaviors that we call the personality (a system) may be stable because socially significant others reward stability and punish change, or because there is some internal drive toward consistency of personality elements. Personality can change when there is a change in a higher-order system (the person gets married and leaves home); when there is a change in a lower-order system (the emotional subsystem is dysfunctional as a result of physical illness that affects the sympathetic nervous system); or as the person matures from the relatively simple patterns of the young child to the complex relationships among aspects of the adult personality.

An important thesis of the systems view is that of interacting systems. Higher-order systems (e.g., the primary relationship) both affect and are affected by lower-order systems (e.g., the person). This reciprocal influence is achieved in part by systems' providing each other with information that change in the system is undesirable (negative feedback loops maintaining stability) or desirable (positive feedback loops promoting change).

A second implication is that the effects of systems are achieved both directly and symbolically. A direct effect of the rival relationship may be to reduce the amount of time spent with the beloved; the symbolic meaning may be that the jealous person is devalued. Further, persons within systems develop ways of interpreting the world through adoption of interpretive constructs that are themselves aspects of those systems. We agree that persons actively construct their world, but note that in the construction of social reality the constructs and meaning dimensions used to do so are themselves products of social structures and of socialization into larger systems (e.g., family, school, culture) (Berger & Luckmann, 1966; D'Andrade, 1984; Gergen & Davis, 1985; Kuhn, 1974; Schutz, 1932/1967). For example, romantic couples may negotiate and adopt meanings about the exclusivity of sexual behavior. These meanings, partly derived from their relationship (system) dynamics, then are used to interpret the degree of threat posed by a future relationship between the beloved and a rival.

Hence, the pattern we call the jealousy complex may be influenced by relatively stable causes that themselves may be aspects of other systems (e.g., the personality, the romantic relationship, culture). The complex itself may also exhibit system-like properties, becoming self-sustaining even if the outside causal conditions change. Finally, the complex may affect higher- and lower-order systems (e.g., the romantic relationship, the emotional subsystem).

Figure 2.1 diagrams a set of relationships among different levels of systems. In this book, we use the term "jealousy complex" to refer to the patterned relationships among thoughts, emotions, and actions exhibited by the person labeled as jealous. We use the term "interpersonal jealousy system" to refer to the system of relationships among the three main actors. Within this triad, there can be three dyadic relationships as well as the triadic relationship. The dyadic relationships we call the "jealous or primary relationship" (jealous and beloved), the "rival or secondary relationship" (beloved and rival), and the "adverse relationship" (jealous and rival). The triadic relationship is called the "romantic triangle." All four relationships are implied when we discuss the interpersonal jealousy system.

Each person in the romantic triangle exists within the context of his or her "support system," or the set of interpersonal relationships with significant others that may have direct or indirect influences upon the interpersonal jealousy system and the jealousy complex. Finally, the larger system of meanings, values, and normative expectations that we call "culture" has its impact upon the other systems within its boundaries.

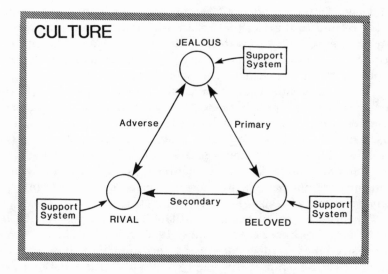

FIGURE 2.1. A schematic diagram of the interpersonal jealousy system embedded within support systems and culture.

THEORETICAL BASES OF OUR DEFINITION

Our definition of jealousy posits that threat to self-esteem and threat to the relationship are the twin psychological situations precipitating the jealousy complex. A variety of theoretical positions support such a stand. At the heart of most of these positions is the question of what it is that is valued about romantic relationships. Most research and theory resolves this question into two broad constructs. The first is the provision of satisfying experiences or resources; the second is the provision of meaning, especially the provision of meaning concerning the nature of and worth of the self. Further, provision of satisfying experience and meaning is restricted in certain ways to romantic relationships; that is, some experiences and meanings are most readily available within the context of a romantic relationship (Knudson, 1985; Levenson & Harris, 1980; Turner, 1970). These restrictions ensure that threats to the development or continuation of satisfying experiences and meanings are especially problematic in romantic relationships.

Provision of Satisfying Experiences

The study of human relationships has yielded two dominating dimensions of interrelationship. The first is variously labeled "power," "dependence," "interdependence," "dominance–submission," and so forth, and is related to the fact that relationships are valued for providing satisfying experiences (rewards, gratifications, need fulfillment, etc.). Acquiring rewards at sustainable costs involves affecting the behavior of others; hence the element of power and interdependence.

The second dimension is variously labeled "love–hate," "attraction," "intimacy," "positivity–negativity," and so on, and refers to affective aspects of relationships (Benjamin, 1974; Carson, 1969; Foa, 1961; Kemper, 1978; Leary, 1957; Schaefer, 1971). Together, these two dominating dimensions are useful in characterizing differences among a wide variety of relationships. (These underlying dimensions are not necessarily those perceived by actors in interpersonal relations; cf. Wish, Deutsch, & Kaplan, 1976.)

Theories of social exchange (Blau, 1964; Burgess & Huston, 1979; Gergen, Greenberg, & Willis, 1980; Kelley et al., 1983) have emphasized the interdependence of actors in relationships, including romantic relationships. Dependence on another for satisfying experiences and desired resources can be symmetrical or asymmetrical. Dependence can refer not only to the experiences provided by the partner, but also to those rewards that result from joint interaction. For example, a person may value his or her partner's humor (for which the person does nothing), as well as their sexual life (which depends on their interaction).

A range of rewards and resources, either conferred by the partner or resulting from interaction, are possible in romantic relationships. Some, like sex, are usually constrained to such relationships; others, like friendship, may be more widely available in other relationships. The nature of the rewards obtained in the relationship is probably idiosyncratic to the needs, values, skills, and resources of each partner, in addition to reflecting emergent properties of close relationships. For example, a person may initially value the partner's physical attractiveness, but may also come to value the ease of communication that may develop over the years.

Perceived threat to the continued development, availability, or quality of these rewards may serve to enhance their subjective value. This could be explained as the operation of supply and demand (Foa & Foa, 1980; White, 1980b), an outcome of arousal of psychological reactance (Brehm, 1972), or the operation of instinctual or learned motives of competition and rivalry (Daly, Wilson, & Weghorst, 1982; McClintock, 1972). For our purposes, it is sufficient to note that there is likely to be a reciprocal relationship between the value of a satisfying experience or resource and the degree of concern about its possible loss, disruption, or reduction.

Intimacy, Attraction, and the Provision of Meaning

The second commonly found dimension of interpersonal relations is that of attraction or liking. This is more than just a simple dimension of approach–avoidance; we assume that it carries a variety of associated meanings. That is, in addition to the resources and experiences that may be available in close relationships, these relationships also provide opportunities to negotiate and abstract meaning about the self (Carson, 1969; Ellis & Weinstein, 1986; Knudson, 1985; Reis, 1985). Other categories of abstracted meaning are also possible (e.g., ideas about men or women, about the nature of love, etc.), but meanings related to the self are assumed to have considerable influence on the course of both individual and relationship development, and particularly on jealousy.

Two aspects of the self are potentially relevant in this process of abstracting meaning from the relationship. The first is "self-esteem," or the degree to which the self, or certain aspects of the self, are valued or derogated. The second is "self-concept," "identity," "self-definition," or "self-schema"—terms that refer to the organized content of knowledge about the self (Coopersmith, 1967; Ellis & Weinstein, 1986; Kuiper & Derry, 1981; Loevinger, 1976; Markus, 1977; Reis, 1985; Rosenberg, 1979; Wylie, 1974). These two are conceptually distinct, as it is possible to have different value orientations toward aspects of self-concept (McGuire, 1984; Scheier & Carver, 1980). A person may know that he or she is a terrible piano player, but such knowledge is only likely to affect self-esteem if the person wishes to become a professional musician.

The degree of attraction in a relationship is related both to enhancement of self-esteem and to affirmation of self-concept. Attraction generally increases if the partner conveys approval or appreciation of some aspect of self. Attraction also generally increases if the partner confirms one's knowledge about oneself (Berscheid & Walster, 1978; Knudson, 1985; Lewicki, in press; Livingstone, 1980; McCall, 1974; Reis, 1985; Rosenberg, 1979; Tesser & Campbell, 1982).

Theoretically, a threat to self-esteem occurs when a person is at risk of valuing aspects of the self less than previously. For example, a lover's comment that the sexual relationship needs improving may threaten the person's current evaluation of the sexual aspect of self. A threat to self-concept is different; the implication is that self-knowledge is incomplete or inaccurate (cf. Harrison, 1977; Holdstock & Rogers, 1983; Luft, 1969; McGuire, 1984; Rosenberg, 1979). For example, the partner may suggest that the person is very defensive about sexual performance. Such information may or may not also threaten self-esteem, depending on the values of the person and on attributions made for the partner's comments.

A threat to self-concept may be in itself aversive, as it increases uncertainty about one's future behavior, including interpersonal behavior (Lewicki, in press; Livingstone, 1980; Markus, Smith, & Moreland, 1985; Orvis, Kelley, & Butler, 1976; Reis, 1985). In addition, we note that people may change their self-concept in the service of protecting or enhancing their self-esteem (Tesser & Campbell, 1982; Tesser & Paulus, 1983).

Information should be most threatening when it challenges both evaluation of and knowledge about self. In our definition of romantic jealousy, threat to or loss of self-esteem implicitly refers to related threats or damage done to the self-concept. We do not assume, however, that threats to self-esteem are always functionally equivalent to threats to the self-concept.

Because of the intimacy of romantic relationships, information obtained or inferred about oneself from one's partner is more likely than information from any other sources to pose a strong threat to self-esteem or self-concept. Romantic partners typically have greater access to information about the self than do other people, especially in areas related to sexual and conflict behaviors (Altman & Taylor, 1973; Backman, 1981; D'Augelli & D'Augelli, 1979; Orvis et al., 1978; Swensen, 1972; Turner, 1970). Hence, their judgments about aspects of self are also likely to have greater informational value. It is not surprising that self-esteem is more vulnerable in romantic relationships, particularly when issues relating to commitment to a relationship are unsettled or when comparison to relevant others (rivals) is likely (Backman, 1981; Braiker & Kelley, 1979; Graziano & Musser, 1982; Kelley, 1983; Knudson, 1985; Reis, 1985; Tesser & Campbell, 1982).

The most threatening information that can be obtained or inferred is that one's partner is romantically attracted to another person, perhaps to a greater extent than to oneself. This information is threatening because it may signal the partner's devaluation of central aspects of self, may imply or reveal inaccuracies in self-concept, and may signal loss or reduction of valued experiences and resources.

Unlike other sources of threat to the relationship, the knowledge or suspicion that one's partner is or may be attracted to another clearly signals the existence of a relevant standard of comparison. The real or potential existence of a rival provides a unique measure against which the jealous person may assess his or her worth. The rival stands as a measure of comparison on those dimensions around which the partners have negotiated the meaning of self-in-the-relationship. Hence, the internal, negotiated reality of the dyad becomes to some extent public and open to renegotiation and disconfirmation. Negotiated self-worth is suddenly faced with a non-negotiated reality: the character and resources of the rival. This forced social comparison is inherently threatening to self-esteem and self-concept (Brickman & Bulman, 1977; Buunk et al., 1984; Harrison, 1977; Ellis & Weinstein, 1986; Tesser & Paulus, 1983; Turner, 1970).

In addition to self-esteem and self-concept, in certain situations the existence of romantic rivals will involve loss of social or communal esteem. The cuckolded husband, for example, may fear the ridicule of others in the community. Because issues of social esteem invariably involve reactions of the larger community (e.g., support systems, institutional representatives), we delay until Chapter 6 our consideration of how issues of social esteem are related to jealousy.

PREVIOUS DEFINITIONS OF ROMANTIC JEALOUSY

A number of definitions of jealousy have been proposed by authors from a variety of academic and clinical disciplines. Often these definitions provide both cause and description, as in this example: "an aversive emotional reaction that occurs as the result of a partner's extradyadic relationship" (Bringle & Buunk, 1985, p. 242). Definitions differ in the extent to which they feature affective, cognitive, behavioral, or situational features of jealousy. They also differ in assumed causes of jealousy. Four causal themes occur repeatedly; jealousy as a reaction to threat to self-esteem; jealousy as a reaction to threat to the romantic relationship; jealousy as a result of possessiveness, exclusivity, and rivalry; and jealousy as a result of the triggering of instinct (cf. Buunk & Bringle, 1987).

We discuss several previous definitions below in order to provide a historical context of our definition and to illustrate limitations in previous approaches that we think our model minimizes.

Definitions Emphasizing Threat to Self-Esteem

Many observers have commented on the threat to self-esteem, or the "narcissistic wound" inherent in jealousy. La Rochefoucauld (1665, quoted in Jones, 1937, p. 268) wrote, "There is more self-love than love in jealousy." Freud (1922/1955) defined jealousy primarily as a normal affective state that

ompounded of grief, the pain caused by the thought of
' loved object, and of the narcissistic wound, in so far as
distinguishable from the other wound [of loss of relation-
..up]; further, of feelings of enmity against the successful rival,
and of a greater or lesser amount of self-criticism which tries to
hold the person himself accountable for his loss. (p. 232)

Margaret Mead (1931) argued that threat to self-esteem is the
defining characteristic of jealousy. Jealousy "is a negative, miserable
state of feeling, having its origin in a sense of insecurity and inferiority" which "merely records the degree of the lover's insecurity"
(p. 41). Based on a review of the available anthropological evidence
of the time, Mead (1931) held that a threat to the relationship and
attending desires for possessiveness merely reflect the degree to
which the self was identified with the form of the relationship:
"However varied the social setting, it will be seen to be the threatened self-esteem, the threatened ego which reacts jealously" (p. 38).

Our last example is from Farber (1973), who noted a crucial
distinction between jealousy and other human "weaknesses" such as
lying, malice, and conceit. These other flaws can be more easily
dissociated from the self, whereas being jealous is a direct threat to
self-esteem: "[A] comforting contrast between himself and his
jealousy is beyond the reach of the jealous person for, subjectively at
least, he *is* his malady: to describe his jealousy is to illuminate his
reduction as a human being" (p. 182).

We have several concerns about definitions emphasizing self-
esteem. Most obvious is the failure to distinguish conceptually between threat to self-esteem and threat to the relationship. These
definitions also do not differentiate threat to self-concept from
threat to self-esteem. The psychodynamic definitions do not clearly
distinguish threat to self-esteem, which can be experienced by the
psychologically mature, from pathologies of narcissism. Such definitions, we think, overemphasize the causal role of intrapsychic, dynamic processes. At the very least, it is unclear whether low self-
esteem is a cause or consequence of jealousy.

Most of the definitions emphasizing self-esteem as a cause define jealousy as an emotion or blend of emotions. This implies that
emotion mediates the relationship between threat to self-esteem and
behavior. This assumption is overly restrictive and is at odds with
the contrary view that cognition precedes emotion (Lazarus & Folkman, 1984; Mandler, 1984). It also leads naturally to concern with
discovering the particular blend that *is* jealousy. This search reflects
reification and not the phenomena. Jealousy is a label given to pat-

terns; different blends of emotions result from the complexity of causal forces involved in generating the patterns.

Definitions Emphasizing Threat to the Relationship

Fear of loss is a widely noted aspect of jealousy within the range of previous definitions (Buunk & Bringle, 1987). Descartes wrote that "Jealousy is a kind of fear related to the desire we have of keeping some possession" (quoted in Davis, 1936, p. 118). Grold (1972) has defined jealousy as a set of feelings that occur when one anticipates "losing our providing source to someone or something else, it is the experience of being left out, rejected, dispensed with, or betrayed" (p. 118). Shettel-Neuber, Bryson, and Young (1978) defined jealousy as "a reaction to an actual or perceived threat by another person to an at least personally recognized, previously established positively valued unit or sentiment relationship" (p. 612). Vuyk (1959, p. 111) has similarly defined jealousy as "the fear of losing something one has to a competitor."

Teismann and Mosher (1978) have defined jealousy "as the emotional state of an actor, consisting of fear and anger and based on a subjective appraisal of a threat of loss of some aspect of a highly valued relationship with a partner to a rival" (p. 1211). Davis (1936) argued that "In every case, [jealousy] is apparently a fear or rage reaction to a threatened appropriation of one's own, or what is desired as one's own property" (p. 396). Daly et al. (1982), who believe that male sexual jealousy is largely instinctual, give a similar definition: "Jealousy may be best defined as a state that is aroused by a perceived threat to a valued relationship or position and motivates behavior aimed at countering the threat" (p. 12). A number of authors have offered similar definitions (Buunk & Bringle, 1987; Clanton, 1981; Pines & Aronson, 1983).

Neu (1980) holds that jealousy is essentially a fear of loss of relationship, but, unlike Davis (1936), does not think that possessiveness is a precondition for its development:

> At the center of jealousy is fear, specifically fear of loss. What is special about [this fear is that it is] connected with what is special about people: while one could lose possession of a thing, one could not lose its affection—it has no affection to give or to be taken away. (p. 433)

At an earlier point in his book, Neu remarks: "To be jealous over someone, you must believe that they love you (or have loved you), but you need not believe that you have a *right* to that love . . . nor need you believe that the other has an obligation [to you] built up over time" (1980, p. 44).

We also have concerns about approaches conceptualizing jealousy as a reaction to threat of loss. The role of self-esteem is secondary at best. Often jealousy is defined as certain emotions that accompany loss, such as fear and anger. Distinctions are not made between complete loss of the relationship and loss of qualities of the relationship, even though the relationship may endure. The role of perception and appraisal processes is not pointed to; most of these definitions assume that threat of or actual loss is a property of the external world, not in part an outcome of appraisal and interpersonal negotiation. We believe our definition is richer in that it points to these aspects.

Ellis and Weinstein (1986) have recently presented a symbolic-interactionist account of jealousy that attempts to encompass both threat to relationship and threat to self-esteem as triggers of jealousy. They define jealousy as "the emotion that people experience when control over valued resources that flow through an attachment to another person is perceived to be in jeopardy because the partner might want or might actually give and/or receive some of these resources from a third party" (p. 341). They also note that the common aspect of all such resources is that of "identity construction and maintenance," a term compatible with the concepts of self-concept and self-esteem. More specifically, jealousy is held to occur when a third party "threatens the area of identification that specifically defines the relationship" (such as sexuality, primacy of self-disclosure, etc.) (p. 341).

We are sympathetic to Ellis and Weinstein's point of view, but the restriction to areas of identification that define the relationship is a premature theoretical statement, especially when considering pathological jealousy or the provision of material resources that make life comfortable but are not central features of identity. We also think that their belief that jealousy is an emotion, rather than a complex interpersonal situation with emotional features, limits their approach. We do agree that cultural, personal, and interpersonal levels of meaning each act to define what is threatened and what threatens.

Definitions Emphasizing Exclusivity, Possessiveness, and Rivalry

Shand (1916) reflected the sentiments of several early 20th-century commentators by supposing that "It is due to the desire of self-love to possess certain things exclusively for self . . . that jealousy principally arises" (quoted by Jones, 1937, p. 268). Spielman (1971) has defined jealousy as an "attitude of vigilant guarding against the threatened loss and an effort to preserve the status quo, to maintain possession" (p. 62). Ausubel, Sullivan, and Ives (1980, p. 295) define jealousy as a composite of fear and anger occurring when individuals "perceive their *exclusive* possession of a source of security, status, or affection challenged by the needs, aspirations, and activities of others." Bernard (1971) and Beecher and Beecher (1971) place similar emphasis on possessiveness. All such definitions contrast with Neu's (1980) contention cited above that possessiveness is not a necessary feature of jealousy.

Solomon (1976), in a comprehensive structural analysis of the major and minor emotions, has also emphasized the exclusive/possessive aspect of jealousy. He stresses that the "direction" of jealousy is toward competition, that the object of the emotion is "another person's competitive gain," and that the associated desire is to gain back whatever was lost. The central characteristic is the right of possession:

> Thus, it is not uncommon that a person will become jealous over an object (including a human "object" . . .) about which, competition aside, he or she has little or no concern whatsoever. It is the claim of possession that is crucial, not the importance of the object itself. (1976, pp. 333–335)

Definitions citing possessiveness, exclusivity, and/or rivalry make the error of labeling variables that affect the likelihood of jealousy or are part of the jealousy complex as "jealousy" itself. For example, possessiveness may reflect various elements of a jealousy complex, such as coping efforts to interfere with the rival relationship or anger at the loss of control over one's partner. It may also be conceptualized as a personality or relationship factor that affects the degree of perceived threat to self or the relationship from rivals, thereby engaging the jealousy complex. It is unlikely that possessiveness is the sole cause of jealousy, let alone a defining feature. Possessiveness may be related to how the person feels or behaves when jealous and may also be a reaction to perceived threat. Likewise, rivalry may be thought of as related feelings, behaviors, and thoughts that some people have if a rival relationship threatens, but we think it is restrictive to assert that rivalry is central to all jealousy.

Definitions Emphasizing Instinctual Reactions

Gottschalk (1936), an early jealousy researcher, held that the possessive feeling and threat to self-esteem that accompany jealousy are secondary, socially conditioned phenomena. He defined jealousy as "a natural, original, instinctive, sexual reaction" (p. 8) that has become adapted to social control forces. William James (1890) asserted that "Jealousy is unquestionably an instinct" (p. 465), a position shared by the sexologist Kinsey (Kinsey, Pomeroy, Martin, & Gebhard, 1953).

Sokoloff (1947), on the basis of clinical experience, differentiated among "jealous reaction," "jealous sentiment," and "jealous complex." The jealous reaction is basically genetic, an "inbred reaction of atavistic nature" that "stems from the adreno-sympathetic system and belongs to the same group of reactions as fear or anger. It is associated but not identical with the instinct of acquisition or ownership" (p. 52). Jealous sentiment, in Sokoloff's view, is a temporary predominant mood state of some children that develops when the jealous reaction is repeatedly stimulated by situational conditions. The jealous complex is supposedly a neurotic extension of the jealous sentiment that is found in adults for which there is some sort of mental predisposition.

It is overrestrictive to define jealousy as caused by instinct. In addition to the problems that are associated with the use of "instinct" as a causal term (Barlow & Silverberg, 1980; Lumsden & Wilson, 1981), recourse to biology in a definition is unnecessary. The idea that genetic factors may be involved in jealousy may have a broad interpretation. For example, individual differences in arousal generated by perceived threat may have genetic components. But this is a far cry from a definition implying that specific motivation or behavior is under genetic control.

Definitions emphasizing instinct usually fail to discuss the content of the instinctual reaction. If jealousy is basically an instinct, its deep genetic structure should be similar if not identical across all people, cultures, and situations. The fact that there is great variability in the content of the jealousy complex and the situations in which it occurs requires a fairly complex theory to link instinct with expression. Problems associated with this attempt are addressed in Chapter 3.

A MODEL OF ROMANTIC JEALOUSY

We now turn to our model of romantic jealousy, which incorporates our definition while providing a more general framework for understanding the causes and consequences of jealousy. This model is interactive in two senses. First, it allows for the possibility that

processes affecting jealousy may combine to produce unique outcomes that otherwise might not be anticipated. Second, it allows for
the possibility that positive and negative feedback loops act back to
influence causes.

Our model is influenced by the metatheoretical scheme of close
relationships developed by Kelley et al. (1983) and by Lazarus's
cognitive–transactional theory of stress and coping (Lazarus & Folkman, 1984; Lazarus & Launier, 1978). We briefly sketch issues that
their work highlights, and then elaborate our model.

Descriptive versus Causal Analyses

Kelley at al. (1983) make a distinction between a "descriptive" and a
"causal" analysis, arguing that much of our understanding of close
relationships is muddied by a failure to make such a distinction. For
example, discussion of the construct of social role may confuse
behaviors, thoughts, and feelings that constitute a role with causes
of the role, as in saying that roles are culturally based norms for the
behavior of people in certain social positions (boss, mother, priest,
etc.). This confuses a cause (cultural norm) with behavior (Peplau,
1983).

Descriptive Analysis

Kelley et al. (1983) argue that a descriptive analysis must precede the
causal analysis. That is, a theorist needs to know what it is he or she
is trying to explain (concrete reality) before trying to explain it
(developing and testing theory). We argue that at present descriptive
analyses of romantic jealousy are largely based on clinical report and
literature, which are biased, and not on more systematic surveys of
what it is that people actually do, think, and feel when jealous. Such
research is vital for future theory development.

A descriptive analysis is intended to reveal patterns of thoughts,
feelings, and behaviors that occur repeatedly within a person ("intrachain events") or between people ("interchain events"). An example
of an intrachain pattern would be appraisal of threat, followed by
fear, followed by attempts to reduce fear. An example of an interchain pattern would be a jealous partner's demanding that the beloved not see an assumed rival, followed by an argument, followed
by renewed pledges of commitment to the primary relationship.
Patterns may be rather commonly encountered in many people or
relationships, as in the first example, or they may be more idiosyncratic to a particular person or relationship.

To be more specific for our analysis of jealousy, patterns of intrachain events that occur in response to perceived threat/loss are what we call the "jealousy complex." Patterns of interchain events between jealous and beloved are part of their "primary relationship system." The patterns of interchain events constitute one major cause of the jealousy complex, and, of course, these interchain events are affected by the intrachain jealousy complex. As mentioned earlier, the intrachain events of the jealous may have characteristics of a self-sustaining system, or their stability may result from the operation of outside causal conditions (the relationship, the romantic triangle, cultural variables, etc.).

One problem of descriptive analysis is identifying elements of the jealousy complex and relevant interpersonal behaviors. This can be done by analyzing diaries of what jealous people think, feel, and do; asking people to write down previous jealous reactions (Bryson, 1977; White, 1981a); observing role plays of jealous behavior (Teismann, 1982); or conducting in-depth interviews or surveys (Francis, 1977; Pines & Aronson, 1981). Much jealousy research has used scales derived from factor analyses of responses to large numbers of items assessing jealous reactions. Unfortunately, these items are usually generated by experimenters on their own, rather than from assessments of the actual behaviors, feelings, and thoughts of jealous people (White, 1984).

A second problem of descriptive analysis is how to identify intrachain and interchain patterns of events. There are a variety of ways to do this with data based on direct observation or self-report, including factor analysis, conditional probability tables, cluster analysis, Q-sort, or multidimensional scaling. To date, however, researchers have largely relied on clinical observation, subjective self-report, or intuition to discuss patterns (when patterns are discussed at all), though there are some exceptions (Hupka & Eshett, 1984; Shettel-Neuber et al. 1978). Note that averages and variabilities of individual elements (e.g., specific feelings, thoughts, or behaviors) are not informative as to how the elements are related to each other.

Causal Analysis

The task of a causal analysis is to specify relatively stable causes of thoughts, feelings, and behaviors and their patterns or interrelationships. For most phenomena in the social world, a great many such causal conditions may be or have been postulated. For example, aspects of jealousy may be related to biology, culture, personality, or relationship. Within each of these categories, a great many theories may compete for our attention. In the area of personality alone, it is possible to generate causal conditions that affect jealousy from psychodynamic, humanistic, learning, social learning, and trait theories.

Causal conditions can be grouped into four general classes. These are properties of each person in an interaction, P and O; properties of the *interaction* of P and O (denoted P × O); and factors in the social environment, such as social norms or the nature of one's support system (denoted E soc). Causal conditions can be causally linked to each other. For example, shyness (a P factor) may lead to leisure-time activities that are largely asocial, such as reading books; such activities reduce the person's social network (an E soc factor).

Various theories can be used to generate P, O, P × O, or E soc causal conditions that may be causally linked to elements of the jealousy complex or to patterns of these elements (the complexes themselves). Generally, it is better to start the search for proximal rather than distal variables—that is, for the causal conditions that most immediately generate the events of interest. For example, attitudes toward love may be more proximal to the jealousy complex than parental modeling of affection, though such modeling may be a cause of the attitudes toward love held by the beloved or the jealous person.

Further, a complete causal analysis should consider the possibility of feedback loops in which causal conditions may themselves be modified by intrachain or interchain events that they initially influenced. For example, demanding commitment as a response to a rival (a coping behavior) may influence the adoption of more general exclusivity norms (a more stable causal condition). Stronger exclusivity norms would then play a role in shaping future jealous reactions.

Cognitive–Transactional Theory of Stress and Coping

Although the language of our model incorporates many features of Lazarus's theoretical approach, we wish to point out some major features of it that we think are particularly important.

First, we adopt the transactional approach to stress. Stress is neither a feature of the environment (e.g., stressful life events) nor of the person (e.g., mature vs. immature defensive styles). Rather, stress is a transaction between the person and the environment that occurs when the press of the environment is perceived to exceed the person's capacity to adapt to it. More specifically, stress occurs to the extent that the threat of a rival relationship is perceived to exceed the person's ability to master the threat.

Second, there are two processes that mediate the transaction between person and environment: "appraisal" and "coping." Appraisals are (conscious or unconscious) judgments about the nature of the environment and one's ability to respond to it. Coping refers to "constantly changing cognitive and behavioral efforts to manage specific external and/or internal demands that are appraised as taxing or exceeding the resources of the person" (Lazarus & Folkman, 1984, p. 141). Coping efforts may be directed at managing the environment ("problem-focused") or directed at managing emotion ("emotion-focused"), or both. Generally, problem-focused coping is more likely if people think they have reasonably effective means to adapt, whereas emotion-focused coping is more likely when such means are not apparent (Folkman & Lazarus, 1980; Moos & Billings, 1982).

Finally, emotions are cognitive–feeling states that are dependent upon appraisal processes and yet influence future appraisal. Emotions refer to "fused components" of thought, impulse to action, and somatic disturbance (Lazarus & Folkman, 1984, p. 275). Anger, for example, is experienced only when there are anger-generating and anger-sustaining thoughts; when there are impulses to damage the object of anger; and when there are somatic accompaniments (e.g., noticeable symptoms of sympathetic arousal, such as a flushed face or sweaty palms).

Hence, emotion is intimately related to both appraisal and coping (cf. Kelley, 1984). Emotion is not an isolated element of the jealousy complex, yet neither is emotion a by-product of other processes with little directive influence. Emotions require appraisal but then influence subsequent appraisal; emotions influence coping efforts but then are modified by those efforts. Approaches to jealousy that overemphasize the often striking and strong emotional aspects may run the risk of obscuring the identity of emotion with appraisal and coping (cf. Berscheid, 1983).

The Model Itself

Figure 2.2 presents our model in schematic form. The jealous, the beloved, and the rival are each represented as having interrelated behaviors (B), thoughts (T), and affects (A). Each person may influence the behaviors, thoughts, and affects of the others, as is represented by the bidirectional arrows between actors. The four classes of stable causal conditions of person (P), other (O), relationship (P × O), and social environment (E soc) are illustrated as influencing and being influenced by the thoughts, affects, and behaviors of actors and by their interpersonal relationships.

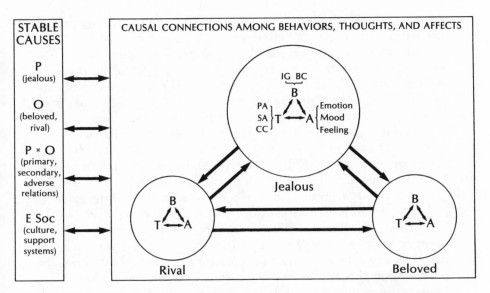

FIGURE 2.2. A schematic model of romantic jealousy. PA = primary appraisal; SA = secondary appraisal; CC = cognitive coping efforts; IG = information gathering; BC = behavioral coping efforts; A = affects; B = behaviors; T = thoughts.

Because of our focus on the jealousy complex, the behaviors, thoughts, and affects of the jealous are further differentiated into the basic elements of the jealousy complex. Each of these elements can influence the other (cf. Bush et al., 1988). "Affect" is a general term that refers to emotions, feelings, and moods. Conceptually, emotions occur when sympathetic arousal is noticeable, whereas feelings are primarily evaluative cognitive states with low levels of arousal. Moods are long-lasting feelings that may color perception for several hours or days (Berscheid, 1983; Mandler, 1984). For obvious clinical, research, and phenomenological reasons, our discussion focuses on emotions, but we do not wish to imply that feelings or moods do not play a role in jealousy.

Borrowing from Lazarus, we differentiate thoughts into "primary appraisal" (PA in Figure 2.2), "secondary appraisal" (SA), and "cognitive coping efforts" (CC). Primary appraisals are judgments that the self or the relationship is threatened or harmed. Secondary appraisals are judgments about what might and can be done to deal with the threat or harm. Both kinds of appraisals can change either in response to new information or in order to manage emotion by distortion of the environment. Cognitive coping efforts include changes in belief and interpretation that function to reduce unpleasant affect or to facilitate behavioral coping efforts

Behaviors are differentiated into "information gathering" (IG in Figure 2.2), a secondary-appraisal process, and "behavioral coping efforts" (BC). These behavioral efforts may be either problem-focused (e.g., improving the relationship) or emotion-focused (e.g., withdrawing from the situation). Problem-focused efforts may be directed at changing the environment or at modifying oneself to increase one's resources to manage the environment, such as by acquiring new skills (Kahn, Wolfe, Quinn, Snoek, & Rosenthal, 1964; Lazarus & Folkman, 1984).

Figure 2.2 diagrams the task that faces those interested in jealousy research or intervention. There is the descriptive task of identifying affective, cognitive, and behavioral elements of the jealousy complex, as well as their patterns. A second descriptive task is to identify interpersonal behaviors that commonly influence the jealousy complex and to identify patterns of these behaviors. Then there is the analytic task of specifying the causes not only of individual elements, but also of their stable patterns.

ELABORATION OF THEORY AND REVIEW OF RESEARCH RELEVANT TO THE MODEL OF JEALOUSY

We are now in a position to be more specific about the elements of the jealousy complex. To do this, we both elaborate our theoretical arguments and review past research through the lens of the model. We first consider primary appraisal, then emotions, secondary appraisal, and coping efforts and their outcomes (this last section includes a discussion of interrelationships among secondary-appraisal processes and coping efforts). For each of these discussions, we first present concepts and theory, tying them into the context of romantic jealousy. We then present a brief review of research related to the theoretical statements. Table 2.1 summarizes the features of appraisal, affect, and coping efforts that we emphasize in our presentation.

Primary Appraisal

Types of Primary Appraisal

Three kinds of primary-appraisal judgments are assumed. The first is a judgment about the potential for a rival relationship to develop;

TABLE 2.1. Major Features of Appraisal, Emotion, and Coping Processes in the Romantic Jealousy Complex

Primary appraisal/reappraisals	Secondary appraisal	Emotion	Coping efforts
Potential for rival relationship	Motive assessment	Anger	Improving relationship
Existence of rival relationship	Social comparison	Fear	Interfering with rival relationship
Threat/harm posed by potential or actual rival relationship	Loss assessment	Sadness	Demanding commitment
	Alternatives assessment	Envy	Derogating partner or rival
	Planning coping	Sexual arousal	Developing alternatives
	Assessing coping outcomes	Guilt	Self-assessment
			Support/catharsis
			Denial/avoidance

here an actual rival relationship is not believed to exist. The second type of appraisal is of whether or not a rival relationship actually exists. The third kind of appraisal is of the degree of threat or harm posed by the actual or potential rival relationship. Conceivably, the causal conditions that influence the appraisal of the potential or actual existence of a rival relationship are not the same conditions that affect assessment of the direction and magnitude of specific threats. For example, relationship dynamics generating deterioration of the primary relationship may thereby influence the perception of the existence of a potential for a rival relationship to develop. Once the person infers this possibility, the degree of threat subsequently appraised may be predicted by personality and cultural variables unrelated to relationship deterioration.

We have emphasized the primary appraisal of a rival *relationship*, rather than focusing on the rival as a person. This is because the rival is only threatening to the extent that the person appraises the existence of a real or potential rival relationship. Characteristics of the rival may affect the primary appraisal of threat, and certainly characteristics of the rival may affect secondary appraisal, emotion, and coping efforts.

A person may become jealous of the advances of a rival even when it would seem to an outside observer (including the beloved) that the beloved has no possible interest in the rival. In most such cases, the jealous person actually has inferred a potential for a relationship to develop (if the rival is persistent enough, if the rival makes the right moves, if the beloved develops new interests, if the jealous is not vigilant, etc.). Sometimes the jealous may not infer such a potential, but may be reacting to other threatening aspects of the rival's actions, such as an affront to communal esteem or status. This difference has obvious therapeutic implications, but it is inappropriate to treat the latter case (theoretically or clinically) as an instance of romantic jealousy.

At this point we make no assumption about the temporal ordering of appraisal of the potential for and appraisal of the existence of a rival relationship. For example, some people continually assess the degree of threat potentially posed by others who have any kind of contact with the beloved. This waxing and waning assessment may be punctuated by judgments that a rival relationship actually does exist.

Primary-Appraisal Research

There is virtually no research on the factors that are related to appraisal of the potential for or existence of a rival or to judgments about the degree of threat posed by a rival relationship. Although there are major conceptual issues in assessment of these appraisals, most researchers have apparently assumed that self-report measures of jealousy reflect primary appraisal. That is, those who rate themselves as very jealous are assumed to have made the judgment that a rival relationship or its potential exists and that it has been appraised as threatening.

Hence it is possible that many of the correlates of self-report measures of jealousy may be linked to any combination of the three primary appraisals we have outlined. But they may also be linked to other aspects of the jealousy complex or of the interpersonal jealousy system that may also be reflected in self-report measures. This ambiguity has led us to review correlates of general, nonspecific jealousy measures in different chapters according to the level of analysis to which the correlates belong. Correlates related to personality are presented in Chapter 4, those related to relationships are presented in Chapter 5, and so on.

There is research pertinent to primary-appraisal processes. Mathes, Phillips, Skowran, and Dick (1982) report that subjects who predicted that they would be upset if their dating partners got involved with another were particularly likely to be threatened when a potential rival (an experimental confederate) asked them for permission to date their partners. This indicates some correspondence between appraisal of potential and appraisal of threat posed by actual rivals.

White (1976) found four variables to be independently related to scores on a scale assessing the degree of relationship threat posed by an actual rival. The more that a rival and a partner were thought to be attracted to each other, and the more traditional a subject's sex-role beliefs were, the greater the threat was perceived as being. Subjects who believed that sex could happen without a high degree of love were less likely to perceive a threat to the relationship. Finally, threat was judged lower to the extent that a partner was perceived to be dependent upon the relationship.

White (1981c) asked 300 romantic partners to indicate the extent to which they noticed the potential for rival relationships and how often they worried about rival relationships. Notice and worry reflect the primary appraisal of threat. Noticing was positively related to worry, and both were predicted by perceived inadequacy as a partner. Sharpsteen and Schmalz (1988) coded subjects' accounts of actual jealousy episodes. Violations of exclusivity expectations, the presence of an actual romantic rival, and flirting were very common features (56–92% of the episodes). Each of these seem certain to engage threat appraisal.

Obviously, more work is needed on identifying the causal conditions that influence primary appraisal. Particular attention needs to be paid to differentiating appraisal of threat to the relationship from appraisal of threat to self-esteem (Bush et al., 1988), as well as to differentiating appraisal of a potential or actual rival from appraisal of the degree of threat immediately posed by these judgments. Both research on pathological jealousy and therapy of jealousy might benefit from differentiating between processes and treatments related to the three primary appraisals we have outlined.

Emotional Reactions

Phases of Emotional Responding

We have found it useful to conceptualize two phases in the process of emotional responding to primary appraisal of harm or threat in jealousy. There is an initial, autonomic stress response characteristic of suddenly perceived threat or harm (Selye, 1976). This so-called "jealous flash" is a common initial experience of the jealous (Clanton & Smith, 1977; Ellis & Weinstein, 1986; Pines & Aronson, 1983) and can be thought of as the physiological component of emotion. In humans this arousal may be due to the interruption, or anticipated interruption, of goal-directed behavior sequences (Berscheid, 1983; Kelley, 1984; Mandler, 1984). Certainly the perception of a rival implies the potential for massive disruption of interaction sequences valued by the jealous, such as sexual behavior, companionship, and provision of resources.

The quality of the emotional response is likely to be influenced by situational factors that suggest plausible causes of arousal and by personal or cultural scripts concerning the nature of jealous reactions (cf. Leventhal, 1980; Read, 1987; Schank & Abelson, 1977; Walster & Walster, 1977). In most cases the initial response is fear or anger, though a percentage of the jealous report heightened sexual arousal (Bohm, 1961; Grold, 1972; Morgan, 1975; Pines & Aronson, 1983). One explanation of this is that the arousal originally accompanying fear or anger becomes associated with sexual cues and produces passion (White, Fishbein, & Rutstein, 1981; Zillman, 1983).

The next and probably overlapping phase of emotional reaction occurs as a consequence of secondary appraisal of the situation, of the operation of emotion-focused coping directed toward reduction of autonomic reactivity, and of the outcomes of problem-focused coping efforts. As the jealous person's understanding of the situation becomes more complex, more subtle and differentiated emotional states are likely. Further, emotion-focused coping that is slower-acting or takes longer to develop can come into play, such as cognitive reappraisal of the threat as a challenge. Problem-solving coping efforts may be successful, leading to feelings of relief, or unsuccessful, leading to depressed mood or fear as the valued inter-action with the partner deteriorates. The results of secondary ap-praisal and coping efforts may so reduce autonomic activity that affect is dominated by feelings and moods rather than by the more intense emotions.

These phases of intense emotion and relatively quiescent feel-ings and moods may alternate. The intensity and frequency of emo-tion may intermittently increase either as jealous persons encounter new obstacles (e.g., a canceled date) or as they generate their own arousal by dwelling on the injustices or threats they are suffering. With each new period of intense emotional reaction, additional at-tempts may be made at emotion-focused coping or at secondary appraisal of the causes of the emotion. These repeated overlays of interpretation and coping may generate very complex patterns of responding to threat and produce the richly variegated clinical pic-ture of the jealous.

This phase distinction is useful because it suggests that initial coping efforts are likely to be directed at managing extreme emotion or autonomic reactivity. Further, to the extent that initial appraisal of threat or harm may be arousing, this phase distinction suggests that initial problem-focused efforts are more likely to be regressive and stereotypical than to be considered and deliberate (Haan, 1977; Lazarus & Folkman, 1984).

Research on Jealous Emotions

Many commentators have supposed that jealousy is a compound emo-tion, a blend of basic or irreducible emotions (Hupka, 1984; Sharpsteen & Schmalz, 1988), though some argue that jealousy is an emotion in its own right (e.g., Mandler, 1984, p. 295). There has been disagree-ment among clinicians and theorists about the elements of the emo-tional compound. Freud (1922/1955) proposed a mixture of grief and enmity; others have suggested grief, anger, and self-pity (Gesell, 1906); fear and rage (Davis, 1936); fear, anger, and love (Arnold, 1960); hate and aggression (Klein & Riviere, 1964); apprehension, anxiety, suspicion, and mistrust (Spielman, 1971); anger, hatred, and envy (Solomon, 1976); anger and fear (Ausubel et al., 1980; Plutchik, 1980); panic, rage, and expectancy (Panskepp, 1982); fear and distress (Bohm, 1961); and fear and envy (Clanton & Smith, 1977).

It should be clear that our approach is not concerned with isolating what the blend actually is. The emotions of the jealousy complex are related to primary and secondary appraisals, which in turn may be affected by a variety of causal conditions at different levels of analysis. The task as we see it is to link particular emotions with different contexts, rather than to identify which emotions "really" constitute jealousy.

A number of studies have factor- or cluster-analyzed emotion ratings of jealous subjects or of subjects who were predicting what emotions they would feel. Resulting factors depend to some extent on what emotions were being rated. Commonly emerging factors are Anger/Revenge, Sadness/Depression, Fear/Anxiety, Envy, Sexual Arousal, and Guilt (Amstutz, 1982; Buunk et al., 1984; Bryson, 1976; Davitz, 1969; Mathes, Phillips, et al., 1982; Salovey & Rodin, 1986; Tipton, Benedictson, Mahoney, & Hartnett, 1978; White, 1985c).

Some researchers have asked subjects to predict how they might react to hypothetical, jealousy-inducing situations. Variations in the situations are then linked to the subjects' predictions. Such research has demonstrated that the intensity and quality of expected emotion are related to focus of attention (Hupka, 1984), degree and quality of threat (Bush et al., 1988; Mathes, Adams, & Davies, 1985), and whether the situation involves a romantic rival versus envy of another's resources (Salovey & Rodin, 1986). On the whole, this approach has not been very informative because subjects are giving predictions of emotion and such predictions may be strongly influenced by social desirability, cultural truisms, and the transparent structure of the stimulus materials. Such research may not yield the complex, interactional effects that might be anticipated in the study of real emotion. For example, Hupka (1984) found that subjects thought that they would be much more fearful when thinking about being alone if a partner left for a rival than when thinking about the way in which the partner ended the relationship—not a surprising finding. Salovey and Rodin (1986) found that people thought they would have more intense emotions if romantically jealous than if merely envious—again not particularly surprising. Such results may or may not mirror the emotional dynamics of real-life jealousy, but we think it preferable to study existing relationships and their jealousy than to complicate the picture by using hypothetical situations, unless the intention of such research is to assess normative expectations.

Other research has correlated emotions with other variables. White (1985c) found that anger was more likely to be reported by jealous high-power partners, whereas depression was more likely to be reported by jealous low-power partners. Buunk et al. (1984) found that only their Anger factor was correlated with a self-description of level of jealousy. This finding was interpreted to mean that people use their level of anger to inform themselves whether they are jealous or not in a jealousy-provoking situation. They also reported that subjects reporting a high degree of self-esteem threat were especially ashamed, fearful, and powerless; anger and self-esteem threat were correlated only for women.

Recent research has focused on assessment of prototypic features of jealous emotions. Shaver, Schwartz, Kirson, and O'Connor (1987) had subjects sort 135 different emotion terms into intuitively appropriate categories of similar emotions. Jealousy was more closely associated with anger than with other basic emotions. However, those authors suggested that jealousy episodes may be complex, so that a particular episode may produce several emotions blended into the experience of jealousy. Sharpsteen and Schmalz (1988) coded subjects' detailed written histories of jealousy episodes. About three-quarters of these episodes included anger, with fear and sadness in 20–30% of the reports. These three emotions were also each found to contribute to the prediction of measures of intensity of jealousy in the episodes. Fear and distrust were linked to ratings of chronic jealousy across many relationships, but anger and sadness were not related to chronic jealousy. Sharpsteen and Schmalz concluded that jealousy can be conceptualized as a blended emotion of fear, anger, and sadness.

Using similar methods, Smith et al. (1988) analyzed episodes of envy and of romantic jealousy. "Jealousy" was found empirically to connote either envy or romantic jealousy, while "envy" always connoted social comparison. Further, a second study indicated that subjects believed that different emotions differentiate romantic jealousy from envy. Envy was believed to be more closely associated with feelings of inferiority, dissatisfaction, self-criticism, and motivation to improve, whereas jealousy was believed to be characterized by suspiciousness, rejection, hostility, fear of loss, and hurt.

Finally, Hupka (1987) presented subjects with various emotion-inducing prototypic scenarios and had subjects indicate their beliefs about the emotions and emotional symptoms associated with each. In the jealousy scenario of an extramarital affair, subjects generally expected that the aggrieved spouse would be shocked, angry, hateful, tense, and overwhelmed.

Based on this review of emotion research and on our survey of the clinical literature, we suggest six basic affective elements of the jealousy complex. Each element is best conceptualized as a set of related emotions, feelings, and moods. Within each set, the affects share certain central appraisals of the situation, while differing in the extent of accompanying arousal as well as in minor features of appraisal. These elements and some of their related affects are as follows:

- Anger (hate, disgust, vengefulness, contempt, annoyance, rage)
- Fear (anxiety, tenseness, worry, distress)
- Sadness (blueness, depression, hopeless, suffering, melancholy)
- Envy (resentment, covetousness, begrudging)
- Sexual arousal (lust, desire, passion)
- Guilt (regret, shame, remorse, embarrassment)

Some of these affects (anger, fear, sadness) are often identified as basic emotions (Ekman, 1984; Izard, 1977; Shaver et al., 1987). Others (envy, guilt) are often thought of as blends of other emotions. However, we believe that the evidence currently supports identifying each of these affective elements as a distinct component of the jealousy complex.

Secondary Appraisal

Types of Secondary Appraisal

In addition to planning coping efforts and assessing the results of such efforts, four appraisal processes are influential in the development of options to cope with the jealousy-provoking situation. These are "motives assessment" (Buunk, 1984; White, 1981a, 1981d), "social comparison to rival" (Bers & Rodin, 1984; Salovey & Rodin, 1984, 1986; Schmitt, 1988), "alternatives assessment," and "loss assessment" (either real or potential loss). These four are conceptualized as information-gathering and interpretational processes that address the questions of "Why is my partner interested in the rival?," "What does my rival have that I don't (and vice versa)?," "What is going to happen to me if I get left?," and "Just what might I lose or have I lost?" These four questions are asked because of the necessity of coping with the threat or loss perceived via primary appraisal.

These four processes may contribute to the primary appraisal or reappraisal of threat or harm. For the time being, however, we wish to emphasize their involvement in the development of coping efforts, the secondary-appraisal process. It is important to think of primary- and secondary-appraisal processes in a functional sense, rather than as nomenclature that yields mutually exclusive categories in which to pigeonhole complex cognitive processes.

The first three questions above were initially derived from Thibaut and Kelley's (1959) concept of "comparison level for alternatives" (CL alt). Their analysis suggests that commitment to a current relationship is related to the degree to which positive outcomes (rewards minus costs) are greater within the current relationship, relative to the level of outcomes believed to be available in the next most attractive relationship (this level is the CL alt). If current outcomes in the primary relationship are close to or below those believed available in the secondary relationship, the person becomes ambivalent about the primary relationship and is more likely to leave (Levinger, 1979). Kelley (1983) has further suggested that commitment is also related to the *variability* in the degree to which the outcomes of a relationship are superior to those of alternatives. A person who is consistently enjoying outcomes moderately superior to those of alternatives is more likely to remain in the relationship than one whose outcomes relative to those of alternatives fluctuate from superior to inferior.

The question of commitment is the central focus of secondary appraisal of the jealous. To develop and gauge the utility of possible coping efforts, the jealous person must assess not only the partner's present and future level of commitment to the relationship, but also his or her own commitment. Within the CL alt framework, assessment of the partner's commitment requires knowledge of the level and variability of outcomes the partner can be expected to receive in both the primary and the rival relationships.

From the point of view of the jealous person, this assessment of the level and variability of outcomes available to the beloved in the rival relationship versus the primary relationship requires knowledge of the partner's unmet needs and motives for (actually or potentially) entering another relationship (motives assessment). It also requires knowledge about the characteristics of the rival or rival relationship that might satisfy those motives, relative to the self and the primary relationship (social comparison). The degree of the partner's perceived commitment to the primary relationship is based on the extent to which the partner's assessed needs are believed to be consistently better satisfied by the self or by the primary relationship.

To assess his or her own commitment, the jealous person needs to gauge the degree to which outcomes in the primary relationship for himself or herself are consistently superior to those available elsewhere (alternatives assessment). This assessment should yield a global estimate of how dependent the person is on the threatened relationship (e.g., "There are plenty of other fish in the sea"). In addition, alternative assessments may highlight specific outcomes that are of greater concern. For example, the jealous may focus the assessment of alternatives on specific features of the relationship, such as degree of sexual satisfaction, level of communicative intimacy, or compatibility of personal habits. Ellis and Weinstein (1986) have suggested that the particular areas of focus may be strongly linked to definitions of self-in-the-relationship.

The perception that available alternatives will not be as satisfactory as the primary relationship influences planning and enactment of coping behaviors. Behaviors that diminish the outcomes upon which one is particularly dependent (e.g., sex, emotional intimacy) are self-defeating and usually less likely to be pursued. The fact that people do pursue behaviors that threaten such rewards does not contradict this assumption, but merely points to the action of other factors that influence coping. Further, those who assess themselves as highly dependent may be more motivated to sustain their current relationships in the face of rivals' threats than those who can obtain valued rewards elsewhere.

Assessment of real or potential loss (loss assessment) as a secondary-appraisal process is inherent in the notion of secondary appraisal. Research on coping has demonstrated that people assess the quality and quantity of real or potential losses, and that such assessments are related to coping efforts (Lazarus & Folkman, 1984). Loss assessment is also suggested by Thibaut and Kelley's (1959) construct of "comparison level" (CL), which is assumed to be a relatively stable expectation about the quality and level of outcomes that should exist in a relationship (Foa & Foa, 1980).

The CL concept suggests that people monitor the degree to which obtained outcomes match expectations, particularly during times of relationship formation or change (Hatfield, Traupmann, Sprecher, Utne, & Hay, 1985; Kelley, 1979; Levinger & Huesmann, 1980). Outcomes are particularly likely to be monitored when the relationship is perceived to be under threat from a romantic rival. If outcomes fall below CL, the jealous person is likely to become dissatisfied with the relationship.

The CL concept also suggests the possibility that either satisfaction with the relationship or the CL itself is affected by the perception of a rival relationship. As mentioned earlier, rewards and resources under threat may increase in subjective value, so that relationship outcomes may be more highly valued than they were prior to the perception of a rival. Given a constant CL, the jealous person should become more satisfied with the primary relationship as existing rewards are valued upwardly. This is one of the reasons why one partner may intentionally induce jealousy in the other—to increase appreciation of the other partner for the relationship (White, 1980a).

The jealous may also assume that expected outcomes should decrease or increase during jealousy episodes. The direction and magnitude of such adjustments may be influenced by cultural, interpersonal, or personality factors. For example, people high in self-esteem may be more likely to think that their partners would respond to their jealous feelings with attempts to reassure and to improve the relationship, temporarily elevating the CL.

These processes of motives assessment, social comparison, alternatives assessment, and loss assessment may serve both primary- and secondary-appraisal functions. In terms of secondary appraisal, they are important in planning coping efforts. With regard to primary appraisal, these four processes provide a more realistic estimate of the degree of threat posed by the rival relationship. If the partner's motives are strong, if the rival has greater resources than the jealous person to satisfy those motives, if the jealous person is greatly dependent on the primary relationship, and if the potential loss is great, then the threat will be considerable.

Research on Secondary Appraisal

Motives Assessment. Four studies have examined motives assessment. Buunk (1984) asked subjects whose partners had had an extrarelationship affair to rate the extent to which six different motives had been present for their partners. These were need for variety, revenge, marital deprivation, circumstances, pressure from the rival, and attractions of the rival. Attributions of marital deprivation and revenge correlated positively with postaffair conflict and jealousy measures. Barr and Hupka (1988) asked subjects to predict their emotions upon discovery of infidelity. Self-blame for the situation was associated with low self-esteem, while anticipated jealousy, anger, and suspicion were highly likely, regardless of attribution.

White (1981a) asked students to list reasons they or their partners might have for going out with another person. Most of these reasons could be classified as desire for sexual variety, attraction to the nonsexual qualities of the rival or rival relationship, dissatisfaction with the primary relationship, or desire for greater commitment. In a second study, 300 subjects in current romantic relationships reported how important each of these four motives were or would be to their partners in forming a rival relationship. Motive ratings were then correlated with a number of jealousy measures. Sexual motives were related to degree of perceived threat from a rival, jealousy, and anger. Perceived dissatisfaction was also related to jealousy and anger. Perceived desire for greater commitment was unrelated to jealousy measures.

White (1981d) employed the same four motives and added an attention motive (e.g., "To see if I really loved partner"), based on evidence that a major reason for inducing jealousy appears to be to gain attention (White, 1980a). As in the earlier study (White, 1981a), sexual and dissatisfaction motives predicted current level of jealousy, but neither commitment or attention attributions were related to level of jealousy.

Social Comparison. White (1981d) asked subjects to indicate which dimensions of comparison they used when worried about losing their partners to rivals. Most responses concerned physical/sexual attractiveness, personality, similarity to partner, job/professional position, willingness to form a long-term relationship with partner, or sensitivity to partner's ideas or emotions. A second group of subjects indicated how favorably or unfavorably they compared to rivals on these dimensions. Those who felt that the rivals were more similar to the partners than they were themselves were more jealous.

Another study asked recently jealous subjects to rate how similar they were to rivals on physical appearance, professional characteristics, social skills, personality, and sexual behavior; as well as to rate how superior or inferior they were to rivals across these categories (Buunk et al., 1984). Subjects who thought the rivals were dissimilar to them and superior in terms of sexual behavior were particularly likely to feel threatened by the rivals. Regardless of similarity to the rivals, women felt more threatened if the rivals were more physically attractive. Also, women felt more threatened if the rivals were dissimilar and superior in social skills, or if the rivals were similar and superior in professional competence. A straightforward interpretation is that when a rival appears both to behave differently and to perform sexually better than oneself, both the relationship and self-esteem are threatened. Given the importance of physical attractiveness in courtship, the greater dependence of women on marriage for status than men, and the importance of social competence for women's self-concept (Berscheid & Walster, 1974; Frieze, Parsons, Johnson, Ruble, & Zellman, 1978; Huston & Ashmore, 1986; Peplau, 1979), it is not surprising that women feel threatened if their rivals are more attractive and more socially skilled. The finding for professional competence may reflect women's fear that their partners would want someone who does work similar to their (the women's) own but at higher pay.

Two studies asked subjects in current relationships, most of whom had current or recent rivals, to rate the importance of various traits to their partners in choosing a romantic partner. Subjects then evaluated both themselves and their rivals on these same traits. Honesty, sincerity, warmth, and intelligence were rated as the most important traits in social comparison; right age, right height, popularity, and activity were rated as least important. Results showed derogation of rivals relative to self-valuation on those traits that had been rated as important to the partners, but less or no derogation of traits that had been rated as less important to the partners (Schmitt, 1988).

Alternatives Assessment. White (1981d) also asked subjects to indicate how difficult it would be to find substitute relationships for their current relationships. Subjects expecting difficulty were more likely to be jealous.

Loss Assessment. To date, there is no research related to loss assessment; this is unfortunate, given the centrality of loss in many conceptions of jealousy.

Coping

The clinical literature on jealousy contains numerous case examples of attempts to cope with normal or pathological jealousy (Ard, 1977; Clanton & Smith, 1977; Morgan, 1975; Mullen & Maack, 1985; Shepherd, 1961; White & Helbick, 1988). We present a number of such examples in later chapters. However, there are a few studies that have used methods other than the case report to assess jealousy coping (Bringle & Buunk, 1985; Clanton, 1981). White (1986a) has reviewed the outcomes of these studies, which are largely based on factor analyses of rationally derived items or on interviews with samples of jealous respondents (Bryson, 1976; Buunk, 1981, 1982; Francis, 1977; Hupka, Jung, & Porteous, 1981; Pines & Aronson, 1983; Shettle-Neuber et al., 1978). In addition, various authors have suggested a number of typologies of jealousy, usually rationally derived without supporting research evidence (Bernard, 1971; Bringle & Buunk, 1985; Bryson, 1977; Clanton & Smith, 1977; Constantine, 1976; Ellis, 1977; Freud, 1922/1955; Neu, 1980; Salovey & Rodin, 1986; White, 1976).

Based on this previous work and on theoretical considerations discussed below, White (1981c, 1986a) has proposed several coping strategies for jealousy. Strategies are associated with superordinate and subordinate goals that may be achieved through a great variety of coping behaviors. Eight strategies have been identified: (1) improving the primary relationship, (2) interfering with the rival relationship, (3) demanding commitment, (4) derogating partner and/or rival, (5) developing alternatives, (6) denial/avoidance, (7) self-assessment, and (8) support/catharsis. A ninth strategy, appraise challenge, may or may not reflect jealousy coping per se. These strategies are discussed in some detail shortly.

We do not claim that the eight strategies above constitute a definitive or exhaustive list of thoughts and behaviors used to cope with jealousy. For example, the jealous can obviously engage in a variety of cognitive strategies, such as humor, projection, and fantasy, to manage emotion (Haan, 1977; Lazarus & Folkman, 1984; Moos & Billings, 1982; Pearlin & Schooler, 1978; Vaillant, 1977). Rather, we focus on the eight strategies listed above because they appear to us either to be derived from the particular interpersonal circumstances of jealousy or to be particularly common among the jealous (Bringle & Buunk, 1985; White, 1981c). Further, many of them are similar in nature to some of the strategies that have been suggested by factor-analytic research (White, 1986a).

Goals of the Coping Strategies

There are several ways to conceptualize coping efforts. They may be under control of stimuli of which the person is unaware; they may be consciously intended; and they may achieve observable outcomes. Further, they may be interpreted by others as plausibly intended to achieve certain outcomes, whether or not they were consciously intended by the jealous person. Much of the coping literature consists of debates concerning which one of these approaches will be most useful in conceptualizing coping; no general solution has yet emerged (Lazarus & Folkman, 1984; Moos & Billings, 1982). Further, there is an even longer history of debate concerning the role of intentionality in human action (Bandura, 1986). This debate suggests that it is useful to distinguish efforts intended to achieve certain goals from the functions or outcomes of efforts. A goal is an intended outcome; an outcome is some alteration in the situation, in other actors, or in oneself.

We use the term "strategy" to denote a cognitive structure organized along lines of superordinate goals, subordinate goals, and associated representations of the behavioral and cognitive efforts that are needed to achieve the goals. Strategies may be consciously derived via problem-solving, but they may also be vicariously learned from the observation of social models. They may also develop as a consequence of observing how one's behavior yields successful outcomes that were not an original intention of the behavior. The person may or may not be able to articulate elements of strategies, but his or her professed ignorance does not mean that such strategies are not operative.

Strategies may be quite primitive and undifferentiated or may be composed of complex associations between superordinate and subordinate goals and particular efforts. (An example of a relatively undifferentiated strategy is the association of the superordinate goal of "avoiding fear" with only two subordinate goals: "hurt threatening others" or "stop thinking of threat." These two subordinate goals themselves may include only a small number of specific efforts believed to yield the goals, such as "yell obscenities" or "get drunk.")

We call strategies that are the result of conscious anticipation and planning "intentional strategies," whereas those that are reflexively enacted we call "reflexive strategies." Most strategies learned via modeling or via effort outcomes will be enacted without much planning, but clearly this does not always hold true. A person may choose to deliberately enact a jealousy coping strategy that is pervasively modeled within the culture.

This distinction between intentional strategies and reflexive strategies is useful in several ways. First, the jealous can convert reflexive strategies into intentional strategies when he or she becomes aware that certain efforts are having a particular desirable result. Second, reflexive strategies may be interpreted by the jealous and others as representing intentional strategies. Intentionality may be attributed to either conscious or unconscious values, plans, or needs of the actor (cf. Bem, 1972; Jones & Davis, 1965). For example, the jealous may observe that emotional displays lead to an improved relationship, and therefore may conclude that he or she (the jealous) must really want to improve the relationship. The beloved may observe that displays lead to assurances of commitment and conclude that the jealous must really need commitment, perhaps because of an unconscious need for commitment from a parental figure. Third, clinically it will often be the case that reflexive strategies can be discussed and modified within clear sociocultural, relationship, and role contexts, whereas intentional strategies may be more influenced by individual attitudes, values, and personality dynamics that affect the course of problem solving.

Superordinate Goals of Reducing Threat/Harm and Managing Emotion. The behaviors and thoughts of the jealous are aimed at either altering the situation or oneself to reduce harm or threat posed by the rival relationship (problem-focused coping), or at managing the affect following perceived harm or threat (emotion-focused coping). Both intentional and reflexive strategies are organized around one or both of these superordinate goals. Behaviors associated with different strategies may be compatible with each other (such as self-assessment and improving the relationship) or may interfere with each other (such as derogating the partner while trying to improve the relationship). However, each of the strategies can be seen as incorporating subordinate goals which themselves are intended to alter the problem situation or to manage affect. For example, a person may intend to improve the relationship to reduce the likelihood that the partner will leave, thereby reducing perceived threat to self or relationship.

Table 2.2 presents a summary of each jealousy coping strategy. It suggests if the superordinate goal of each strategy is likely to be altering the situation, managing affect, or both. Subordinate goals are listed for each strategy along with some examples of specific behavioral or cognitive coping efforts. In our discussion below we elaborate each strategy and give more examples from among the great many actual behaviors or thoughts that may achieve, or be intended to achieve, the subordinate goals of that strategy. Therefore, when discussing each strategy, we first start with the subordinate outcomes or goals around which specific behaviors and thoughts are organized.

The Eight Coping Strategies

Improving the Relationship. The goal of behaviors that improve the primary relationship is to make it more attractive to the partner than the secondary relationship. This can be done by increasing the partner's rewards or lowering the partner's costs (Kelley, 1979; Thibaut & Kelley, 1959), or by insuring greater consistency in the level of outcomes (Kelley, 1983). Examples include making oneself more physically attractive; doing more of the household chores; going more often than usual to entertainment the beloved likes; inquiring more often about the beloved's state of satisfaction; giving compliments to the beloved; demanding less time or attention from the beloved; and engaging more regularly in intimate, supportive communication.

Interfering with the Rival Relationship. The goal of interfering with the rival relationship is also to make the primary relationship relatively more attractive than the rival relationship. This is done by increasing the costs or lowering the rewards of the rival relationship. Again, a great many behaviors may be enacted toward achieving such interference. Dropping hints that the rival has unsavory attri-

TABLE 2.2. Jealousy Coping Strategies

Strategy	Superordinate goals	Subordinate goals	Examples of efforts
Improving relationship	Situation	Increase P's[1] rewards Decrease P's costs	Improving physical appearance Doing more of the housework
Interfering with adverse relationship	Situation	Decrease P's or R's rewards Increase P's or R's costs	Physical violence Inducing guilt
Demanding commitment	Situation, affect	Erect barriers to leaving primary relationship	Propose marriage Threaten violence
Derogation	Affect	Devalue primary relationship Discredit P + R threat to self-esteem	"Realizing" partner no longer ideal Provoking P to rejection
Developing alternatives	Affect, situation	Develop alternative sources of esteem and resources	Turn towards children Get involved in work
Denial/avoidance	Affect	Alter focus of attention	Get drunk Pretend oneself is unaffected
Self-assessment	Situation, affect	Develop new understandings of self and situation Develop new skills	Read a pop book on jealousy Change expectations about relationship
Support/catharsis	Affect	Diminish feelings through supported expression	Commiserating with a friend Individual psychotherapy
Appraise challenge	Affect, situation	Personal or relationship growth	Couples counseling Renegotiating relationship

Note. Strategies are cognitive organizations of superordinate and subordinate goals with specific behavioral and cognitive efforts associated with those goals.

[1]P = partner; R = rival.

butes, interrupting conversations between the rival and the beloved, inducing guilt in the beloved for seeing the rival, verbally or physically assaulting the rival or beloved, and withholding affection are all instances of decreasing the rewards or increasing the costs to either the beloved or the rival of the rival relationship.

These two strategies of improving the relationship and interfering with the rival relationship are usually what is meant by "jealous competition," a category of coping often mentioned by jealousy researchers (Bringle & Buunk, 1985; Clanton & Smith, 1977; White, 1986a). "Competition" can be carried out through either or both of these two strategies.

Demanding Commitment. The goal of demanding commitment is to force the partner into a choice that would erect social (e.g., marriage) or emotional (e.g., guilt) barriers to leaving the primary relationship (Levinger, 1979). A positive choice may enhance the self-esteem of the jealous as well. Commitment can be demanded in a number of ways, such as proposing marriage; stopping contraception without informing the beloved and conceiving a child; engaging in intimate self-disclosure about one's feelings while signaling that one can no longer tolerate the emotions induced by the rival relationship; pretending that one also has another potential partner who desires a committed relationship; and getting friends of the beloved to push the idea of a more committed relationship.

Derogating the Partner and/or Rival. The goals of derogation of the partner are to devalue the primary relationship and to discredit the beloved as a source of reliable information about the self. Devaluing the relationship may reduce the degree of threat over potential loss of the relationship and help in managing related affect. Discrediting the beloved may reduce the threat to self-esteem as well as manage affect. An example of devaluing rewards of the relationship is the "realization" that the partner is not as pretty or handsome as once thought or that the relationship is too demanding. An example of discrediting the beloved is the emerging belief that the partner cannot be trusted or is too manipulative.

The goal of derogation of the rival is to reduce the social comparison threat to self-esteem (Rosenberg, 1979; Salovey & Rodin, 1986; Schmitt, 1988; Suls & Miller, 1978; Tesser & Campbell, 1982), either by downplaying the rival's attributes or by inventing dimensions of comparison on which the self is clearly superior to the rival. For example, fantasies that one would be a better parent for yet-unborn children than the rival may help maintain esteem in the face of other, more easily confirmed disadvantageous comparisons between oneself and the rival. In addition, derogation of a rival may act to preserve a sense of certainty about the continuation of the relationship, since the rival's threat is less potent. This function is probably most likely if the beloved is perceived as pursued by the rival, rather than reciprocally attracted to him or her.

Derogation may be either cognitive or behavioral. Noticing and evaluating the beloved's peccadillos, engaging in fantasies about unworthy aspects of the rival, and name calling are more cognitive means of derogation. Manipulating the partner into some humiliating situation, inducing the rival to behave in antisocial ways, and demonstrating to rival or partner some previously hidden talent or resource (thereby establishing a new dimension of comparison) are behavioral avenues to derogation.

Developing Alternatives. The goal of developing alternatives is to secure alternative sources of esteem, desired interpersonal experiences, or valued resources—perhaps especially those aspects of esteem, interaction, or resources that are appraised as lost, damaged, or under threat. Developing alternatives reduces dependency on the primary relationship for affirmation of both self-esteem and self-concept, as well as for satisfying exchange. Alternatives may be developed by seeking new romantic partners, turning to friends or to one's children, getting more involved in work, getting a pet, calling up an old lover, joining a hobby club, and so forth.

Denial/Avoidance. The goal of denial/avoidance is primarily to manage negative affect consequent to perceived harm/threat (Haan, 1977; Lazarus & Folkman, 1984; Moos & Billings, 1982; Vaillant, 1977). A wide range of depth of denial is implied, from convenient rationalization to psychotic distortion of reality. Avoidance implies physically or psychologically removing one's attention from stimuli that engender unpleasant affect, such as walking out on a date, getting drunk, or engaging in tasks that demand constant attention (e.g., a fast and furious drive in the car). Denial/avoidance here is not meant to encompass impression management techniques to make the *beloved* think one is less affected than one actually is. Impression management may be associated with other goals, such as improving the relationship or interfering with the rival relationship (Buunk & Bringle, 1987; Hupka et al., 1981).

Self-Assessment. "Self-assessment" is our term for what Lazarus terms "inward-directed coping" (Lazarus & Folkman, 1984, p. 152). As discussed earlier, inward-directed efforts may be problem-focused in the sense that one tries to change oneself in order to better manage the environment that is perceived as threatening. Inward-directed change may also result in reappraisals that serve to manage affect (cognitive reappraisals) or in interpretations of events that suggest different coping strategies (secondary appraisal or reappraisal of degree of threat/harm). Examples of self-assessment, problem-focused coping efforts include undergoing psychotherapy in order to develop the skills to make the partner more satisfied with the relationship; reading books on how to make oneself sexier and hence more able to attract new lovers; reading pop psychology books for clues on how to be a better person; and taking up meditation so that stress is reduced, allowing for a calmer approach to the partner.

Self-assessment that primarily results in cognitive reappraisals (which reduce aversive affect) often involves self-conscious attempts to change self-concept and values. For example, moving from a concept of love that is passion-oriented to one that is oriented toward intimate self-disclosure may result in less anxiety concerning sexual performance. Moving from a concept of oneself as being relatively unlovable to a concept of being lovable may reduce depression over the possible loss of the primary relationship. Thinking of oneself as mainly interested in career rather than relationships may reduce the anxiety over perceived rejection.

Self-assessment also refers to changes in the way the person constructs meaning about the actions of the beloved or rival, and is akin to the concept of "reframing" popular in some systems-oriented therapies (Hoffman, 1981; Sherman & Fredman, 1986). The same events are given a different interpretation in a way that reduces unpleasant affect or suggests coping efforts not previously considered. For example, interpreting a rival's actions as indicating a sincere, platonic interest in developing a friendship with the beloved may fit the observed facts as well as or better than inferring a romantic interest. Thinking of the beloved's tendency to flirt at parties as a way in which he or she prepares for heightened sexual pleasure with oneself may not only fit the facts as well, but lead to quite a different emotional reaction to flirtation.

As these examples suggest, self-assessment refers to a variety of internal changes. These can be conceptualized as one category because the different functions are intertwined. That is, any self-assessment behavior or thought has simultaneous elements of preparing oneself to act on the environment, of managing affect, and of suggesting new interpretations of events in a way that allows for planning new coping efforts. For example, psychotherapy of jealousy may have all three elements of action, interpretation, and reduction of emotion.

Support/Catharsis. The strategy of support/catharsis is directed toward the management of emotions through their safe expression. Often such feelings are expressed to friends who can support the effort (Wills, 1985). (Additional instances of turning to friends, we believe, are related to other coping strategies or to appraisal—e.g., to gather information about the partner's motives.) We use "catharsis" in its literal sense as a cleansing discharge of emotion, resulting in more stable and less dysphoric emotions and moods. Of course, displays of emotion do not always result in catharsis, but here again we wish to differentiate between a strategic goal and an actual outcome. "Support/catharsis" refers to an attempt to reduce unpleasant affect through discharge, particularly in the presence of supportive others. It does not refer to acting out or other emotional displays where the intent is to avoid unpleasant affect, intimidate the partner, or manage impression.

Appraise Challenge. The jealous person may discover aspects of self or relationship that are perceived as presenting a challenge to personal or relationship growth which go beyond the particulars of the jealousy situation. For example, a jealous man may realize that his adoption of a rigid masculine sex role is not only related to his current jealousy but is also related to many other problems in his life. His jealousy poses a challenge to change his concepts of masculinity and masculine behavior, but this change is related to much more than his current jealousy. A jealous woman may realize that she and her husband have poor communication as a consequence of trying to resolve her jealousy, but see that the communication is poor for many other aspects of their life together. Her jealousy leads to a challenge to change the communication pattern, but this change extends well beyond the particulars of her jealousy.

The appraisal of challenge may enable the person to more effectively cope with jealousy, but that is not perceived as the only or primary goal. Appraising challenge may lead the jealous away from an overly narrow concern with the particulars of the jealousy situation. In this regard it differs from self-assessment, where the goal is to manage the particular jealousy situation or its associated emotion. Challenge appraisals suggest that certain changes in and of themselves are valuable or lead to valuable outcomes that are not focused on the jealousy. For example, better marital communication may or may not affect the jealousy, but it may reduce conflict in other areas.

In terms of our concept of coping strategy, appraising challenge results in the development of new subordinate goals, such as better communication or becoming less sex-role stereotyped. Once these other goals are developed, the particular coping efforts to achieve them are not conceptualized as jealousy coping per se as the superordinate goals of managing the jealousy situation or reducing jealous affect are no longer operative. However, the act of developing other subordinate goals may have consequences for reducing (or increasing) threat to self-esteem and relationship, or for managing emotion. For example, a focus on improving marital communication may improve the relationship for the beloved, may lead to a greater sense of control and predictability for the jealous, and may reduce the dependence of the jealous on the beloved for self-esteem.

A Cultural Cautionary Note. We would like to reiterate that culture plays a profound role in shaping the jealousy complex. This raises the question of the generalizability of our coping strategies. We do not expect that the specific behaviors and thoughts commonly used to cope within one culture will necessarily generalize to another. We do assume that the processes of appraisal, emotion, and coping operate universally. For the time being, we assume that our eight functional coping strategies are classifications at an appropriate level of abstraction to augur for universality. Cultures may differ in the extent to which derogation or self-assessment or improving the relationship is a valued coping solution, but we hold for now that the eight strategies will prove useful for meaningfully classifying coping efforts across cultures.

Research on Coping with Jealousy

Most of the research on coping has employed factor analysis of face-valid coping items given to jealous subjects. There are major problems with such studies. First, the coping factors that emerge depend on which behaviors just happened to be chosen by the researchers for rating by subjects. Second, the resulting factors often have items measuring thoughts and emotions as well as coping efforts per se. Not only do these factors likewise depend on just what thought and emotion items the researchers decided to include; it is also unclear whether the resulting factors are really assessing coping efforts, patterns among elements of the jealousy complex, or cultural expectations about what the jealousy complex is. Third, questionnaire items are often a mix of specific behaviors ("get drunk") and categories of behavior ("express jealousy"). It is hard to know what to make of correlations among such questions, let alone how to interpret the factors that result.

Bryson (1976) reported three factors that have elements of coping: Need for Social Support ("talk to close friends about my feelings"), Confrontation ("confront the other person directly," "ask my partner to explain the situation"), and Reactive Retribution ("start going out with other people," "make critical comments about my partner in front of other people"). Shettel-Neuber et al. (1978) showed subjects a jealousy-inducing videotape vignette and asked them to predict how they would have reacted. Coping responses depended to some extent on the attractiveness of the rival.

Sharpsteen and Schmalz (1988) coded subjects' reports of actual jealousy episodes, and reported that over half tried to conceal their jealousy and over one-third kept their feelings to themselves. Both can be interpreted as denial/avoidance strategies. Francis (1977) interviewed 15 couples and reported that denial, threat, monitoring the partner, competition, and renegotiation of the relationship were common coping attempts. Schmitt (1988) found that subjects derogated actual romantic rivals on traits they thought were important to their romantic partners, but did not derogate partners on less important traits; these results suggest selectivity in derogation that functions to maintain self-esteem (Tesser & Campbell, 1982). Buunk (1986) reported that highly jealous subjects were more likely to use physical or overt aggression, both of which are forms of interfering with the rival relationship. Buunk (1981) asked partners in sexually open marriages to indicate the extent to which various thoughts and behaviors reduced marital jealousy. Four emergent factors were Independence (becoming less dependent on partner), Acceptance (expressing and accepting jealousy), Trust, and Communication. In our terms, Buunk's Independence factor relates to our strategy of developing alternatives; Acceptance is an aspect of self-assessment; and Trust and Communication relate to improving the relationship.

In what appears to have been a follow-up study, Buunk (1982b) asked a sample of earlier subjects to indicate how frequently they had engaged in 13 "jealousy coping" efforts selected for face validity. He reported three factors of Avoidance, Reappraisal, and Communication. Though a direct translation is not warranted, these factors appear to us to be related to our strategies of denial/avoidance, self-assessment, challenge, and improving the relationship.

Salovey and Rodin (1988) factor-analyzed 15 face-valid coping items and reported three factors: Self-Reliance (which appears to assess attempts to manage emotion by inhibition, such as "refraining from anger"), Self-Bolstering (attempts to feel good about oneself), and Reducing the Importance of the Situation. The latter may reflect coping similar to our denial/avoidance. All three appear to be emotion-focused coping efforts. Self-Reliance and Reducing Importance were associated with less jealousy reported toward friends and in school or work situations; their association with romantic jealousy was not reported. Self-Reliance and Self-Bolstering were associated with less depression in these domains, while only Self-Reliance was associated with less anger. In general, it appears that conscious attempts to inhibit or prevent negative emotions were the most powerful of the three methods of managing jealous affects.

Schmitt (1988) focused on the use of derogation as a strategy in romantic jealousy. Not surprisingly, derogation was the most strong for those attributes of romantic rivals that were perceived as important to the beloved. Schmitt points out that these results may reflect a need to see the primary relationship as more secure than it may actually be (the rival is thus seen as less threatening to the relationship), as well as a need to reduce self-esteem threat.

Research on the Relationships between Secondary Appraisal and Coping

Only one study has examined relationships between secondary-appraisal processes and coping efforts. White (1981d) reported the degree to which motive attribution, alternatives assessment, and social comparison were related to each of seven coping strategies. Improving the relationship was more likely if attention was a perceived motive for partner involvement. Interference was more likely if the rival's nonsexual attraction was the motive. Denial was less likely if a sexual motive was perceived, but more likely if rival attraction or attention was the perceived motive. Developing alternatives was more likely if rival attraction was the motive. Interference was more likely if the jealous person thought his or her personality compared favorably to that of the rival or if the rival was perceived as being more similar to the partner. Denial was less likely if the rival was more similar, whereas derogation was more likely. Derogation was also more likely if the rival was seen as more intelligent than onself.

SUMMARY

We have defined jealousy as a *complex* of behaviors, thoughts, and emotions resulting from the perception of harm or threat to the self and/or the romantic relationship by a real or potential rival relationship. A distinction has been made between the intrapersonal complex of relationships among thoughts, emotions, and behaviors of the jealous person, and the interpersonal system of relationships among actors within the jealousy triangle. Theoretical support for our definition is offered through a discussion of the twin dependencies between romantic partners for self-esteem and for the provision of satisfying experiences and resources. We have selectively presented previous definitions of jealousy to provide a frame or reference for our model and to illustrate weaknesses in previous approaches.

We have then presented our model of jealousy, which incorporates our definition while outlining the larger contexts of the jealousy complex and of the surrounding intrapersonal and interpersonal systems. This model draws on the metatheoretical scheme of Kelley et al. (1983) and on Lazarus's cognitive–transactional theory of stress (Lazarus & Folkman, 1984). We have differentiated the affects, behavior, and thoughts of the jealous into the primary elements of the jealousy complex and elaborated our conceptualization of these elements. Previous jealousy research related to these elements has been reviewed. The resulting elaborated model of jealousy, we believe, will be useful in integrating previous theory, clinical observation, and basic research. It also points to gaps in our empirical knowledge and provides a process-oriented framework that we hope will have a high degree of generalizability to different cultures.

3

The Sociobiology of Jealousy

The theory of evolution through natural selection (Darwin, 1871) has exerted a profound influence upon science and the general public alike. It is common for the layperson to assume that jealousy is just "natural" and reflects some kind of biological imperative (Clanton & Smith, 1977; Hupka, 1981). In addition, sociobiologists have tried to link both human and animal jealousy with genetic determinants. In this chapter we outline their basic approach. As we shall see, there are enormous conceptual and methodological problems in validating sociobiological hypotheses; in fact, there is no empirical work that directly links jealousy with genes. Given the lack of research and the popularity of evolutionary explanations for human behavior, we devote much of our discussion to specifying a number of cautions about genetic explanations for jealousy.

Darwin himself presented a stark image of the savage, sexually jealous male animal:

> There can be little doubt that the greater size and strength of man, in comparison with women, together with his broad shoulders, more developed muscles, rugged outline of body, his greater courage and pugnacity, are all due in chief part to inheritance from his half-human ancestors. These characteristics would, however, have been preserved or even augmented during the long ages of man's savagery, by the success of the strongest and boldest men, both in the general struggle for life and in their contest for wives; a success which would have ensured their leaving a more numerous progeny than their less favored brethren. . . .
>
> [Men] originally lived in small communities, each with a single wife, or if powerful with several, whom he jealously guarded against all other men. (1871, pp. 325, 394)

Darwin's comments have several features that permeate later sociobiological thinking. First, physical characteristics (broad shoulders) are lumped together with social or psychological characteristics (courage). Second, it is the male who has been shaped to be jealous (via competition); this suggests that gender differences in jealousy will have a genetic base. Third, the jealousy of modern-day humans is similar to that of distant ancestors stretching back to prehuman species. Fourth, the mechanism of natural selection (greater probability of survival of one's genes because of better fitness for the environment) for specific traits accounts for the genetic basis of jealousy. Males inherit a specific capacity for aggressive, sexual jealousy in response to real or potential threats to their sexual access to mates. Fifth, social structures are derivative from biological inheritance.

We will not catalog here the great variety of social scientists and social commentators who have accepted the basic Darwinian sketch of human jealousy since the rise of evolutionary theory, except to note two very influential authors. Westermarck (1936), one of the early sociologists of the family, reviewed the anthropological and ethological evidence of his day and concluded that male jealousy was instinctually aggressive and competitive, noting that jealous violence served to prevent promiscuity. Kinsey and his associates (Kinsey et al., 1953) also reviewed ethological reports while commenting on their own landmark American study, which seemed to show that (1) males had a greater drive for sexual variety than females and (2) jealous males were more sexually threatened and aggressive than jealous females. They concluded, "While cultural traditions may account for some of the human male's behavior, his jealousies so closely parallel those of the lower species that one is forced to conclude that his mammalian heritage may be partly responsible for his attitudes" (1953, p. 411).

MODERN SOCIOBIOLOGICAL THEORY OF JEALOUSY

Sociobiology is an emerging field that attempts to integrate research and theory in ethology, comparative psychology, population biology, and evolutionary theory. Although it is wide-ranging, its basic premise is that both animal and human social behavior is ultimately under genetic control. That is, specific behaviors—or, more correctly, capacities for such behaviors—are inherited via genetic transmission.

These inherited potentials are the result of natural selection that favored their expression in specific ecologies. Those individuals who expressed certain specific behaviors were more likely to have surviving progeny than individuals who did not have the genetic capacity for such behaviors. Sociobiologists acknowledge that behavioral "genotypes" (genetically coded behavior patterns) interact with specific environments to produce behavioral "phenotypes" (actual behavior) (Lumsden & Wilson, 1981; Wilson, 1975).

Although sociobiology has only been a distinct academic specialty for less than two decades, it has generated a great deal of controversy both within and outside of academia, especially for the attempt to explain human behavior. Sociobiology has been criticized from within evolutionary biology (e.g., Gould, 1978, 1980), as well as from without by feminists, psychologists, and anthropologists. Criticisms have been raised at the technical, conceptual, and moral/political levels. This controversy cannot be reviewed here (interested readers are referred to excellent edited volumes and reviews by Barlow & Silverberg, 1980; Caplan, 1978; Fetzer, 1985; Lewontin, Rose, & Kamin, 1984; Rose, 1982; Sahlins, 1976; and Wade, 1976). Many of the cautions we raise later about genetic explanations of jealousy, however, have been more generally raised about the general application of sociobiological theory to human behavior.

Modern sociobiological accounts of romantic jealousy derive from the theory of "parental investment" (Trivers, 1972) and its derivative, the concept of "paternity confidence" (Daly et al., 1982; Kurland, 1979). We consider each in turn, along with their implications for jealousy.

The Theory of Parental Investment

"Parental investment" refers to the energy expended by parents to produce and nurture offspring. More accurately, the term refers to the decrement in future reproductive potential as a consequence of present effort (Trivers, 1972; Wilson, 1975). The more energy that is expended in raising current progeny, the less energy there is available for producing and nurturing other offspring. It is immediately apparent that if investment is high, it is evolutionarily advantageous for the parent to insure the survival of current progeny. Those parents who do so will be more likely to pass along their parental genes. If investment is low, it is evolutionarily advantageous to have numerous offspring in order to insure survival of the genes through force of numbers, rather than through insuring the survival of a small number of highly invested offspring.

One of the facts of biological life, at least for mammals, is that eggs are scarce while sperm are plentiful. Because females transmit their genes through their eggs, they must insure that their relatively few offspring will survive. Hence, maternal investment will necessarily be high. Males, on the other hand, have a different reproductive strategy. In order to insure survival of their genes, they attempt to sire as many progeny as possible. To do so, they cannot afford to put much energy into raising any one offspring; rather, they limit paternal investment and redirect their energy into impregnating as many females as often as possible. The catch is that all other males of the species are driven by the same dynamic for a limited pool of females. Hence, males compete for access to females in order to inseminate as many as possible. Females do not compete to be inseminated, but may compete to secure paternal investment in their progeny. (In some species paternal investment is as high as or higher than maternal investment, and in such species the females may be the aggressive competitors for the male. See Trivers, 1972, and Wilson, 1975).

According to natural selection theory, females who invest highly in their young are more likely to pass along their genes to future generations, establishing females of the species as the primary caretakers of the young. Males who successfully compete to sire many progeny are more likely to have their genes transmitted; hence males are established as the sexually competitive gender with little caretaking of the young.

These differing reproductive strategies, according to the theory, have the consequence of favoring secondary sexual characteristics that give each gender an edge in its own strategy. For females, for example, small body size relative to appetite permits greater energy expenditure for gestation and lactation than for body maintenance (Hrdy & Williams, 1983). Males, however, should benefit from physical and psychological traits that aid in competition for females, largely via aggression and display. Hence, species in which maternal investment is high and paternal investment is low should be marked by sexual dimorphism, or anatomical and psychological differences between genders.

Another result of the difference in reproductive strategies is that active competition among males results in increased variability in the distribution of female mates to males. The most successful males may mate exclusively with several females, whereas many males may not have access to females at all—a situation reminiscent of Darwin's guess about early human social structure (Lancaster, 1985; Trivers, 1972; Wilson, 1975). Dominance hierarchies and territoriality may evolve to reduce the energy directed toward competition by the most fit males so that they may put more energy into mating and defense of the social group, which itself is made up of a substantial number of their progeny (Wilson, 1975). It is tempting to generalize from such data by offering biological justifications for human dominance hierarchies and polygyny (males' having multiple mates) (Barash, 1977; Kurland, 1979; Rose, 1982; Sahlins, 1976).

However, paternal investment is more likely if monogamous pair bonding is advantageous. As Wilson notes (1975, pp. 330–334), monogamy is more likely when environmental pressures can be better overcome by two adults defending territory and securing food, or, as is especially the case for humans, when the young are not able to care for themselves for a long time.

Sociobiologists acknowledge that human paternal investment is markedly higher than that of any other mammal, including our closest genetic relatives, the primates (Alexander & Noonan, 1979; Lancaster, 1985; Kurland, 1979; Symons, 1979; West & Konner, 1976; Wilson, 1975). The theory would predict that if parental investment is high and closer to that of the female, sexual dimorphism should diminish. And, indeed, compared to most other mammals including the primates, male and female humans are generally much more alike in body size, weapons of aggression, sexuality, bond formation, and behavioral levels of aggression and nurturance (Hrdy & Williams, 1983; Kurland, 1979; Lancaster, 1985; Rossi, 1985; Symons, 1979).

The Problem of Paternity Confidence

However, greater paternal investment poses a problem of genetic transmission to males that is not faced by females. The dilemma is this: Females almost always will know that the offspring they are investing in are their own because of the fact of live birth. Males, however, have no such assurance based on the act of birth alone. If a male were to invest highly in the offspring of another male, it is the other male's genes that have a greater likelihood of survival, not those of the investing male. Hence, in terms of survival of the individual's genes, high levels of paternal investment will be a viable pattern only if "paternity probability" is also relatively high. This is the probability that the young invested in by the male are in fact his offspring."Paternity confidence" is the individual male's assessment of paternity probability. (To use the term "assessment" does not imply consciousness at all, but rather some decision process that results in greater likelihood of investment.) If paternity confidence is high, males are more likely to invest in their own offspring (West & Konner, 1976). If confidence is related to actual probability, then, evolutionarily, mechanisms of assuring paternity confidence are likely to become genetically established.

Explanation of Jealousy

The sociobiologists are now in a position to explain male sexual jealousy. As Symons (1979) puts it, "the ultimate function of male jealousy is to increase the probability that one's wife [note the human term for mate] will conceive one's own rather than someone else's child" (p. 242). Daly et al. (1982), in the most explicit statement of the sociobiological perspective, believe that

> *Homo sapiens* [have evolved] certain psychological propensities which function to defend paternity confidence. Manifestations include the emotion of sexual jealousy, the dogged inclination of men to possess and control women, and the use or threat of violence to achieve sexual exclusivity and control. We will refer to this behavioural/motivational complex as male sexual jealousy. (p. 11)

Or, as the recognized founder of sociobiology puts it, "the theory [of parental investment] suggests that a particularly severe form of aggressiveness should be reserved for actual or suspected adultery" (Wilson, 1975, p. 327). Wilson then goes on to discuss how human adulterers (especially females) are treated harshly in many cultures. Finally, Kurland (1979) previews an extended discussion of avuncular care of sister's offspring with the statement, "For those species in which the male's relative parental investment approaches that of a female, a male will be selected to guard against 'cuckoldry'—that is, against the probability that he might invest in offspring which are not his" (p. 149).

Note that these suggestions contain, explicitly or implicitly, many of the same assumptions present in Darwin's position: There is a genetic basis for gender differences in jealousy; jealousy of modern-day males is rooted in prehistorical ancestors' patterns; natural selection shapes jealousy; social structures are derivative from genetic facts; and specific psychological and behavioral propensities are inherited.

It is instructive to understand the kinds of evidence offered by the sociobiologists when they hypothesize that male jealousy is the primary means of insuring paternity confidence. First, analogies are made to infrahuman species, with the explicit or implicit assumption that if other animals' "jealousy" is genetically controlled, so must be that of the human animal. Second, note is made of gender differences between modern-day men and women in jealousy. Third, it is noted that male sexual jealousy is often related to conflict and murder. Fourth, evidence is marshaled that there is a universal or nearly universal practice of male constraint of female sexuality, while the reverse is rarely the case. Fifth, human concerns with paternity confidence found in anthropological descriptions or in literature are cited as evidence of the likelihood of biological involvement (Alexander & Noonan, 1979; Daly et al., 1982; Kurland, 1979; Symons, 1979; Trivers, 1972; Wilson, 1975). All of these arguments are arguments by analogy or after-the-fact reasoning.

Other Methods of Insuring Paternity Confidence

In addition to direct uses of threats or violence to control mates by jealous males, a number of other means of insuring paternity confidence have been suggested. These include control of territories and dominance hierarchies, which act to keep other males away from females (backed up by threat of violence); familiarity with the mother; patterns of previous mating with the mother; recognition of familial traits in the offspring; and females' alerting dominant males to mating attempts of other males (supposedly inducing jealousy) (Cox & Le Boeuf, 1977; Hrdy & Williams, 1983; Trivers, 1972; Wilson, 1975). In addition, Alexander and Noonan (1979) suggest that the continuous sexual receptivity of the human female strengthens paternity confidence, as rival males have no clues as to ovulation (which in all other mammals is strongly linked with female receptivity), thus favoring the mate who has intercourse more frequently than rivals.

Another suggestion is that the problem of paternity confidence can be circumvented by the "avunculate"—the social pattern of males' investment in the progeny of sisters rather than, or in addition to, investment in their own children (Irons, 1979; Kurland, 1979). Since one's own offspring have half of each parent's genes, usually investment would be in one's own progeny rather than in a sister's, who has a quarter of one's own genes. However, if paternity probability is such that the likelihood of one's own genes in offspring approaches that of one's genes in a sister's children, then the avunculate will develop, as one's own genes may be more likely to be transmitted through the sister's progeny than through a mate's progeny.

Cross-culturally, avuncular investment is more likely to the degree that women have multiple sexual partners (Kurland, 1979). It is quite another proposition to suppose that some genotype in humans for the expression of avunculate social roles interacts with particular cultural environments to produce a complicated social system in which males invest in their sisters' children. However, the notion of genetic determination of the avunculate pattern is interesting, because it suggests that genetically controlled behavioral patterns other than male aggressive sexual jealousy may be capable of insuring genetic transmission.

Summary of the Sociobiological Argument

According to the theory of parental investment, females will direct their energy toward the care of their own offspring, while males will have little paternal investment and will attempt to mate with as many females as possible. Sexual dimorphism results, which helps the female in the role of raising progeny and the male in competition for females. The extension of this to humans is the most atavistic of metaphors: Male jealousy is sexually oriented and aggressively competitive, and coupled with strong urges for sexual variety. Some sociobiologists adopt this basic metaphor (Symons, 1979).

However, most sociobiologists note that human males invest heavily in their own (or their sisters') offspring, but that to do so they must be assured of relatively high paternity probability. Assessment of this probability is paternity confidence. High male investment explains the relatively weak sexual dimorphism in humans, while the necessity of paternity confidence has led to human males having sexual jealousy marked by violence and consistent attempts to restrict the sexual behavior of women. Presumably as a leftover from the remote phylogenetic past, the sexual motivation and behavior of men are not genetically restricted, as polygyny is accepted, condoned, or advocated in the great majority of cultures. Female jealousy is centered more on concerns related to paternal investment than on male extrarelationship sexuality per se, as greater paternal investment should increase the chance of survival for the female's offspring.

In short, sociobiological theory holds that female jealousy is marked by fear and anxiety over losing the relationship and by an interest in the nature of the rival relationship, whereas male jealousy, focusing on the sexual threat of the rival, is marked by competitiveness and aggression, and is much less affected by situational factors suggesting that the mate is still interested in maintaining the primary bond (Barash, 1977; Daly et al., 1982; Farber, 1973; Irons, 1979; Symons, 1979; Trivers, 1972; Wilson, 1975). As we shall see in Chapter 5, these gender differences have been noted in contemporary research. Leaving aside the fact that some of the sociobiological arguments were developed in order to explain gender differences in human data, does this fit between genetically based theory and human data imply that human sexual jealousy is under genetic control?

There are a great many objections to making the leap from the plausible fit of the theory to human data to the inference that genetic mechanisms actually determine the nature of human jealousy. We have already noted the use of analogy and after-the-fact explanations by sociobiologists; these are weak forms of argument and are usually considered prescientific (Kaplan, 1964; Popper, 1965). In the next section we discuss further objections. Some of these accept the sociobiologists' basic premise that specific human behaviors are under genetic control; others suggest the inapplicability of such genetic models to human jealousy, however applicable they may be to animal behavior patterns.

OBJECTIONS AND CAUTIONS CONCERNING THE SOCIOBIOLOGICAL ARGUMENT

Objections and Cautions That Accept the Premise of Genetic Control

Why Are Wives More Likely to Be Killed Than Rivals?

Male sexual jealousy is much more likely to result in aggression toward or death of the beloved than in aggression toward or death of the rival. The pattern is not universal; in many cultures the rival is as likely or more so to be the object of aggression. But, without a doubt, in Western cultures it is the female beloved and not the male rival who is usually killed. This poses a problem for upholding the concept of paternity confidence. Killing the beloved should lower the survival chances of children, as well as decrease the chances of future pair bonding. This would make it less likely for aggression to become genetically established. It is possible that the greater likelihood of murder of the mate results from complex interactions among actual paternal probability, probability of survival of existing progeny, and probability of forming new relationships. However, no sociobiologist has posited such interactions. Greater sophistication of models may or may not solve this problem.

Inappropriate Generalization to and from Other Species

If human jealousy is so closely linked to our remote ancestors among the mammals, then it should show some similarity to behavior in genetically closely related species such as the primates. Lancaster (1985) surveyed gender differences among the primates in dominance patterns, attachment, mating and sex, and morphology. She concluded, "The demands of sexual selection and paternal investment strategies fall differently on each sex [among primates] *and these patterns are highly species specific* . . . it is *virtually impossible* to generalize about what male or female primates do" (p. 22; italics added). The sociobiologists have inappropriately generalized, both from humans to other primates and vice versa.

For example, there is ample evidence that female monkeys and apes are promiscuous, even in species with sexual consortships (Hrdy & Williams, 1983; Lancaster, 1985). Female primates are frequently sexually assertive, not just passive objects of male advance. Females have even been observed killing the young of other females and forming special sexual attachments with nondominant males (Hrdy & Williams, 1983). All of these data, based on modern field observation methods, are at odds with the general picture of genetically determined gender differences in sex and jealousy supposed by the sociobiologists.

Hence, though it may be that human jealousy is genetically determined, to generalize from other primates (let alone other mammals) to humans is not defensible. Human patterns per se have to be determined and then, if possible, linked to genetic mechanisms. This is a monumental task for the sociobiologists, given the incredible diversity of the jealousy complex and the great variety of situations that elicit it cross-culturally—a diversity vastly greater than among primates.

Failure to Consider Other Means of Securing Paternity Confidence

A great many means of securing paternity confidence other than male aggressive jealousy can be supposed. As mentioned earlier, only the avunculate and female sexual receptivity have been proposed for humans in any detail. Yet sociobiologists must consider alternatives and explain via genetic modeling why these other forms are not observed. Failure to do so leaves the sociobiologists in a very weak logical position, since any plausible story can be formulated to explain the development of current patterns (Gould, 1980).

We would like to present a short list of plausible methods of security paternity confidence that do not require aggressive male jealousy. First, natural selection might have favored those males who did not direct aggression toward females, thus reducing the likelihood that females would avoid that male and accept another. Second, natural selection should have favored males who were particularly sensitive to subtle cues that the female mate was ovulating—cues that may also have been selected to be discernible only in a close, sustained relationship. Third, natural selection might have favored males who, once a pair bond formed, would only be sexually attracted to their mates. This would reduce competition among males, allowing for maximal investment in their own offspring. Fourth, natural selection might have favored males who would be willing to cooperate and negotiate for paternity rights, thus freeing them of the energy expenditure and risk of aggression while insuring paternity confidence. Fifth, natural selection might have favored expression of recognizable traits of offspring that were more similar to paternal traits than maternal, thus insuring that males could identify paternity. For example, offspring might more closely resemble their father than their mother in hair color or distribution, smell, or physiognomy. Sixth, natural selection might have favored females who experienced disgust or pain in mating with any other male but the primary-bond male, but who experienced great pleasure in mating with him, thus increasing paternity confidence. Seventh, natural selection might have favored males who were more likely to invest in female offspring than in male offspring. Daughters will always pass along the father's genes, but the problem of paternity probability would make it less likely that sons would pass along the father's genes. Daughters, then, should be especially treasured by fathers, who would naturally want them to be impregnated by as many fit males as possible.

More possibilities could be suggested, but the point we are trying to make is that sociobiologists need to elaborate in detail just why these other methods do not appear to be prominent. It is not sufficient to say that male aggressive jealousy must have been the best solution; this needs, at the very least, to be tested in mathematical models against other possibilities. Otherwise, the sociobiologists will have less of a defense against the thesis that aggressive male jealousy is the result of cultural conditioning.

Adoption of the Pleistocene Fallacy

Silverberg (1980) comments on what he calls the "early Pleistocene behavioral fixation"—that is, the assumption that contemporary traits stretch back to outcomes of natural selection affecting ancestors several hundred thousand years ago. There are several problems with such an assumption. First, there is very little evidence for any behavioral traits in such remote ancestors; we are lucky enough to have a few bone fragments. Sociobiologists rely on generalizing from other modern mammals (which is hard to defend; see above), about whom we have no evidence of behavioral traits for their remote ancestors.

Second, sociobiologists make assertions about patterns of primitive humankind that are at variance with what is known about remaining hunter–gatherer cultures. Leacock (1980) notes that modern Western culture is much more competitive than the great majority of hunter–gatherer cultures. Since it is estimated that about 95% of the history of *Homo sapiens* was spent in hunting–gathering and the remainder in agricultural and industrial societies (Leacock, 1980; Wilson, 1975), assertions that competitiveness characterized human evolution must be taken very cautiously. Leacock further notes that sociobiologists explain wife swapping in terms of harsh environments that demand cooperation, a demand that overrides the genetic propensity for jealousy to insure paternity confidence. Yet if most extant hunter–gatherer societies are marked by cooperation rather than competition, it might be expected that paternity confidence would have been less of an issue in prehistory than it is today among competitive societies.

Third is the possibility that substantial evolution could have taken place in human beings in a relatively short period of time. A leading sociobiologist suggests,

> The theory of population genetics and experiments on other organisms show that substantial [biological] changes can occur in a span of less than 100 generations . . . Two thousand generations, roughly the period since typical *Homo sapiens* invaded Europe, is enough time to create new species and to mold them in major ways . . . it would be false to assume that modern civilizations have been built entirely on capital accumulated during the long haul of the Pleistocene. (Wilson, 1975, p. 569)

Failure to Consider the Impact of Culture on Genetic Change

Durham (1979) cites several examples of how cultural practice can affect human genotypic distribution. For example, cultures in which there is high milk or alcohol consumption have much higher frequencies of genes that control for enzymes involved in the metabolism of lactose and alcohol. At least with regard to jealousy, sociobiologists have not examined the possibility that non-genetically based cultural practices have led to selection for traits genetically related to the development or expression of jealousy. For example, it could be that the extension of private property norms to sexual property (Davis, 1936)—a wholly cultural development—could have led to natural selection for aggressively jealous males, as their response would have been supported by social norms and hence more likely to lead to survival of progeny.

Objections and Cautions That Do Not Accept the Premise of Genetic Control

Human Genes' Control for Plasticity Rather Than Specificity

Several critics have pointed out a paradox in the sociobiological argument. The great advantage that has led to the dominance of *Homo sapiens* is the capacity to learn, to adapt flexibly to situations. Cultural evolution is the collective aspect of this plasticity of behavior. Humans have a survival advantage because their specific social behaviors are *not* under genetic control, but under the control of the processes of socialization and learning. While the human genotype allows for this plasticity, the content of behavior cannot be under specific control. If it were, the survival advantage conferred by plasticity (and, hence by cultural evolution) would be erased. Thus, human beings differ greatly from all other species, including other primates, in that genes do not control for specific behaviors or their potential.

To claim that jealousy or any other behavior pattern is specifically genetically determined is thus a major error (Durham, 1979; Gould, 1978, 1980; Lewontin et al., 1984; Rose, 1982; Sahlins, 1976; Silverberg, 1980). As Gould (1978) notes, there is no direct evidence for genetic control of any specific human social behavior. Such evidence could come from twin studies, breeding studies (ethically impossible), or sophisticated neuropsychological studies; but such studies have not been done to test sociobiological theories of jealousy, and their success at establishing genetic bases for a few other behavior patterns (schizophrenia, intelligence) is mixed (Lewontin et al., 1984).

Confusion of Functional and Genetic Outcomes

Evolutionary biologists have long made a distinction between anatomical structures that have a common genetic ancestry, such as the

hands of humans and baboons, and anatomical structures that perform similar functions but that have no genetic ancestry, such as the
wings of birds and insects. Given this traditional distinction, it is
something of a surprise that sociobiological arguments generally do
not take into account the possibility that similar patterns between
humans and other species may serve similar functions but may not
be genetically related or genetically determined. Male aggressive
jealousy may serve to enforce monogamy and instill paternity confidence in both humans and some primates, but this does not imply
that these jealousies share a common genetic heritage.

An exceptionally clear example of the power of this error is
found in Barash's (1976) study of mountain bluebirds. He reasoned
that male birds might be more alarmed by the intrusion of other
males before the female mate laid its eggs than after, due to a need
to establish paternity probability. He studied two nests, making
three observations over 10 days. The first observation was made
prior to egg laying, the others afterwards. For each observation he
placed a stuffed male bluebird near the nest while the male was out
foraging. During the first observation, the male in each pair was
aggressive toward the stuffed competitor and somewhat less so
toward the female. During the second and third observations, the
male was less aggressive toward both the rival and the female.
Barash concluded:

> The decline in male–female aggressiveness during incubation and
> fledgling stages could be attributed to the impossibility of being
> cuckolded after the eggs have been laid . . . The results are consis-
> tent with an evolutionary interpretation. In addition, the term
> "adultery" [of the female] is unblushingly employed . . . as I believe
> it reflects a true analogy to the human concept. . . . It may also be
> prophesied that continued application of a similar evolutionary
> approach will eventually shed considerable light on various human
> foibles as well. (1976, p. 1100)

Here we have not only inappropriate generalization from one
species to another, but a total lack of consideration of the possibility
that the prevention of bluebird adultery and human adultery may be
functionally similar, not genetically similar. In addition, any good
experimental scientist will have winced at Barash's methodology,
since he confounded the initial presentation of a strange object (a
stuffed bird) with his observational period. He should have had some
nests where he presented the stuffed bird for the first time after egg
laying, to rule out the possibility of habituation to the initially

strange stuffed bird. Aggression in the bluebird may be due to unfamiliarity rather than to the sexual threat of a stranger.

We think that the confusion of functional and genetic similarity is the primary error made in the major sociobiological treatise on jealousy by Daly et al. (1982). They support a genetic argument on three grounds: Jealousy leads to aggression in many species; males and females differ in their patterns of jealousy; and males almost universally constrain female sexual behavior (a claim that can be debated—see Ford & Beach, 1951; Leacock, 1980). Since all three of these grounds appear true to Daly et al., and since paternity confidence is related to animal jealousy, they conclude that human male jealousy is genetically determined. However, all three can be true for functional reasons as well as for genetic reasons. Aggression is certainly one way to control the beloved and the rival, especially if males are larger and more genetically or socially aggressive; male and female jealousy can differ because of functional differences in male and female roles; and restriction of female sexual behavior may function to preserve systems of patrilineal inheritance (Hupka, 1981).

Failure to Consider Reciprocal-Interaction Explanations

Genotype and culture may mutually influence each other: Genotype may affect social behavior, while social behavior (especially collective, institutionalized behavior patterns) may affect genotype. At best, sociobiologists acknowledge that the expression of phenotype is a joint result of genotype and environment, as we have mentioned earlier.

For example, it is true that human males are generally larger than human females—a difference partly genetically determined. There may also be a genetic component to general activity levels, including physical aggression (Maccoby & Jacklin, 1974; Rossi, 1985). It is plausible that, given greater size and activity level, threatened males are more likely than threatened females to respond with aggression. This may have influenced the development of social institutions such as male dominance over females in economic structures, as males would be more successful at threatening and killing deviant females (Leacock, 1980). These economic structures could then have influenced the subsequent natural selection for males. Aggressive male sexual jealousy may be nothing special in and of itself, but may instead reflect the coevolution of genetically determined male aggressiveness and male-dominated social structures, each reciprocally influencing the other.

Lack of Emphasis on the Ability of Culture to Override Heredity

The ability of culture to override heredity may be best introduced by a simple example. In corn, height is almost 100% heritable within a certain environment. Take one handful of corn seed at random from a sack of corn and plant it in good rich soil, and then take another random handful and plant it in barren soil. At maturity, measure the height of all corn plants. Within each plot of soil (rich, barren), the variability in height is almost entirely under genetic control, based on the distribution of genes controlling for height in the original seed. However, the corn grown in the rich soil is 4 feet taller than the corn grown in barren soil, far exceeding the average difference of corn within each plot. Even though height is controlled for by genes and is nearly 100% heritable, environment can override genetic factors.

Now, imagine that it is possible to measure jealousy within a population—say, the population we are most familiar with, Western culture. Further imagine that we find (through experiments that are actually not possible with humans) that all of the variability in jealousy within Western culture is due to differential distribution of jealousy genes. We now notice that in another culture (gender, society) there is much more or less jealousy, or that it is qualitatively different in the feelings or behaviors of the jealous. We then conclude that since we have already determined that jealousy is under genetic control, these differences betwen cultures (genders, societies) must be due to genetic differences between them. We fail to take into account that even if jealousy were 100% heritable within our culture, this does not mean that major differences between populations in the jealousy complex are attributable to genetic differences. To return to our corn example, this would be like concluding that the difference in height between the plants in rich and in barren soil is genetic, which it cannot be, given the way in which seed was chosen.

Of course, our predicament is that there is actually no way to determine the extent to which human traits are heritable and affected by environments. To do so, we would need to breed humans. The next best thing would be to take identical twins (preferably separated at birth) and randomly assign them to different social environments. Neither of these can be done, and hence it is impossible to determine for humans what we can determine for animals: the extent to which our genes are overridden by environment (Gould, 1980; Lewontin et al., 1984).

However, there is certainly sentiment on both sides of the

question. As we have seen, the sociobiologists would generally argue that genes override culture. Perhaps the most eminent population geneticist of the century took the opposite view, arguing that "the transmission of culture short-circuits biological heredity" (Dobzhansky, 1951, p. 387). Certainly most anthropologists would take this view (Sahlins, 1976; Silverberg, 1980). The interesting question is this: Why is the debate so hotly joined?

The answer lies in the inclination of humans to defend existing social arrangements in terms of their naturalness, whether ordained by God or by biology. Whether or not individual sociobiologists intend to offer a defense of the human status quo, it is clear that those with an interest in defending existing arrangements take up sociobiological arguments (Gould, 1978; Leacock, 1980; Lewontin et al., 1984; Sahlins, 1976; Whitehurst, 1977).

The defense of jealous actions is often an example of this justification through naturalness. There is a long tradition of allowing men to kill their wives and rivals because of the belief that they cannot help themselves, due to a biological imperative—an imperative that is much less likely to be invoked in defense of jealous women. At less extreme levels, one of the difficulties in working therapeutically with the jealous is that both they and their mates and friends may adopt the position that jealous feelings and actions are only human nature and therefore cannot be modified. In our own experience, it is not unusual for a jealous client to make allusions to popular press accounts of the sociobiology of jealousy or to books like the best-selling *The Naked Ape* (Morris, 1967). As another example, there are a number of cultural practices of insuring paternity confidence that reflect male dominance, including sewing up the vaginal lips in the husband's absence. Though there are no systematic data on this, we are relatively sure that the men (mostly) who resort to such tactics would be likely to defend their actions in terms of naturalness or biology.

SUMMARY

Sociobiologists have attempted to explain human jealousy from the point of view of the theory of parental investment and the concept of paternity confidence. At first glance, their arguments seem plausible and appear to give an account of continuity between animal and human jealousy. However, closer examination of their specific arguments, and of underlying assumptions regnant in the field of sociobiology, leads to a number of objections. We have presented objections we think are relevant to the study of jealousy; additional critiques have been offered elsewhere.

We offer two sets of objections. The first centers around the failure to develop sophisticated models of genetic transmission based on human data. The second centers around the inapplicability of genetic deterministic models to jealousy per se and to human social behavior in general. Our review leads us to conclude that at present there is little evidence for a specific genetic basis for human jealousy. Such evidence may be exceedingly hard to come by because of the methodological and conceptual problems that plague sociobiology. We are prepared to accept the premise that genes code for the plasticity of behavior of humans, and that this very plasticity is revealed in the diverse patterns of the jealousy complex found cross-culturally. We are also prepared to accept the idea that genes may be involved in the determination of the general processes of stress and coping (e.g., the nature of sympathetic activation) that we argue are involved in the specific case of romantic jealousy. However, we are not prepared to accept a genetic basis for gender differences in jealousy or for any range of specific jealous feelings, actions, or thoughts.

4

Personality and Jealousy

In this chapter we focus on theory and research related to personality characteristics and developmental antecedents of adult romantic jealousy. The psychoanalytic tradition is the only major approach to personality theory that has offered systematic explanations of jealousy. Accordingly, in this chapter we first overview psychoanalytic approaches to jealousy that emphasize the Oedipal conflict and the projection of anxiety-provoking sexual impulses. Such approaches not only have been influential among therapists, but have found their way into the popular press (cf. Clanton & Smith, 1977). Our intention is to outline the general tenor of the analytic approach; detailed analyses would involve us in the often arcane language of analytic theory, which is beyond most readers and which might obscure the central points. (Friday, 1985, provides extended but accessible discussion of the psychoanalytic perspective.)

We next review relevant research on sibling rivalry and other developmental aspects of jealousy. Analytic, trait, and learning theories suggest that childhood experience with parental or sibling rivals may be influential in establishing patterns of adult jealousy. With the exception of case histories, we know of no research on actual patterns of parent–child rivalry for the other parent (e.g., Vollmer, 1946; Waletzky, 1979). However, patterns of sibling rivalry or sibling jealousy have been studied, and we review this research, which is suggestive of how adult patterns may be related to childhood experience. Unfortunately, there is very little research that actually links sibling rivalry to adult jealousy. Furthermore, research on sibling rivalry to date is not very helpful in assessing psychoanalytic hypotheses about the developmental aspects of adult jealousy.

Next, we summarize research on trait correlates of jealousy measures. The bulk of this research concerns self-esteem. We end this section with a comment on recent research on attachment styles in adult relationships, which appears to offer a promising new research direction. There has been little theory, and virtually no research, on jealousy from humanistic, existential, or cognitive paradigms of personality; these paradigms are therefore absent from our discussion.

PSYCHOANALYTIC THEORY AND JEALOUSY

Jealousy is an interesting phenomena for analytic theorists, since both the idea of actual or possible infidelity of the partner and associated emotions such as rage and anxiety are conscious. Unlike other conflicts against which one is defended, jealousy is often associated with actions and thoughts that appear to increase the psychic pain. A jealous lover may seek out confirmation of his or her worst fears and act to drive the beloved toward the rival, or may become obsessed with painful images of the beloved in the sexual embrace of the rival. From the analytic point of view, the tendency of the jealous to dwell on ideas of infidelity and to act to increase the emotional trauma appears paradoxical. This paradox is typically resolved, as we shall see, by assuming that jealousy is *itself* a defense (or a result of defenses) against even more troubling ideas and affects (Fenichel, 1935; Jones, 1937).

Freud (1922/1955) postulated three types of jealousy: "normal" (or "competitive"), "projection," and "delusional" (or "paranoid") jealousy. Rather than consider them as discrete, he suggested that the processes of each could interpenetrate, yielding complex unconscious determinants of conscious affect, thought, and action. Other analytic theorists have mainly elaborated on one of these three types or sought commonalities among them. We discuss each type below.

Normal Jealousy

Freud (1922/1955) considered normal jealousy a compound emotion consisting of grief over actual or potential loss of the beloved, a narcissistic wound, anger at the rival, impulses to compete, and self-criticism. Normal jealousy occurs when the person believes that a rival exists, and always reflects a contribution of the "earliest stirrings of the child's affective life," which are based on the Oedipus complex and on sibling rivalry. The excessive emotionality of jealousy occurs because it unconsciously rekindles repressed unresolved Oedipal and sibling conflicts. Since these conflicts are ubiquitous, Freud thought that those who show little evidence of jealousy have undergone particularly severe repression of the childhood conflicts. Accordingly, these deeply repressed conflicts would be all the more powerful in the unconscious (Freud, 1922/1955).

The Oedipal situation and sibling rivalry pose the prototypic dilemma involved in normal jealousy—the perception that a rival is competing for the beloved and, particularly in the Oedipal situation, that the beloved favors the rival. The emotional circumstances are different for males in the Oedipus complex than for females in the Electra complex. The male child loves the mother and fears (castration anxiety) and hates the father/rival. The female child both loves the mother/nurturer and fears and hates her as a rival, while loving the father. In adulthood, women may be more ambivalent about rivals than males, who are more likely to feel only negative emotions toward the rival (Francis, 1977). The conflict with the rival parent is repressed and, ideally, the child identifies with the same-sex parent as a resolution of the conflict.

Freud complicates this picture by suggesting that the pre-Oedipal child is bisexual, with attractions to the same-sex parent as well as the opposite-sex parent (Freud, 1926/1959). These feelings are also repressed but may emerge again in the form of conscious or unconscious attractions toward one's rival in adult jealousy. Though homosexual attraction is the primary feature of delusional jealousy, this formulation suggests that it plays a role in normal jealousy as well.

While repressed Oedipal and sibling conflicts are aroused by the similarity of the romantic triangle to the childhood situation in normal jealousy, some people are observed to be continually involved in adult romantic relationships in which jealousy and associated dramas recur as central themes. The general analytic interpretation is that there is a character pathology attributable to difficulties in the passage either through pre-Oedipal stages or through the Oedipal conflict. These pathologies may manifest themselves in two ways. First, and more characteristic of problems of the Oedipal resolution itself, the person demonstrates the "repetition compulsion" of seeking out adult situations in which the repressed anxieties of childhood may be mastered, albeit not entirely successfully because the true conflict remains repressed. In this regard, jealousy joins a long list of other recurring neurotic patterns supposedly aimed at indirectly mastering unconscious anxieties (Fenichel, 1945; Freud, 1933/1964; Horney, 1937; Klein & Riviere, 1964).

The second manifestation is through character pathology that leaves the person chronically needing self-aggrandizing love from others and suspicious of rivals. Freud pointed to the "narcissistic wound" in jealousy, and others have elaborated the contribution of primary narcissism and its pathology to jealousy. Fenichel (1935), for example, suggested:

> [P]eople who are particularly inclined to jealousy are precisely those who are incapable of deeper love. . . . The mixture of depression, envy, and aggressive tendencies betrays a particular intolerance for such a loss. The fear of loss of love [is] a severe impairment of their self-regard and under certain circumstances a dissolution of the ego. (p. 143)

Behind Fenichel's position is a central psychoanalytic assumption that fixation at earlier stages of psychosexual development will affect progression through later stages. Narcissistic pathologies are thought to reflect fixation at the later oral stages (oral-sadistic) that is largely due to undergratification and parental aggression (Kernberg, 1975; Kohut, 1968), or to result from overgratification and overvaluation by parents (Millon, 1981). In the former case, the infant's sexual drives are supposedly turned onto the image of itself as a protection against deprivation and associated affect. This fixation colors the subsequent passage through the Oedipal conflict, deepening the need for love and increasing fear of and anger at the parental rival. As adults, those with this pathology not only need admiration from others to support a fragile sense of self-worth; they also characteristically distrust and envy others (Kernberg, 1975; Wollheim, 1971). Indeed, Sharpsteen and Schmalz (1988) report that subjects who rated themselves as chronically jealous were more likely to have large elements of fear and distrust of others in actual jealousy episodes. Such people enter into romantic relationships to bolster self-esteem and self-concept, but when doing so unconsciously relive their pre-Oedipal and Oedipal situation of experiencing loss of love and dependency upon aggressors. They are not trying to master unconscious Oedipal conflicts residual from childhood so much as they are trying to maintain a fragile sense of self and defend against self-hate. Failure to do so may result in psychotic episodes.

One of our cases involved a 32-year-old professional woman with a history of jealousy. In the 5 years preceding our contact, she reported a total of 12 "serious" romantic relationships in which she experienced herself as deeply in love; sexual relations (usually problematic) had developed in all but one relationship. These relationships had varied from 2 to 8 months in duration. She reported that she was moderately to intensely jealous in all of the relationships and that her jealousy had been a significant factor in all of her breakups. She also reported an intense dislike of her mother, whom she blamed for the divorce of her parents when she was 8; this dislike was coupled with idealized descriptions of her father, who had been rather preoccupied with his profession (similar to hers) while she was a child. She was an only child. Therapy proceeded in part by focusing on similarities in patterns of behavior and emotion between her relationships with her parents, both current and retrospected, and her romantic relationships. For example, in most of her relationships she maintained somewhat idealized views of her lovers while focusing her anger on female interlopers. Most of the breakups appeared to have been initiated by boyfriends who were scared off by her demands and by her presumption that serious rival relationships existed. Developing more realistic relationships with her parents appeared to have special therapeutic benefit.

This woman's dilemma, which is atypical in the presentation of jealousy as centrally involved in a good many relationships, can be interpreted as stemming from unresolved Electra conflicts coupled with a need to be loved to overcome feelings of low self-worth. She appeared to have some capacity for intimacy, which suggests, from the analytic view, that her narcissism was not extreme. She did not meet the *Diagnostic and Statistical Manual of Mental Disorders*, third edition (DSM-III) criteria for Narcissistic Personality Disorder.

Freud (1922/1959) also commented on the relationship of jealousy to group life. First, sibling jealousy produces anxieties and guilt, due to actual behavior or aggressive impulses toward one's siblings. These are defended against by developing love (reaction formation) for and identifying with the siblings; such defenses are consciously experienced as group or communal feelings. In addition, sibling rivalry can result in a displacement of anger toward siblings (due to the injustice of not being favored by the parent) into anger over and concern with social injustice. Concern with justice can also be seen as a reaction formation defending against the hopeless wish for an unjust exclusive consumption of parental love. Sibling jealousy animates sibling bonding and social concern. In adult life, group situations resemble the sibling situation as group members consciously or unconsciously desire the exclusive attention of the idealized group leader (parental figure). This wish is untenable and threatens consciousness with the repressed ideas and affects of earlier sibling rivalry. It is resolved, as in childhood, by identifying and bonding with other group members, as well as with the group leaders. This line of thinking has been influential in later psychodynamic formulations of group processes (e.g., Gibbard, Hartman, & Mann, 1978).

In addition, Freud supposed that romantic lovers make a demonstration against the power of the group—namely, that they can be independent of it. This rejection of the group is experienced as shame; hence lovers hide displays of affection from the public. Further, Freud supposed that "feelings of jealousy of the most extreme violence are summoned up in order to protect the choice of a sexual object from being encroached upon by a group tie" (1922/1959, p. 72). This formulation suggests a broader view of jealousy as functional in maintaining pair bonding against the divisive forces of others' claims on the loyalties of mates (cf. Davis, 1936).

Projection Jealousy

Projection jealousy occurs as a consequence of one's own infidelity or from impulses to such infidelity. The behavior or impulses lead to guilt, which may be conscious as well as unconscious. Projection is a defense against the guilt raised by heteroerotic attractions toward others. The intensity and quality of the guilt are related to pre-Oedipal precursors and Oedipal dynamics of the superego. Very harsh superego attacks increase the need for defense through repression, denial, and projection. When this projection is onto the beloved, the conscious experience is that the beloved is or may be attracted to a rival. The jealous may then attack the beloved rather than attacking themselves, or may identify with their partners and attempt to manage their own unconscious conflict by managing the presumed attractions of the partners (Jones, 1937; Klein & Riviere, 1964; Waelder, 1951). For example, the jealous may attempt to restrict the beloved's access to others as a symbolic means of limiting the guilt resulting from their own actions or wishes (Downing, 1977).

Freud (1917/1963) illustrated projection jealousy with a case history of a 53-year-old woman happily married for 30 years. She became violently jealous after reading an anonymous letter suggesting that her husband was having an affair. The jealousy persisted even though the woman claimed not to believe the letter, which appeared to have been written to her by a disgruntled maid in order to provoke trouble. Freud interpreted the fear as a disguised wish for a sexual relationship with her son-in-law, which could not be admitted to consciousness and which had been defended against by projection onto the husband. The jealousy was intractable, as it itself was a defense. To overcome the jealousy would have meant recognizing an even more troubling desire for a somewhat incestuous sexual relationship. As might be expected, Freud recommended that therapy proceed by enabling the woman to recognize her own desires rather than by disputing her accusations.

Delusional Jealousy

As in projection jealousy, in delusional jealousy erotic impulses are projected; however, in delusional jealousy these impulses are homoerotic. Freud (1911/1955) first formulated delusional jealousy in his famous Schreber case, in which he supposed that Schreber's psychotic paranoia and jealousy were defenses against homoerotic wishes. Later he extended the analysis to suggest that all delusional jealousy is a defense against homoerotic impulses (Freud, 1922/1955). Freud believed that the homoerotic impulse is much more anxiety-producing (because of a stronger superego attack) than heteroerotic impulses; therefore the defense against it should be more rigid and more likely to involve serious distortions of reality (delusional), to keep it from emerging into consciousness. As in projection jealousy, the impulse is projected onto the beloved and the person becomes jealous, but the hidden wish is even more refractory to therapy and the person is even less approachable through rational means. Such jealousy is thought to be attended by paranoia, presumedly because paranoia is another result of defense against homoerotic impulses (Fenichel, 1945; Jones, 1937). Further, the unconscious attraction to the same-sex person may involve deeply repressed sexual feelings for the same-sex parent.

A number of analytic theorists have reiterated this thesis that homoerotic wishes generate both normal and delusional jealousy (Barag, 1949; Ferenczi, 1921; Jones, 1937). For example, Brunswick (1929) interpreted a case of a woman's extreme and paranoid jealousy as reflecting a projection of homosexual attachment derived from a sexual relationship in infancy with her older sister. Lagache (1947, 1949) noted that consciously homosexual patients became jealous. Accepting the general analytic notion that jealousy must be a defense, he suggested that jealousy must obviously defend against something other than homosexual wishes in openly homosexual male patients. His solution was that jealousy is a defense against "latent" or "passive" homosexuality, which supposedly involves a condensation of castration anxiety and wishes to be the wife for the father. The wish to be penetrated by the father is more frightening than the desire for adult homoerotic gratification; hence jealousy in conscious homosexuals is a defense against realizing the latent wish for the father. However, contemporary analytic thought has tended to downplay the role of homosexuality in both paranoia and jealousy (Lacan, 1977), perhaps due to the influence of research on paranoid states and changes in societal attitudes toward homosexuality.

Several theorists have suggested additional conflicts for which jealousy may act as a defense. Ovesey (1955) suggested that nonassertive males fear they are homosexual and that their jealous delusions are a defense against this fear, not against homoerotic impulses per se. Riviere (1932), in a particularly detailed and convoluted analysis, suggested that jealousy is a defense against unconscious impulses to steal from and humiliate others. Her patient sought affairs with married men in which she could totally dominate them, but when she was successful at seduction she became anxious. The anxiety lessened when she came to believe that others were trying to steal her lover. The interpretation was that oral-sadistic urges first generated the stealing of the lover as a symbolic despoiling and humiliation of the mother. These impulses were then defended against by projection onto supposed rivals. Fenichel's (1935) emphasis on pathologies of narcissism likewise focused on fixation at the oral-sadistic stage as a central dynamic in jealousy.

Further Developments in Ego Psychology and Object Relations Theory

As was the case in much of analytic theory, later formulations of jealousy moved from concepts of defense against instinctual impulses toward recognition of interpersonal conflicts and needs and their resolution via ego processes. Horney (1937) suggested that "basic anxiety" of isolation and helplessness results from disturbed interpersonal relationships in childhood and later. One (of many) neurotic needs that attempts to overcome basic anxiety is a need for unconditional affection and love, a need impossible to satisfy. Neurotic jealousy results from a "constant fear of losing possession of the person . . . any other interest that person may have is a potential danger" (1937, p. 129) to the defense against basic anxiety. This sounds like a narcissistic disorder, except that it is now disconnected from the concept of oral-sadistic fixation. Recent discussions of extreme lovesickness or "limerance" (Tennov, 1979; see Chapter 5) draw on similar notions of needs for unconditional affection expressed romantically to compensate for insecurities.

Object relations theory stresses the ego's role in differentiation of self from objects (other people) and the separation of positive and negative affects (splitting) (Hartmann, 1958; Kernberg, 1975). Klein and Riviere (1964) emphasized that jealousy recapitulates what are called "depressive" and "persecutory" anxieties of infancy. The angry, undergratified infant directs anger and infantile fantasies of destruction at the bad mother (or the part-object of the breast), and then becomes depressed when it believes it has also destroyed the good mother (inability to integrate positive and negative affect). This depressive anxiety is primitively defended against by projection away from self (failure of differentiation) to the outside world and is experienced as persecution. Klein and Riviere (1964) argued that in adults the feelings of worthlessness stemming from potential or actual withdrawal of love by the beloved result in depressive anxiety, which is defended against by projection onto a rival, either resulting in or intensifying an existing jealousy:

> When anyone unconsciously feels himself deficient in love and good-ness, and fears that this deficiency may be discovered and exposed by his lover–partner, or may hurt her, then he begins to be jealous and to look for lack of love in that partner, so as not to see it in himself, and to see wickedness in a rival instead of in himself. (p. 43)

Notice that, rather than a defense against instinctual impulses, the approach supposes a defense against feelings of worthlessness that result from engagement of primitive ego processes. Even psychologi-cally normal adults will engage in the primitive processes of splitting and projection, but these processes are exaggerated if depressive and paranoid anxieties were particularly severe in infancy. Somewhat similar formulations have been offered by Sullivan (1953) and Schwartz (1963).

Schmiedeberg (1953) suggested a number of pathological pro-cesses that lead to jealousy. His analysis considerably extended the range of conditions promoting jealousy, from the earlier notions of defense against Oedipal and instinctual anxiety to a variety of fixa-tions and interpersonal conflicts. These include the following:

1. Jealousy as an attempt to deny and compensate for a schizoid inability to love.
2. Jealousy as a result of conscious or unconscious stimulation by a narcissistic partner who is gratified by the jealousy (cf. Bergler, 1956).
3. Jealousy as a technique to destroy a relationship to avoid the envy or gain the sympathy of parents, siblings, or friends.
4. Jealousy as an oral-dependent fixation. Jealous possessive-ness is symbolic of swallowing the mother and represents a

solution to other anxieties originally unrelated to the perception of a rival.

5. Jealousy as an anal-retentive fixation. The desire to control the beloved through jealousy is a solution to other anxieties; this desire stems from learning to control parents by holding in feces.

6. Jealousy as a reflection of fear of and competitiveness toward women by men. The subjugation of women is a symbolic castration, which may also be achieved by displacement onto the supposed rival and subjugation of the rival.

7. Jealousy as a reflection of the woman's desire to possess the potency and masculinity of the male partner of her rival.

8. Jealousy as a denial of and reaction formation to males' fears of impotence. Possessiveness and bullying are attempts to demonstrate potency.

9. Jealousy as a result of masochistic needs for humiliation.

More recent accounts have expanded this list. Seidenberg (1967), for example, suggests that men equate their partners with their own mothers, with whom they have earlier identified in the wish for sexual freedom (the childhood wish that the mother have two lovers). Jealousy then results from the perception of a desire for sexual freedom in one's partner, due to the unconscious equation of mother and beloved. Docherty and Ellis (1976) report cases of morbid jealousy in patients who witnessed their own mothers in the act of adultery. Seeman (1979) presents case histories of five jealous women who are interpreted as having identified with their husbands' greater freedom and opportunity. This identification was in part due to low self-esteem, itself promoted by situational and cultural circumstances. Identification supposedly led to vivid fantasies of their husbands' seducing others, or of themselves as their husbands in the act of seduction. These fantasies were their means of unconsciously overcoming feared romantic rivals. The identification with the husbands also allowed for expression of homoerotic and narcissistic needs. Further, jealousy provided a secondary gain of adding mystery and excitement to otherwise humdrum marriages: Both sexual desire and behavior increased as a result of the jealousy.

Contributions of Other Analytic Schools

As suggested by our coverage, the bulk of psychoanalytic theory comes out of Freudian instinct theory and from ego psychology and its Kleinian object relations variant. Theorists such as Fromm, Sullivan, and Murray mention jealousy only in the briefest terms, such as Sullivan's suggestion that jealousy "is invariably a very complex, painful process involving a group of three or more persons . . . [Unlike envy] it does not concern itself with an attribute or an attachment, but, rather, involves a great complex field of interpersonal relations" (1953, p. 348). Adler (1928) described a jealous character trait growing out of sibling rivalry, which manifests itself in a great many situations in addition to romantic relationships, which has "a thousand shapes," and which is "an especially well-marked form of the striving for power" (pp. 177–178). Adler's focus was on the ways in which the jealous may limit, dominate, or degrade their partners. He believed that this indicates a pathological exaggeration of the normal drive to master the world and achieve actualization of the self, and that this pathology is due to extreme feelings of inferiority during childhood.

Jung's school of analytic psychology, perhaps the major competitor to the Freudians, has likewise failed to produce systematic coverage of jealousy. One major abstract of Jung's works fails to index jealousy at all (Rothgeb & Clemens, 1978). In his autobiography, he merely mentioned that "the kernel of all jealousy is lack of love" (Jung, 1961, p. 137). However, the prevalence of jealous themes in myth and religion suggests fertile ground for Jungian analysis (Downing, 1977). The ego-alien yet coherent actions that often occur when people are jealous can be interpreted as an aspect of the shadow archetype. This archetype organizes the denied, devalued, or undeveloped aspects of self (e.g., possessiveness). The shadow may have particular force in the unconscious when rivals appear. In Jungian psychology, romantic relationships in part involve projection of the masculine side of self (animus) onto male partners (for women) or of the feminine side of self (anima) onto female partners (for men). The more deeply repressed the anima or animus archetype is, the more the person seeks an opposite-sex partner to compensate for the undeveloped aspect. A rival threatens this compensation, which is countered by the shadow. This formulation suggests that individuals who conform strongly to sex-role stereotypes should be most jealous; however, the scant data indicate that this is true for men but not women (see Chapter 5).

The Relationship of Analytic Concepts to Our Model of Jealousy

As is true for many other aspects of analytic theory, there is little evidence outside of case histories to support the basic hypotheses of the influence of Oedipal conflict and of jealousy as a defense. Although it may be possible to design such studies (cf. Luborsky, 1977), contemporary jealousy researchers are not explicitly guided by analytic theory.

However, there are points of intersection between analytic concepts and our model. First, most of the analytic concepts have to do with the primary appraisal of threat or harm. Simply put, because jealousy is a defense or because of repetition compulsion, some people may be more likely to perceive a potential or actual relationship in the face of ambiguous information, or to appraise more harm or threat from an actual rival. Second, the secondary-appraisal processes of motive assessment and social comparison should be related to certain analytic constructs. If jealousy is a defense against one's own impulses, then the perception of the partner's motives may be affected. If the superego attack is not overwhelming, the jealous may perceive the beloved as having motives the person himself or herself has (but does not recognize); if the attack is stronger, then the nature of the person's own motives may be disguised through distortion of the partner's motives. A similar pattern may be found for social comparison. The jealous may be less likely to compare themselves to rivals on certain dimensions if those dimensions are those on which they (unconsciously) judge themselves as unworthy. A person who feels that he or she is very unlovable may be more concerned with a rival's material possessions, for example, than with a rival's basic worth as a lovable human.

A third possibility is that to the extent that jealousy is a defense or a replaying of the Oedipal situation, the jealous may be more likely to plan or enact coping efforts that validate their perceptions rather than reduce the jealousy. In terms of our set of suggested coping strategies, we would expect more coping efforts aimed at interfering with the rival relationship (as a test of the partner's attraction toward it), demanding commitment (again as a test), or derogating the partner and rival (which supports the jealous person's suspicions).

Finally, it is possible to interpret some of the relationship correlates presented in Chapter 5 as having a defensive function or reflecting Oedipal or pre-Oedipal outcomes. For example, depending on one's partner for one's own self-esteem does correlate with jealousy, and this may be construed as an aspect of narcissism. The desire for exclusivity in relationships may partly be a residue of the Oedipal situation. Being more dependent on the relationship, another correlate, emotionally resembles childhood dependency, and this may stir repressed Oedipal conflicts. It may be possible to generate analytic explanations for many of the other correlates and gender differences, and these explanations would compete with social-psychological and cultural models. However, since there is little research linking childhood conflicts and experiences to adult jealousy, such explanations of known correlates remain theoretical.

SIBLING RIVALRY AND DEVELOPMENTAL ANTECEDENTS OF ADULT JEALOUSY

Sibling rivalry and how to handle it are common themes in books and articles on child care (Dunn, 1984; Griffin & De La Torre, 1983; Watson, Switzer, & Hirschberg, 1972). It is common for older siblings, particularly first-borns, to react to a birth with increased negativism, withdrawal, sleep problems, or toileting problems (Dunn, Kendrick, & MacNamee, 1981; Field & Reite, 1984; Nadelman & Begun, 1982). Estimates of the percentage of siblings showing such reactions range from 50–93% (Dunn, 1984, p. 95). The different problem areas are not strongly correlated; neither is there a strong relationship between the degree of affection shown toward the newborn and the frequency of problems. Most of these problems disappear after 8 months or so, with the exception of fearful, anxious behavior (Dunn & Kendrick, 1982). Sometimes the hostility results in sustained physical abuse of one sibling by another (Green, 1984).

In addition to its potential role in later adult romantic jealousy, sibling jealousy has also been regarded by some theorists as a major influence on personality formation (Adler, 1928; Levy, 1934; Winnicott, 1977). Given the practical problems of child raising and these theoretical interests, there is surprisingly little research on sibling rivalry. Further, the bulk of this research has used measures of physical or verbal aggression as indicators of jealousy. The practical reasons for this practice are obvious, but nonetheless the equation of aggression with jealousy is limiting and has probably retarded interesting work in this area. Like jealous adults, jealous children act, think, and feel in a variety of ways that are not aggressive or overtly competitive.

Research on Sibling Rivalry

Research on aggression per se generally finds that physical aggression begins to decline fairly rapidly after the preschool years. After 6 years or so, empathy begins to attenuate aggressive responses, as does the ability to attribute intention to others' acts. As the child matures, both physical and verbal aggression are more likely to be due to insults and threats to self-esteem than to struggles over possession of objects (Maccoby, 1980; Maccoby & Jacklin, 1974). It might be expected that aggression as an aspect of sibling jealousy would conform to these general patterns.

Early research on sibling rivalry involved analyses of mothers' responses to straightforward questionnaires, observations of children in nursery schools or at home, reports on problem children dealt with by social agencies, or clinical case reports (Foster, 1927; Levy, 1934; McFarland, 1937/1938; Obendorf, 1929; Ross, 1931; Sewall, 1930; Sokoloff, 1947; Vollmer, 1946). Most researchers explicitly or implicitly assumed that most if not all fighting between siblings was due to rivalry for parental affection and favors. This assumption is common in modern child guidance manuals, but it is not supported by later research (Banks & Kahn, 1982; Dunn, 1983; Maccoby, 1980). Most sibling aggression is not attributable to sibling rivalry for parental attention.

The earlier research can be easily summarized. First-borns were reported to have more problems with siblings, especially if the second child was born 18–36 months later, and especially if there were only two or three children in the family (Foster, 1927; McFarland, 1937/1938; Ross, 1931; Sewall, 1930). Sibling jealousy appeared to be more pronounced in families that had other problems of interpersonal adjustment or that were poor; such families had more limited resources to meet each child's needs (Foster, 1927; Sewall, 1930). Parental favoritism was found to foster jealousy (Foster, 1927; Ross, 1931; Vollmer, 1946). Pronounced sibling jealousy often accompanied other behavioral problems, such as "negativism" and "fearfulness" (Foster, 1927; McFarland, 1937/1938; Ross, 1931; Sewall, 1930).

Modern research on sibling jealousy is part of a larger interest in sibling relationships, including questions of how such relationships are reciprocally related to parental relationships, how roles are differentiated in the family, and the long-term impact of sibling relationships upon social role taking and personality (Dunn, 1983, 1984; Dunn & Kendrick, 1982; Lamb & Sutton-Smith, 1982; Scarr & Grajeck, 1982). It is beyond the scope of this book and our expertise to review this literature. However, some recent research is focused specifically on sibling rivalry.

At the outset it is apparent that, like romantic jealousy, sibling jealousy is a complex process and is probably related to culture, developmental progress, family dynamics, temperament, and idiosyncratic development of sibling relationships (Dunn, 1983). Simple approaches utilizing structural variables, such as birth order, gender, family size, and family spacing, are unlikely to be of much value in accounting for sibling relationships, including sibling jealousy (Dunn, 1983; Scarr & Grajeck, 1982). However, recent research has confirmed earlier findings that first-borns, especially boys, express more ambivalence, distress, and hostility about their siblings (Koch, 1960; Nadelman & Begun, 1982). First-borns tend to be especially verbally aggressive and are more likely to adopt a disciplinarian role toward their younger siblings (Dunn, 1984; Koch, 1960; Sutton-Smith & Rosenberg, 1970). Sibling jealousy is less common or problematic in larger families; in general, children appear to be more emotionally secure in larger families (Dunn, 1984). This may be partly due to increased opportunities for children to have some needs met by their siblings in addition to their parents. There is some indication that sister–mother relationships are more strongly affected by birth of a sibling than are brother–mother relationships (Henchie, cited in Moore, 1969).

Temperament may affect relations with siblings. Dunn (1984) reports that first-born children who were anxious and withdrawn before the birth of the second-born children usually displayed little affection for their siblings. Lamb (1978) studied pairs of siblings when the second-born was 12 months old, and again at 18 months. The behavior of the *second-born* in each pair at 12 months was a better predictor of the first-born's behavior 6 months later than was the first-born's behavior at the original assessment. Sociable babies helped produce affectionate older siblings.

Fearfulness and anxiety, which may be related to temperament, are especially likely to persist well after the birth of the sibling (Dunn et al., 1981; Dunn & Kendrick, 1982). One study found that 38% of children showed a marked increase in fears in the year after the birth (Dunn & Kendrick, 1982). A child who reacts to the birth of a sibling by withdrawing is particularly likely to have a conflicted, hostile relationship with the sibling for several years (Dunn & Kendrick, 1982). An older sibling who imitates behavior of the newborn is particularly likely to show affection and interest over the next 14 months (Dunn & Kendrick, 1982).

Some research has considered the effects of differential treatment of children by parents. Dunn and Kendrick (1982) reported that a few situations of differential treatment were particularly likely to upset children. "Naughty" behavior increased threefold while the mother was occupied with the newborn (bathing, cuddling, feeding, etc.). Contrary to conventional wisdom in child care manuals, breastfeeding in itself was not particularly upsetting, relative to other kinds of attention. Also, decrease in the mother's play with the older sibling was associated with increased negative behavior. One reason why most negative behavior declines after 8 months may be that the mother becomes increasingly able to play with the older child and/or needs less time to care for the baby's basic needs.

Other research has focused on differential treatment and its effects over a longer time span than the first months of the younger sibling's life. First-born children generally get more attention than later-borns when they are alone with their mothers, but less attention than later-borns when the siblings are present (Dunn, 1983). In one study, if a mother was particularly playful with a first-born daughter before and immediately after the birth of the second sibling, then both children were relatively likely to be hostile toward each other over the next 14 months. This hostility was increased if the mother was also warm and playful with the second-born as well (Dunn & Kendrick, 1981).

Bryant and Crockenberg (1980) found that sibling aggression decreased and prosocial behavior increased to the degree that the mother was responsive to each child's needs. This pattern did not hold if one child's expressed needs were being met while the other's were being neglected. The relativity of attention, rather than its absolute level, was linked to unpleasant reactions from the child who was receiving relatively less attention. Research has also indicated that discussion with the first-born of the needs and feelings of siblings is associated with less aggression toward the siblings (Dunn, 1983). This may be due to increased capacity to tolerate the frustration of unmet needs, as well as to the increased attention and status that may accompany such discussions.

Kendrick and Dunn (1983) reported that mothers more consistently punished aggression of a first-born son toward a sibling than similar aggression of a first-born daughter. Punishment of a son for aggression was associated with *increased* aggression toward the sibling over the next 6 months. For daughters, it appeared that aggression toward the siblings was much more stable and independent of mothers' behavior.

The father's behavior also affects sibling relationships. Close relationships between the father and the first-born (regardless of sex) were found to be associated with more hostility between siblings over a year's time. However, to the extent that the first-born had a close relationship with the father, conflict between the first-born and the mother was reduced after the sibling's birth (Dunn & Kendrick, 1982).

The sex of siblings further complicates the picture. Some studies have found that same-sex siblings are more jealous, whereas others have found that opposite-sex siblings are more jealous (Abramovitch, Pepler, & Corter, 1982; Moore, 1969; Stewart, Mobley, Van Tuyl, & Salvador, 1987). Henchie (cited in Moore, 1969) found that male infants evoke more negative responses from brothers than from sisters.

Summary of the Research

Sibling rivalry or jealousy is typically measured by aggression toward a sibling, though children may also show withdrawal, increased negativism, sleep disturbance, and behavior disorders after birth of a sibling. Early interest in and imitation of the newborn are correlated with less jealousy, whereas early withdrawal is related to more. First-borns, particularly males, are likely to be especially jealous, perhaps because they experience a greater relative reduction in attention than later siblings do. Males are more likely to be punished for aggression toward a sibling, which acts to increase their subsequent aggression. Sibling rivalry appears to be more likely in families with limited capacities to address the material and psychological needs of the children. Differential attention promotes rivalry and may be difficult to avoid during infancy of the next-borns. Rivalry is reduced if parents can meet one child's needs while not neglecting the other's. It appears that close relationships and play between children and each parent may exacerbate rivalry, perhaps because there are more opportunities for each child to observe relatively greater attention being given to the other. Children with anxious temperaments may be particularly jealous.

Relevance to Psychoanalytic Theory

Analytic thought concentrates on Oedipal rather than sibling rivalry, so the research on sibling rivalry is less pertinent than research on parent–child rivalry (currently nonexistent) would be. The finding that differential treatment promotes sibling rivalry is consistent with analytic theory and, by extension, supportive of the notion that differential treatment of the child and the spouse promotes child–parent rivalry. (Of course, analytic theory is not the only school of thought to make this supposition.) Aside from this rather general agreement with theory, the research evidence is not central to analytic assumptions. There is no evidence that sibling rivalry is resolved by bonding with siblings. Positive rather than negative attitudes before and at birth predict later bonding, but this does not directly address the assumption of unconscious resolution of later conflicts. Birth order and temperament are not concerns of analytic explanations of jealousy.

Developmental Antecedents of Adult Jealousy

Whether or not the early learning history of the siblings–parent triad is related to aspects of romantic triads is largely untested. White (1977) reported that first-borns were no more likely to describe themselves as jealous than later-borns. If sibling rivalry does condition adult jealousy, first-borns in general should have been more romantically jealous, since, as we have seen, they are more likely to show sibling jealousy. This contrary finding suggests that if there are contributions of sibling rivalry to later jealousy, they are likely to be complex rather than straightforward. In general, the study of sibling relationships is still so young a field that there is as yet little evidence that sibling relationships affect any adult behaviors outside of familial relationships (Banks & Kahn, 1982; Dunn, 1982; Lamb & Sutton-Smith, 1982).

We have found two studies relating childhood antecedents to adult jealousy. Hindy, Schwarz, and Brodsky (1989) assessed self-report of current relationship jealousy. (Note that such reports may reflect a stable personality component: Those disposed to be jealous should be more likely to report jealousy in a current relationship.) A number of child-rearing practices of subjects' parents had been assessed in a study conducted 3–5 years earlier. These assessments were averages of reports not only from the subjects, but also from a sibling and from both parents of each subject. This procedure reduced the possibility that retrospective reports of childhood antecedents would be affected by the subjects' current level of jealousy. What is striking about Hindy et al.'s results is that a large number of curvilinear associations were found, whereas the number of linear associations was quite low. That is, both high and low degrees of a particular childhood antecedent were more likely to be related to jealousy than medium degrees. We can only briefly summarize the most notable findings.

First, male relationship jealousy was much more strongly related to childhood patterns than was female jealousy. Males were more jealous if their mothers had been especially high or low in inconsistent or lax use of discipline, or in the use of withdrawal of love as a punishment. Males were more jealous if their fathers had been high or low in rejection of them, hostility, and enforcement of family rules. They were less jealous if their mothers and fathers had been high or low in accepting individuation and the children's needs and in positive involvement.

From these results, it appears that three different patterns of child raising may affect adult male jealousy. In the first, mothers are inconsistent and lax in their discipline and use withdrawal of love to punish, while fathers are rejecting, hostile, and rule-oriented. In the second, mothers are consistent and strict in their discipline and punish by means other than withdrawing love, while fathers are accepting, are friendly, and avoid enforcement of the rules. In the third, parents produce high or low self-esteem by being either particularly accepting or nonaccepting and especially enjoying or not enjoying their children's individuality. In the positive case, a child when adult has a core of security and may be less dependent on romantic partners to provide self-esteem. However, extreme parental acceptance may produce a narcissistic sense of grandiosity (Millon, 1981). In the negative case, a child when adult may avoid close relationships and hence may also be less dependent; in the extreme, the person may develop narcissistic defenses against self-hate conditioned on parental enmity (Kernberg, 1975; Kohut, 1968).

The first pattern seems to fit the Oedipal image of the castrating father and the mother who vacillates between attention to the husband and attention to the child. If this pattern persists into adulthood, romantic rivals may be seen as hostile and competitive and may provoke anger. The second suggests a family in which the son is conflicted about the mother because she provides both love and punishment, while the father is friendly and supportive. Adult romantic jealousy may be focused on the unreliability of the mate, and there may be less concern with aggressive rivals. Jealous depression over the mate's unreliability may be more likely than jealous anger. The third pattern seems more related to what the analytic theorists describe as pathologies of narcissism. Adult rivals would threaten a grandiose self-image that may defend against underlying self-hate, with the jealous being easily suspicious of the commitment of the beloved.

Hindy and Schwarz's (1986) results were quite different for females. None of the mothers' child-rearing behaviors predicted relationship jealousy, and the effects for fathers' behaviors were much weaker. Females were more jealous if fathers were high or low in wanting to control daughters' behavior, enforcement of rules, and intrusiveness into daughters' lives. They were less jealous if fathers were high or low in promoting autonomy. Two patterns seem involved here. The first is that of the father as a controlling and intrusive rule maker who requires an obedient (low-autonomy) daughter. The other is a permissive and needy father who is perhaps threatened by autonomy. Although neither pattern is transparently related to analytic suppositions, the second seems closer in that the daughter may have a special, close relationship with the needy father and may defensively project Electra-like desires for such a special relationship onto rivals. Finally, Hindy and Schwarz found no relationship between parents' satisfaction with their own marriage and their children's adult relationship jealousy.

Bringle and Williams (1979) had college students and their parents fill out identical questionnaires that assessed dispositional jealousy (the tendency to be jealous in nonromantic as well as romantic situations, discussed in the following section); numerous jealous behaviors and feelings; and the use of denial-like defenses versus intellectualizing or ruminating about threats (repression-sensitization). Both parents' dispositional jealousy predicted to their children's jealousy, and the correlation between parents and children was higher for same-sex than for opposite-sex parents. Fathers who were more dispositionally jealous had offspring who were more likely to use repression. Both males and females were likely to have jealous feelings if both parents had a high degree of jealous feelings, while females were more likely to behave in jealous ways if they had fathers who had a high level of jealous behaviors.

There are a number of possible interpretations for these results, but they do suggest that parents provide models and create emotional situations that can affect their children's jealousy. The finding that fathers' jealousy is associated with children's repression also ties into the projective jealousy hypothesis. Jealous fathers produce jealous children, who are also more likely to deny and repress their feelings, theoretically increasing the likelihood of projection. Finally, Kosins (1983) gave undergraduate and psychotherapy clients scales assessing current relationship jealousy and sibling conflict history. No relationship was found between romantic jealousy and sibling rivalry.

PERSONALITY TRAIT CORRELATES OF JEALOUSY

Several studies have reported correlations between measures of different personality traits and jealousy measures. Most of this work has been rather ad hoc. There has not been any systematic jealousy research based on a specific personality theory, though there is some systematic work in identifying personality correlates of the propensity to become jealous (Bringle & Buunk, 1985). In addition, several studies have investigated the possible link between self-esteem and jealousy. In this section the research on dispositional jealousy and on self-esteem is reviewed first, followed by a brief summary of the outcomes of other trait-oriented research.

Dispositional Jealousy

Bringle and his colleagues have reported a series of studies on individual differences in "the propensity to behave emotionally in jealousy situations," which they have termed "dispositional jealousy" (Bringle, 1981, 1986; Bringle, Renner, Terry, & Davis, 1983; Bringle, Roach, Andler, & Evenbeck, 1977, 1979; Bringle & Williams, 1979). This research has used the Self-Report Jealousy Scale (SRJS) as the measure of dispositional jealousy (Bringle et al., 1979; see the Appendix to the present volume). Questions on this scale assess how jealous the person is, or anticipates how jealous he or she might be, in romantic, work, family, and school situations. The assumption is that people who are jealous in all four situations have a personality disposition to become jealous. The subscales are in fact moderately correlated, and the total scale is moderately correlated with a simple self-report of oneself as jealous (Bringle et al., 1979; White, 1984).

Two studies have attempted to determine the relative contributions of situation, disposition, and their interaction to jealousy (Bringle et al., 1983). In both studies, dispositional jealousy was measured, and subjects were then presented with different jealousy-related situations. They were asked to predict their emotional reactions and how threatened the relationship described in the situation would be. Results showed that dispositional jealousy was related to these predictions, but that situation and person–situation interactions were equally strong or stronger predictors. The strength of these predictors differed dramatically with the nature of the sample situations, suggesting caution in drawing conclusions. Unfortunately, this work is of unknown generalizability to actual jealousy situations, but it does support the straightforward assumption that one's concept of oneself as jealous in many situations is related to actual jealousy.

Self-Esteem and Jealousy

We and others have defined jealousy as in part a reaction to threat to self-esteem (see Chapter 2). This does not necessarily imply that people high in self-esteem are less likely to become jealous than people with low self-esteem. It is certainly possible that jealousy acts to reduce self-esteem, creating the illusion that insecure people are more jealous (Bush et al., 1988). Although it may be argued that people low in self-esteem are particularly sensitive to further erosion of self-regard, the case is not that clear-cut. People high in self-esteem may be more sensitive to esteem threats in many circumstances (Berscheid & Fei, 1977; Bringle, 1981; E. Jones, 1937; S. C. Jones, 1973; Tesser & Paulus, 1983; Tetlock & Manstead, 1985).

One problem in establishing the link between jealousy and self-esteem is that the jealousy situation may lead to lowered self-esteem. In either clinical or research assessment, it may appear that people with low self-esteem are jealous, but the causal direction is ambiguous. For example, Sharpsteen and Schmalz (1988) found that respondents felt inadequate and vulnerable in one-third of reported jealousy episodes. This may reflect problems of pathologies of narcissism, as well as the ordinary narcissistic wound of normal jealousy.

Another problem in assessing the role of self-esteem in jealousy is that people's evaluations of themselves depend upon personality and situational variables that focus attention on different self-attributes (Buss, 1980; McGuire & McGuire, 1982; Wicklund, 1980). Because self-esteem is a summary, global evaluation of self, the aspects of self that are under evaluation are likely to influence overall self-evaluation. Consider the person whose romantic partner has been asked out by another suitor. This fact may not be related to self-evaluation if the person is at work and work-related competencies are affecting self-evaluation at that time. It may threaten self-evaluation if the person focuses on unfavorable comparisons with the rival (the rival is smarter, more attractive, etc.). It may enhance self-evaluation if the person focuses on the implication that the partner is desirable, and therefore the person himself or herself must be desirable to attract such a partner. The theoretically more interesting question then becomes what situational, personality, relationship, and/or cultural factors direct attention to esteem-enhancing versus esteem-threatening aspects of the jealousy situation. Global self-esteem is just one of many variables that can affect the focus of attention.

This conceptual problem has its methodological counterpart. If global self-esteem is measured in the usual ambiguous assessment situation, in which attention is not particularly directed toward relationship-related self-esteem, then the self-esteem score should not be strongly related to jealousy measures. If self-esteem is measured in the context of the jealous situation, then it should be more related to jealousy (Holroyd, 1985).

Another conceptual problem is that self-esteem is related to other variables that affect the jealousy complex. For example, people high in self-esteem generally score as more in love with their current partners (Dion & Dion, 1975). Since love is somewhat correlated with jealousy measures (see Chapter 5), those high in self-esteem may be more likely to score as jealous. On the other hand, people with high self-esteem may compare themselves more favorably with rivals, and hence their secondary appraisal of the degree of threat from rival relationships may be low. As a consequence, they may be less jealous. A number of such hypotheses could be made in regard to competing effects of self-esteem on different elements of the jealousy complex. It should not be surprising if the overall effect of self-esteem is weak.

In fact, the evidence for a relationship between global self-esteem and jealousy measures is extremely mixed (Bringle & Buunk, 1985). Several studies have found no correlation between self-esteem and jealousy (Amstutz, 1982; Buunk, 1981, 1982a; Hansen, 1982; Mathes & Severa, 1981; Shettel-Neuber et al., 1978; White, 1981b, 1981e). Others have reported modest negative correlations (Amstutz, 1982; Bendedictson et al., 1977; Bringle, 1981; De Moja, 1986; Hupka & Bachelor, 1979; Jaremko & Lindsey, 1979; Rosmarin, Chambless, & LaPointe, 1979; Stewart & Beatty, 1985; White, 1981c, 1981e).

Examination of the actual scales used as measures of jealousy in the studies cited above suggests that self-esteem is likely to correlate with factors derived from factor analyses of face-valid jealousy items. Usually these factors concern anticipated reactions to hypothetical jealousy-inducing events. It is difficult to know what such factors are assessing (White, 1984). They may be measuring general coping traits, reports of elements of the jealousy complex, or beliefs about what people are like when jealous. For these reasons, it is difficult to interpret the meaning of correlations between such factors and global self-esteem measures. The problem is further compounded by the fact that social desirability is only rarely controlled for. The tendency to present oneself favorably leads to inflated reports of self-esteem and deflated reports of anticipated or potential jealousy (White, 1984).

On the other hand, those scales that ask for direct self-reports of how jealous the person is generally show no or weak correlations with self-esteem. Such reports are central to self-evaluation, since they are reports about the nature of the self ("I am jealous"). These data are more informative in suggesting that global self-esteem is not strongly related to jealousy. However, self-reports of jealousy are reports of perceptions that may not be related to all relevant elements of the jealousy complex or to the perceptions of the partner or other observers (Buunk & Bringle, 1987; White, 1984).

The data reviewed in Chapter 5 suggest that self-esteem measures more closely related to the romantic relationship are stronger predictors of jealousy. Specifically, research has shown that both the perception of oneself as an inadequate partner and the degree to which one's self-esteem is dependent upon the partner's evaluation of oneself predict jealous behavior and emotion. Also, White (1981c) has shown in a path analysis that global self-esteem is related to perceived inadequacy as a partner, which in turn is related to jealousy. In that analysis, perceived inadequacy completely accounted for the observed correlations between global self-esteem and jealousy.

In another attempt to relate self-esteem more closely to the jealousy context, Holroyd (1985) had subjects whose partners were involved with another complete a self-esteem scale twice—once to assess self-esteem while they were thinking about the rival relationship, and again to assess retrospected self-esteem prior to the development of the rival relationship. Analyses showed that for males retrospected self-esteem was negatively related to jealousy, whereas it was positively related for females. At face value, this suggests that males who thought they had low self-esteem prior to the rival relationship were more likely to become jealous, and that low-self-esteem females were less likely to become jealous. Current, relationship-related self-esteem was negatively related to jealousy for females and unrelated for males. Again at face value, this suggests that currently jealous females were likely to deprecate themselves. Holroyd's data, while obviously constrained by problems of interpretation of correlations, do suggest that measures of self-esteem related to the relationship may be more likely to correlate with jealousy measures.

In general, the data indicate that for the samples of college students typically used in previous research, global self-esteem is not very closely related to self-report of romantic jealousy. It may be more strongly related to particular emotions, behaviors, or thoughts of the jealous, but even here the evidence is hard to interpret. Future research would benefit from more sophisticated approaches to self-concept and self-esteem. Global self-esteem measures, if used at all, should be joined by measures more sensitive to aspects of self that are salient in the relationship.

Other Trait Measures

Several studies have reported correlations between trait measures and jealousy measures, though to date there is only one report relating jealousy to comprehensive personality inventories (Bringle & Buunk, 1985, 1986; De Moja, 1986; Hindy & Schwarz, 1986; Mathes, Roter, & Joerger, 1982; White, 1984) To summarize this research briefly, repressors score as less jealous than sensitizers. Screeners (who filter out environmental complexity) are less jealous than nonscreeners. Subjects high in trait anxiety are more likely to be jealous, as are those high in neuroticism (emotional lability). Some evidence suggests that those with an external locus of control are more jealous, as are those who are dispositionally dogmatic or insecure. Machiavellianism (the tendency to manipulate people) is uncorrelated with jealousy.

In the one systematic study, Hindy, Schwarz, and Brodsky (1989) correlated results from three standard personality inventories with self-reports of current relationship jealousy. These inventories assessed, in part, personality styles/disorders, psychological needs, and traits. Unfortunately, statistical techniques were not used to control for the overlap among these constructs. As with child-rearing antecedents, male jealousy was curvilinearly related to a number of measures; however, for females, the more numerous personality correlates were mostly linear. To summarize only the stronger correlates, males were more jealous if they were high or low in narcissism and needs for exhibition and expressiveness; also, the more paranoid and alienated they were, the more jealous they were. They were less jealous if they were high or low in submissiveness and deference. Females were more jealous if they were high or low in paranoia, noncomformity, and psychotic symptoms; they were also more jealous if they were less inhibited, were less well-adjusted, had low tolerance for anxiety, and had strong needs to aggress and to be taken care of. The resulting image of the paranoid, narcissistic, low-impulse-control, alienated male often found in the clinical literature (see Chapters 7, 8, and 9) can be constructed out of these results, as can the image of the neurotic, suspicious, emotionally variable woman conflicted over aggression and neediness, which is also a feature of the clinical literature.

The correlations reported for trait measures are generally low. This research has not made use of recently developed methods (such as repeated sampling over time and situations) that might demonstrate a stronger effect of personality variables (Peterson, 1988). Much of the work does not use multivariate techniques to control for related constructs (e.g., repression–sensitization and trait anxiety are highly correlated). Further, it is unclear for many of these traits whether the correlations represent the use of defensive mechanisms that influence self-report (e.g., repressors may deny or repress jealousy experiences) or whether they genuinely indicate some relationship between the trait and actual emotion, perception, or behavior (e.g., repressors may be more likely to develop projection jealousy).

Attachment Styles

Recent research on attachment styles and close relationships is somewhat more promising. This research is based on Bowlby's seminal work on the development of affectional bonds in infancy and childhood (Bowlby, 1969; Hazan & Shaver, 1987). Three types of attachment styles have been described: secure, anxious/ambivalent, and avoidant (Ainsworth, Blehar, Waters, & Wall, 1978). Of interest here is the anxious/ambivalent style, characterized as wanting intense, emotional contact yet fearing rejection. This style may have a temperamental component; recall that temperamentally anxious children are more jealous of siblings. This style is also reminiscent of manic or limerant love styles (Lee, 1977; Tennov, 1979; Chapter 5, this volume).

Hazan and Shaver (1987) report that agreement with a paragraph describing the anxious/ambivalent style in adult relationships (about 25% of their sample) was related to a wide variety of relationship-related variables, including a self-report measure of relationship jealousy, in both college and general population (newspaper survey) samples. Further, this style was correlated in expected ways with retrospective accounts of childhood attachments. Future jealousy research might benefit from attention to attachment styles, with work directed at understanding how such styles are related both to personality and to the situational context of the adult romantic relationship.

SUMMARY

Psychoanalytic theory has linked adult jealousy to narcissistic characteristics, to repetition compulsion of Oedipal and sibling rivalry, and to projection of sexual impulses. Outside of case histories, there is little evidence for or against these propositions. Two studies have attempted to link adult jealousy to parental factors. Results are somewhat supportive of the analytic propositions regarding narcissism and the Oedipal conflict, and are more generally supportive of the notion that parents' jealousy is related to their children's adult jealousy and defensive styles.

There is even less research on sibling rivalry than on adult romantic jealousy. The existing research indicates that sibling rivalry is probably related to temperament, to the experience of absolute loss of attention and resources, and to opportunities to witness siblings getting relatively more attention or attention. These findings have little bearing on analytic theory of adult jealousy. There is no research on links between sibling rivalry and adult jealousy.

Trait research has been relatively unsystematic. Research supports the notion that some people are disposed to become jealous in a variety of situations, but the importance of this disposition in affecting normal jealousy remains unclear. The link between self-esteem and jealousy is tenuous. In view of our conceptualization of jealousy as a complex, self-esteem may be differentially related to a variety of elements of the complex; hence, no simple statement is possible. Further, it appears that aspects of self-esteem more specifically related to the romantic relationship will prove to be more specifically related to aspects of the jealousy complex. Research on other traits is rather sparse, but the evidence available partially conforms to the often-encountered clinical picture of the narcissistic, macho jealous male and the histrionic, anxious jealous female. However, it must be emphasized that much more work within the trait approach is necessary if we are to have any confidence in the utility of trait constructs to predict romantic jealousy.

Recent research on attachment styles suggests that children who are anxious and ambivalent about their parents may be anxious and ambivalent about their romantic partners and may thus be susceptible to jealousy. It is easy to speculate that such styles would be related to aspects of primary appraisal, secondary appraisal, and coping efforts of the jealous. Research in this area appears promising.

5

Relationships, Gender, and Jealousy

Romantic relationships form the major arena in which jealousy is played out. Though culture, personality, and perhaps biology contribute to the dynamics of jealousy, it almost always occurs within the context of a love relationship. Jealousy may seem alien to the relationship or, conversely, may appear to flow from its very fabric. In this chapter we first use our model to sketch five characteristics of relationships that are likely to influence the development and nature of the jealousy complex. We discuss what it means to conceptualize a relationship factor as a cause of jealousy, and then review jealousy research on relationship-related variables and processes. This review links previous research to the characteristics of relationships that are proposed to influence jealousy.

The volumes of relationship-related hypotheses that have been generated by clinicians and assorted social scientists and social philosophers are not reviewed in detail here, because this literature is so extensive and because in this area there is a need to concentrate more on data and less on theory. The research on specific variables that have been correlated with jealousy measures is reviewed, together with concepts and processes such as equity norm maintenance and impression management, for which there are data directly related to jealousy.

RELATIONSHIP CHARACTERISTICS LIKELY TO INFLUENCE THE JEALOUSY COMPLEX

Our model of jealousy suggests that it is a multifaceted reaction to threats to self-esteem or to the romantic relationship. Appraisal

103

processes yield judgments about the potential for a rival relationship to exist, about the actual existence of a rival relationship, and about the degree of threat or harm posed by the rival relationship. From this model, five characteristics of relationships that are likely to be related to jealousy can be abstracted. These characteristics have to do with the nature of what is threatened or lost, the nature of protection against threat or of the means to recuperate from loss, and the likelihood of rival relationships. These characteristics may themselves be either the products or the producers of other relationship factors. It is possible to generate a large number of relationship factors (not to mention cultural and person factors) potentially related to these characteristics. Such a task is beyond our scope, since our primary aim is to explain jealousy, not to explain the development of these five characteristics. Inherent in our model, however, is the supposition that these characteristics play an important role in shaping the jealousy complex. Part of this role may be to mediate the influence of other relationship factors.

The five relationship characteristics proposed to particularly influence jealousy are as follows:

- Investments and rewards
- Salience and evaluation of dimensions of self-concept
- Security for investments and rewards
- Security for self-esteem and self-concept
- Potential for a rival relationship

Investments and Rewards

The more valued the romantic relationship, the more likely it is that a person will try to maintain it, be vigilant toward threats to the relationship, and experience strong emotional reactions to loss or threat of loss. Generally, relationships are more valued to the extent that investments of time, energy, or resources have been made and to the extent that the partner and the relationship provide rewarding experiences. The quality of the investments or rewards may partly determine the specific experience of jealousy and the coping efforts made in the face of threat or loss. For example, relationships in which sexual satisfaction is central to one partner may sensitize that partner to sexual threats from rivals and may foster sexually competitive coping efforts. In addition, the valuation of investments and rewards is not static and may be modified by aspects of one's jealousy. When sad, the jealous person may devalue past investments and elevate past rewards, whereas just the opposite may occur when the person is angry.

Salience and Evaluation of Dimensions of Self-Concept

Relationships can be characterized by the extent to which different dimensions of self-concept become salient to or evaluated by oneself. Both salience and self-evaluation are particularly likely to be influenced by the partner's overt or covert evaluations of self or the relationship, and these evaluations are at least partly grounded in the interactional nature of the relationship. Failure of a partner to take one's advice may imply that one's supportive capacities are not good; the partner's complaints that the relationship is boring implies that one is boring. Certain aspects of self may often be salient (e.g., sexuality, lovableness, verbal intimacy skills); others may emerge in particular contexts or developmental periods (e.g., parenting skills, provision of support in crises).

Like the valuation of investments and rewards, the salience and evaluation of particular dimensions of self-concept are not static, but are influenced by elements of the emerging jealousy complex. For example, appraisals of the meaning of the partner's attractions to others are likely to be bidirectionally related to the salience of specific aspects of self, and coping efforts may be aimed at re-establishing self-esteem or self-concept along specific dimensions.

Security for Investments and Rewards

The concept of "vulnerability" is used to explain individual differences in the reaction to stressors. Our use of the term follows that of Lazarus and Folkman (1984), who suggest that vulnerability is a relationship between the things people seek to maintain (commitments) and the resources they have to ward off threats to those commitments. People are vulnerable when they are not able to protect aspects of themselves and their lives that are rewarding or otherwise meaningful. Vulnerability is affected by both personal and relationship processes.

Partners develop arrangements to prevent or minimize loss to their rewards and investments, and thereby reduce vulnerability. We call these arrangements "security." Hence, security is a form of resource to reduce threat or loss, but it is a resource that relies on negotiation with the partner and is not a resource independent of the partner's actions, as are personal resources such as skills or physical appearance. The overt or covert negotiation of security may occur either in anticipation of threat or in reaction to it. Various forms of security are negotiated or borrowed from the larger culture, such as exclusivity norms, professions of appreciation for the investments of the other, or beliefs that each partner is uniquely suited to the other.

Failure to provide security yields "insecurity" about the future supply of rewards, protection of investments, and ability to recoup losses while staying in the relationship. Insecurity, in this sense, increases the perceived vulnerability of investments and rewards to actions of rivals. Insecurity is a particularly problematic type of vulnerability, as it stems from the failure of the partner to enter into desired security arrangements; it is just this failure that can rightly or wrongly imply the potential of the partner's forming a relationship with another.

The kinds and degree of security are related to the nature of the investments and rewards. Security for the investment of emotional energy may be different from the security for a satisfying sexual relationship. Violation of different forms of security may have differing effects on the jealousy complex. For example, violation of exclusivity norms is a breach of security with potentially different consequences from those of challenges to the belief in one's unique ability to provide the beloved with emotional support.

Security for Self-Esteem and Self-Concept

In Chapter 2, we have discussed the theoretical bases for the central role played by threats to self-esteem and self-concept. We have suggested that a romantic attraction between partner and rival may signal devaluation of central aspects of self and imply inaccuracies in self-concept. Now we simply point out that the form of security for self-esteem and self-concept may influence the form and intensity of the jealousy complex.

As is the case with vulnerability of investments and rewards, to reduce vulnerability of the self, partners negotiate security for salient dimensions of self-concept and for self-esteem. Both salience and self-evaluation are influenced by the nature of the interaction with one's partner. Failure to negotiate security promotes insecurity of self-esteem and self-concept. Hence, insecurity of self will reflect relational dynamics as well as personality dynamics. Overemphasis on personality roots of insecurity may promote theoretical and clinical difficulties.

Negotiated security for self-esteem may also function as security for investments and rewards, as is the case for exclusivity norms. This is parallel to the dual function of many coping efforts (see Chapter 2): to protect rewards and investments, and to protect self-esteem. Hence, jealousy is a major impetus in the development of security, and as a result may function to stabilize developing relationships. For example, the coping efforts of demanding commitment and improving the relationship can lead to stronger exclusivity norms and to the belief that one's relationship is superior to potential alternatives. Jealousy can play a constructive as well as a destructive role in relationships.

The Potential for a Rival Relationship

Relationship factors influence both the perceived potential for a rival relationship to develop and judgments that such a relationship actually exists. As we have noted earlier, the nature of motives attributed to partners for their interests in others is related to various indices of jealousy. The perception that one's partner is dissatisfied or has strong needs that cannot be met within the relationship is related to the perception of a rival relationship. This perception is in turn likely to be related to more distal relationship factors, particularly those predictive of relationship dissatisfaction and dissolution. As noted earlier, the unwillingness of a partner to negotiate security for investments, rewards, and self-esteem may itself signal that the potential or actuality of a rival is high.

CONCEPTUALIZING RELATIONSHIP FACTORS AS CAUSES: MATCHING AND EMERGENT FEATURES

It is more difficult to conceptualize causal conditions that are the result of interpersonal relationships than those thought to arise from individual or cultural factors. In addition to information-processing biases that favor simple person attributions (Fiske & Taylor, 1984), this difficulty exists because relationship factors influencing an individual's behavior may either result from *matching* characteristics of partners or *emerge* from repeated interaction (Kelley et al., 1983).

"Matching" refers to the relationship between properties of each partner. These properties may be similar or dissimilar, or they may be complementary or noncomplementary. Depending on the variable being considered, both similarity and complementarity may facilitate or hinder rewarding interaction. For example, two people with similar attitudes are more likely to be attracted to each other than two people with dissimilar attitudes (Berscheid & Walster, 1978). A man with a traditional masculine sex-role orientation and a woman with a complementary, traditional feminine sex-role orientation are more likely to have satisfactory interactions than if they differ in orientation (Huston & Ashmore, 1986; Peplau, 1983). These attitudes and sex-role orientations may exist prior to the development of the relationship, yet their juxtaposition produces a variety of consequences, and their matching only occurs as the result of a relationship. Hence, the degree of similarity or complementarity between properties of two partners is a cause different from the properties themselves.

A causal condition that is generated by reciprocal interaction is one that has emerged from the relationship. Such emergence is marked by circular causality, in which the actions of each partner influence and are influenced in turn by the other (Bandura, 1978; Watzlawick et al., 1967). A great many examples of emergent causal conditions can be generated, but many of these can be classified as emergent norms or role expectations that regulate interaction. For example, out of past interaction, the romantic couple may arrive at more or less explicitly shared rules about the acceptable degrees of extrarelationship intimacy (an exclusivity norm). Or, out of past interaction, they may arrive at shared expectations about the tasks that each partner is to perform (he does the laundry, she pays the bills). Although cultural norms and role expectations may influence the development of these emergent rules, it is clear that cultural causal conditions alone are unable to explain the variability of patterns seen in close relationships (Ashmore, Del Boca, & Wohlers, 1986; Peplau, 1983).

For many of the variables related to jealousy, it is unclear at this stage whether they represent person factors, the result of matching, or emergent properties of the relationship. For example, the self-concept that one is inadequate as a partner may be a property of the jealous person that is relatively chronic and stable across many different romantic partners (a person factor). Or it may emerge from the interaction between the jealous and the beloved well in advance of any perception of a rival and may be unique to that relationship. Or this self-concept may be a result of the matching of pre-existing attributes of the partners (she has lots of friends, he is a loner).

The distinction between person and relationship factors that we are trying to make is necessary for the theoretical specification of causal conditions and is vital in the therapy of romantic jealousy. It should be obvious that a therapist who conceptualizes jealousy as a result of person factors (e.g., unresolved Oedipal complex, narcissistic personality disorder) will be less effective if the client's jealousy crisis is primarily caused by emergent properties of the couple's interaction.

In the following review, for many correlates of jealousy (e.g., perception of oneself as an inadequate partner), it is impossible to know the extent to which the variable as assessed represents a person or a relationship variable. Given the status of current research, it is useful to consider that the label given to a particular research variable may be conceptualized both as a person factor and as a relationship factor, with potentially independent effects on jealousy. Part of the existing theoretical and therapeutic confusion about relationships results from the fact that phenomenologically similar processes may result from person forces, relationship forces, or both. People may think themselves to be inadequate for very different reasons.

REVIEW OF RESEARCH ON JEALOUSY-RELATED VARIABLES AND PROCESSES

The remainder of this chapter summarizes research on variables and processes that have been specifically concerned with romantic jealousy. This review of individual variables or jealousy-related relationship processes is followed by a review of gender differences in elements of the jealousy complex. The chapter concludes with consideration of the impact of the beloved, the rival, and the adverse and secondary relationships on jealousy.

Relationship Status and Length

Research evidence is not consistent in relating relationship status and length to jealousy. Macklin (1972) found jealousy to be a particular problem for cohabiters; other research has found jealousy more problematic for serious or exclusive daters (Braiker-Stambul, 1975; Bringle & Gray, 1986; White, 1985b). Still other studies have found no relationship between status or length of relationship and jealousy (Bush et al., 1988; Buunk, 1981; White, 1981e). Mathes (1986) found that higher jealousy scores were positively related to continuation of the relationship over a 7-year period. This mixed picture is not surprising, given that markers such as status, stage, or length are likely to be correlated with a wide variety of relationship variables, some positively and some negatively related to jealousy. Further, the concept of stage or status does not capture the complexity of relationship development (Braiker & Kelley, 1979; Graziano & Musser, 1982; Huston, Surra, Fitzgerald, & Cate, 1981; Levinger & Huesmann, 1980). Hence, it is not useful for theory development to concentrate on relationship status, stage, or length per se; rather, causal conditions that covary with these gross markers should be examined.

Relationship Satisfaction and Commitment

There is a large and often conflicting literature on the conceptualization of both satisfaction and commitment. "Satisfaction" most frequently is used to refer to the level of positive feelings about the relationship; "commitment" refers to the stability of, and attachment to, the relationship (Kelley, 1983; Lewis & Spanier, 1979; Rusbult, 1980, 1983). Commitment to the relationship has already been noted as the central focus of secondary-appraisal processes in jealousy (see Chapter 2). Needless to say, a large number of methods have been used to assess satisfaction and commitment.

Satisfaction

Some studies have reported that increased satisfaction is associated with less jealousy (Bringle, 1986; Bringle, Evenbeck, & Schmedel, 1977; Buunk, 1981, males only; Jenks, 1985). Hansen (1983), however, found no relationship, and Rosmarin and LaPointe (1978) reported that those high and low in satisfaction were more anxious about the potential for a rival relationship than those moderately satisfied. Buunk (1982b) reported that satisfied partners were less likely to cope with jealousy by avoidance and more likely to attempt open communication.

Commitment

Buunk (1982a) asked subjects to indicate the likelihood that they would engage in various extrarelationship sexual behaviors; these responses can be thought of as a measure of commitment. Commitment was strongly negatively correlated with an anticipated-jealousy measure. In contrast, Hansen (1982) found that a "future of marriage" item, assessing degree of motivation to maintain the relationship, was positively correlated with anticipated jealousy in men.

Bush et al. (1988) reported that a measure of perceived relationship security was uncorrelated with a dispositional measure of jealousy, but was negatively correlated with current level of relationship jealousy (personal communication). Perceived security dropped in response to imagining a jealousy-provoking situation.

We think that satisfaction and commitment are more likely to be associated with low levels of jealousy, because both are probably related to high levels of security for investments, rewards, and self-esteem. In addition, the stability of a relationship (commitment) is likely to suggest a low potential for a rival relationship to develop.

Dependence On the Relationship

"Dependence" refers to the extent to which the person believes that the outcomes in the current romantic relationship are superior to those in the next most available relationship (Thibaut & Kelley, 1959). In our terms, dependence is related to the degree of rewards received and the vulnerability of those rewards. Dependent partners are receiving comparatively high rewards (compared to those available elsewhere). Since those rewards are not readily available elsewhere, dependent partners are vulnerable to disruption of those rewards by rivals. Those who are highly dependent are likely to infer threat in the primary appraisal of the rival relationship, to try to improve the relationship, or to demand commitment as a means of reducing the threat to the relationship (Berscheid & Fei, 1977; Bringle & Gray, 1986; Clanton & Smith, 1977; Foa & Foa, 1980).

Several studies have demonstrated that dependent partners are more likely to be jealous. White (1981b, 1981e) reported that a Dependence Scale correlated positively with female but not male jealousy; in both studies, females rated themselves as more dependent than males. Amstutz (1982) replicated these findings and also reported that dependent partners were more likely to maintain positive feelings about their partners and relationships despite becoming jealous. This is consistent with the finding that dependency promotes idealization of romantic partners (Dion & Dion, 1975; Kanin, Davidson, & Scheck, 1970; Kemper, 1978). Other researchers have used a variety of ad hoc scales to assess dependency, and all have found that the more dependent are more likely to be jealous (Bringle, Evenbeck, & Schmedel, 1977; Bringle & Gray, 1986; Buunk, 1982a; Bush et al., 1988). Hindy, Schwarz, and Brodsky (1989) identified both attachment/dependence and jealousy as correlated aspects of lovesickness.

Bringle and Gray (1986) reasoned that jealousy might be influenced by the kinds of rewards partners exchanged, such as love, status, information, money, goods, and services. Subjects indicated the degree to which they gave and received different kinds of rewards in their romantic relationships. Two anticipated-jealousy scales were used; one asked how upset the person would be if the partner had an affair, and the other assessed anticipated jealousy in minor events (e.g., seeing one's partner kissing a stranger at a party). Various composite measures of the quality and quantity of exchange were not significantly related to scores on either scale. We would expect, however, that the kinds of rewards upon which one is dependent should influence such aspects of the jealousy complex as emotion and coping efforts.

Relative Dependence and Power

"Relative dependence" refers to the degree to which one partner is dependent upon the relationship compared to the other. Relative dependence can range from one partner's being highly dependent while the other is not very dependent, to both partners' being equally dependent. Relative dependence is closely linked to power in a relationship. Generally, the person closer to leaving the relationship (the less dependent) is the more powerful. This relationship appears to hold across a wide variety of interpersonal relationships (Blau, 1964; Frieze et al., 1978; Gillespie, 1971; Huston, 1983; Thibaut & Kelley, 1959; Waller & Hill, 1951). Relative dependence is not static, but obviously depends on the nature and relative availability of rewards outside the primary relationship (Peplau, 1979).

Note that relative dependence is different from absolute dependence. Relative dependence may lead to a concern with the meaning of one's position relative to that of one's partner. Such a concern is not generated by the absolute level of dependence. For example, in early dating, neither partner may be particularly dependent on the other. Yet one partner may be more eager to continue the relationship; this is an indication of relative dependence. Even though the absolute level of dependence is low, the more eager partner may feel more vulnerable and hence may be more susceptible to jealousy than the less eager partner.

Relative dependence is linked to vulnerability of investments, rewards, and self-esteem, as well as to estimates of the potential for a rival relationship to form. If the partner is perceived as less dependent than oneself, this should increase the perceived likelihood that he or she will leave the relationship for a better alternative (Hill,

Rubin, & Peplau, 1976; Levinger, 1979; Rusbult, 1980; White, 1980b, 1981c). Insecurity may be relatively high, and a relatively dependent partner may often be in the position of trying to achieve security in the face of the other partner's indifference (Berscheid & Fei, 1977). Primary-appraisal vigilance may be high, and generally we would expect social comparison outcomes to be unfavorable. Relatively dependent partners should be more depressed when jealous, as they would stand in greater danger of losing a valued relationship.

Several studies have found that the relatively dependent are more jealous. White (1981c) found that responses to the question "Who would you say is more involved in your relationship, you or your partner?" were related to the current level of jealousy for both sexes. Bringle et al. (1983) found that relative involvement averaged across three previous relationships predicted anticipated jealousy. In another study, more involved women (but not men) reported intentionally inducing jealousy more frequently. This was interpreted as an indirect power tactic to make the beloved think the person was less dependent, presumably equalizing power (White, 1980a). Relative dependence has predicted jealousy even when absolute dependence was held constant (Bringle & Gray, 1986; White, 1981b), but Amstutz (1982) did not replicate this effect.

Relatively more dependent partners have been reported to be more depressed and intropunitive when jealous, whereas relatively less dependent partners are more angry and vengeful. The effect of relative dependence on emotion accounted for most of an observed gender difference that women were more depressed and men were more angry when jealous (White, 1985c). Women rate themselves as relatively more dependent than do men (White, 1981b, 1985c).

Equity in the Relationship

"Equity" refers to equivalence between the relative gain (or loss) between two or more actors in a relationship. Roughly speaking, the "equity norm" is an expectation that people will benefit from relationships roughly in proportion to what they put into them (Walster, Walster, & Berscheid, 1978). Thus, if two people are contributing equally to a relationship, they should be enjoying equivalent outcomes. If one person is contributing more, that person should be enjoying a relatively greater outcome.

Violations of equity lead to distress and attempts to restore the balance. Attempts to restore equity can be either psychological or material and can be directed at changing the level of one's own or the partner's inputs (e.g., putting in less effort, demanding more effort from the partner) or at changing the level of one's own or the partner's outcomes (e.g., idealizing the partner's qualities to give a sense of better outcomes for oneself, sabotaging the partner's outcomes).

The equity norm has been found to be useful in predicting interpersonal exchanges in a variety of different kinds of relationships, such as parent–child, romantic, business, and exploiter–victim relationships (Hatfield et al., 1985; Walster et al., 1978). In romantic relationships or close friendships, the equity norm may be supplanted by communal or equality norms favoring altruism and sharing without regard to need (Clark, 1985; Clark & Mills, 1979). However, in the long run, underbenefited romantic partners may return to an emphasis on equity (Hatfield et al., 1985; Kelley, 1983).

There are several reasons why underbenefited partners may be more jealous. In order to restore a balance of *psychological* equity, the underbenefited individual may devalue the outcomes the partner is believed to be receiving from the relationship, or may upwardly re-evaluate his or her own outcomes. The latter may increase the sense of dependence, which is related to jealousy; the former may increase the sense of relative dependence, which is also related to jealousy. Also, attempts to restore equity by demanding greater investment by the partner may enhance the potential for the partner to seek relatively less costly rewards elsewhere. For example, it is not un-usual for American women to demand more intimacy, which is costly for men, who then seek less demanding romantic relationships (Peplau & Gordon, 1985).

Equity violations, especially if chronic, are also related to the five characteristics of relationships that we suggest influence jealousy. In terms of investments and rewards, the underbenefited individual has relatively greater investments in the rewards generated by the relationship. Indications that the partner is further decreasing in-vestment because of a rival may generate equity-restorative acts that are interpreted as jealousy (e.g., derogating the rival or seeking alternatives). The underbenefited person may perceive his or her rewards to be vulnerable, since the person may think the partner more capable of investment (to produce greater relationship re-wards), and hence potentially able to invest surplus time, energy, and other resources elsewhere.

Many of the investments in romantic relationships are related to personal attributes often central to self-concept, such as mainte-nance of physical attractiveness and efforts to be emotionally sensi-tive (Hatfield et al., 1985). Further, what is rewarding in relation-ships is a function of core values, which are inherently related to self-concept. Achieving equity often requires that the partners make judgments about the relative worth of the different kinds of investments and rewards (Foa & Foa, 1980; Hatfield et al., 1985). Hence, equity restoration may be threatening to self-esteem and self-concept. Being consistently underbenefited may imply that the partner devalues one's investments, which in turn threatens self-esteem. This implication may sensitize the underbenefited to the potential for the partner to achieve more valued rewards elsewhere. Hatfield et al. (1985) conclude from their review of equity research that inequitable relationships are less stable and presumably more likely to be ended in favor of rival relationships.

There is some research suggesting that the underbenefited are more likely to be jealous. A Relative Effort Scale (e.g., "Who spends more time and energy maintaining your relationship?") was found to be positively related to both chronic and relationship jealousy, with those who thought they put relatively more effort into their relationships being more jealous (Amstutz, 1982; White, 1981b). This effect was independent of relative dependency, suggesting that relative effort has merit as a separate construct. Those who thought they put relatively more effort into their relationships were more likely to feel insecure, anxious, confused, and angry at themselves when jealous, and also to feel more sexually attracted to the beloved (Amstutz, 1982).

In another study, subjects who were asked to imagine a jealousy-provoking scene involving their partners subsequently rated themselves as relatively more involved (Bush et al., 1988). This is an example of a more general possibility that perceived threat and jealousy-related variables may be mutually influencing each other. Those who are relatively more involved (underbenefited?) may be more likely to perceive threat, and those who perceive threat may subsequently view themselves as relatively more involved.

Though the research is sparse at this time, the ubiquity of the equity norm and the probable involvement of equity processes in the jealousy-influencing characteristics of relationships suggest that both research on equity and jealousy, and clinical attention to equity processes, would be fruitful undertakings.

Perception of Oneself as an Inadequate Partner for the Beloved

Although the research reviewed in Chapter 4 shows no clear relationship between global self-esteem and jealousy, the perception of oneself as an inadequate partner appears related to jealousy. This aspect of self-concept is more relevant to jealousy than is global self-esteem. Adequacy as a partner may be a salient aspect of self in many kinds of interactions with the partner. Further, perceived inadequacy increases vulnerability of self-esteem, as the partner is viewed as more likely to develop an attraction for a rival.

The perception of oneself as inadequate is likely to affect and be affected by a number of elements of the jealousy complex. For example, Bush et al. (1988) found that perceived inadequacy increased in response to imagining a jealousy-provoking situation. Although it is possible that a jealous person may perceive of himself or herself as inadequate for a particular partner, yet may not negatively evaluate himself or herself for this attribute, it is likely that perceived inadequacy may be associated with self-blame, insecurity, and anxiety (Berscheid & Fei, 1977; Bush et al., 1988).

A Perceived Inadequacy Scale (e.g., "I wish I were a different person so that my relationship would be better") has predicted chronic and relationship jealousy in a number of studies (Amstutz, 1982; White, 1981b, 1981c, 1981e). In addition, Amstutz (1982) reported that those who felt inadequate were more likely to be angry at both their partners and themselves, and anxious, insecure, confused, and guilty about being jealous; they also tended to pay more attention to and to be more sexually aggressive with their partners.

Roy (1977) reported that in most of her 150 cases of abused women, jealousy was closely related to sexual problems in the relationship and to the husbands' doubts about their own sexual adequacy. We later discuss the pathological aspects of such insecurity, but note for now that the perception of sexual inadequacy may result from mismatching of the partners' sexual needs and practices or may emerge from a deteriorating sexual relationship.

Self-Esteem Dependence

"Self-esteem dependence" refers to the extent to which a person's self-esteem is affected by the partner's evaluation. This variable is related to vulnerability of self-esteem and self-concept. It follows from our definition of jealousy as a reaction to perceived threat to self-esteem (self-concept) that those who are more dependent on the beloved for their sense of self-worth are more vulnerable to real or implied rejection. Further, self-esteem dependence is a normal characteristic of many romantic relationships, and hence is likely to frequently influence the jealousy complex (Dion & Dion, 1973, 1975; Kelley, 1983; Knudson, 1985; Lee, 1977; Levenson & Harris, 1980).

A Self-Esteem Dependency Scale (e.g., "I would feel terrible about myself if my partner didn't respect me") has been positively related to chronic jealousy (Amstutz, 1982; White, 1981b, 1981e). The more esteem-dependent subjects appeared to be more confused, anxious, insecure, and intropunitive when jealous (Amstutz, 1982). Mathes and Severa (1981) reported that items measuring "separate identities" (e.g., "Do you and your partner do everything together?") were negatively related to jealousy.

Exclusivity Norms and Expectations

Exclusivity norms or expectations may be directed at either sexual or nonsexual exclusivity. Nonsexual exclusivity concerns nonsexual exchange, such as intimate self-disclosure, advice giving, support or help in adverse circumstances, recreation time, and so forth. Both kinds of exclusivity expectations can be thought of as ways in which both self-esteem and the relationship become protected from outside interference (D'Augelli & D'Augelli, 1979; Levinger, 1979). Hence, they are security for investments, rewards, and the self. These norms appear to be very widespread and powerful, which probably attests to their ability to provide security for a great range of investments, rewards, and aspects of the self.

To date, jealousy researchers have only studied sexual exclusivity expectations. However, several observers have speculated that violations of nonsexual exclusivity expectations or norms should also engender jealousy. For example, Bringle and Buunk (1985) advise that violations of "specialness" are likely to trigger jealousy. Lewin (1948, pp. 99-100) suggested that a rival relationship promotes jealousy by breaching the "barrier between one's intimate life and the public," indicating that certain kinds of information should be held exclusively within the relationship. Clinically oriented observations that violations of nonsexual exclusivity promote jealousy are common (e.g., Clanton & Smith, 1977; Constantine, 1976; Farber, 1973; Mazur, 1977). The sociologist Georg Simmel (1950) also observed that the loss of the feeling of "uniqueness" or exclusive sharing of intimacy often led to jealousy.

A Sexual Exclusivity Scale (e.g., "I expect my partner to be sexually faithful to me") has been found to be a strong predictor of jealousy (Amstutz, 1982b; White, 1981b, 1981e). White (1976) found that sexual exclusivity expectations were a stronger predictor of male than of female anger over the partner's involvement with a rival. However, Pines and Aronson (1983) reported that belief in monogamy was negatively correlated with current jealousy. It is likely that the stronger the exclusivity norm, the more secure and less jealous partners should be. However, violation of that norm (or expectations) should lead to intense jealousy, as investments, rewards, and aspects of self considered safe are unexpectedly exposed to threat.

Love and Jealousy

There has been substantial interest in the last two decades in the social psychology of love and romantic relationships (Berscheid & Walster, 1978; Brehm, 1985; Kelley, 1983; Rubin, 1970). These recent developments stand alongside a vast literature on romantic love that is more clinical, subjective, or philosophical in nature (Ortega y Gasset, 1957; Otto, 1972; Pope, 1980; Solomon, 1976). In this section research related to love and jealousy is reviewed. Most of this research can be seen as related either to the types of investments and rewards made in the relationship, or to the dimensions of self that become salient and influenceable in love relationships.

Loving versus Liking

Rubin's Love Scale, which is based on a concept of romantic love as a blend of attachment, caring, and intimacy (Rubin, 1970), has correlated to some extent with a variety of jealousy scales. His Liking Scale, which assesses respect for the partner, has not often correlated with jealousy. Pfeiffer and Wong's (1987) study was an exception, these authors report that liking was negatively related to suspicion and worry about a rival relationship and to checking-up (information-gathering) behaviors. Correlations between love and jealousy have generally been higher for measures of anticipated jealousy than for measures of the current level of jealousy or of specific jealous reactions (Bush et al., 1988; Mathes, 1984; Mathes, Roter, & Joerger, 1982; Mathes & Severa, 1981; Pfeiffer & Wong, 1987; Rosmarin & LaPointe, 1978; White, 1976, 1984, 1985b).

Correlations with global measures of love may be weak because these measures fail to capture the multidimensionality of love. There is some evidence, for example that the attachment aspect of love may correlate more highly with jealousy (Hazan & Shaver, 1987; Mathes, Roter, & Joerger, 1982).

Attitudes toward Love

Love researchers have measured various attitudes toward love (Brehm, 1985; Kelley, 1983; Knox & Sporakowski, 1968). For example, Dion and Dion (1973) report three major attitudes: idealism

("There is only one real love for a person"), cyni(
love is an outmoded and unrealistic concept"),
("Even if not as strong, a previous love affair may s{
love"). Idealism is similar to the concept of rom
1985; Murstein, 1974). The romantic ideal is that o'
and that once lovers find each other they will live tog̶e̶t̶h̶.̶.̶
Love will overcome all obstacles.

There is mixed evidence that romanticism is related to jealousy
(Hansen, 1982; Lester, Deluca, Hellinghausen, & Scribner, 1985;
White, 1976). For example, White (1977) found no correlations between idealistic, cynical, and pragmatic attitudes toward love and
current levels of jealousy, whereas Lester et al. (1985) and De Moja
(1986) found modest correlations between jealousy and romantic
attitudes toward love.

Attitudes toward Jealousy

Jealousy is commonly thought to be either a sign of personal insecurity or a sign of true love (Clanton & Smith, 1977; Sommers,
1984). Research has indicated that the latter belief is weakly to
moderately correlated with jealousy self-reports; the former belief
has not been found to correlate with jealousy (Greenberg & Pyszczynski, 1985; Pines & Aronson, 1983; White, 1976, 1985b). One
study reported that a jealous partner portrayed in jealousy vignettes
was more harshly evaluated when the errant partner was in love
with the rival than when he or she was having a casual affair
(Hartnett, Mahoney, & Bernstein, 1977). Obviously, attitudes toward the jealous will depend on the context of the jealousy.

Types of Love and Jealousy

Various authors have proposed qualitatively different types of romantic love (Brehm, 1985; Hazan & Shaver, 1987; Kelley, 1983; Lee, 1977;
Sternberg, 1986; Tennov, 1979; Walster & Walster, 1978). One common distinction is between "passionate" or "erotic" love and "companionate" or "conjugal" love. Passionate love is intense, sexualized, and
romantic, whereas companionate love is more characterized by trust,
friendship, and stability. No research has distinguished between these
two types of love and jealousy per se. Mathes (1984) reported that
sexual attraction to one's partner was higher among those who anticipated they would be quite jealous in a jealousy-inducing situation.

Lee (1977) has suggested six types of styles of love: *eros* (physical
attraction), *ludus* (desire for uncommitted relationships), *storge* (com-

mitted attachment, low in passion), *mania* (intense romantic love needing repeated reassurance of reciprocation), *agape* (altruistic love), and *pragma* (love based on utilitarian considerations). White (1977) reported that current relationship jealousy was correlated with *eros*, *storge*, and *mania*, and negatively related to *ludus*. Chronic jealousy was correlated with *mania* and negatively related to *ludus*. Three major clusters of jealous emotions identified were anger/revenge, anxiety, and depression. *Eros* was associated with jealous anxiety, while *ludus* was negatively related to anger and depression. *Storge* was linked to anxiety and depression. *Mania*, the closest type to passionate love, was associated with all three emotions.

Taken at face value, these data suggest that people who do not want commitment experience little jealousy. This finding is consistent with research reviewed earlier, which found that jealousy is minimized if the person is not dependent on the relationship for self-esteem and the rewards of the relationship. People with a history of jealous relationships are more likely to be manic (passionate) lovers. Jealousy in a current relationship is positively related to passion, physical attractiveness of the partner, and attachment.

One of the phenomenological similarities between romantic love and jealousy is the experience that the lover is never quite sure about the beloved. Does the beloved really love him or her (love)? Does the beloved love another (jealousy)? Lee's (1977) *mania*, the type closest to passionate love, is characterized by repeated needs to be reassured. Tennov (1979) presents a number of compelling biographical accounts suggesting that manic, or as she calls them "limerant" lovers desperately need repeated assurance that their partners love them. This need for reassurance may have personality predictors, but it is also probably related to beliefs and experience that intense, sexualized attraction is short-lived. Something so ephemeral should need constant monitoring. The loss or threatened loss of passionate love to a rival should, like all losses, engage the jealousy complex. The ephemeral quality of passionate love should serve to intensify the sense of threat and to motivate urgent coping efforts. The constant monitoring and questioning that are characteristic of both passionate (manic, limerant) love and the jealousy of passionate lovers can thus be seen as extreme forms of the normal secondary-appraisal processes of information gathering, motive attribution, and social comparison. Coping efforts of the jealous manic lover may be more extreme or more primitive as a function of heightened primary appraisal of threat.

Based on Bowlby's (1969) attachment theory of personality development, Hazan and Shaver (1987) differentiate among "secure," "avoidant," and "anxious/ambivalent" attachment styles in romantic love. Anxious/ambivalent lovers are somewhat similar to Tennov's limerant lovers, who often perceive themselves as more willing to be intimate than their partners and who are anxious that their partners will reject them. Anxious/ambivalent partners reported greater past or current jealousy than avoidant lovers, who reported more jealousy than secure lovers. Although Hazen and Shaver conceptualize attachment styles as personality variables, it may be that how secure, avoidant, or anxious/ambivalent one feels about one's partner is partly due to the nature of the relationship.

Erotic Orientation

Very little research has been done on jealousy differences between partners with homoerotic and partners with heteroerotic orientations. Research and commentaries on gay and lesbian relationships generally cite jealousy (or cite many of the jealousy-related variables we are reviewing) as a problem, just as it is in relationships among the heteroerotic (Bell & Weinberg, 1978; Blasband & Peplau, 1985; Morris, 1982; Peplau, Cochran, Rook, & Padesky, 1978; Peplau & Gordon, 1983; Silverstein, 1981). For example, Blasband and Peplau (1985) and Silverstein (1981) report that jealousy is a frequently cited reason for having a closed rather than an open gay relationship. Jealousy may be a greater problem for gay male couples than for lesbian couples, as gay men generally have more sex partners than heterosexual men or women or lesbians (Brehm, 1985), though this appears to be changing with the advent of AIDS. Lesbian women may particularly fear that the beloved will seek a heterosexual relationship to escape the stigma and stresses associated with lesbian relationships (Morris, 1982).

White (1985b) found that jealousy was more likely to be cited as a cause of relationship breakup for gay college couples than for heterosexual couples or lesbians, but his sample of homoerotic subjects was small and probably not representative. Larson (1982) has reported that gay men appear to be less jealous than heterosexual men in response to their partners' involvements with others.

Sexual Lifestyle

Sociologists and social psychologists have been interested in alternative sexual lifestyles such as open marriage, communal sexuality, and "swinging" since these lifestyles began gaining public attention in the 1960s. Occasionally, research into such lifestyles has included questions about jealousy. In our terms, most of this research is related to the relationship characteristics of vulnerability and the potential for rival relationships.

Swinging

Swinging is usually initiated by husbands out of boredom or desire for sexual variety; wives are usually reluctant to go along. However, once swinging is initiated, wives report as much satisfaction with the lifestyle as husbands, or more (Smith & Smith, 1973).

As might be expected in spite of self-selection biases serving to screen out the highly jealous from swinging, jealousy appears to be the major problem for swingers. Swingers try to prevent jealousy by adopting security-providing norms, such as not permitting contact outside of sex parties and swinging only with other married couples (Denfeld, 1974; Smith & Smith, 1970; Varni, 1974). Despite such efforts, up to a third of swingers soon drop out because of their own or their spouses' jealousy.

Gilmartin (1977) found that his swinger subjects differentiated between "body-centered" and "emotion-centered" sex and believed in psychological but not physical monogamy. Jealousy was likely only when a spouse suspected emotion-centered sex; otherwise, couples who had a stable swinging lifestyle appeared to have little jealousy and a high degree of sexual and relationship satisfaction within the marriage. However, Denfeld (1974) reported that marriage counselors who had advised swingers reported a good deal of jealousy, mostly resulting from the husbands' comparing themselves to other men. Bartell (1970) surveyed 280 swingers and also reported that men were more threatened than women by social comparison to other men. In fact, less than a quarter of men at swinging parties engaged in sex. Feelings of inadequacy and lack of perceived commitment from spouses also seemed to foster jealousy. Jenks (1985) found that swingers as a group were more liberal than nonswingers, but otherwise were not noticeably deviant except for swinging. The swingers also rated themselves as less jealous than did nonswingers.

Group Marriage

Unlike swingers, partners in group marriages display commitment to ongoing relationships among the partners that extends beyond sexuality to child raising, income earning, and recreational activities. Most group marriages define themselves to some extent as communal, though most commune members probably do not define themselves as being in a group marriage with sexual sharing the norm.

Although the literature on group marriage and communes is too diverse to review here, indications are that romantic jealousy is a significant problem in communes in general and especially in group marriages (Constantine & Constantine, 1974; Kanter, 1972; Ramey, 1974). For example, Ramey (1974) suggests that the inability of most group marriages to accommodate single parents or single adults is related to adoption of security-providing norms that reduce jealousy. Such groups stress the primacy of the pair bond in spite of sex outside of the primary pair. Constantine and Constantine (1976) surveyed 30 group marriages and reported that jealousy was a problem for 80% of respondents. This percentage did not vary much as a function of stability of the relationships or age of the participants.

One exception to this general pattern is the report of Pines and Aronson (1981) on the Kerista commune in San Francisco. The Keristans practice "polyfidelity" which can be seen as an extension of the usual norm of monogamy to cover a small group of people married together. Sexual relations outside the group are rare and provoke intense negative reactions from the other partners. The Keristans appear to be remarkably free from jealousy among themselves. This probably stems from several procedures: an elaborate process by which one gradually develops commitment to the group before sexual relations can occur; group norms that encourage talking about and resolving antagonistic emotions; and posted rosters about who may sleep with whom any particular night (deviations are frowned upon and rare, though a person may freely choose not to have sex with the assigned partner that night).

In summary, the evidence is unclear about whether people within alternative sexual lifestyles have any more or less of a problem with jealousy than the traditionally monogamous do. Self-selection biases are likely to be strong both in starting such relationships and in dropping out. Those who remain may be less jealous than the average person. Whether or not this is due to some person factor or represents security-providing arrangements that develop between partners over the course of experimenting with such lifestyles is not known.

Sex-role Orientation and Androgyny

A sex role consists of regularly occurring gender differences in thoughts, feelings, and behaviors that are observed in task performance or social interaction (Huston & Ashmore, 1986; Peplau, 1983;

Staines & Libby, 1986). "Sex-role orientation," as we use the term here, refers to prescriptive expectations about how men and women should behave, think, and feel (differently) in certain situations. These expectations may be properties of the person or may emerge from interaction. "Androgyny" (Bem, 1974) refers to the capacity to perform either masculine or feminine sex roles according to the needs posed by the situation. This concept requires thinking of masculinity and femininity as two dimensions, not as opposite ends of a single dimension of masculinity–femininity.

Bringle, Roach, Andler, and Evenbeck (1977) reported that subjects high in dispositional jealousy were somewhat more likely to report feminine role behaviors and to have more conservative attitudes toward women. White (1981e) found that conservative attitudes toward women were related to male but not to female jealousy.

Amstutz (1982) studied 553 subjects and reported a number of findings involving androgyny. Androgynous men were *more* jealous than other men, whereas androgynous women were *less* jealous than other women and androgynous men. Feminine males and masculine females reported feeling more inadequate as partners for their loved ones; this finding might occur as a result of mismatch of partners' sex-role orientations. Feminine subjects (male or female) reported that their self-esteem was more affected by their partners' actions than that of other subjects, and that they regarded themselves as relatively more dependent than their partners. Androgynous and feminine subjects rated themselves as more dependent on their relationships than masculine subjects. Most of Amstutz's (1982) findings can be understood in light of sex-role-related differences in relationship values and power. However, it is not at all clear why androgynous men should be the most jealous while androgynous women are the least jealous.

Inducing Jealousy

White (1980a) studied subjects who admitted having intentionally induced jealousy in their current romantic partners. Five motives for inducing jealousy were found: to test the strength of the relationship; to get a specific reward (such as more time, attention, more dates, etc.); to inflict revenge because the partner was seeing another; to bolster self-esteem; and to punish the partner. Testing the relationship and getting a reward were much more common than the other motives. The most popular method of intentionally inducing jealousy was to discuss or exaggerate current attractions to others, followed by flirting, dating others, fabricating rivals, and talking about former romantic partners. Women were more likely to report inducing jealousy than men, and were more likely to induce jealousy if they were relatively more involved. These differences are partly due to women's use of bases of power, which are indirect (manipulative) and personal (based on interaction rather than on concrete resources such as money) (Howard, Blumstein, & Schwartz, 1986; Johnson, 1976).

As the list of motives for inducing jealousy suggests, inducing jealousy is probably related to all of our jealousy-influencing relationship characteristics. Jealousy induction is a powerful technique, to the extent that the partner's investment, rewards, and self-involvement are high and vulnerability is also high. Induction may be a way of increasing rewards or reducing the vulnerability of the inductor, and of course induction is more plausible to the extent that the potential for a rival appears to exist.

Impression Management by the Beloved

How the beloved responds to accusations by the jealous influences the nature of the emotions and coping efforts of the jealous. Previous research has shown that couples in conflict differ in their attributions for the conflict: The aggrieved partner is more likely to attribute the problem to stable causes within the beloved, while the erring partner may be more likely to attribute the conflict to unintended, unstable, or situational causes (Kelley, 1979; Orvis et al., 1976). Schlenker (1980) has documented how manipulation of attributions for one's behavior is a major aspect of impression management. The importance of manipulating such attributions is suggested by research linking attributions for a partner's involvement with another to various indices of jealousy (Buunk, 1984; White, 1981a, 1981d) and by research indicating that conflicted relationships may be "repaired" if less threatening attributions for conflict are achieved (Duck, 1984).

Although it may be interesting to speculate how impression management is related to the jealousy complex (Buunk & Bringle, 1987), there is only one relevant study. Hupka, Jung, and Silverthorn (1987) asked subjects to read jealousy-inducing vignettes (portraying flirting or sexual involvement with a rival) while imagining themselves as either the jealous partner or the erring partner. Subjects then rated 22 different explanations for the errant behaviors that were provided. Factor analysis of the 22 explanations yielded three factors: Justifications, Excuses, and Apologies. These factors are consistent with Schlenker's (1980) analysis of different types of accounts or explanations that are used to manipulate impressions. Apologies involve acceptance of blame and requests for pardon ("I'm sorry I hurt you; please give me another chance"); excuses that acknowledge the harm to another but minimize responsibility for it ("I know you're angry, but he kept forcing himself on me'"); and justifications that acknowledge some responsibility but minimize negative intent or consequences ("I needed something to make me feel good; it wasn't meant to hurt you"). In our terms, apologies appear to acknowledge the jealous partner's vulnerability and promise greater security; excuses acknowledge vulnerability but do not extend security; and justifications signal denial of vulnerability while perhaps promising some greater security, since the erring partner acknowledges some control over the event.

Hupka et al.'s results were the same, regardless of assigned role as the jealous or erring partner. Apologies were by far the preferred explanations, followed generally by excuses and then by justifications. Jealous role players preferred justifications to excuses if they wanted to end the relationship. Hupka et al. (1987) suggest that if the relationship cannot be terminated on friendly grounds (apologies), it is preferable to become an adversary (justifications) than to minimize the partner's responsibility (excuses).

Justifications were preferred if the partner and rival had sex, especially if the jealous role player wanted to end the relationship ("It's my life; you've got no right to be jealous"). This finding is consistent with Schlenker's (1980) suggestion that justifications are more likely if the partner is seriously harmed, especially justifications that place blame for the partner's reactions on the partner. This is equivalent to denial of both vulnerability and chances for increased security; it is not surprising that jealous individuals may find it easier to break with those who deny both vulnerability and security than with those who may confirm vulnerability and/or promise future security.

GENDER DIFFERENCES IN ROMANTIC JEALOUSY

Several gender differences have been found in jealousy research. While such differences may be intrinsically interesting, they are relevant to understanding jealousy insofar as they suggest that certain cultural, biological, and relationship factors that produce gender differences may also be influencing jealousy. Gender differences in jealousy research, though statistically significant, may not explain much of the variability of subjects' responses (Bringle & Buunk, 1985; White, 1984). This would be expected if gender correlates with cultural, biological, or relationship variables that influence jealousy, some of which increase jealousy and some of which decrease jealousy (Ashmore & Del Boca, 1986).

The number and range of gender differences in jealousy raises the question whether the label "jealousy" means the same thing to men as to women (Bringle & Buunk, 1985; Clanton & Smith, 1977; White, 1981b, 1984). Here, the arguments we raise in the next chapter about the need for understanding the cultural meaning of jealousy apply to understanding how the subcultures of men and women influence expectations and scripts concerning the jealousy complex. For now, we note that many of the gender differences reviewed below may result from fundamentally different conceptions of jealousy.

Which Is the Jealous Sex?

White (1985a) found that American television comedies were more likely to portray women as jealous, whereas dramas were more likely to portray men as jealous, especially if violence was used. This is consistent with the popular "caveman" stereotype of jealousy, which presumes a sexually savage male (Clanton & Smith, 1977).

However, most research has reported no gender differences in the level of self-reported jealousy, and those studies finding a difference are not consistent in finding one gender to be more jealous than the other (Bringle & Buunk, 1985; Buunk & Bringle, 1987; White, 1984). Different results have been found with the same subjects, depending on the nature of the jealousy measure used (Hupka & Eshett, 1988). More reliable gender differences are observed when elements of the jealousy complex are studied individually, as documented below.

Differences in Focus of Threat: Sexual versus Relationship Threat

One of the best-documented gender differences is that men are more threatened by the sexual aspects of the rival relationship, whereas women are more threatened by the potential loss of the primary relationship. Teismann and Mosher (1978) found that men role-playing a jealousy situation were more likely to discuss the sexual aspects of the rival relationship; women were more likely to focus on issues of loss of time and attention. White (1985a) found that television portrayals of men's jealousy were more sexually focused (e.g., themes of sexual infidelity) and that women's were focused on wanting to know about the rival relationship and worrying about the loss of the primary relationship. Gottschalk (1936) reported that 80% of jealous central European men he interviewed expressed a sexual threat (fantasies, doubts about sexual adequacy, etc.), compared to only 22% of the women. Women were more likely to discuss relationship-oriented themes, such as the communication and emotional exchange between partner and rival. Buunk (1984) reported that male jealousy was more strongly related to attribution of the partner's need for sexual variety, whereas female jealousy was more strongly related to the degree of attraction perceived between the rival and the partner. Much of the clinical material presented in later chapters, as well as data we discuss in our chapters on culture and sociobiology, also suggest that male jealousy is more centered on sexual aspects of the rival relationship, while female jealousy is more focused on fear of loss of the primary relationship and on the emotional qualities of the rival relationship (Bringle & Buunk, 1985; Clanton & Smith, 1977; White, 1981a, 1981b).

Perhaps related to these gender differences in the nature of the appraisal of threat, research indicates that jealous men (or men whose partners have had affairs) are more likely than jealous women to break off a relationship. White (1985b) reported that men were more likely to report initiating the breakup if they were jealous. Hill et al. (1976) found that couples were more likely to break up if the woman had an interest in another than if the man did. Analyses of divorce cases and breakups in American, English, and Dutch samples show that men complain more about infidelity, though they are less likely to encounter infidelity than women (Buunk, 1987; Levinger, 1965, 1966; Thornes & Collard, 1979).

Differences in Secondary-Appraisal Processes

The gender difference in focus of threat noted above is also found for secondary-appraisal processes. Females are more concerned about their partners' motives for affairs and are more likely to attribute both sexual need and the attractions of the rival relationship as motives. Males are more likely to attribute a desire for a more committed relationship and a need for attention as motives; jealous males are also more likely to consider alternative relationships. Males become more jealous than females if they think their partners are having an affair for the sex or for revenge on them. Females appear to become more jealous than males if they think the marital relationship has been damaged (Buunk, 1984; White, 1980a, 1981b, 1986b).

White (1981d) asked jealous partners to indicate how favorably they thought they compared to their rivals on several dimensions. Males were more likely than females to compare themselves favorably to their rivals on dimensions of intelligence, similarity to the partner, and sensitivity. Men who rated themselves as more intelligent than the rivals were more likely to be jealous, as were women who rated themselves as more sensitive to their partners. Women who rated themselves unfavorably in terms of personality or willingness to form a long-term relationship were also more jealous.

Differences in Emotions

Bryson (1976) found that males who watched a videotape of a jealousy situation were more likely to indicate they would get angry at themselves, whereas females were more likely to forecast becoming anxious, confused, depressed, fearful, betrayed, and angry at the partner. Amstutz (1982) used the same items as Bryson but failed to find sex differences for actually jealous subjects. White (1985c) used currently jealous respondents (respondents whose partners were actually involved with others). Females rated themselves as more depressed, while males rated themselves as more angry. Hupka and Eshett (1988) asked subjects to imagine that they had just discovered their romantic partner passionately kissing another at a party. Females were more likely to predict they would be fearful, but not more angry, disgusted, surprised, sad, or jealous.

Differences in Coping Efforts

Many of the gender differences in actual or anticipated coping suggest that females are more oriented toward solving relationship problems or directly expressing their emotions, whereas men are more oriented toward developing alternative sources of rewards and esteem or indirectly managing their painful emotion; however, the data are not entirely consistent. Bryson (1976) reported that females were more likely to predict they would seek social support and use face saving and denial. On specific items, males were more likely to say they would get drunk, get more sexually aggressive with others, and try to get a friend to talk to the beloved. Females were more likely to say that they would try to get even. Amstutz (1982) reported that males were more likely to use derogation and seek alternative partners. Buunk (1982b) reported that females were more likely to avoid the situation while blaming themselves; Francis (1977) interviewed 15 couples and reported that jealous men were more likely to use denial. Buunk (1986) reviewed data from a number of clinical and research sources and concluded that men were more likely to bolster their self-esteem when jealous and to behave in more dominating and aggressive ways. He also reported that jealousy and denial were more highly correlated for men than for women.

In one study of sexually open marriages, subjects' perceptions of the importance of techniques for reducing jealousy intercorrelated differently for men and women. For men, the importance given to marriage primacy, restricted intensity of the rival relationship, and visibility of the partners' affairs were highly related. For women, the importance of visibility and open mate exchange were correlated, as were restricted intensity and invisibility. Taken at face value, these patterns indicate that males wanted to know about the rival relationships, and wanted to know that these were not intense or threatening to the marriage. Females either wanted visible partner swapping or wanted not to know about affairs that were supposedly of low emotional involvement for their husbands (Buunk, 1980). In a similar study, subjects were asked how effective different coping efforts had been in reducing actual jealousy. Females thought that open communication was more effective than did males (Buunk, 1981).

White (1981d) asked jealous dating partners to rate how often they had used different coping strategies. Females were more likely to improve the relationship and demand commitment; males were more likely to use denial and avoidance. There were also gender differences in relationships among strategies. Demanding commitment was more strongly related to improving the relationship and interfering with the rival relationship for women than for men, whereas derogation was more strongly related to developing alternatives and self-assessment for men than for women. One interpretation of these differences is that coping efforts for women are more focused on relationships, while those of men are more oriented toward individual action.

Holroyd (1985) found in a New Zealand sample that currently jealous women were more likely to self-assess, improve the relationship, and demand commitment, but not less likely to use denial. Intercorrelations among coping effort strategies varied across gender. For males, interference was negatively related to improving the relationship, but the two were unrelated for females. For females, self-assessment correlated with improving the relationship; these strategies were unrelated for males. For males, developing alternatives was negatively correlated with improving the relationship, but just the opposite relationship was true for females. These differences in correlations among coping strategies are not the same as reported by White (1981d).

Finally, Weghorst (1980) reported one of the very few field studies of jealousy. Male and female confederates approached heterosexual couples and gazed at the opposite-sex partner while avoiding eye contact. Compared to those who later told an interviewer they were not jealous, jealous women avoided eye contact and were unlikely to speak with the rival; jealous men looked much more at the rival. After the confederate had left, jealous women were more likely to discuss the incident with their partners than were the nonjealous women.

Differences in Relationships among Secondary-Appraisal Processes, Jealousy Self-Reports, and Coping Efforts

Gender differences in the patterns of relationships among motive attribution, emotion, and jealousy have been reported. Attribution to the attractions of the rival relationship was related to current jealousy for females but not males. Attribution to a sexual motive was linked to male but not female anger, while attribution to the attractions of the rival relationship was associated with female but not male anger (White, 1981a, 1981d).

White (1981d) found a number of gender differences in the relationships among (1) attributions for a partner's interest in another and coping efforts, (2) social comparison outcomes and coping efforts, and (3) alternatives assessment and coping. For example, women were more likely to improve the relationship if they attributed dissatisfaction with the relationship to their partners; this relationship did not hold for men. Men who felt more sensitive than the rivals to their partners were more likely to interfere but less likely to self-assess. Females who thought that establishing an alternative would be relatively easy were more likely to demand commitment; again, this relationship was not found for men. These results illustrate that jealousy is by no means a simple phenomenon. The variety of different gender patterns (correlations among variables) supports our contention that it is useful to think of jealousy as a pattern or complex of elements.

Explanations for Gender Differences

Many of the gender differences described above may be due to sex-role and power differences within romantic relationships (Brehm, 1985; Bringle & Buunk, 1985; Buunk, 1986; Clanton & Smith, 1977; Peplau & Gordon, 1985; White, 1981b). For example, since women have greater interpersonal skills and value the process of relationship more than men, they might be more expected to try to improve the relationship, demand commitment, or be particularly concerned about the emotional and communication aspects of the rival relationship (Frieze et al., 1978; Huston & Ashmore, 1986; Mahoney & Heretick, 1979; Peplau & Gordon, 1985). Power dynamics within the couple have also been discussed as a relationship factor likely to influence jealousy (Bringle & Buunk, 1985). For instance, White (1985c) has shown that partners who have relatively more power within the relationship are more likely to feel angry when jealous, whereas those with less power are more likely to feel sad and depressed.

Not only do sex roles and power have a direct impact on individual elements of the jealousy complex; they are also likely to influence the jealousy-related relationship characteristics previously outlined. Males and females differ in degree and types of investment and rewards in relationships. They also differ in the degree to which different dimensions of self are salient in and influenced by relationships. There are gender differences in the vulnerability of investments, rewards, and self; these differences in vulnerability are in part due to different forms of security favored by men and women. Finally, men and women may differ on which variables influence their estimates of the potential for a rival relationship to develop.

Gender differences in the jealousy-influencing relationship characteristics can help explain why men are more focused on sexual threat and women are more focused on relationship threat. Females may be more likely to invest emotions and value intimacy, whereas males may be more likely to invest money and value sexual relations (Frieze et al., 1978; Huston & Ashmore, 1986). Hence, women may be more likely than men to link emotional investment and intimacy, and men may be more likely to link material input and sexual availability. If so, women may be more likely to compare the emotional investments of themselves and their rivals and to be concerned with the potential loss of intimacy; men may compare themselves to their rivals on financial status and be concerned with potential loss of sexual favors. Men's sexual self-concept and self-esteem may be more salient than other central dimensions of self within the relationship, while women's self-concept as nurturant and succorant may be more salient (Ashmore et al., 1986; Gross, 1978; Maccoby & Jacklin, 1974; Peplau & Gordon, 1985).

These differences should influence relevant dimensions of social comparisons and choice of means of seeking security for self-concept. For example, men may be more likely than women to seek sexual exclusivity norms to protect their sexual self-concept, whereas women may be more likely to seek nonsexual exclusivity norms that protect their opportunities to display nurturance or protect intimacy of self-disclosure. Hence, violation of sexual and nonsexual exclusivity norms may to some extent pose threats to different aspects of self for men than for women.

Gender differences in normative attributions for partners' involvement may differentially affect estimates of the potential for rival relationships. Males may be more attentive to females' unhappiness with the intimacy of the primary relationship as an indicator of the potential for a rival relationship, while females may be more attentive to males' lack of interest in sex as an indicator of potential rivals. Given the differences in investments, rewards, and self-concept, this may lead men to link the experience of a sexually threatening rival with partners' dissatisfaction with the relationship; women may be more likely to link the experience of a relationship-threatening rival with partners' lack of sexual interest.

This discussion suggests that observed gender differences in jealousy may in part be due to gender differences in investments, salience of self, security for self and investments, and estimates of the potential for a rival relationship. Future research might benefit from systematically linking gender differences in these characteristics to elements of the jealousy complex.

IMPACT OF THE BELOVED, THE RIVAL, AND THE SECONDARY AND ADVERSE RELATIONSHIPS ON JEALOUSY

The great bulk of jealousy research focuses on the jealous person or on the primary relationship. There is little work on aspects of the beloved, the rival, or the secondary and adverse relationships. Past research is briefly reviewed here, followed by some suggestions for future research.

Research to Date

The Nature of the Threat Posed by the Rival

In Chapter 2 we suggested that the jealousy complex may differ if the threat is primarily to self-esteem rather than to the existence or quality of the relationship. We and others have also suggested that coping efforts can be seen as directed at maintaining the relationship or maintaining self-esteem (Bringle & Buunk, 1985; Bryson, 1977; Clanton & Smith, 1977; White, 1976, 1981d, 1986b).

Mathes et al. (1985) sought to test White's (1981b) model of jealousy as resulting from threats to self-esteem or the relationship. In one study subjects were presented with vignettes that depicted different kinds of loss of a romantic partner: no loss, fate (accidental death), destiny (partner leaves for professional reasons), rejection, loss due to a romantic rival. Threat to the relationship was measured by asking subjects how lonely they would be if they experienced these conditions; threat to self-esteem was measured directly by asking how much subjects thought their self-esteem would suffer. Results showed that loneliness was expected to be high in all loss situations, but that self-esteem would suffer most if there were a rival, next most if the subject were rejected, still less if destiny were the reason, and least in an accident of fate.

In the second study subjects read the same vignettes (except for no loss), but this time rated how depressed, anxious, angry, and jealous they would be. Anger and jealousy were low for fate, moderate for destiny, higher for rejection, and highest for loss due to a rival. Anxiety was moderate in all vignettes. High scorers on an anticipated-jealousy scale were more likely to say they would have intense emotions. Mathes et al. (1985) interpret their results as a confirmation of White's (1981b) theory, and surmise that anxiety characterizes both types of loss (self-esteem, relationship), whereas anger is more closely associated with loss of self-esteem and depression with loss of relationship rewards. This suggestion is broadly consistent with research on the interpersonal antecedents of depression and anger (Averill, 1979, 1982; Ilfeld, 1977; Jones, 1973; Leary, Barnes, & Griebel, 1986).

The degree of attraction between the partner and the rival has been shown to correlate with the perceived degree of threat to the primary relationship and with jealous anger (White, 1976). These findings also support the idea that primary appraisal of threat may generate both threat to self-esteem (assessed by anger ratings) and threat to relationship (directly assessed). Both anger and perceived threat correlated with conflict over the rival relationship.

Hupka and Eshett (1988) attempted to distinguish between jealous reactions to threats to self-esteem and reactions to threats to social esteem. Subjects rated how afraid, angry, disgusted, jealous, sad, and surprised they would be in response to a vignette in which a spouse was seen passionately kissing another at a party. In one condition the embrace was observed by only the jealous; in another it was observed by others at the party as well, thus introducing the threat to social esteem in addition to the self-esteem threat. Subjects thought they would feel more sad if the partner were unobserved and would be more disgusted if the partner were observed.

Characteristics of the Rival

Shettel-Neuber et al. (1978) manipulated physical attractiveness of a rival in videotape vignettes portraying the rival kissing the beloved at a party. Subjects anticipated that they would be more angry at the beloved and embarrassed if the interloper was unattractive than if he or she was attractive. Perhaps kissing an ugly rival signaled that the primary relationship was under greater threat than if the kiss could be attributed to physical attractiveness per se. Males were more likely to think they would develop alternatives (an esteem-maintaining coping strategy) if the rival were attractive than if unattractive, whereas the opposite was true for females. This is consistent with the notion discussed earlier that male jealousy is more focused on sexual self-esteem threat while female jealousy is more closely related to relationship threat. For males, self-esteem threat may be greater if the rival is sexy; for females, a partner's attraction to an unattractive rival may be attributed to their good relationship (since it isn't the sex), and this may be particularly threatening to the relationship and self-esteem.

One survey of subjects whose partners had affairs found that if a jealous partner actually knew the rival, jealousy was weaker if the rival was liked. This might reflect greater security if the rival was a friend; the attenuating impact of positive aspects of the adverse relationship; or the possibility that those highly jealous were more likely to derogate the rival, leading to retrospection that the rival was disliked (Buunk, 1978). In the Hupka and Eshett (1988) vignette study described earlier, the rival was portrayed as either a servant, a stranger, a business partner, a senior business partner, or a close friend of the jealous person. The effect of the rival's status depended on whether or not others at a party saw the rival kissing and embracing the beloved. If others saw the embrace, all anticipated emotions were most intense if the rival was of equal status (the business partner) and least intense if the rival was a close friend.

However, if only the jealous witnessed the embrace, emotions were most intense if the rival was a close friend and least intense if the rival was a stranger. One explanation is that in the public condition subjects assumed that the embrace was just for fun if the friend was the rival, whereas if a business associate was the rival it was assumed that a serious public play for the beloved was being made, perhaps posing social as well as self-esteem threat. In the private condition, the embrace of a close friend could have signaled loss of security or actual loss of the relationship.

Suggestions for Future Research

It is likely that many characteristics of the rival and the beloved and characteristics of the rival and the adverse relationship will be correlated with different elements of the jealousy complex. To avoid rampant empiricism in future research, we suggest that the following factors are particularly likely to mediate the relationship between such characteristics and the jealousy complex:

1. The nature of primary relationship investments or rewards that are threatened. A rival, for example, who seeks verbal intimacy may pose a different threat than does one who seeks sexual intimacy.

2. The dimensions of self-esteem and self-concept that are threatened. A rival relationship characterized by strong intellectual camaraderie poses a different threat than does one characterized by pursuit of similar spiritual values.

3. The degree to which existing security arrangements for investments, rewards, and self-esteem are threatened or broached. A rival relationship that is above board and can be monitored by the jealous poses different security issues than does a secret affair.

4. The degree to which specific coping efforts may plausibly protect self-esteem or the relationship. Improving the primary relationship, for example, may seem unlikely if the rival relationship is deemed to have a greater potential to satisfy the partner. Instead, the jealous may try to interfere with the rival relationship.

These factors are likely themselves to be related to characteristics that are described below.

Characteristics of the Beloved

The needs and motives of the beloved, as perceived by the jealous, have been found to be related to jealousy. It would be useful to link actual attributes of the beloved (such as actual motives, love, satisfaction, and commitment) to the partner's perception of needs and motives in an attempt to understand the bases for such perceptions. Intentionally inducing jealousy may be related to a variety of partner variables, such as sex-role orientation, attitudes toward love, and feelings of inadequacy as a partner. Susceptibility of the beloved to different kinds of influence should influence the selection of such coping efforts as demanding commitment and self-assessment (Howard et al., 1986; Huston, 1983). Standards by which the beloved assesses the worth of the jealous and of the relationship, and how such evaluations are conveyed, should be related to the degree of primary appraisal of threat posed by a rival. Finally, research needs to be addressed to ways in which the beloved copes with actions and emotions of the jealous, and how such efforts in turn affect the jealousy complex.

Characteristics of the Rival

Since we argue that social comparison to the rival is an essential element of secondary appraisal, it follows that actual attributes of the rival and the rival's attempts to manipulate social comparison outcomes will be important. Since we argue that jealousy may follow perception of a potential relationship, it may be that certain characteristics of rivals are more likely to engender this perception. For example, the ubiquity of the physical attractiveness stereotype suggests that attractive persons may elicit fear of potential trouble. It would be interesting as well to study cases in which the romantic rival is of the same gender as the beloved, since this might bring into focus the impact of comparison processes. Do men become more or less sexually threatened when their sexual rivals are women or men? What do women think about the kind of relationship threat posed by a male rival? Although we have stressed the perceived motives of the partner and the resources of the rival, it would be useful to assess perceptions of why the rival is attracted to the beloved. Some motives may flatter the jealous or increase the sense of security of the primary relationship, perhaps mitigating jealousy. For example, if a rival's interest is based on refusal of the partner to pay attention to him or her (as with the rival who believes the beloved is playing "hard to get"), this may lead to anger at the rival but may reduce the level of threat.

Characteristics of the Secondary Relationship

A good deal of effort needs to be focused on actual characteristics of the relationship between the beloved and the rival, as different from the jealous person's perception of that relationship, which may not be congruent with reality. (The lack of congruence need not be defensive or delusional; it may result from reasonable inference in the face of the partner's refusal to discuss the rival relationship.) Obvious characteristics, including matching between the partner's needs and the rival's resources, satisfaction with the rival relationship, and whether or not it is sexually or emotionally intimate, need to be studied. Rivals may be jealous as well, and hence the variables and processes we have discussed in relation to the jealous and the primary relationship may also have their impact on the rival's jealousy complex. The coping efforts of the jealous and the coping efforts of the rival should not only effect their own reactions to appraised threat, but each other's as well. It is possible that stable patterns of triadic relationship develop. What the jealous does affects the beloved, which affects the rival, who then copes in ways that affect the beloved, which affects the jealous, and so forth. The behavior of the jealous and the rival may become synchronized even in the absence of any explicit communication between them.

Characteristics of the Adverse Relationship

We have already cited Hupka and Eshett's (1988) vignette study showing gender differences in reaction to a jealousy-inducing event if the rival is a close friend compared to other statuses. Pines and Aronson's (1981) report on the Kerista commune suggests that good friends can share lovers and remain good friends under certain social conditions; additional evidence suggesting this is presented in Chapter 6—namely, that brothers and sisters in some cultures may share spouses or lovers. The effects of rivalry on existing friendships must be distinguished from those of developing a friendship with a rival. We have already hypothesized that rivals may unknowingly become synchronized in their actions; however, outside of the literature on group marriage, little is known about how often jealous rivals explicitly negotiate sharing of the beloved, or about what conditions promote such negotiation (Pines & Aronson, 1981; Smith & Smith, 1973). Another untested possibility relates to the Freudian notion that jealousy may be the result of projection of unconscious homosexual impulses toward the rival.

There are certainly self-disclosure issues between the rival and the jealous if they are both sexually or otherwise intimate with the partner. Rivals may press the beloved for such information, reducing each one's security of self-esteem, or they may cooperate in security arrangements by insisting that no such information be disclosed.

Finally, it would be interesting to know how two rivals cope by developing a friendship; they may do so to increase security or to develop an alternative relationship. There is certainly anecdotal evidence that rivals may decide to limit or end their relationships with the beloved in order to maintain friendships.

SUMMARY

The research on relationship aspects of jealousy is complex and often contradictory. These difficulties stem from conceptual problems in distinguishing between relationship causes and personality factors and from consequent ambiguity in measurement. They also stem from lack of coherent theory about what aspects of relationships will be relevant for jealousy—a problem that is understandable, given the state of theory development in close relationships and the relative infancy of jealousy research itself (Bringle & Buunk, 1985; Clanton, 1981; Kelley et al., 1983).

We have reviewed the research on a good many variables that are plausibly relationship-related and that are correlated with various measures of the level of reported jealousy or elements of the jealousy complex. Most of these variables seem to be related to one or more of five central features of romantic relationships: the nature of rewards and investments; the salience and evaluation of dimensions of self-concept; security for investments and rewards; security for self-concept and self-esteem; and the potential for rival relationships. As will be subsequently seen, these aspects of the primary relationship appear important to clinical concerns as well.

We suggest that future theory development and research will profit from attention to these features. Since each of these features is relevant to the broader study of close relationships and gender, such attention will foster the development of links between these literatures and those on romantic jealousy (Ashmore & Del Boca, 1986; Berscheid, 1983; Brehm, 1985; Buunk & Bringle, 1987; Kelley et al., 1983; Ickes, 1985b). Development of means to assess these features should sharpen the conceptual debate over relationship versus personality. For example, the nature of security arrangements that emerge from the relationship can be distinguished from the desire for such arrangements. The latter may be more closely related to personality than the former.

It is also important to move jealousy research away from its conceptual and methodological focus on the jealous person toward theory and research that encompass the interpersonal jealousy system. No doubt this is difficult to do for practical as well as theoretical reasons, but a broader focus should reap benefits for jealousy therapy as well as for theory.

Finally, much of the reviewed research has used "as-if" methodologies of role playing, vignettes, or measurement of anticipated reactions. The problems with generalizability of these methods outweigh the obvious benefits of their simplicity for most research purposes. Except for studies designed to assess normative expectations or to generate hypotheses, it is important that jealousy research be conducted as much as possible with subjects who are really jealous; who are in existing romantic relationships; or who otherwise can inform the researcher about what jealous people, their partners, and rivals actually do, think, and feel when jealous.

6

Culture and Jealousy

We have emphasized that it is necessary to take culture into account when trying to understand jealousy. In this chapter we hope to demonstrate why this is so. First we review cultural variations in elements of the jealousy complex—primary and secondary appraisal, emotion, and coping. Our purpose is not to present an exhaustive ethnographic review, but rather to demonstrate the range of behaviors, thoughts, and feelings exhibited by people labeled as "jealous" in the language of various cultures (or exhibited by partners of adulterous spouses). This review raises some conceptual issues regarding the nature of threat and coping.

Next we present the scant existing cross-cultural research on jealousy, which we follow by presenting some cultural-level variables that might be expected to be cross-culturally related to jealousy. The purpose of this discussion is largely to generate hypotheses for future research. We end the chapter with a review of suggestions for future cross-cultural work on jealousy.

JEALOUSY AND PROBLEMS
OF THE HUMAN CONDITION

We think that jealousy is likely to be strongly influenced by culture because it is involved in major existential dilemmas of social life—dilemmas for which different cultures supply an overwhelming variety of solutions. Lutz and White (1986) have suggested five such basic problems of social relationship or existential meaning that appear to be universal and that are typically expressed in emotional terms. These are the problems of interpersonal conflict, or others' violations of cultural or personal expectations; intrapersonal conflict, or one's own violation of cultural or personal expectations; danger to one's own physical and psychological self (as well as those of significant others); actual or threatened loss of significant relationships; and "positive problems," including rewarding bonds and receipt of valued resources.

We can see immediately why the cultural aspects of jealousy are both complex and compelling. Jealousy involves all of these five basic problems. The jealous person may be in interpersonal conflict with the partner and the rival (at least), and in intrapersonal conflict if jealous emotion or coping violates personal expectations and codes. Jealousy not only may reflect danger to the psychological self (threat/loss to self-esteem), but may also entail risk to the physical self. Jealousy likewise involves the risk of loss of valued relationships. Its primary context of the romantic or marriage relationship inherently links it with the positive problems of rewarding relationships.

DEFINITION OF CULTURE

At this point we should say what we mean by "culture." In line with most anthropological thought (Jahoda, 1980; Kroeber & Kluckhohn, 1952; Swartz & Jordan, 1980), we assume that culture has three major elements: ideas, beliefs, and values; patterns of behavior; and products of behavior (e.g., tools, art). In line with the Kelley et al. (1983) model of causal conditions and interaction presented in earlier chapters, we conceive one element of culture to be repeated patterns of intrapersonal or interpersonal chains of thoughts, feelings, and behavior—patterns that are common to a number of members of the culture and that may be predicted on the basis of socialization practices, place in social structure, or other cultural-level forces. That is, the basic patterns may be fairly well predicted without any knowledge of the personality of the person or the interaction history of actors.

Among the major influences on culturally common intra- and interchain sequences of events are background causal conditions called values, beliefs, and ideas. These give meaning to the behavior patterns; organize the display of particular thoughts, feelings, and behaviors; and allow the person to choose among different options for intra- and interpersonal behavior. Groups differ in the extent to which members share (consciously or unconsciously) certain values, ideas, and beliefs with members of other groups. These differences help demarcate cultures from each other.

The background causal conditions of the culture, particularly shared ideas, beliefs, and values, guide the interpersonal and intrapersonal sequences of events that yield tangible products, including architecture, art, tools, recreational devices, ornamentation, and so on. It is not surprising that groups of people with differences in causal conditions and in characteristic intrapersonal and interpersonal sequences produce different products.

Collectively, all three elements constitute culture. From a systems perspective, neither element is *a priori* the most fundamental. Cultural products may influence the development of ideas; repeated sequences of behavior may become the basis for valued ideals; and the development of new products certainly alters patterns of behavior.

CULTURAL VARIATION
IN ROMANTIC JEALOUSY

Jealousy per se has not been a focus of ethnographic report or ethnological comparison among cultures. Hupka (1981) has presented a discussion of jealousy compatible with our approach and reviewed some cultural variations. We have drawn on many of his examples in our review below and will return to his observations later. However, in our presentation here, we use the elements of the jealousy complex outlined in Chapter 2 to categorize various ethnographic accounts. Although we think that our model provides a useful basis for such categorization, we want to make it clear that the original sources have no particular categories guiding reports of jealousy. Further, many of the ethnographic reports given below are concerned with cultural patterns and rules regarding premarital and extramarital sexual relations. It is often not clear whether the reactions of actors in such situations are culturally recognized as part of "jealousy." For example, exacting a financial penalty from a person who has had sex with one's wife is common, but it is rarely mentioned whether this demand is considered a "natural" part of being jealous. There is no easy way around this problem. Since the purpose of our review is to demonstrate cultural variation, we have elected to discuss ethnographic accounts that are ambiguous as to whether or not the described behaviors are related to "jealousy" as it is locally understood in the culture.

Primary Appraisal of Threat to Self/Relationship

As Hupka (1981) notes, there is substantial cultural variation in the kinds of evidence that lead to a primary appraisal of threat to self or

relationship. Most of the ethnographic reports concern what constitutes evidence of an actual sexual liaison between one's spouse and a
rival. However, A. B. Ellis (1890) recorded that a man of the Daho-
mey of Africa may evaluate a lower-status neighbor's praise of his
wife's beauty as a threat to his social rank and become offended and
angry. Among the Pawnee of the American Plains, a request by
another male for a cup of water from one's wife is clearly a signal
that the other man is after the wife (Weltfish, 1965).

The Saora of India require the husband actually to witness the
extramarital intercourse before he can accuse his wife of adultery;
the highly promiscuous Dobu of equatorial Africa merely require
personal suspicion; and the Zuni woman is led to the evidence by
gossip among villagers (Hupka, 1981). Apache men who leave the
encampment are likely to ask close blood relatives to spy on their
wives. Their secret reports form the basis for the presumption of the
wives' guilt (Goodwin, 1942). Mead (1931) reported that the Dobuan
husband watches his wife while she works the fields and counts her
footsteps if she goes into the bush. Too many footsteps mean a
possibility of a secret sexual liaison. On the other hand, the Trobri-
ander man of the South Pacific may return home from a long canoe
voyage to find that his wife has new children. This is "cheerfully"
accepted as proof that intercourse has nothing to do with pregnancy
(Malinowski, 1929, p. 193).

The Plateau tribes of Zimbabwe assume that death of the child
or the mother during childbirth is evidence of adultery. The dying
mother or mother of a stillborn is asked for the name of the lover,
who is always held as guilty (Gouldsbury & Sheane, 1911). Conversely, the Yao of Africa believe it is the husband's infidelity soon
before or during pregnancy that can cause injury to mother or child
(Maire, 1953).

The ancient Hebrews had a practice whereby a husband who
suspected his wife of adultery would bring an offering of barley meal
to a priest. The priest placed the meal in the wife's hand, uncovered
her head, and then put dust from the tabernacle into a jar of bitter
holy water, which the wife then drank. If she were innocent there
would be no harm, but if she were guilty her belly would swell and
her thigh rot. If found innocent, she was assured she would conceive
shortly (Murstein, 1974).

In many societies, one's wife may have sex with another man
under certain circumstances that apparently lead to no threat to self-
esteem, social standing, or the marital relationship. The Ammassalik
of Greenland reach mutual agreement between two families to exchange mates. Husbands, as noted in Chapter 2, also practice a

"putting out the lamp" ritual. The good host is expected to make his wife available for a guest by turning down the lamp at an appropriate time. A husband who does not share his wife is likely to be publicly scolded for being mean, inhospitable, and stingy. Also, a wife who is slow to respond to the guest is scolded by the husband (Mead, 1931; Mirsky, 1937b). The Chukchee of Siberia have a similar practice in which married men make arrangements with men in different communities for reciprocity of wife lending (Neubeck, 1969b). The polyandrous Toda of southern India have a custom of *mokhthoditi*, which allows both husbands and wives to take on lovers if mutual consent is given by all parties and an annual fee is paid to the spouse (Rivers, 1906). The Lesu of New Ireland (Melanesia) have a system in which the wife's lover gives her gifts, which are turned over to the husband. As long as this payment is made, there appears to be little jealousy among most men, though the occasional husband chooses to fight the rival (Neubeck, 1969b).

Mead (1931) discussed the complicated sexual institutions of the Banaro of New Guinea. In addition to his or her own formal spouse, each man or woman has three "goblin" spouses during a lifetime. Before formal marriage, the bride-to-be has sex with a ceremonial friend of her father-in-law while the prospective husband has sex with the wife of the ceremonial friend. During ceremonial occasions husbands may exchange wives with their own ceremonial friends; wives may bear the friends' children as well as their husbands'. According to Mead, these arrangements are rarely if ever accompanied by jealousy. No threat to self or relationship exists within these traditional arrangements.

Among the Nayar of Central Kerala (southern India), a matrilineal society, husbands do not live with their wives but remain in their natal households. Ritual group marriages allow women to have from 3 to 12 or more husbands at one time, all of whom have sexual relations with her. Jealousy among these husbands, who are not necessarily related, is apparently rare (Gough, 1961).

Ford and Beach (1951) have identified 17 societies (out of 139 surveyed) in which extramarital relations are extremely common though formally socially disapproved. For example, marriage for the Bena of Africa is supposed to carry rights of sexual exclusivity. But, for both sexes, adultery is something of a game and extramarital liaisons are quite frequent. If discovered, the adulterous spouse is verbally abused but soon all seems forgotten, and the offending spouse appears to be more careful in the future in order to be a better game player.

The Pagan Gaddang of the Philippines and the Qolla Indians of

Peru both practice a spouse exchange in which both husbands and wives must agree to the exchange before threat ceases to be inferred from the extramarital attraction. For the Qolla, the first step is for the husbands to agree with each other. The women typically disagree with the proposed exchange. Both couples then have a dinner together and get very drunk, after which each woman has sex with the other's husband. In the morning the women "discover" what has happened and then give their assent to the spouse exchange on a more permanent basis (Symons, 1979).

Most available ethnographic evidence suggests that multiple wives in polygynous societies do not become jealous unless the husband shows favoritism to one wife or her children that is not in accordance with cultural prescriptions about how attention and rewards should be distributed among wives. Given that the husband follows these prescriptions, wives, particularly first wives, seem to favor polygynous marriages for the household help, friendship, or prestige that accompanies multiple-wife households (Irons, 1979; Kurland, 1979; Mead, 1931; Murstein, 1974; Swartz & Jordan, 1980; Symons, 1979). Mead (1931) reported a case in which a husband was brought to a native court by his first wife because he *refused* to take other wives, even though they had been married 3 years! The court ordered him to marry again within 6 months. According to Davenport (1965, cited in Symons, 1979), wives in one Melanesian group not only are not jealous of concubines, but regard them as status symbols for both their husbands and themselves. Such data suggest that wives' primary appraisal in polygynous societies is directed towards husbands' deviations from clearly defined rules about resource and power distribution among wives.

Similarly, in most societies in which polyandry is acceptable or the norm, the multiple "husbands" (who are usually brothers or brothers-in-law) tend to show little jealousy, as long as status differences are observed, such as greater respect for the older brother (Ford & Beach, 1951; Kurland, 1979; Neubeck, 1969b).

We think these examples of great cultural variation in the contexts that engender jealousy have two simple themes uniting them. Cultures in part define the stimuli that are appraised as posing harm or threat to self-esteem or the relationship. Hence, Apache men appraise threat if small favors are offered to a wife by another man, whereas the Dobuan husband appraises threat by counting the number of steps the wife takes into the bush. Cultures also prescribe actions of the rival and spouse that minimize perceived threat in situations that otherwise might be appraised differently. The Qolla practice of wives' disagreeing with exchange proposals and becoming drunk before the exchange may reduce threat to husbands' self-esteem, while the Toda practice of *mokhthoditi* provides control over access to wives. As we discuss later, the particular cues that signal threat or harm and the particular actions of spouse or rival that reduce these appraisals are understandable in light of larger cultural definitions of the meaning of self and of romantic/marital relationships.

Secondary Appraisal of Threat

Motives Assessment

Ethnographic reports suggest that societies prescribe solutions to the problem of assessing partners' motives. The Toda have few restrictions on premarital or extramarital sex. It is recognized that the basis of such liaisons for both men and women is sexual desire. However, while a Toda man or woman "naturally" assumes that the partner's desire to be with another stems from the desire for sexual variety, this attribution apparently is not threatening to self- or social esteem, and in itself does not mean that a marriage relationship is under threat (Rivers, 1906). The Apache also seem to assume that affairs are solely undertaken for sexual pleasure. However, the Apache, unlike the Toda, strongly disapprove of both premarital and extramarital sex. Even trivial signs of attraction to another are likely to be attributed to sexual desires, and such an attribution engenders extreme jealousy (Goodwin, 1942).

A great many cultures tend to attribute male extramarital liaisons to a natural biological inclination that is rarely invoked to account for female adultery. This biological explanation is usually accompanied by norms granting greater freedom to the male—the so-called "double standard" (Buunk, 1986; Christensen, 1963; Ford & Beach, 1951; Murstein, 1974, Neubeck, 1969b; Symons, 1979). Although this belief is well known in contemporary Western society, it is neatly captured by the Kgatla (African) proverb, "A man, like a bull, cannot be confined to a kraal" (Schapera, 1941, p. 204). It is perhaps not surprising that revenge is a common motive ascribed for female adultery among the Kgatla (Schapera, 1941).

However, there are societies in which female sexual desire is a commonly attributed motive. The aboriginal women of Western Arnhem Land (Australia) are most likely to take lovers if their husbands are old and not sexually satisfying. Women of some parts of Melanesia complain bitterly if frequency of intercourse drops from the usual once a day or more to once every 5–10 days. It is justifiable for women to take lovers or leave their husbands if they are not having marital sex at least once every 10 days or so (Symons, 1979).

A number of other reports point to the importance of the motive attribution process in reducing jealousy. Malinowski (1929) discussed examples of males of various native cultures selling their wives' sexual favors to white men with no apparent jealousy. The wives' motives are clear and not threatening to the husbands. Jealousy of Apache men while their wives are engaged in war dances with other men is reduced by war chiefs, who emphasize that the women are dancing merely to conform to ritual requirements (Goodwin, 1942). Mead (1931) reported that the Natchez Indians of North America so prize premarital sexual relationships that women who do not have many partners are suspect and held in disfavor. Presumably, a Natchez male does not concern himself with the motives of a premarital partner who has relations with others as much as with the motives of a partner who does not have other sexual partners.

The Kaka allow nephews free sexual access to their uncles' wives. If a man discovers his wife having sex with another man, he first finds out whether the other man is a nephew or not. If he is a nephew, no loss of self-esteem or relationship is implied, and no jealous behavior seems to follow. Sex relations involving a nephew are on the order of paying a social call (Reyburn, 1962).

The Kgatla of Africa developed an interesting motive for extramarital liaison after the coming of the Western missionaries and the ending of polygyny. They believed that since the coming of the missionaries fewer children were being born. This, coupled with the absence of men for periods of time from the village (to work), fostered the additional belief that many women were sexually dissatisfied. As a consequence of these beliefs, the adulterous male could plead that he was doing both the tribe and the women involved a valuable service, one that was apparently approved by the elders. If these selfless motives were accepted, jealousy would be minimized (Schapera, 1941).

In some societies adultery is the normative first step in changing husbands. For example, the Zuni husband who discovers his wife's affair (which is usually not well hidden) rarely reacts with anger or violence, but interprets it more or less as the expected first step of separation leading to a divorce, which was usually anticipated by both parties (Benedict, 1961). In American middle-class culture, adultery is often taken to signal a desire for divorce (Bernard, 1971; Levinger, 1966).

The ethnographic record suggests that cultures affect the motive attribution process in fundamental ways. First, there may be strongly held beliefs about the "normal" causes of attraction between rival and partner. Second, cultures differ as to which causes are appraised as threatening. In general, it appears that causes over which the jealous has control or that are not linked to self-definition are less likely to lead to jealousy. Finally, adultery may be recognized as a legitimate method to terminate a marriage.

Social Comparison, Alternatives Assessment, and Loss Assessment

Scattered reports point to cultural variation in these other secondary-appraisal processes. Mead (1931) reported that on the east coast of Africa, girls fatten themselves to make themselves more attractive, in order to secure and keep husbands. A woman who is unable to put on much weight is "haunted" by the fear that a fatter woman would be more appealing to her husband and might lead to his desertion.

Although many authors have discussed the element of sexual social comparison in Western cultures (Clanton & Smith, 1977; Zetterberg, 1966), the Kaka of Africa are much more explicit about the importance of sexual comparison. Both sexes play a game of extramarital sex called *wandja*, in which men attempt as many extramarital contacts as possible while suffering no cuckoldry themselves. If a women is adulterous, it implies to the Kaka that the husband is less potent. Indeed, groups of women commonly mock men for the size of their genitals. It is not surprising that genital size and general potency are important dimensions of comparison with rivals (Reyburn, 1962).

Alternatives assessment is most clearly seen in the several cultures that require the father of an adulterous wife to make another daughter available as a replacement wife. In such cases, the wronged husband is typically expected to have some choice in the matter, depending on his evaluation of the other daughters as suitable alternatives (Ford & Beach, 1951; Murstein, 1974; Neubeck, 1969b; Symons, 1979).

Loss assessment is similarly most explicit in many cultures that have arrangements to award compensation to the jealous spouse, usually the husband (Hupka, 1981). Compensation may be decided by rule or may to some extent be a matter of negotiation among the injured party, the rival, and/or family and friends of the erring spouse.

According to Harris (1974), the aggressive Yanomamo (Venezuela and Brazil) male becomes enraged when he discoveres an affair, because he considers the uncompensated value of gifts and services that should have been given to him by his rival for having sex with his wife. Presentation of such gifts immediately after the extramarital affair apparently reduces such anger, suggesting that the "loss" perceived when cuckolded is a loss of payment for rented services. The Bakongo of Africa have a similar property orientation. It is accepted that the rival male has used the husband's property and therefore must pay "rent." The amount demanded depends to some extent on the length of the affair and the value of the wife and is set by the husband (Weeks, 1914).

Several societies require that the adulterous wife's dowry be returned by her family (Hupka, 1981; Murstein, 1974; Neubeck, 1969b), thereby insuring that the in-laws will aid in controlling the wife. The dowry may be demanded even if, as among the Plateau tribes, the husband also has the right to kill his wife (Gouldsbury & Sheane, 1911).

Other examples of cultural rules determining the extent of loss assessment are found among the Verre, Birwana, and Sumbwa of Africa. In one form of marriage, the husband pays for sexual rights and his lineage acquires rights to the children. In another form, less payment is made for sexual rights only; the children remain with the mother's kin group. The price demanded of an adulterer may vary according to the form of marriage (Maire, 1953). In other cultures, the bride price is paid over a period of time, and the amount of compensation that is demanded of an adulterer is partially based on how much of the bride price has been paid (Maire, 1953).

Jealous Emotions

Jealous emotions are not much discussed in ethnographic reports, reflecting a general neglect of emotion by anthropologists (Lutz & White, 1986). We found 117 accounts of adulterous, promiscuous, or other potentially jealousy-inducing situations in a total of 46 different cultures (including ancient Western cultures such as the Hebrews or Greeks). Only 63 of these accounts discussed emotion, and of these only 9 reported more than one emotion felt by the jealous. Anger was by far the most commonly reported emotion (appearing in over half the emotion accounts), followed by fear or anxiety and then by sadness or depression. No sex differences in likelihood of emotion were found. However, it would be an error to make too much of these data, given the nature of the ethnographic records available to us.

Jealousy Coping

We have used our typology of functional coping strategies to order and illustrate a wide variety of coping efforts. As we have discussed earlier, the same behavior may have elements of more than one strategy, so our ordering is somewhat arbitrary. We found no accounts that we felt could be interpreted as examples of improving the relationship, self-assessment, or support/catharsis. Whether this means that those strategies are infrequently used or merely hard to detect is unanswerable from the data. Many of the specific behaviors reported below may seem strange or puzzling as to origin, even though their function in reducing threat or harm may be apparent. Since the ethnographic accounts very rarely discuss or even speculate on the origins of specific behaviors, we cannot do so.

Interference with the Rival Relationship

As mentioned earlier, cuckolded husbands in many cultures demand money or valuable property from their wives' lovers (or sometimes the wives' families); these cultures include the Bakongo (Weeks, 1914), the Yanomamo (Harris, 1974; Irons, 1979), and the Maori of New Zealand (Mishkin, 1937). If a Bakongo adulterer cannot pay the compensation, he has to work the husband's fields as well as his own, generally insuring exhaustion and lack of energy for pursuing women. In the 1800s, the Hidatsa Indians of North America allowed the husband whose wife eloped with another man to seize all the property of the rival *and* of the rival's friends, apparently enlisting the friends' aid in preventing the elopement (Matthews, 1877). The ancient Romans fined both the wife and the lover, while men were generally free to have extramarital sex. A cuckolded husband had to have witnesses before a fine could be demanded, and Roman law gave him the right to hold the rival for 20 hours while witnesses were rounded up (Murstein, 1974).

The most violent jealous behavior, that of killing a spouse or rival, is the most extreme form of interference with the rival relationship. Since a person's death usually has a great impact on a social network, it is not surprising that in many cultures it is not necessarily the jealous spouse who may rightfully kill the adulterous spouse or rival; friends, relatives, strangers, or officials can take part as well. For example, the ancient Hebrews would stone to death a married woman and her lover if the affair took place in the city. If in the country, it was assumed the woman had been raped but that no one had heard her screams; hence only the man was killed (Murstein, 1974).

Examples of justifiable homicide are very common, and almost without exception involve the male as the justified party. The king of the Plateau tribes of Zimbabwe executes males caught with any of the wives of his harem. The offending wife is often grossly mutilated but, if she survives the ordeal, is sometimes allowed to live (Goldsbury & Sheane, 1911). The Ammassalik husband is likely to attack a man who has sex with his wife without either the benefit of the lamp ritual mentioned earlier or an agreement of wife swapping. Murder is apparently not at all unusual in such circumstances (Mirsky, 1937b). In earlier times, Apache husbands apparently routinely killed their rivals and mutilated their wives (by cutting off the end of the nose) to make them unappealing to other potential interlopers (Goodwin, 1942). The 19th-century Antakerrinya (Australia) husband cut or burned his unfaithful wife (Taplin, 1879). In 11th-century Britain an adulteress would forfeit her nose and ears (Murstein, 1974). Daly et al. (1982), Hupka (1981), Mead (1931), Neubeck (1969a), and Murstein (1974) present a number of other examples of jealous males' culturally justified aggression. We merely wish to point out that such aggression is functional in ending the threat to the relationship and perhaps in maintaining self- or social esteem.

It is relatively rare for groups to condone a jealous female's aggression toward a guilty husband. Female aggression toward a rival is more likely (Hupka, 1981). One exception is the Tokopia (western Polynesia). If a husband is out all night with another woman, the wife strikes him with a stick on the back and legs when he returns, and also pinches his flesh until the skin is broken. The husband suffers this quietly and passively (Firth, 1936).

A hundred years ago, Samoan wives would seek out women who had had sex with their husbands and bite these rivals on the nose, reducing their attractiveness (Turner, 1884). The Dakota female, unlike the male, has approval for assaulting a rival female (Mirsky, 1937a). Among the usually nonviolent Pueblo Zuni a wife may fight a rival if the husband deserts her, though this is not the usual pattern. The two women call each other names and black eyes are exchanged (Benedict, 1961). Much more dramatic are the Toba Indians of Bolivia. The jealous wife is expected to attack the rival; an observer in the 1920s note that these "fights continued for several hours, often for a whole night, during which the two enraged women beat each other with their hands, scratch each other with nails or with big cactus thorns which they have tied at the wrists (Karsten, 1925, pp. 19–20).

In addition to fines or aggression, a number of means have been employed to make the rival relationship costly to partner and/or rival. A suspicious or aggrieved Pawnee male may try to inhibit his rival by bewitching him, hoping to make him suffer for his attraction to the jealous man's wife (Weltfish, 1965). A much more public tack is taken by Murngin women of Australia, whose only legitimate recourse to affect an erring husband's behavior is to repeatedly heap scathing abuse upon him in public (Warner, 1937). In ancient Greece, a woman who had committed adultery knew that, if caught and not killed by her husband, for the rest of her life she could not attend public sacrifices without risking rough handling from passers-by (Murstein, 1974).

Another form of interference is the use of devices to prevent intercourse between a wife and a rival. Chastity belts were relatively common among medieval European and British nobility, and may still be purchased today in some Western countries. Other cultures have practiced infibulation (the stitching and buckling together of the labia majora), foot binding, the use of vaginal plugs, and clitoridectomy to reduce the woman's sexual motivation (Daly et al., 1982; Kurland, 1979; Murstein, 1974; Symons, 1979).

By the late 19th century, Pomo Indian men of California had developed an elaborate ritual, apparently to instill in women great anxiety if they contemplated having an affair—an anticipatory form of interference. A special chief presided over a secret society of men whose sole purpose it was to perform these rituals. The rituals included solemn fire-and-brimstone speeches to the women by the chief, threatening all kinds of natural and supernatural retributions for infidelity; devil dances in which mock combat was staged between the forces of supernatural evil who could attack unfaithful women and the village men; and threatening women with secretly defanged rattlesnakes (Powers, 1877).

Demanding Commitment

Observers in the 1800s noted that the Maori of New Zealand valued women who were courted by many men; women were generally allowed as many premarital sex partners as they liked. Since men were also free to choose their own mates, inevitably rivalries would develop. Physically carrying away the woman, if achieved, amounted to a successful demand for commitment, as the woman either stayed with the man or killed herself. Carrying her off was no easy task, as she and her relatives might violently resist. It was not uncommon for the woman to be injured, sometimes severely (Thomson, 1859).

It has also been reported that a jealous Maori woman might strangle her children, apparently to stop her husband from taking another wife or continuing an affair (Yate, 1835).

Hupka (1981) mentions a number of societies in which a woman's recourse for her husband's infidelity is to demand commitment by threatening to leave the marriage. In other cultures the wife cannot leave without great problems, effectively cutting off this coping tactic. For example, if the Murngin wife runs away in response to her husband's infidelity, her male kin hunt her down and return her to her husband, who usually beats her (Warner, 1937).

Jealous Dobuan spouses, as a last resort, stage an attempted suicide. This arouses great anxiety in the unfaithful spouse, as a suicide is cause for revenge by the dead spouse's relatives. If the spouse has not yielded to any other form of threat to stop an affair, this tactic usually succeeds (Benedict, 1961).

Derogation

New Zealand Maori society of the 1800s allowed for polygyny. One early report held that a wife who feared for her status would invent lies about another wife in an attempt to derogate her, easing the threat to status (Yate, 1835). The Bena of Africa almost exclusively react to discovered adultery by sarcasm and derogation (Ford & Beach, 1951). Many of the reports we categorize elsewhere have elements of sarcasm and verbal abuse directed toward the partner or rival, but it is difficult to know whether these serve the functional strategy of reducing threat to self-esteem or are merely means of making it unpleasant for the secondary relationship to be maintained.

Developing Alternatives

Several cultures have practices whereby the jealous spouse can gain community approval for certain ways of dealing with a jealousy-provoking situation (Hupka, 1981; Murstein, 1974; Neubeck, 1969b). Conceptually, we suggest that the jealous individual can be thought of as turning to the community for self-esteem maintenance to repair the loss of self- or social esteem occasioned by the rival relationship.

For example, a jealous Maori husband in the 19th century had the option of ritual spear combat in the presence of relatives of the rival. Physical assault was minimized, and apparently the ritual allowed the husband to regain stature (Thomson, 1859). The Ammassalik husband can challenge his rival to a drum and singing match in which both men bash heads and make fun of each other. Sessions can last all night and may continue intermittently for years. These matches provide community entertainment and hence garner communal approval. Over the months or years, the initial bitterness is often transformed into a pleasant show (the head bashing is dropped) enjoyed by the principals. From one point of view this ritual can be seen as a communal way to contain violence, but from the perspective of the individual it allows for the rebuilding of self- and communal esteem (Mirsky, 1937b). The Hidatsa Indian husband of the 1800s could gain great esteem if he gave his wife to her lover along with a valuable gift (Matthews, 1877).

According to Mirsky (1937b), an Ammassalik husband who has just lost his wife to a rival may then steal the wife of another man not involved in the affair in order to insure basic survival in a harsh environment. Presumably several considerations enter into the choice of which of many possible alternative wives to steal.

Hupka (1981) found that divorce or desertion is the most common means for women of different cultures to cope with unfaithful husbands, either by threatening to leave unless the husbands stop their affairs or by actually leaving. Ammassalik women appear to have perhaps the most liberal opportunities. If a husband is unfaithful, the wife has the right and the support of the community to run away or "permit" herself to be carried away by another man (Mirsky, 1937b). Among the Navaho, adultery is the most frequent grounds for divorce for both sexes (Aberle, 1961).

Denial/Avoidance

The Zuni wife typically says nothing to her husband if an affair is discovered, even if the infidelity is flagrant. She confronts him only if he persists or if the affair or she herself becomes a focus of local gossip (Benedict, 1961).

The Dakota Indian husband and wife live in a group with brothers, sisters, cousins, and their spouses and children. If one of these kin has an affair with the wife of another, the husband is expected to show no anger or bitter emotion, but rather to gracefully give up his wife to the rival, apparently hiding true feelings. At this point, the whole group makes evident its censure of the offending couple, and they must leave the group for another (Mirsky, 1937a).

As mentioned earlier, the Kaka allow nephews free sexual access to their uncles' wives. If the uncle returns home and discovers his wife and nephew having sex, the nephew calls out, "It's me," and the uncle pretends thereafter not to know what is going on (Reyburn, 1962).

Reappraisal as Challenge

Because extramarital intercourse is socially sanctioned, the Toda husband can easily assume that his wife's pregnancy is by another man (perhaps his brother). According to Hupka (1981), a pregnancy is experienced as a challenge to the husband to insure that a ceremony called *pursutpimi* was carried out. This ceremony establishes the *legal* paternity of the husband through the act of his presenting his wife with a bow and arrow. Actual paternity is of little interest to the husband.

As mentioned above, the most commonly esteemed behavior for a 19th-century Hidatsa husband whose wife had eloped with another was to invite the wife and rival back to his lodge and present his wife to her new lover. A valuable gift to the new couple would signal even greater merit. While this pattern shows the function of developing an alternative source of esteem (community approval for this selfless act), to carry out the ceremony seems to have been regarded as a challenge to rise above the situation (Matthews, 1877).

Issues Raised by the Ethnographic Evidence

The cultural variations we have reviewed suggest some issues important to theory development, to which we now turn.

Anticipatory versus Reactive Coping

We have argued that coping efforts function to reduce perceived threat/harm to self-esteem and relationship or to manage affect. Several of the examples above can be thought of as "anticipatory" coping. That is, no rival or even a potential for a rival is thought to exist currently, but coping is instigated to prevent the development of rivals. Conceptually, such anticipatory coping may work directly to manage the emotion that arises at the thought of a rival developing. Much of the time, however, the culture provides examples of the bad things that happen when rivals develop, and the person may use anticipatory coping as insurance against such developments without experiencing aversive affect.

All of the eight coping strategies in our typology may be used to prevent development of a rival relationship. The choice of anticipatory strategy should be affected by cultural prescriptions for strategies to be used after a rival relationship develops. For example, almost all of the cultures reviewed have some form of physical, financial, or symbolic punishment that is meted out to individuals who violate cultural practices regarding sexual exclusivity. Hence, it is not surprising that the use of socially sanctioned threats is a common means for the jealous person to prevent a rival relationship from developing, as well as to pressure a partner or rival to end such relationships.

Threat to Self-Esteem versus Threat to Social Esteem

Social esteem concerns the evaluation of self by others. It is possible to conceptualize situations in which a person may be concerned about a threat to social esteem, but may be relatively unconcerned about a threat to self-esteem. There is a long-standing controversy regarding the differences between shame (loss of social esteem) and guilt (loss of self-esteem) (Izard, 1977; Kemper, 1978; Lewis & Spanier, 1979). Experimental studies have attempted to demonstrate the unique causes and effects of threat to self-esteem versus threat to social esteem, as well as the use of different strategies to maintain self versus social esteem. This research has generally validated the conceptual distinction between the two, though of course controversy remains (Greenwald & Breckler, 1985; Leary et al., 1986; Tesser & Paulus, 1983; Tetlock & Manstead, 1985).

Our position is that jealousy involves threats to *self*-esteem only—a position consistent with Mead's (1931) conclusions about jealousy and social esteem. Of course, it is possible that knowledge of communal disapproval may lead to consideration of internal standards, resulting in a threat to self-esteem; hence, threats to communal esteem may be linked to threats to self-esteem. However, it is plausible from the ethnographic evidence that a person may appraise a threat to communal esteem from being cuckolded, but may experience no threat to or loss of self-esteem. In such cases, the person may behave in such a way as to reduce the loss of communal esteem. Such coping, however, we do not consider part of the jealousy complex. In these cases the threat to communal esteem is bound up with the community's values and expectations regarding marriage or other institutionalized relationships (Turner, 1970). Issues of communal esteem maintenance may overlap with the jealousy complex, but we believe it is useful to think of self-esteem processes as conceptually distinct from (though interactive with) communal esteem processes.

The distinction is based on the degree to which behavior is

generated by the internal processes of perceived threats to self and relationship, versus the degree to which behavior is generated by role expectations and the consequences of the failure to fulfill such expectations (e.g., the role of the cuckolded husband). The difference has been wonderfully portrayed by Marcello Mastroianni in the movie *Divorce, Italian Style*. His wife has an affair with another man, but for various reasons this is of little personal concern to Mastroianni's character. However, in the setting of rural Sicily he is expected to kill the rival as well as his wife. All sorts of strong social pressures are put on him to do so against his personal wishes. The character finally develops a plan to appear to have avenged himself without actually creating mayhem.

The experience of finding oneself expected to behave in a jealous way while not actually feeling very jealous has been commented on by several authors (Bohm, 1961; Clanton & Smith, 1977; Mead, 1931; Safilios-Rothschild, 1969; Seidenberg, 1967). The problem is that the behaviors required to maintain communal esteem may be the same behaviors used by the actually jealous. A truly jealous Sicilian may easily kill his wife and her lover. This is why it is important to make the argument that *jealous* behaviors are best understood as the pursuit of functional strategies to reduce threat to self or the relationship. Similar behaviors that are solely serving the function of maintaining social esteem are not coping with jealousy, but with the desire to maintain a certain social standing in the face of social disapproval.

A related question is the strategy of turning to the community for self-esteem maintenance. We have discussed examples of this above under "Developing Alternatives." If a ritual such as the Ammassalik drum challenge serves the function of building self-esteem lost as a result of being cuckolded, then engaging in the ritual is a strategy for coping with jealousy. However, if such a ritual is engaged in solely because of a need to fulfill a role obligation or to garner public favor in the absence of a threat to self-esteem, then engaging in the ritual is not part of the jealousy complex.

Threat to Social Status/Rank versus Threat to Self-Esteem or the Relationship

Social status or rank is determined in large part by a person's placement within defined hierarchies. Social esteem may or may not accrue to the person who occupies a particular status or rank. In our ethnographic review above, we have mentioned instances in which the partner's involvement with another may be perceived as a threat to social rank.

As with our distinction between social esteem and self-esteem involvement in jealousy, we hold that reactions to threats to rank should not be conceptualized as jealousy, except insofar as they affect appraisals concerning threat to self-esteem or to the relationship. Losing status may certainly lead to negative self-evaluations (Kemper, 1978; Tesser & Paulus, 1983). If loss of self-esteem following from status loss occurs as a result of the partner's attraction to another (or the rival's attraction to the partner), then jealousy is involved. Also, marriage in most cultures has strong implications for the person's social standing (Hupka, 1981; Swartz & Jordan, 1980; Turner, 1970). Hence, one quality of a marriage relationship *is* its status-giving nature. A threat to this quality would trigger reactions we call the jealousy complex.

Because a threat to status from a rival relationship is likely to threaten self-esteem and relationship quality as well, in real life we would predict that all or most such instances of status threat are correctly labeled as part of the jealousy complex as jealousy is defined within the culture. Part of what "jealousy" means in such situations involves reference to status and feelings about status threat. However, by no means are all rival relationships threats to status; hence, attempts to cope with rival relationships may usually carry no implication for social status.

Demanding Compensation

A number of cultures have arrangements by which the husband can be compensated for his wife's sexual relations with another man, either before or after the actual liaison (we found no instance of a wife's being compensated). Although cultural-level variables that support such practices may be suggested, the question here is how to conceptualize compensation. Although the act of demanding and getting compensation certainly has the function of pointing to and supporting certain cultural values and beliefs, at the level of the individual we think that compensation has elements of the two coping strategies of interfering with the rival relationship and demanding commitment.

Compensations are costs for engaging in a secondary relationship. Knowledge that compensation will be demanded may decrease the likelihood that a rival relationship will be contemplated; payment of compensation may increase the likelihood that extrarelationship liaisons will not be repeated. Compensation can also be a means of demanding commitment from the partner, especially if relatives and friends share in paying the compensation. They may be expected to use persuasive means to insure commitment.

It is also possible that paying compensation attenuates threat to self-esteem by making the resolution of the problem related to the worth of the relationship, especially as we have seen in terms of sexual access or lineage. Putting a price on these rather more tangible aspects of relationship is a much more easily negotiated process than putting a price on some intrapsychic loss or the pain of certain emotions. Although it may be that jealousy can be viewed as a reaction to loss of sexual property (Davis, 1936; see following discussion), it may also be true that the property metaphor is easily adopted because it enables a person to translate the threat to self-esteem into a much more manageable and less self-referent transaction over property.

CROSS-CULTURAL JEALOUSY RESEARCH

Aside from the ethnographic literature, few cross-cultural studies of jealousy have been reported. We briefly review these reports before discussing cultural-level variables that we think are important in affecting the quality and frequency of jealousy.

Hupka and Ryan (1981) rated 92 cultures in the Human Relation Area Files (which contain information on over 300 societies; see Barry, 1980) for the severity of *male* responses to adultery (verbal abuse was rated as low in severity; nonviolent termination of marriage was rated as being of intermediate severity; beating and disfigurement were rated as high in severity). Three cultural variables were found to be significantly correlated with this severity measure: importance of marriage for social status, importance of private ownership of property, and restriction of sex to marriage. Importance of personal progeny (e.g., for inheritance and material support) was not related to severity. Though the data are open to interpretation, they are consistent with our model, in that both importance of marriage and restriction of sexuality have direct implications for jealousy's being a reaction to perceived threats to relationship and/or self-esteem. Private property norms may act to define situations in which threat is perceived. We return to these three cultural factors later.

Hupka et al. (1985) studied 2,091 university students in Hungary, Ireland, Mexico, the Netherlands, the Soviet Union, Yugoslavia, and the United States. Each student completed a jealousy questionnaire, and the responses were factor-analyzed separately for each culture. Three factors were found that were similar in all seven cultures: Threat to Exclusive Relationship, Dependency, and Self-Deprecation/Envy (the only exception was the Hungarian sample, which did not yield the Dependency factor). Examples of items defining these factors are "When my partner pays attention to other people, I feel lonely and left out," "When I see my lover kissing someone else, my stomach knots up" (Threat); "I often feel I couldn't exist without him/her," "Losing my lover prevents me from being the kind of person I want to be" (Dependency); "Most of my friends have a more exciting love life than I do," and "I feel empty inside when I see a successful relationship" (Self-Deprecation/Envy).

Some cultures had unique factors. A Distrust factor was found for Mexicans; a Threat to Sexual Exclusivity factor was found for the Netherlands; and Hungary, Ireland, Mexico, and Yugoslavia produced Aversion to Partner Autonomy, which had different items defining it for each culture. Hupka et al. (1985) explain their results by assuming that the three factors of Threat to Exclusive Relationship, Dependency, and Self-Deprecation/Envy capture global interpersonal concerns, but that cultures differ a great deal in the situations that are associated with or trigger the concerns.

In our view, these results indicate that some interpersonal issues have similar meaning across different cultures, whereas other issues have particularistic meaning (Lutz & White, 1986). Whether or not dependency is related somehow to the jealousy complex in each of the seven national samples, students by and large seem to share a concept of dependency as a major interpersonal theme (cf. Kelley & Thibaut, 1978; Wish et al., 1976). However, merely finding that "dependency" and "threat to exclusivity" are two separate factors in a factor analysis does not mean that both are necessarily part of some invariant thing called "jealousy."

We think that both exclusivity and dependency may be related to indicators of jealousy in different cultures if (1) cultural definitions of self and of romantic relationships are similar, (2) cultural definitions of exclusivity and dependency are similar, and (3) exclusivity and dependency are linked in similar ways with definitions of self and of romantic relationships. For example, the self-concept and self-esteem of American and Irish males may have a strong element of sexual competence or prowess (similarity in cultural definition of self). They may also share a belief in the importance of female sexual faithfulness in relationships (cultural similarity in exclusivity beliefs). They may also share a belief that their partners' interest in others implies that they are incompetent lovers (similarity in linkage of self-esteem to exclusivity beliefs). When these three sets of similarities are in place, then we would expect that American and Irish males would be similar in major aspects of the jealousy complex: Appraisal of partner interest in another leads to threat to self-esteem, which leads to coping efforts to reduce threat to self-esteem.

Buunk and Hupka (1987) reported an analysis of specific questionnaire responses from the same students whose complete data we have just been discussing (Hupka et al., 1985). These responses concerned specific situations that were expected to elicit sexual jealousy. The six situations were partner's flirting with another, kissing another, dancing with another, hugging another, having sex with another, and having sexual fantasies about another. Averaged across all cultures, flirting and having sex elicited strongly negative reactions, while the other situations yielded neutral reactions (neither strongly positive or negative). Across all cultures, women were most upset by their partners' kissing another, whereas men were more upset by their partners' having sexual fantasies about another.

However, there was also a good deal of variation among the cultures. For example, Yugoslavian students were particularly upset by flirting, but the least concerned about kissing and sexual fantasies. Sexual fantasies were the most upsetting to the Dutch, who were otherwise relatively unaffected by kissing, dancing, and hugging. Russian students were the most negatively reacting group, regardless of specific situation.

As with the Hupka et al. (1985) study, such data can be explained by assuming that for some situations (flirting, sex) there is cross-cultural uniformity in the extent to which definitions of self and relationship are related to these specific events. For other events, cultures differ in the extent to which the situation has implications for self or the relationship.

CULTURAL FACTORS IN JEALOUSY

Conceptual Issues

Before discussing cultural factors we think are important in understanding jealousy, we feel it is important to make clear our assumptions about the role of culture in emotion. Anthropologists of emotion have suggested several conceptual issues about which it is important to be precise (Boucher, 1979; Levy, 1984; Lutz & White, 1986; Shweder, 1985). Lutz and White (1986), for example, present five conceptual dimensions regarding emotion: "materialism–idealism," "positivism–interpretivism," "universalism–relativism," "individual–culture," and "romanticism–rationalism." The materialism–idealism dimension refers to whether or not emotions are conceived as material things with inherently biological properties, such as nervous system configurations, cardiovascular configurations, and muscular involvement, or whether emotions are regarded as personally and socially constructed ideas or evaluative judgments. Materialism requires that the "emotion" of jealousy be relatively invariant, whereas idealism suggests great variability across person, culture, and situation. Our position is that jealousy cannot be defined in terms of its physiological properties, but is inherently a culturally created set of propositions regarding relationships among interpersonal relationships and self-evaluation. However, the emotions felt by the jealous (e.g., anger, sadness, and fear), though not bound invariantly into a complex emotion called "jealousy," themselves can be conceptually and empirically distinguished to some extent at the physiological/muscular level.

Positivism supposes that scientific method and observation will discover the "true" nature of the world, whereas interpretivism assumes that both articulated and nonconscious theories and assumptions about the world create the data that the positivists assume is inherently "natural." A positivist approach assumes that jealousy is not basically a product of historical period or culture; interpretivism assumes no transhistorical stability of jealousy, as the meaning of emotion is constantly renegotiated between actors and between observers (scientists) and actors. Our approach is positivist in that we assume that jealousy is inherently a perception of and reaction to threat to (or loss of) self-esteem and/or the romantic relationship, and interpretivist in that we assume that what constitutes self, the romantic relationship, threat, and the relationships among them posed by a rival relationship is negotiated and hence not invariant across time and culture.

Universalism—relativism refers to the position that it is possible to develop laws or understandings that apply across cultures or persons, versus the position that each person or culture is so uniquely arranged that it cannot be understood by reference to any system standing outside of it (i.e., general laws are not possible, but lawful regularities may exist within each culture or personality). We are universalistic in assuming that people in all cultures can experience themselves or their relationships as being under threat from a rival relationship, and that there is some underlying regularity in the consequences of such threat. However, we are relativistic in the

sense that the surface, observable features of the underlying processes of threat appraisal and coping can be best understood by
references to the particular culture.

The individual–culture dimension refers to whether emotion is
held to be primarily a property of individuals that is best studied at
the level of the individual (methodological individualism), or whether
an emotion is thought to be a property of a culture in which individuals may participate. We attempt to bridge this dichotomy by referring to the jealousy complex as a property of the individual (conceptually and methodologically), while speaking of the interpersonal
jealousy system to capture the aspect of jealousy as a creation of a
culture.

The romanticism–rationalism dichotomy refers to underlying
value assumptions about the worth of emotions. Our own view is
that jealousy is neither good nor bad, but certainly leads to behaviors
that may be evaluated as good or bad within the culture. Jealousy
may lead to a "good" result, such as partners' deepening their relationship, or to a "bad" result, such as murder. Understanding the
bases for such cultural evaluations then becomes an important aspect of understanding the jealousy complex in that culture.

Cultural Factors

Jealousy as a Violation of Sexual Property Norms

Davis (1936) distinguished between the "jealousy of rivalry" and the
"jealousy of trespass." In the former, two or more rivals did not
consider that they "owned" the beloved, but were competing for
ownership. Davis devoted most of his discussion to the latter concept, arguing (1) that cultures vary in the extent to which sexual
favors of a partner are considered the "property" of the other
partner; (2) that each culture has rules about how such property can
be borrowed or trespassed upon; and (3) that each culture has prescriptions about the consequences of trespassing upon sexual property.

This formulation can explain a great deal of the cultural variation we have described. Further, it suggests that sexual property
norms constitute an instance of more general property norms. There
should be a rough alignment between treatments of sexual and
nonsexual property. For example, a culture like the Apache, in which
private property norms are very strong, should be more likely to
produce frequent and intense jealousy than cultures like the Toda, in
which private property is minimized. Hupka and Ryan (1981), as

mentioned, reported that the importance of private property correlated with the severity of jealousy. Fromkin (1957) and Whitehurst
(1971b, 1977) have employed Davis's proposition to explain American male jealousy as an extension of the primacy of private property
ideals in American culture. Mead (1931) noted that the Dobuan are
particularly jealous and have a strong emphasis on personal property.

Jealousy and the Assertion of the Self

Mead (1931) commented in her ethnographic review of jealousy-
inducing situations that "however varied the social setting, it will be
seen to be the threatened self-esteem, the threatened ego which
reacts jealously. Situations involving this self-esteem will, however,
take widely different forms" (p. 38). She then discussed variations in
the conventions on which personal reputation and self-esteem are
based. We have incorporated the notion of self-esteem threat into
our definition of jealousy, but our concern here is with the more
fundamental requirement of the sense of self.

Whatever else it entails, it appears that jealousy and its resolution certainly act to delineate and differentiate the self from the
rival, from the partner, and from other relevant actors. This seems
to require a coherent notion of self. Our speculation is that jealousy
should be more common or more intense in societies that are atomistic in the sense of presenting strong models for the self as a distinct,
potentially alienated entity (Guthrie & Tanco, 1980; Parsons, 1951).
Hence, it should not be private property norms that generate
jealousy as much as the attachment of sense of self to the ownership
of such property.

More generally, cultures differ in the extent to which a sense of
self is differentiated from networks of kinship, friendship, and tribal
relationships. Who one is is defined in terms of personal attributes
(the atomistic self) or network relationships (the extended self).
Threats to (or loss of) self-esteem or self-concept may be more
salient and difficult to cope with for the atomistic self, who cannot
refer to a social network of others for purposes of appraisal and
coping in the same way as the extended self can. For example, an
American, with a relatively atomistic sense of self, may infer that the
partner's attraction to another signals failure of the self to satisfy
the partner; a Toda, with a greater sense of extended self, may infer
that the partner's attraction to another signals failure of the
partner's family to prepare him or her properly for the role of
marriage. The American may then concentrate on changing the self

in order to better satisfy the partner (the coping strategy of improving the relationship), whereas the Toda may enlist the aid of family elders to encourage the beloved's family to enforce expected role behavior (the strategy of demanding commitment).

Jealousy and the Importance of Marriage

As mentioned earlier, Hupka and Ryan (1981) reported a correlation between male jealousy and the importance of marriage as a means of achieving socially valued goals. Our discussion of the wives' reactions to polygyny in polygynous cultures also supports the idea that it is the instrumental value of marriage that is related to jealousy. Jealousy among wives is low as long as the husband follows cultural convention in distributing resources and power among the wives. Deviations are seen by the disadvantaged as impediments to the instrumental goals of being married (access to resources, friendship, sexuality, inheritance, etc.).

The role of the importance of marriage is rather straightforwardly related to our definition of jealousy. The more important the primary relationship is, the more likely it is that threats to/losses of such relationships will evoke attempts to reduce threat or loss. Within the context of the romantic triangle, such threats/losses promote the reactions we call the jealousy complex.

There are a variety of factors that make marriage an important institution (Murstein, 1974; Parsons, 1951; Swartz & Jordan, 1980; Turner, 1970). The relevant literature is too large to review here, but such factors include social and geographic mobility, industrialization, religious systems, and sex-role prescriptions affecting cultural and individual choices about the value of marriage.

Jealousy and the Regulation of Sexuality

Hupka and Ryan (1981) also reported a correlation between male jealousy and the extent to which sex was restricted to marriage. Our own ethnographic review provides examples as well. Conceptually, sex can be considered a valued experience that, if restricted to particular social forms, increases the value of those forms (e.g., marriage) and hence makes threats to them from rival relationships more likely to promote jealousy.

The underlying question, however, is why sexuality is restricted to certain forms in societies; this question demands examination of the reasons why sex is a valued experience (Turner, 1970). Although the orgasm can be seen as having inherently desired characteristics, it is also clear that the meaning given to orgasm and sexuality more generally can vary tremendously—from simple relief, to play, to expressions of love, to expressions of dominance or disgust, and to attempts to fulfill divine procreational functions. In order to understand why sexuality is restricted to marriage or any other form, it is necessary to understand the meaning of sexuality within that form and then the ways in which such meaning is related to larger cultural values. An example is the meaning of female sexuality in southern Mediterranean marriage (Safilios-Rothschild, 1969). Female sexual behavior is heavily laden with religious meaning concerning procreation. Extramarital sex for women thus carries connotations threatening the parallel system of religious beliefs in a way that male extramarital sexuality does not. The restriction of female sexuality serves the function of preserving a pervasive system of religious belief.

By extension, it will be useful to examine the meaning of a partner's extrarelationship sexuality in order to understand the emotions and coping that may follow. This examination of meaning is what we refer to as part of secondary appraisal of the partner's motives—an appraisal that may be highly influenced by cultural meaning systems attached to sexuality.

Jealousy and Competition

Much of our ethnographic review and many of our causal suggestions have focused on threat to or loss of an already established relationship. The ethnographic evidence is scant concerning premarital competition for mates or sexual partners, especially the ways in which such competition is related to jealousy.

Whitehurst (1971b, 1977) has suggested that a competitive ethos is related to jealousy, especially in the sense that competition is the means by which personal worth is established. For example, it is not so much the acquisition of wealth per se that signifies merit; rather, it is the assumption that one has acquired wealth through being a superior competitor. Several Western authors have also commented on what appears to them as the pervasive presence of the element of competition in jealousy (Baute, 1978; Bohm, 1961; Farber, 1973; Mazur, 1977; Spielman, 1971).

It would seem useful to investigate how cultural variation in general competitiveness or in expected competitiveness for mates is related to jealousy. Our assumption is that a real or potential failure in such competitiveness is problematic if self-esteem is based on the comparison of worth through competition. If competition is found to be related to jealousy cross-culturally, of course, this would promote attention to cultural, economic, and political factors that may influence the competitive orientation.

Jealousy as a Means of Maintaining Male Dominance

Kurland (1979) has noted that matrilineal/matrifocal societies typically condone or favor premarital and extramarital sexuality, whereas patrilineal/patrifocal societies generally have strong sanctions against premarital and extramarital sex, especially the latter. Ford and Beach (1951) reached similar conclusions. Those societies in which women hold relatively greater power are likely to be societies that allow women greater sexual freedom, and these societies appear to be relatively low in both male and female jealousy as well. As shown earlier, sanctions against inappropriate female sexual behavior are particularly violent and usually enacted by males.

Our interest here is in the function of both male and female jealousy in maintaining male control over socioeconomic and political structures, such as control over the family and access to valued employment. A man who feels jealous over a wife's potential for meeting other attractive men at the workplace may (and often does) demand that the wife remain at home or that her conditions of employment minimize such potential (e.g., that she work only with women or children). Female jealousy may have aspects of minimizing women's threat to established male dominance by alienating women from each other. For example, one of us (White) once consulted with a police force that was having problems with women joining the force because the male officers' wives were jealous. By fighting over access to men, women are less likely to act to promote adoption of roles that lead to greater power for women if such roles also increase the chances of their husbands' having affairs.

Hence, jealousy has the potential for being related to the sexual politics (Millett, 1970) of a society. We suggest that societies in which traditional patterns of male dominance are threatened are those in which both male and female jealousy are relatively intense and pervasive, and constitute foci of particular interest by members of the society.

In this light it is interesting to note that prior to the 1960s, American mass media presentations of jealousy usually described it as an aspect of love, however problematic, and hence implied that women should be accepting of male jealousy. With the onset of the sexual and cultural revolution of the 1960s, jealousy as a theme of the mass media declined, only to emerge in the early 1970s as a sign of a neurotic or unliberated personality (Clanton & Smith, 1977, p. 15). Our explanation is that the feminist critique in the late 1960s and early 1970s changed to some extent the portrayal of jealousy as supportive of male dominance to a portrayal of jealousy as indicating failure to adapt to cultural change.

Jealousy and Lineage

Although Hupka (1981) reported a nonsignificant correlation between importance of personal progeny and male jealousy, we think that the hypothesis is worth further assessment. Specifically, we suppose that jealousy will be related to lineage under the following conditions: (1) to the extent that symbolic and/or material inheritance is wholly prescribed as flowing to one's children, whether male or female; (2) to the extent that self is invested in one's symbolic or material inheritance; and (3) to the extent that the value of the marital (or similar) relationship is based on the determination of lineage. The first two will together foster threat to self-esteem, while the third may foster threat to the relationship.

If male biological lineage is important, men should be particularly concerned with paternity confidence—an issue we have discussed at length in our chapter on sociobiological approaches to jealousy. Here we want to point out that if paternity confidence is a salient issue for men, then men in the culture should be more likely to monitor the potential for rival–partner attraction, to make mistakes in appraisal of threat, and to use anticipatory coping efforts that restrict the access of rivals to one's mate.

A Clinical Note

We think that each of the cultural factors we have been discussing is an important consideration for assessing and treating jealousy. Each factor may condition the appraisals and coping efforts of the jealous. In addition, each factor may be more or less salient as a particular issue of the jealous person or of the primary and adverse relationships. For example, a husband's religious beliefs about women's sexuality may be involved in his desire to restrict his wife's relationships with other men, or a wife's belief that her husband's affectionate attention belongs solely to her may lead to a sense of violated contract if he is attentive to other women. It may also be possible to appropriately depersonalize some of the conflict between the jealous and the beloved by attributing their difficulties to cultural issues and posing choices about the extent to which they want to adhere to socialized beliefs and expectations.

SUGGESTIONS FOR FUTURE
CROSS-CULTURAL RESEARCH ON JEALOUSY

We would like to suggest potentially useful areas for future cross-cultural research on romantic jealousy. Many of our suggestions are based on suggestions made by cultural anthropologists interested in the ethnopsychology of emotion (Boucher, 1979; Levy, 1984; Lutz & White, 1986; Shweder, 1985).

Ethnotheoretical Models of Emotion

There is a need for elaboration of the schematic meaning of words such as "jealousy." A number of methodologies are available (Izard, 1977; Lutz & White, 1986; Shaver et al., 1987). The meaning of jealousy for the jealous person includes expected interpersonal precipitants; intrapersonal thoughts, feelings, and behaviors that are expected of jealous persons; and interpersonal behaviors (including the expression of emotion) expected of the jealous. Cross-cultural comparisons can then be made more systematically along dimensions of meaning. Different cultures may emphasize certain dimensions of meaning or may yield more or less unique dimensions. The conceptual elements of the jealousy complex offer one way of ordering meanings (e.g., what constitutes primary appraisal of threat or harm, what it is that is threatened or harmed, what feelings go with what types of threats, what people may do to effect such threat or harm, etc.).

Levy (1984) cautions that lexical studies are insufficient, as some emotion words may be finely differentiated but rarely experienced (e.g., "anger" for the Tahitians), whereas other emotions may be commonly experienced but rarely talked about or differentiated (e.g., Tahitians often appear to feel guilt but have no word for it). Observational studies of which emotions go with what situations within a culture are needed as well.

Cultural Expectations about Other Actors
within the Interpersonal Jealousy System

A similar analysis is needed of what jealousy means for the partner, the rival, and significant others (e.g., children, family of origin, and close friends). Special attention should be given to their roles in resolving the culturally undesirable aspects of the jealousy complex.

Cultural Evaluations of Elements of the Jealousy Complex

Also needed is an elaboration of the moral meaning of jealousy. Cultures can be compared as to their typical moral judgments for different aspects of jealousy. Is it proper to show anger? Which kinds of perceived threat are naturally justifiable and which are signs of weakness or misguided thinking? Which kinds of coping strategies or behaviors are valued?

Linkage of Elements of the Jealousy Complex to Social Institutions

Many of the research hypotheses we have offered earlier can be used to link particular elements or configurations of elements to social institutions. This may be done within the culture by asking informants how certain elements are related to major social institutions, or it may be done on the basis of cross-cultural variables selected from a theoretical point of view. For example, patterns of inheritance can be linked to coping strategies on the basis that some coping strategies are more likely than others to signal enforcement of inheritance systems.

Developmental Aspects of Jealousy

We also see a need for research on the methods and content of socialization of children into the meaning of romantic jealousy, including moral meaning. Although parental reaction to sibling rivalry or Oedipal conflicts may or may not be related to adult jealousy, children may be expected to model adult behavior even though the modeled behavior is not produced until after childhood. Our concern here is not with general socialization practices and their relationship to elements of the jealousy complex (e.g., whether withdrawal of love as a punishment leads to denial/avoidance in adult jealousy), but rather with the specific socialization of romantic jealousy. For many societies, an interest in developmental aspects would lead to a concern with media presentations (White, 1985a). In the broader context of lifespan development, additional questions would concern the ways in which elements of the jealousy complex are expected to be modified as a consequence of maturing into older age groups.

SUMMARY

We have attempted to show why the study of romantic jealousy requires understanding of broader cultural contexts. To do so, we have discussed common social and existential dilemmas inherent in jealousy and have reviewed cultural variations in elements of the jealousy complex using our model of jealousy. This review has led us to discuss the difference between threats to self-esteem and threats to social esteem, as well as the difference between threats to social status and threats to self-esteem or the romantic relationship.

Aside from ethnographic reports, only three cross-cultural studies (by Hupka and his colleagues) exist. Despite methodological and conceptual difficulties, they generally support our model of the jealousy complex. We have also discussed five dimensions of the debate over how to conceptualize and study emotions and have presented our position on each with regard to romantic jealousy and our model. We have emphasized our generally constructionist approach, which requires the consideration of cultural meaning of jealousy before the content of the jealousy complex can be understood.

We have then offered some general hypotheses linking cultural-level factors to romantic jealousy, including jealousy as a violation of sexual property norms, as an expression of the alienated self, as a function of the importance of marriage and of the restriction of sex to marriage, as an expression of a society's competitive ethos, as a means of maintaining male dominance, and as a consequence of certain patterns of inheritance. Finally, we have presented some suggestions of areas for future ethnopsychological research on jealousy.

7

Pathological Jealousy and Delusions of Infidelity

> Not only can man's being not be understood without madness,
> it would not be man's being if it did not bear madness within
> itself as the limits of our freedom.
>
> Lacan (1977)

The pathological extensions of jealousy occupy an important though ambiguous position in contemporary psychiatry. A number of terms are in current usage for these disorders, including "pathological jealousy" (Tiggelaar, 1956), "morbid jealousy" (Shepherd, 1961), "the jealousy–paranoic syndrome" (Retterstol, 1967), "the Othello syndrome" (Todd & Dewhurst, 1955), "the erotic jealousy syndrome" (Langfeldt, 1961), and "conjugal paranoia" (Revitch, 1954). The boundaries of these states have been drawn differently by various writers, though all overlap to some extent. "Pathological" and "morbid" are the designations with the broadest connotations and are employed in this chapter as the favored terms.

Pathological jealousy is approached from a number of perspectives to highlight its various aspects. A phenomenological model of the jealousy complex is employed to clarify the borderline between normal and pathological jealousy. Delusions of infidelity, because of their importance, are considered separately. The categories of "reactive" and "symptomatic" jealousy are offered as a basis for providing a clinical perspective on pathological jealousy. This multifaceted approach is incompatible with theoretical precision, but, we hope, not with clarity and clinical utility.

Jealousy, even in its normal variants, can be a furious passion attended by dramatic alterations in the individual's state of mind and behavior. Ordinary and otherwise unremarkable individuals in the grips of jealousy may be prey to experiences that at other times they would consider totally alien to their normal character. Jealousy can make sufferers doubt their own sanity and can evoke similar misgivings in their friends and relatives. The jealousy complex in normal individuals may include well-recognized psychopathological elements. On the other hand, it is no less true that many of the abnormalities of mental state manifested in pathological jealousy are also to be found in normal jealousy (Tiggelaar, 1956).

Given the extreme nature of such jealousies, it may be wondered what constitutes a pathological extension and how it may be recognized. The distinction between normal and pathological jealousy, though ultimately resting on theoretical assumptions, has practical implications for management and treatment. Fortunately, in clinical practice the marginal cases, though of great interest, are far outweighed by those in which the pathological nature is glaringly obvious. This assertion needs illustrating at the outset, particularly for those not familiar with pathological jealousy in its full-fledged form.

A rather shy and sensitive individual who worked as an accountant presented with problems of jealousy. His marriage had not been marred by any major conflict or incompatibilities. He had no previous history of psychiatric disorder, but for some weeks before the eruption of the jealousy he had been troubled by an alteration in his usual mood, with ill-defined perplexity combined with an uncertainty and uncharacteristic suspiciousness of those around him.

One morning at breakfast, he looked across at his wife and suddenly "remembered" an incident that had occurred soon after they were married. This memory was of his wife deep in conversation with a man at the office Christmas party and their subsequent disappearance for some considerable time. He thought he remembered her confusion and inability to explain the extended absence when she returned to the party. Later, when driving to work, he was ruminating on this recollection when he saw a colleague in a red station wagon. It came to him in a flash that this man was the man at the party and that he must have been having an affair with his wife since. This revelation came as a sudden and totally convincing intuition. When questioned later, he claimed that the man's car had, in some obscure manner, been connected to his realizing that its driver was both the man at the party and his wife's lover.

He sat in his car in a state of distress and shock, and during this time everything fell into place for him. He realized that this affair had been going on for years, that everyone at work and in his home neighborhood knew about it, and that this explained their attitude of pity and contempt, which he now recognized for the first time. He also realized that his children lacked any resemblance to him and must, perforce, be the offspring of his wife's lover. He drove home to confront his wife with his newfound knowledge. His wife was puzzled and confused by his accusations, thinking at first he was joking. Her response simply confirmed him in his suspicions. He spent the day in an agony of distress, quite convinced that he now knew the truth and his life was in ruins. Later that afternoon, he attempted to kill himself with a large overdose of analgesics.

When he recovered from the self-poisoning, he remained convinced of his wife's infidelity. He accepted that the color of the man's car was a somewhat bizarre reason for attributing adultery, but he nevertheless insisted he was correct. The memory of his wife at the party had no correspondence with any actual event as far as could be established, and certainly could not have involved the colleague he named. Following a course of treatment that included antipsychotic medication, his convictions about his wife's infidelity receded. Some months later when questioned, he denied ever entertaining such suspicions and dismissed his previous beliefs as absurd, implying that his doctors had misunderstood what he had said.

Another patient began in his 70s to accuse his wife, then in her 80s, of persistent infidelity. He accused her of having relationships with several neighbors, a number of local shopkeepers, and various workmen who passed through the neighborhood. He watched his elderly and physically limited spouse constantly, even resorting to binoculars to follow her movements around the local shopping center. He would almost invariably bang on the door of the lavatory when she went to the toilet, demanding entry and accusing her of having a man in there with her. He claimed that men entered their marital bed at night and had intercourse with her while he lay sleeping beside them. The disparity between the frail old lady and the outlandish behavior attributed to her was gross and bizarre.

These cases are examples of pathological jealousy that most of us would recognize as falling outside of the normal range, however generously the limits of normality are drawn.

THE DISTINCTION OF NORMAL FROM PATHOLOGICAL JEALOUSY

The recognition of pathological states of mind, in jealousy or any other disturbance, does not depend on superfine insight or the trained observer's capacity to see subtle clues and obscure signs invisible to the layperson. Clinical training and experience should broaden our understanding and knowledge of the normal range, and of necessity should narrow what will be regarded as pathological. There is research evidence to support the capacity of adequate clinical training to produce this broadening of acceptance and recognition of the normal range (Copeland, Kelleher, & Smith, with Gourlay, 1975). Those lacking either professional or personal experience are likely to view an honest and straightforward account of jealousy as indicative of major mental disorder. Inexperienced clinicians see pathology in almost every case of jealousy that presents itself, because they are dazzled by the phenomena and sensibly wary of the very real potential for violence.

Pathological jealousy has been regarded as synonymous with delusional jealousy by some authors (Dominik, 1970; Krafft-Ebing, 1905; Todd & Dewhurst, 1955). This has the advantage of focusing on those cases in which the abnormalities of mental state are most florid. In forensic material, where legal as well as psychiatric frames of reference are operative, delusional and pathological jealousy are likely to correspond (Mowat, 1966). There are, however, difficulties with defining pathological jealousy by the presence of delusion. It displaces the problem from defining pathological jealousy to defining delusions of infidelity, which is a formidable problem in its own right. The second objection is that confining the pathology of jealousy to delusional states is too restrictive either for clinical or for heuristic purposes.

Jealousy has been considered pathological in the absence of delusional beliefs when the individual responds with abnormal facility and intensity to situations that appear, however remotely, to put the partner's fidelity in question (Mairet, 1908; Shepherd, 1961). This raises the question of how the abnormal facility and intensity of such pathological jealousy may be recognized.

One approach to this distinction is to contrast the responses of the normal individual with those that are claimed to characterize the pathological individual. Oppenheim (1912) suggested that the abnormal individual searches for jealous conflict, in contrast to the normal person, who has it thrust upon him or her. In addition, the normal person attempts to find a solution to the jealousy, but the pathological individual takes a morbid pleasure in willfully prolonging the suffering. This distinction depends on an appeal to unconscious motivations and to an ability to divine when individuals really mean the opposite of what they say. Jealous individuals, however pathological, do not in our experience proclaim their pleasure in the pangs of jealousy.

Vauhkonen (1968), in his excellent monograph, summarizes the work of Jakobsen on the distinctions between the responses of those normally and those pathologically jealous. The healthy individual expresses jealousy only when there is clear evidence, whereas the morbid person regards even slight signs as conclusive evidence and reacts forcefully. The pathologically jealous do not learn from their mistakes and harbor suspicions against many, whereas the normally jealous do modify their behavior in response to circumstances and focus their jealousy on a single rival. Pathological jealousy is considered to be subject to periodic exacerbations, virtually whatever the external circumstances, whereas the normal person depends on the vicissitudes of the actual relationship. These distinctions have a good deal to recommend them when one is dealing with clear-cut examples. A jealous reaction in a healthy, well-adjusted individual exposed to unequivocal evidence of infidelity can on these criteria usually be distinguished from the responses of someone who periodically accuses all and sundry of flagrant misconduct with his or her partner without real evidence and who persists in these convictions despite overwhelming evidence to the contrary. The problem is that in practice the jealous reactions of normal individuals are often not so reasonable and circumscribed. Equally, pathological jealousy may not be expressed with such convenient flamboyance.

Several distinctions have been suggested by psychoanalysts, based on their views of the genesis of jealousy. Freud (1922/1955) distinguished between normal and pathological jealousy on the basis of the mental mechanisms postulated to underlie the jealousy. He considered what he termed "competitive" jealousy to be universal though not "completely" rational; jealousy that he assumed to be based on projection was viewed as pathological. Kaplan and Sadock (1985), in their influential text on clinical psychiatry, employ a Freudian approach, claiming that the difference between normal and pathological jealousy is similar to that between normal grief and pathological mourning. They argue that the occurrence of pathological jealousy in adult life is related to unresolved early childhood attachments and may involve the projection of unconscious extramarital sexual impulses onto the partner, which emerge clinically as delusions of infidelity. This distinction, based on psychodynamic theory, is not derived from any observable aspects of jealousy, but on assumptions and causal speculations about what brings the jealousy into being. It makes what is already a difficult distinction into a matter for uncheckable and irrefutable assertions based on theoretical preconceptions.

Boranga (1981), drawing on the work of Lagache (1947), states,

> [J]ealousy remains within the bounds of normality as long as it expresses a situation of conflict which the individual is capable of controlling and overcoming in the evolution of their [sic] personality. It becomes pathological when it assumes the characteristics of a personality fixation which is expressed in the amorous relationship by way of a demand for the complete submission of the partner. (p. 48)

This distinction would draw the boundaries of the pathological very widely, and, as Boranga admits, would still leave the borderline between the normal and the pathological vague and indistinct.

That the distinctions between the normal and the pathological jealousy complex are difficult to draw should occasion no surprise, given the variety of phenomena, often experienced with great intensity, that characterize both normal jealousy and its pathological variants.

PATHOLOGY AND THE JEALOUSY COMPLEX

The pathologies of the jealousy complex can be approached descriptively by examining the way in which aspects such as judgments and feelings are disturbed. This enables distinctions between pathological and normal jealousy to be made by examining the separate elements of the jealousy complex for evidence of pathology. Thus, if the judgments on which the jealousy is based are the results of a pathological process—say, delusions—then the jealousy itself is best regarded as pathological. The question of the separation between normal and pathological jealousies can then be resolved by a descriptive analysis of the various aspects of the jealousy complex (i.e., appraisals, affects, and coping efforts).

To divide and make distinctions among aspects and parts of a lived experience involves rending apart what is a continuous process. This becomes clear when, for example, one considers the desire to hurt the partner that is found so often in jealousy. This desire is usually intimately connected with a predisposition to act aggressively and arises out of feelings of anger and humiliation, which in turn are inseparable experientially from the judgment that betrayal has occurred. To describe in a manner that can be generalized involves making distinctions, but those divisions are creatures of convention rather than the reflections of reality. This caveat should be kept in view during the oversimplifications that follow.

The jealous individual's attention is focused on the actual or supposed loved one and the presumed rival. The central object of jealousy is the partner, with the rival usually occupying a subordinate role. That the loved one is the primary object for jealousy becomes obvious when jealous behavior is examined. It is the partner and not the actual or supposed rival who is most frequently accused, checked on, and attacked.

Jealousy emerges in a real situation where the context and the individual's pre-existing states of mind interact to release the emotion. The situation may allow for an obvious connection to be made to the jealousy, as, for example, when the lover is discovered in the intimate embrace of another. The context is, however, often ambiguous and dependent in part on the meaning attributed to it by the jealous individual. The divining of a changed attitude, a subtle alteration in sexual responsiveness, an unexplained absence, a suspicious hair on the lover's clothing—all these are examples of events that may provide the context for the suspicions. When such ambiguity is present, then the emergence of jealousy will depend on an interaction between the events and the individual's predispositions and vulnerability to become suspicious.

Appraisals

Jealous individuals are often not immediately aware that their emotions are dependent on their prior judgments, not only as to their own rights and perogatives, but also, on occasion, on moral and ethical imperatives as these apply to their partners. When we talk with jealous people, the judgments rapidly become overt. They will talk of the betrayal of trust, of their pain and indignation at being deserted, and of the fear of losing love. These and many other complaints of the jealous all depend on such appraisals. Betrayal is only possible when loyalty is due; indignation is justified by an assumption of moral right; and love can only be lost if it is judged to have been possessed. Jealousy involves an objection to loss, and this objection derives from a judgment that one had the other's love to begin with and that the loss of this love is imminent (Ellis, 1977; Neu, 1980; Tellenbach, 1974).

The judgments central to arousing and sustaining jealousy may arise from morbid—that is, pathological—states of mind. Thus, when delusions of infidelity are present, they constitute a criterion for the recognition of pathological jealousy. The judgment of the lover's infidelity may also be considered morbid when it has the characteristics of an obsessional phenomena or an overvalued idea (see later discussion).

Feelings and Affects

The jealous may be wracked by intense affects, which are usually painful and distressing. Empirical studies reviewed in Chapter 2 suggest that anger, fear, sadness, envy, arousal, and guilt are the predominant affects associated with jealousy. Tiggelaar (1956) stated that a central feature of jealousy is a feeling of pain and grief, permeated by a sense of oppression and anxiety. Sadness is present in most experiences of jealousy. The fear of a future that is depleted and empty usually leads to sadness. Sadness may well be muted, because jealousy is a state in which loss is feared rather than accepted, and sadness is likely to predominate in jealousy only when hope is abandoned. Jealousy is primarily a state of excitement and activation that is still directed at the future and at changing that future, rather than a state of passive and sad acceptance.

The feeling of shame is commonly experienced as part of the jealousy complex. This may arise from the feared exposure of personal deficiencies and deviations to the judgment of others, bringing with it a threat to social prestige and reputation. Shame is related to protecting the reputation of one's public persona, but equally is related to preserving important aspects of one's personal life and private relationships (Straus, 1966). Jealousy brings with it a feeling of shame not just because of the exposure of private vulnerabilities, but because of the feared destruction of the development and unfolding of the love relationship.

Anger is nearly always present, if not pre-eminent, in the feelings of jealousy. Jealousy involves anger at the beloved and, as a secondary theme, anger at the rival. Feelings of being humiliated and diminished are frequently expressed in jealousy. There is a sense of losing out to a rival and being exposed as inadequate in the eyes of the world. Self-esteem, or the lack of it, contributes to the subject's vulnerability to the jealousy complex and to the experience of jealousy.

The feelings associated with the jealousy may be morbid in their origins. In depression, for example, the associated feelings of guilt and worthlessness can lead the sufferer to expect (or even to believe he or she deserves) disloyalty and desertion from the lover, and to find such a betrayal whether or not it is actually present. Depression, which is often associated with both feelings of worthlessness and a sense of anger and suspicion, provides a medium in which jealousy may readily develop and grow. The insecurity and inferiority considered by Mead (1931) to be critical to the genesis of jealousy are frequent accompaniments of major depression.

Jealousy may give expression to feelings whose origin is unrelated to the sexual or other activities of the inamorata. The pathology here lies in the displacement of feelings from their actual object onto an unrelated or inappropriate object. Those who are subject to the pain and distress associated with feelings of insufficiency and personal inadequacy may find themselves easy prey to jealousy. Poor self-esteem or blows to an individual's sense of adequacy in one area may be shifted to find expression in the realm of the person's erotic and love relationships (Tiggelaar, 1956).

In one of our cases, the loss of an arm in an industrial accident totally disrupted the patient's self-esteem and ushered in an intense jealousy of his wife. His own feelings of insufficiency and depletion led him to become convinced that his wife's view of him must have changed as dramatically and disastrously as his own self-appraisal. In fact, his wife's attitude to him had not altered significantly. Nevertheless, he no longer felt lovable, so he believed he was no longer loved and must eventually be deserted. The step from this to jealousy was a small one soon taken. Here the feelings generated by a reversal in one sphere of life found expression in the inappropriate guise of jealousy. The jealousy in such situations does not express the reality of the relationship, but the displacement of feelings from unrelated areas. As a result, the displaced feelings cannot be resolved by simply attending to the jealousy or to the relationship itself.

The feelings evoked by the suspicions of infidelity may also be abnormal by virtue of the ease with which they are provoked and by their intensity. Extreme lability of mood and excitability characterize major mental disorders such as mania, and in more muted form may be found in certain unusual personalities. This predisposition to emotional overreaction may occasionally lead to the initiation of the jealousy complex and to abnormally intense feelings in association with the state, once it is established.

Desires

The desires of the jealous may be complex and contradictory, as are so many other aspects of this painful passion. The desire to expose the partner's infidelities (e.g., for confirmation of threat appraisal) jostle for a place alongside the desire to put the jealousy to rest by proving the suspicions groundless. The wish to hurt often coexists with sexual desire, as does a wish to be rid of the troublesome partner with the fear of losing him or her.

Jealousy may be considered pathological when the desires aroused are grossly inappropriate or perverse. Lagache (1947) stated that love usually involves both the desire to dedicate oneself to the lover and, in contrast, the desire to possess and subjugate the beloved. The love that asserts its rights and seeks submission Lagache termed *amour captatif*, and the love that wishes to give itself *amour oblatif*. In practice most love partakes of both types, but Lagache considered that the greater the dominance of *amour captatif*, the greater the tendency to jealousy. In some relationships the desire to control may become the central feature. The individual uses the lover to establish his or her own sense of adequacy and satisfy the will to power. The lover becomes a means to an end and a victim of the domination. Such tyranny in love is doomed to failure and all too often leads to jealousy. The desire for mastery and the will to power are not themselves pathological, but the attempt to satisfy them in the context of a love relationship is grossly misplaced. The jealousy arises from the frustration of displaced desire that cannot find resolution in the concrete reality of the relationship, for its unacknowledged origins and aims lie elsewhere. Hahn (1933) considered such "tyrannical jealousy" to form a separate category of pathological jealousy.

Jealousy offers the opportunity for the expression of both voyeuristic desires and those sadomasochistic desires directed at subjecting the partner to humiliation (see Chapter 8). Here the satisfaction of the perverse sexuality may be the covert agenda that contributes to the jealousy's being sustained or recurring.

Imagination and Fantasy

Imagination and fantasy may play a prominent role in jealous thoughts. The activation and agitation so characteristic of the individual in the grips of jealousy are often manifested in vivid imaginings and fantasies. Tolstoy (1889/1985) describes the power of imagination in jealousy thus:

> I lost all control over my imagination: it began to paint for me, in the most lurid fashion, a rapid sequence of pictures which inflamed my jealousy. . . . They were all of the same thing; of what was

happening there, in my absence, of her being unfaithful to me. I was consumed with rage, indignation and a kind of strange drunken enjoyment of my own hurt pride as I contemplated these pictures. . . . I couldn't tear myself away from them, I couldn't erase them from my mind and I couldn't stop myself dreaming them up. But that wasn't all: the more I contemplated these imaginary pictures, the more I believed they were real. (p. 25)

In this extract, the compulsive quality, the specifically visual nature of the imagery, and the way the imaginings create a compelling view of reality are all highlighted.

In jealousy, the dividing lines between imagination, belief, and the certainty of experienced reality often become vague and ill defined. The fascination of jealousy for the psychopathologist lies in large part in the ease with which otherwise normal individuals in the grip of this passion can generate beliefs in a manner and of a type that would in other circumstances be regarded as clearly delusional.

Behavior

Checking (secondary-appraisal, information-gathering strategy; see Chapter 2) is an almost universal behavior among jealous people. Checking their lovers' accounts of their movements; checking that they are where they say they are and with whom they say; cross-checking, rechecking; checking the mail, checkbook stubs, and credit card returns for payments to restaurants, motels, or florists—life for jealous individuals is an unending task. Nothing is irrelevant. A clue or even final confirmation may be waiting in the next mail delivery, in a husband's coat pocket, in a wife's purse. A jealous patient complained that what she resented most was the sheer waste of time and effort in which her jealousy involved her because of her checking on every aspect of her husband's life. The jealous inspect their lovers' clothes for telltale hairs, undergarments for semen stains, bed linen for the marks of extramarital engagements. The compulsion to check often causes them to feel disgust at their own activities, but nevertheless they find it difficult to resist. Perhaps jealousy's one virtue is that it encourages an interest in all one's partner's activities. Jealousy, like love, focuses intense attention onto the lover.

Inquisitional cross-questioning of a lover by a jealous partner is frequent. It may be a form of information gathering, a form of aggression, and/or a coping method of interfering with the rival relationship. The questioning often involves an attempt to catch the partner out in some inconsistency or outright lie that will expose the hidden truth. Alternatively, the jealous individual will try to obtain an outright confession by various stratagems. Jealous people often claim that the truth would put their minds at rest. Attempts to threaten or cajole admissions from partners are relatively common. Not infrequently, harassed lovers satisfy their jealous partners by admitting or even inventing acts of infidelity. This may produce temporary respite, or sometimes violent reaction. What it practically never does is to satisfy, for no confession is sufficiently full, just as no evidence of innocence can fully convince.

The assumption is occasionally made that the more extreme examples of spying and cross-questioning are to be found only in morbid jealousy. "Normal people just don't behave like that." In clinical practice, we find that some checking and interrogating occurs in most relationships afflicted with jealousy. Otherwise normal and well-balanced individuals will find themselves inspecting their partners' clothing, listening in on their phone conversations, or even following them or turning up unexpectedly where they suspect their erring partners of having an assignation. They are ashamed of such spying and realize how ridiculous it makes them. This inhibits many from disclosing such behavior without sympathetic questioning.

Behaviors on the part of the jealous person that are aimed at attaining reassurance are equally common and may alternate or even coexist with behaviors aimed at exposing the suspected infidelity. The quest for reassurance, like that for the true account of the infidelity, is unending. Such activities can never produce the desired result, for any assurance is inevitably called into question and the repetitive, unvarying demands for further reassurance continue without respite (see the discussion of excuses and justifications in Chapter 5).

The partners of the jealous often ask whether they should continue to provide the reassurances that are incessantly demanded. One wife was asked repeatedly by her husband whether she still loved him and was requested innumerable times each day to hold him, cuddle him, kiss him, and assure him of her continued fidelity and total commitment. If she neglected any minor attention or gesture of affection, such as a kiss at breakfast, an assurance of love over toast, or an avowal of continued devotion prior to leaving for work, then her jealous spouse was thrown into a paroxysm of distress and jealous doubt. Here the wife was occupied for several hours each day in reassuring her husband. As a result, he was rendered pathetically dependent but still doubting, and she was exhausted; any spontaneous affection that might have existed for her husband was buried in the constant professing of undying devotion.

Jealousy, with its associated angry feelings, judgments of betrayal, and destructive fantasies, is all too often involved with behaviors aimed at hurting or harming the lover. This area of the behavior of jealousy is discussed in more detail in the chapter on violence. The behavior in jealousy, on occasion, takes on bizarre and violent forms.

Traditionally, in psychiatry the attribution of pathology has been separated from the characteristics of behavior itself. A diagnosis of mental illness is based not on what people do, but on the mental state that accompanies the actions. There is virtually no human act, however unusual or awful, that cannot be perpetrated by a mentally normal individual. Matricide, for example, is one of the rarest and most shocking of individual acts of violence. Those who kill their mothers are usually mentally ill, but not always. Greed, anger, and viciousness may on occasion be the best available explanation for those who commit such a crime and in whom no significant abnormality of mental state can be discerned. The behavior in jealousy, however extreme, must remain dubious grounds for the attribution of pathology. Behavior is often a good reason for suspecting the presence of pathological jealousy, but the final decision must rest on the state of mind that underlies the activities.

Relationship

Normal jealousy can be regarded as a pathology of relationship. As discussed in Chapter 5, the initiation and progress of jealousy often reflects the nature of the relationship as much as or more than it reflects any actual acts of infidelity. In pathological jealousy the relationship may also play a part. This is true even in delusional jealousy. The delusions may have their necessary cause in an illness such as schizophrenia, or the pharmacological effects of a drug like cocaine, but the reasons why it is infidelity rather than persecution or religiosity that forms the delusional content are usually to be found in the history of the sufferer's relationships. The relationship is where pathology manifests itself in jealousy. Deviant and disturbed relationships may well generate jealousy and are therefore often usefully regarded as part of the pathogenesis of jealousy rather than as signs of the pathology itself.

The exception to this rule is an "erotomanic" relationship, or a relationship that exists only in the mind of one would-be partner. "Erotomania" is used to describe a situation where the patient has a delusional conviction that another is secretly enamored of him or her, though prevented from expressing this love openly, does so through subtle hints and signs comprehensible only to the patient (de Clerambeauit, 1942; Enoch & Trethowen, 1979; Mullen, in press-b). It is a belief in the love the other has for oneself that is central.

Those with erotomanic attachments not infrequently become jealous of the partners of their objects of affection. One of our patients was convinced that her previous psychiatrist was in love with her and that he revealed this passion in such ways as his choice in neckties and the hidden meaning in his questions and comments. For example, she was convinced that behind the inquiries as to her health lay declarations of undying devotion. This lady kept her bags packed and waited nightly for her lover to carry her off to a new life. She suffered intense jealousy of the man's wife and on a number of occasions wrote her vituperative letters.

A young man we encountered had been convicted of a horrific attack on a young woman into whose face he had thrown acid. This man accused the victim of having deserted and betrayed him by taking up with another man. The young lady, however, said that she didn't even know her attacker and had only seen him on a couple of occasions when he had come to the store at which she worked. The man gave a story of having fallen in love with the girl "at first sight," a year previously. He said he regularly waited outside the store where she worked to see her come and go from work. He said that, being a shy and retiring person, he had never had the courage actually to approach her and speak to her. He claimed, however, that she had looked at him on a number of occasions, and he believed she was aware of his interest (if not the extent of his love). A week before the attack, the young woman was picked up by her boyfriend from work. The watching would-be lover was devastated by this. He felt that the young woman had knowingly betrayed him and was flaunting her infidelity before him. Here no relationship existed except in the hopes and dreams of the hidden admirer; nevertheless, jealousy emerged and with it dreadful violence. Taylor, Mahendra, and Gunn (1983), in their study of erotomania, have documented the frequency with which this delusional disorder may be associated with criminal violence, not infrequently because of the emergence of jealousy as part of the erotomanic state.

Jealousy may also create pathology in the other partner or may interact with existing psychopathology (Turbott, 1981). The effects of being the object of jealousy can include the development of emotional and psychological problems that can become disabling in their own right. Depressive and anxiety disorders may occur in those subjected by their partners to jealousy. A number of our cases were only recognized following suicide attempts by their distraught partners. The beloved may increasingly limit their own activities to pander to their partners' jealousy. They are then at risk of becoming isolated and housebound. Hafner (1979) has described the coexistence of morbid jealousy and agoraphobia in the partner. In one of our own cases referred for treatment of agoraphobia, it emerged that the husband's jealousy was the prime reason for the patient's remaining confined to the house. She feared that any attempt to go out in public unaccompanied would initiate another round of questioning, accusations, and abuse.

The consideration of the various elements in the jealousy complex allows a structured approach to the question of pathology to be developed. In practice, most cases show a number of morbid features. The initial disorder may, for example, start in a depressive mood disorder, but may develop to produce disturbances in most of the other elements of the complex. The model does, however, allow for a systematic approach to the pathological extensions of jealousy, albeit somewhat simplified.

DELUSIONS OF INFIDELITY

One of the fascinations of pathological jealousy for academic psychiatry is that it provides a critical test for theoretical and practical attempts to distinguish the morbid state of mind called "delusion" from extreme variants of the normal range of beliefs. The question of the relationship among jealousy, pathological jealousy, and delusional jealousy confronts us with the general problem of the genesis and structure of delusions (Tiggelaar, 1956).

Delusions may occur as persistent or ephemeral phenomena in any major mental disorder and can emerge in a wide variety of conditions that disrupt brain function. Delusions of infidelity, as a result, are found across the full range of major mental disorders and psychosyndromes arising in organic brain disorders. The specific features of delusional jealousy in the context of these various conditions are discussed later under the heading of "Symptomatic Jealousy." Delusions of infidelity may also emerge in the context of the reactions of individuals rendered vulnerable by personality deviation or disorders of mental state such as depression.

Delusions have traditionally been regarded as a defining feature of mental illness—as "the mad thoughts that madmen think" (Maudsley, 1867). Even in antiquity, delusions were seen as synonymous with mental illness. Socrates is said to have declared, "[D]on't think a slight error implies madness for just as they call strong desire love, so they name a great delusion madness" (Xenophon, ca. 380 B.C./1923).

Krafft-Ebing (1905) distinguished two types of delusion in pathological jealousy. The first was a delusion of infidelity, when the lawful wife was believed to be deceiving the patient; the second was a delusion of jealousy, if it was merely a mistress who was suspected. This extension of moral judgment and civil status into the furthest reaches of psychopathology is only of historic interest. The use of the term "delusion of infidelity" is, however, to be preferred to "delusion of jealousy," as the abnormal belief is about supposed infidelity (Shepherd, 1961).

Jealousy puts in question the very possibility of distinguishing the normal from the pathological state of mind by objective criteria rather than by the arbitrary application of socially sanctioned limits. Thomas Szasz is an exponent of the view that mental illness is a myth and that features such as delusions arise from the arbitrary labeling of nonconformist beliefs by institutional psychiatry. Szasz (1960) claims that calling something a mental symptom "involves rendering a judgment which entails a covert comparison, or matching of the patients' ideas, concepts or beliefs with those of the observer and the society in which they live" (p. 114).

Psychiatrists have on occasion attempted to avoid the social relativism attributed to psychiatry by such commentators by claiming that abnormalities such as delusion are defined not by the content of the phenomenon but by its form. It is not a delusion because of what a person believes and whether that belief is true or false, but because of the form of the mental experience that is associated with the expression of this particular belief.

The content of delusional beliefs is often fantastic, or at the very least inherently unlikely. The characteristics of the form usually attributable to delusional experiences have been summarized by Mullen (1985) as follows:

1. They are held with absolute conviction and are experienced as self-evident reality, not merely as opinions or beliefs.
2. They are not amenable to reason or modifiable by experience.
3. They are experienced as of great personal significance.
4. They consist of convictions that are highly personal and idiosyncratic, and that are not likely to be shared even by those of a similar social and cultural background.

To these criteria may be added the following:

5. The beliefs often emerge in a manner that cannot be understood by others, and the connections between the supposed

foundations and the emergent belief may be incomprehensible to all except the deluded individual.

6. The beliefs extend to explain wide areas of the patient's experience, becoming a source of new and idiosyncratic knowledge. The delusion becomes the central organizing factor around which the patient understands his or her personal existence and the world in general.

The utility and potential limitation of these factors as the defining characteristics of delusion can be exemplified by an examination of jealousy and delusions of infidelity:

1. Jealousy in an otherwise normal individual may carry with it an absolute conviction of the infidelity of the partner. The jealous subject may well present the accusations of infidelity as accomplished facts, though to an outsider this overriding conviction may appear to be based on the flimsiest of evidence. In deluded subjects the convictions are often presented not only as self-evident realities, but with a vehemence and contempt for any quibble or contradiction offered by others; this sets them apart from the normal in degree if not in kind.

2. The beliefs in normal jealousy may not be amenable to reason and are often far from being modifiable by experience. The jealous can reinterpret almost any occurrence to confirm their suspicions. In normal jealousy, for some of the time the self-evident truth of the betrayal dominates the experience, alternating at other times with genuine doubt about the extent of the infidelity. In normal jealousy, an absolute conviction about the partner's infidelity may apparently coexist with a desire to be proved wrong or a wish to dismiss the conviction as a product of jealousy rather than a product of the partner's actual behavior. This double bookkeeping, in which two apparently incompatible world views alternate and even coexist, is also found in many deluded subjects, who both proclaim their total conviction in their ideas and simultaneously accept that they are mentally ill and that those very convictions arise from that illness.

A number of writers have considered the truth or falsity of jealous individuals' accusations against their partners as the touchstone by which pathological jealousy can be recognized. (In so doing, they justify the criticisms leveled at psychiatry by Szasz and others.) This, in cases of delusional jealousy, makes the definition of delusion dependent on its content rather than its form and leaves the clinician with the problem of deciding what, if any, justification there is for .

the suspicions. Retterstol (1967) has argued that the line between normal and pathological jealousy should be drawn on the basis of the "actual facts" and the patient's lack of amenability to reason. Hoaken (1976) has suggested that when there is no actual provocation, then the jealousy is morbid or pathological; this again implies a distinction based on the actual facts of the partner's behavior.

The first problem with using the correctness of the jealous individual's accusation as a criterion either for the pathology of the jealousy or the presence of the delusion of infidelity is that the "actual facts" may be just as obscure to the clinician as they are to the patient. Odegaard (1968) noted the frequency with which the spouses of patients who separated, on his advice, from their pathologically jealous partners subsequently became sexually involved with or married the subjects of their ex-spouses' "delusions." In one of our cases, the patient had repeatedly accused her husband of having an affair with her best friend. He, in response, had repeatedly denied any connection to this woman. She took to questioning him repeatedly, checking up on him, and searching for clues in the most obscure places. When at the husband's insistence they came for help, she could only advance as evidence of infidelity a change in his manner toward her, an alteration in his sexual technique, and an intuition about her husband's relationship to this friend. The husband expressed amazement at her accusations and, when interviewed, totally denied any validity to the charges. The couple agreed on treatment and considerable progress was made. They were discharged some months later, with the jealousy in abeyance and the wife expressing considerable gratitude for the help she had had to overcome what she termed her "delusions." Three months later, the wife came back to the clinic in a distressed state: The husband had left with the best friend, revealing that they had indeed been having an affair the whole time.

The other problem with using the truth or falsity of the beliefs as a defining characteristic is that patients may believe that their partners are having affairs for bizarre and extraordinary reasons. Nevertheless, they may be correct in their central hypothesis about the partners' extramural activities (Mullen & Maack, 1985). Jaspers (1946/1963) noted that a delusion may be correct in content without ceasing to be a delusion and that such correctness is most frequently seen in the delusions of jealousy. This is a difficult concept to grasp, because it goes against the common usage of the word "delusion" to designate an error or false belief. It can only be clarified by an example of a case in which delusional beliefs partook of the truth.

A patient of ours with a schizophrenic illness realized for the first time that his wife was unfaithful when he noticed that the lights on a Christmas tree in his home were flashing on and off in synchrony with the lights on a tree placed in the window of a neighboring house. He regarded this correspondence in the flashing lights as incontrovertible proof of his wife's having had a long-standing affair with the neighbor. There are many reasons for attributing adultery to one's partner—some may be cynical enough to do so on the grounds of statistical probability—but when it comes to Christmas tree lights this particular reason is incomprehensible in the sense that it is impossible to understand the connection between the event and the knowledge derived from it. There is little doubt about the morbid nature of this man's experience, which is known technically as a "primary delusional experience" (Schneider, 1959). The man's belief arose therefore from a delusional experience, but in fact his suspicions about the wife's relationship to the neighbor were substantially correct. Here, then, we have the situation of a delusional belief with an essentially correct content. Jealousy in normal individuals may arise from false accusations and erroneous judgments. Baseless jealousy should not be viewed as necessarily delusional jealousy, and correct accusations may arise from delusional beliefs. The truth or falsity of the beliefs about the partner's infidelity therefore forms an unreliable basis for a distinction between pathological and normal jealousy and does not help clarify whether a delusion of infidelity is present. What is of some assistance is the deluded subject's capacity to ignore all contrary evidence and argument and to reinterpret events that appear entirely innocent as incontrovertible proofs of infidelity.

3. Jealousy is usually experienced as of great and often overriding personal significance. The feared loss often strikes at the very core of the jealous individual's existence. In these aspects, the experiences of normal and pathological jealousy appear quite similar.

4. The idiosyncratic nature of the beliefs and their incongruity with the views of those from a similar social and cultural background are often employed as defining features of delusion. They may be of considerable practical value in recognizing delusion, and, even more importantly, in excluding delusion where the beliefs (however bizarre they may seem to the clinician) do in fact reflect the views of the individual's cultural environment (Kraupl Taylor, 1979). In jealousy these criteria are of little value, given the ubiquitous nature of jealousy and the popularity of infidelity in most social and cultural backgrounds. Viewed from a theoretical perspective, incongruity

with social and cultural norms is always shaky ground for the definition of delusion.

5. The way in which the ideas emerge and the reasons for continuing to hold the beliefs are often of central importance in recognizing delusional thinking. The jealousy is likely to be delusional in a person whose partner's infidelity is conclusively revealed by lights on a festive tree, or in one (like another of our patients) whose belief in the continuing adultery of his wife was repeatedly confirmed by the order of the numbers on tax codings sent to his office by the income tax office. Delusion is recognizable when the emergence of the conviction is clearly bizarre and beyond understanding, and the evidence adduced is idiosyncratic and outside of all usual rules of logic and correspondence.

Jealousy involves judgments about the fidelity of the partner that in an otherwise normal individual may arise from interpretations of subtle changes in the lover's behavior and manner; these, though convincing to the individual, may be difficult to explain to an outsider. A jealous individual may divine evidence of the alienation of the partner's affections from nuances of their interaction that would be invisible except to the eye of love. The suspicious lover may well be correct in his or her interpretation of these tenuous and refined changes in the relationship; equally, the lover may be totally mistaken. This divination of infidelity, right or wrong, is not of itself evidence of delusion—or if it is, then most jealous individuals fall into delusion at some time during the progress of the passion.

6. Delusions in major mental disorders have a tendency to spread to contaminate wide areas of patients' beliefs and experience of the world. Delusion usually brings with it an extensive change in the sufferers' world view. Their horizons fundamentally alter. Thus, in typical persecutory delusions, the patients not only believe themselves to be the victims of the nefarious activities of the supposed persecutors, but they see evidence for the malevolent machinations in a vast variety of trivial and mundane occurrences and in events both personal and apparently unrelated. Thus the color of the cars in the street, the latest presidential speech, the way the man sitting across the aisle crosses his legs, and the advertisement on television all carry intense personal meaning referable to the central persecutory idea.

In addition to such interpretations, the delusion may spread to affect the sufferers' judgments and beliefs about wide areas of their lives. This extension is an important dimension of the delusional experience (Kendler, Glazer, & Morganstern, 1983). In delusions of infidelity, this extension can occur, and the patients' jealousy becomes the starting point for a spreading system of delusional beliefs and misinterpretations. Persecutory beliefs are the most common, with convictions that the errant lovers are poisoning the patients or that the supposed rivals are orchestrating their constant harassment. Hypochondriacal preoccupations with bodily decay and disintegration may also occur in association with delusions of infidelity, and perhaps represent a morbid extension of the worries about aging and loss of attractiveness that occur in normal jealousy. The pathological nature of the jealousy is readily apparent in cases where the central belief in the partners' infidelity has been elaborated and extended to encompass a generalized persecution or other bizarre beliefs and interpretations. These extensions are, however, the exception rather than the rule in pathological jealousy.

The deluded individual does harbor morbid beliefs, but suspicion and doubt are what dominate his or her state of mind, rather than the comfortable certainty of conviction. Delusions usually emerge from doubts and suspicions centered on the actions and motivations of other people. The delusional system may initially resolve the patient's uncertainty, but in time becomes a source of fresh suspicion. The jealous and the deluded share a world of suspicion and distrust in which they constantly examine and interpret the actions of other people for confirmation of their fears.

Between delusion proper and the errors and mistaken beliefs of us all is sometimes inserted a type of belief about the world termed the "overvalued idea." An overvalued idea can be defined as a solitary belief that comes to have enormous personal significance and in which there is intense emotional investment (Fish, 1967; Mullen, 1985). These beliefs are generally associated with an abnormal personality and grow in a comprehensible manner out of adverse experience (McKenna, 1984). There are convictions, particularly in the area of religion and politics, that in normal individuals may be invested with great significance and become the focus of considerable emotion. Overvalued ideas are very similar to such beliefs, but are idiosyncratic and isolating in that they concern mundane and personal matters and are usually demonstrably false, at least to others if not the believer. Jaspers (1946/1963) considered overvalued ideas to merge into delusion-like ideas, though they were usually distinguishable by their comprehensible development from the interaction between the personality and environmental stresses. Jaspers noted that belief in a partner's infidelity may have the characteristics of an overvalued idea, and McKenna (1984) has gone so far as to attempt to reformulate the core syndrome of morbid jealousy in terms of an overvalued idea. In our opinion, the concept of overvalued ideas, far from clarifying the difficulties, adds to the problems of distinguishing normal jealousy from its morbid variants. The problems of a falsity criterion have been discussed; once this is removed, little remains to distinguish an overvalued idea from the jealousy of the commonality.

The foregoing discussion illustrates the difficulty in producing a phenomenological description of delusions of infidelity that will provide a clear and simple distinction between the beliefs common in normal jealousy and the delusions of pathological jealousy. No single factor can be relied upon as a foolproof guide. In practice, many cases create little problem, given the bizarre nature of the beliefs and the history of their emergence and extension. In some situations, however, it is impossible for a clinician to be certain whether he or she is dealing with a delusional phenomenon or a flamboyant expression of normal jealousy. In situations where doubt exists, the presumption of normality should always be made.

PREVIOUS CLASSIFICATIONS
OF PATHOLOGICAL JEALOUSY

Defining the boundaries of pathological jealousy is a problem. The protean manifestations of jealousy, and its complex interaction with a wide range of mental disorders, frustrate attempts to provide a simple and consistent classification. In practice, most of the substantial attempts at classifying pathological jealousy employ a mixture of descriptive, clinical, and causal elements, resulting in overlapping categories that can produce as much confusion as enlightenment.

Mairet (1908) proposed one of the first classifications of jealousy, postulating four basic variants. He recognized a "normal" or "physiological" jealousy involving the understandable reaction to an actual threat to the relationship. He termed an excessive reaction, one that is out of proportion to the actual or implied threat to the relationship, "hyperesthetic" jealousy. This jealousy of the hypersensitive, he believed, often runs a course marked by remissions and exacerbations. Delusional developments were thought to emerge on occasion out of hyperesthetic jealousy. Mairet continued to apply Esquirol's (1838/1976) concept of "monomania" to a group of pathological jealousies marked by delusions of infidelity without other abnormalities of mental state. Mairet recognized that in some cases of monodelusional jealousy the delusions may extend to involve ideas of a more generalized persecution. Mairet's fourth category was one in which delusions of infidelity form one part of a generalized and florid psychiatric state, usually with hallucinations and delusions of persecution, and frequently in the context of obvious affective disturbance of a depressive or manic variety. Mairet's classification used a mixture of casual, descriptive, and clinical categories that does justice to the complexity of pathological jealousy, even if not to the reader's desire for clarity.

Jaspers (1910), in a classic paper, used morbid jealousy to illustrate his views on the distinction between process and development in mental disorders. The essence of developmental jealousy is that it is understandable as an extension of the habitual manner in which an individual reacts to and elaborates his or her experiences. For all its pathology, it remains part of the individual's human destiny. The problem with making any such judgment is that we rarely know other human beings, and certainly not our patients, in the degree of detail required to establish such a distinction. We know only about particular aspects of another person; the whole person escapes us. When apparent changes occur in patients, these may reflect not something new, but the revelation of aspects of them previously hidden from us. The recognition of developmental jealousy in practice relies almost as much on the absence of evidence for any new process in the form of mental disorder that can account for change as it does on a positive understanding of how the jealousy arises from pre-existing tendencies and traits.

A process can include a variety of major mental disorders and physical illnesses that, by disrupting the functioning of the brain, cause disturbances in the mental life. When something such as schizophrenia or mania is termed a "process," the assumption is made that it represents, at least in part, a disruption of the biological basis for mind and behavior. A process starts at a definable point in time. It arises without an adequate precipitation to explain its emergence and has a course with a dynamic and an autonomy of its own. The emergence of a process, rooted in biological change and dysfunction, leads to a break in the normal development of personality and mental life. The process, having an autonomy of its own, compromises the autonomy of the sufferer. In mania, for example, as the disorder runs its course, the patient can do little to control or guide the profound alterations that are wrought in his or her state of mind. The patient's choices become limited and, to an extent, determined by the disease process. A number of examples of jealousy emerging as part of a process are given later in the section devoted to symptomatic jealousies.

A third way in which jealousy can be conceptualized is as a reaction (Jaspers, 1946/1963; Lagache, 1947). A reaction follows a genuine precipitating factor that can be related in time to the jealousy's emergence. There is an understandable relationship between the content of the experience and that of the abnormal jealous reaction. Finally, the course of the jealousy is tied to the evolution of the precipitating factor.

This division into development, process, and reaction had a profound influence on European psychiatry far beyond the discourse on pathological jealousy. The categories should be regarded as ideal models, not mutually exclusive descriptions of clinical reality. Jaspers' (1910) original clinical examples make clear the extent of overlap among the categories. Unfortunately, this flexibility and recognition of the interactive potential of the model have not always been apparent in the subsequent use of the concepts.

The classification of jealousy proposed by Jaspers was used by Lagache (1947) as the basis for his own extensive work on jealousy. He further elucidated Jaspers' model within the light of his own theoretical preconceptions, but left the basic structure unchanged. Ey (1950) also used Jaspers' classification with minor modifications as the basis for his contribution to the literature on pathological jealousy.

Shepherd (1961), though not committing himself to a classification as such, made clear in the text of his classic paper, and even more clearly in his wealth of case histories, that he regarded pathological jealousy predominantly as a symptom of disorder rather than as a disorder or phenomenon in and of itself. Shepherd noted that "between the extremes of a florid delusional state and a morbid readiness to react in a jealous fashion, there must be inserted a universe of clinical variants" (1961, p. 691). He further suggested that a number of general factors entered into the features of every case. These included the following:

- The nature of associated clinical conditions
- The patient's personality structure
- The age and sex of the patient
- The nature of the relationship
- The phasic tendency and reactive potential of the jealousy

A number of attempts have been made to develop simpler classifications of pathological jealousy. Mooney (1965) proposed a division into "excessive," "obsessive," and "delusional." Cobb (1979) suggested that for simplicity, jealousy could be divided into "neurotic" and "psychotic" types. Such divisions are difficult to apply in practice. The jealousy that may arise under stress in a neurotic individual with, say, a paranoid or sensitive personality can include delusions of infidelity, just as the jealousy emerging in someone with a schizophrenic disorder may have all the hallmarks of a jealous reaction without delusional (psychotic) development.

The classifications of Jaspers (1910) and Lagache (1947) categorize pathological jealousy as (1) reactions, (2) a result of personality development, and (3) a phenomenon associated with organic and functional processes. The categories of reaction and development overlap and can be combined with little loss of discrimination, and perhaps some gains in clarity. The jealousies arising from processes may all be subsumed under the label of "symptomatic." This process of bowdlerization allows a division of pathological jealousy into the two broad, and to some extent overlapping, categories of "reactive" and "symptomatic."

PROPOSED CLASSIFICATIONS OF JEALOUSY: NORMAL, PATHOLOGICALLY REACTIVE, OR SYMPTOMATIC

With the above historical precedents in mind, we suggest a threefold classification of jealousy as normal, pathologically reactive, or symptomatic. Figure 7.1 presents a simplified decision tree for making the assessment of type of jealousy using our scheme. In Chapter 9, we discuss issues of differential treatment based on this assessment. We have already discussed the differentiation of normal from pathological jealousy. The sections that follow focus on further specification of pathologically reactive jealousy and symptomatic jealousy. We review clinical diagnoses and symptom patterns that are likely to be related to pathologically reactive and symptomatic jealousies but unlikely to be encountered as part of the clinical picture in normal jealousy.

Reactive Jealousy

Normal jealousy is reactive in the sense that it is a response to an actual or suspected infidelity. Pathological jealousy can be reactive in exactly the same manner. The provocations giving rise to pathological jealousy may in no way differ from those that result in normal jealousy, but the distinction lies in the nature of the reaction and its relationship to the initiating events.

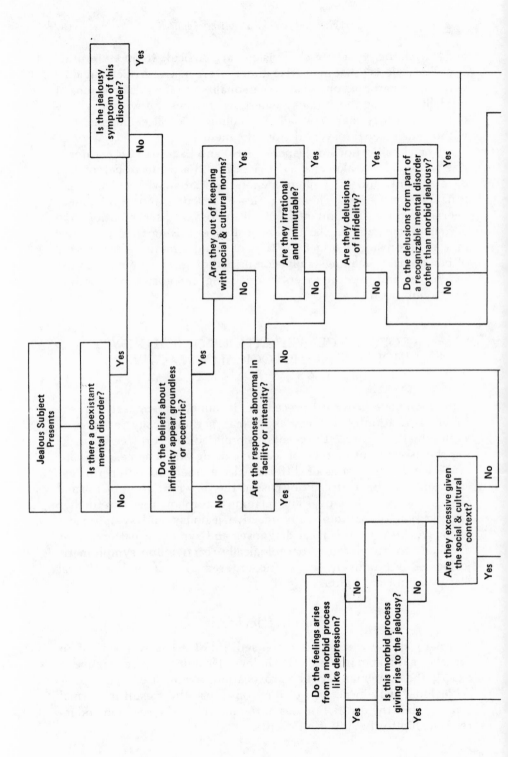

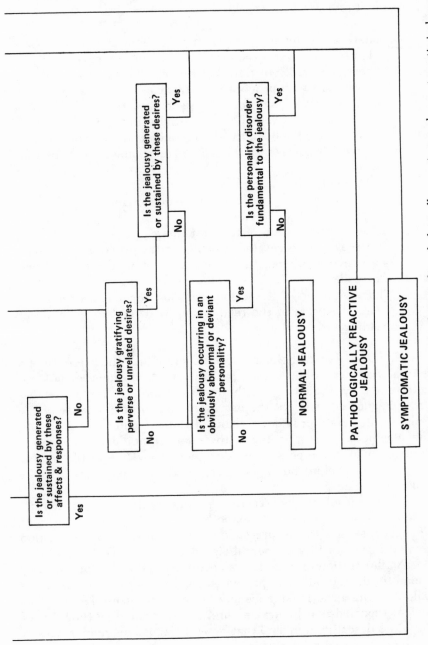

FIGURE 7.1. A simplified decision-tree for the assessment of normal, pathologically reactive, and symptomatic jealousy.

Jealousies that are pathologically reactive share the following characteristics:

1. There is a provoking event that can be understandably related to fears about the partner's past or future infidelity.
2. There is a predisposition that renders the subject unusually sensitive to such provocations; this can be either:
   a. A deviation from normal personality structure. This can be in the direction of oversensitivity and poor self-esteem, or, alternatively, in the direction of a superficially aggressive self-confidence that covers unacknowledged vulnerability.
   b. A mental disorder.
   c. A previous experience of desertion or infidelity that has sensitized the individual.
   d. Any combination of the first three.
3. There is an exaggerated response to the provocation, and an excessive ensuing disturbance in state of mind and behavioral turmoil.
4. The evolution of the jealous reaction depends on the situation or aspects of the relationship that tend to maintain or reinforce the jealousy.

The course of pathological reactions to which the presence of a mental disorder predisposes a patient will be influenced, but not determined by, the course of the mental disorder. The mental disorder in such cases is not the necessary and sufficient cause of the jealousy; it merely provides a changed state of mind that increases the likelihood of responding with jealousy should a provocation occur. Similarly, the personality deviations provide a fertile soil for jealousy to develop, but a provocation is still necessary for the jealousy to emerge.

Thus pathologically reactive jealousy differs from normal jealousy, which is itself reactive, both in the facility and intensity of the response and in the presence of an underlying predisposition created by personality or mental disorder.

An illustration of pathologically reactive jealousy is provided by a man in his mid-30s who presented for help with overcoming his jealousy, which was making his marital relationship intolerable. This patient reported that his waking life was dominated by thoughts of his wife's deserting him, and that he was plagued by vivid images of her having sexual relationships with other men. He was in danger of losing his job because his work was disrupted by his ruminations and by frequent absences during which he would rush home to check that his wife was alone. The wife was confined to the house, literally locked in, and fearful of saying or doing anything that would provoke another paroxysm of jealousy. He accepted in the interview that his suspicions were, at the very least, exaggerated and probably totally groundless, but he added that he probably would not retain that insight the next day at work.

This man had grown up in impoverished circumstances, the only son of a single mother who lavished all her attention on him. He was of above-average intelligence, but had had minimal formal education as a result of frequent absences and poor local schooling. He remained very sensitive about this educational deficit; despite this, he had been successful as a salesman. His personality was superficially outgoing and aggressive, but with an underlying sense of personal and social inferiority. He had an exquisitely developed sense of his own rights and prerogatives, though not of his responsibilities. This engendered frequent conflict, which usually left him feeling he had been denied his entitlements. He had been married for the first time in his mid-20s to a 17-year-old. He talked in an animated fashion of how beautiful she was, even producing a photograph from his wallet during the interview. This marriage had ended in less than a year when she left him for another man. He claimed to have had no warning of her leaving, denied any problems prior to the desertion, and specifically denied any jealousy on his part. Following this, he had been despondent, isolated himself, and drank to excess. He had only recovered after meeting his present wife some 4 years later. The second marriage seemed to be successful for the first few years. He curbed his drinking and returned to a successful career in sales.

The problems with jealousy had commenced suddenly a few months previously. His wife was working as a secretary and was in the habit of getting a lift home with her boss in his car. Her husband had returned early from his work and seen them together in the car. He had not mentioned this to his wife initially, but had ruminated at length on the incident. He began following his wife, checking on her at work, and trying to question her surreptitiously about her relationship to this man. Finally he confronted her and accused her of infidelity. In the extended argument that followed, she denied his specific accusations, but was induced to reveal a degree of closeness and sexual attraction to her boss. He demanded she leave the job; she refused. The next day she returned from work to find her husband unconscious on the bed, having overdosed and left a note accusing her. He required only brief hospitalization. From this time forward, she gave up her job and attempted to comply with the husband's demands to avoid all possible temptation. He took the view that if she worked or even left the house unaccompanied, she might fall prey to an adulterous urge. She became a prisoner. This did not assuage his doubts or jealousy, which continued and increasingly disrupted his own life.

This case illustrates a number of features of a pathologically reactive jealousy. There was a provocation that could justify some suspicion, though not the extreme response. The man's character structure left him vulnerable to any threat to self-esteem or potential desertion. The experience of his first wife's leaving him had also left a specific sensitivity to potential infidelity. The ensuing jealous reaction had been grossly exaggerated and disruptive. The failure of the jealousy to resolve itself, despite the second wife's compliance to a regimen of virtual solitary confinement, is of interest. The wife was herself a person with fragile self-esteem and very considerable dependency needs. She was as frightened of losing her husband as he was of losing her. She was not blessed by obvious good looks and had always felt second-best to the beautiful first wife. The husband's jealousy had been gratifying to her vanity and increased her sense of security. It became clear in treatment that she had contributed to some extent to the maintenance of his jealousy by ambiguous responses and vague hints of hidden secrets. She was in fact flattered initially by the attention and passion, but soon found herself literally trapped in a situation from which she could not escape.

The previous experience of infidelity was critical in this case example. This is the most frequent type of sensitizing experience in our case material. Docherty and Ellis (1976) have suggested that the witnessing of maternal extramarital relations by adolescents may be a specific etiological factor for the development of later pathological jealousy. They believe that it may not be necessary actually to see the act; strong fantasies of maternal infidelity by a seductive or flirtatious parent may be effective causes. No examples of this have appeared in our case material.

The most common disturbance of mental state that predisposes individuals to a jealous reaction is a depressed mood. In depression there is a lowering of self-esteem, often combined with an increase in sensitivity to rejection. The loss of libido and reduced sexual performance that are ubiquitous in both major depressions and dysthymic disorders can also feed into fears that a partner will seek satisfaction elsewhere. The depressed individual is thus rendered peculiarly vulnerable to a pathological jealous reaction.

The relationship of personality traits to the disposition to develop the jealousy complex is discussed in Chapter 5. It has been difficult to empirically verify the relationship between pre-existing character traits and the emergence of jealousy in normal subjects. Even self-esteem, which appears so critical in clinical practice, has not been clearly associated with jealousy in the studies to date. An association between pathological jealous reactions and personality disorders has frequently been asserted, though never systematically demonstrated.

A number of personality deviations or disorders have been claimed to predispose the development of morbid jealousy. The recent revision of DSM-III (DSM-III-R) notes that morbid jealousy may develop in those with so-called Paranoid Personality Disorders. This syndrome is said to include suspiciousness, mistrust, hypersensitivity to offense, and a restricted cold affectivity. Vauhkonen (1968) presented several case histories of the pathologically jealous and noted the frequency of what he referred to as "sensitive" and "narcissistic" characters. The sensitive characters correspond to the Kretschmers' (E. Kretschmer 1918/1952; W. Kretschmer, 1974) "sensitive" personality type. These are individuals with a delicate emotional life, who combine deeply felt sensibilities with a touchy, self-willed arrogance. The latter feature is rarely apparent except on close acquaintance. These individuals are quick to take offense and painfully aware of their vulnerabilities. The narcissistic characters correspond to the Kretschmers' "sthenic" type, who have an overt self-confidence with an expansive manner and domineering approach, but their toleration of frustration is low and their actual self-esteem is precarious. Vauhkonen believed that narcissistic characters need to regard their spouses as worthless and unfaithful so as to inflate their own vulnerable self-esteem.

Pathological jealousy may emerge on the basis of an interaction between a deviant personality and the experience of a threat to the relationship. The description of personalities vulnerable to such developments frequently include oversensitivity to threat or offense, a superficial arrogance covering a consciousness of personal vulnerability, and a lack either of personal warmth or of appropriate emotional expressiveness. The pathological element in these jealousies is introduced both by the morbid predispositions and by the exaggerated response. In practice, it is the disparity between the provoking event and the individual's response that usually raises the question of a pathological reaction. The recognition of an abnormal response has been discussed earlier under the heading of "Pathology and the Jealousy Complex." The extent to which the evolution of the reaction depends on the situation that evoked it is often difficult to be certain of, as the emergence of the jealousy changes the relationship from which it arose. The presence of a pathological jealousy produces alterations in both of the protagonists and in their interaction. The progress of the jealousy is often related as much to these alterations and adjustments as it is to the original provocation.

Pathologically reactive jealousy may be accompanied by delusions of infidelity. In such cases the suspicions give way to delusional convictions about the partner's infidelity. The concept of a psychotic reaction or psychogenic psychosis, though long established, remains somewhat contentious, particularly among American and British psychiatrists (Faergemann, 1963). Wimmer (1916, cited in Faergemann, 1963) stated that psychogenic psychoses are a group of clinically independent psychoses that are caused by psychic traumatization in individuals with a psychopathic predisposition. In the area of jealousy, this implies that pathological jealousy characterized by delusions of infidelity may on occasion be caused by the impact on a vulnerable personality of a situation or conflict that puts the partner's fidelity in question. The psychogenic or reactive psychosis has the characteristics of reaction already described; delusions are the excessive response to the provoking state of affairs. It may be that delusional developments only occur in those with some innate predisposition, but this could equally be claimed about any reaction, whatever its form.

Jaspers (1963) suggested that in a true delusional reaction we are able to understand (1) the intensity of the provoking experience as sufficient to explain the patient's breakdown; (2) the purpose of the psychosis in furthering the interests of the patient; and (3) the content of the psychosis in terms of the provocation. In assessing reactive delusions of infidelity, the third criterion can usually be met, but the first two may present problems. The provocation may be intensely traumatic for the jealous individual, but appear trivial when recounted to an observer. Equally, the benefits of delusional jealousy to the sufferer, or to the romantic relationship, can be difficult to discern (this contrasts with reactive prison psychosis, where the secondary gain is usually obvious). Jaspers' attempts at theoretical clarity does not translate well into the clinical realities. Paykel (1982) has commented that the first criterion seems irrelevant, the second asks too much, and the third is untestable. Lewis (1934) gave his opinion that not a single patient was likely to fulfill all the criteria.

Delusions of infidelity do seem to occur in both reactive and symptomatic jealousy, and our theoretical structure had better reflect this rather than attempt to make the clinical realities conform to the dictates of theory (see Figure 7.1).

Symptomatic Jealousy

Jealousy may form part of the clinical picture in a wide variety of psychiatric disorders. Jealousy can be considered as symptomatic when its occurrence is dependent on the presence of a mental disorder, and the jealousy is a manifestation of this underlying pathology. The course of jealousy in this situation is intimately linked to the progress of the disorder that was its necessary, if not sufficient, cause. The jealousy will usually form a part of a wider syndrome and will be manifested alongside, and entwined with, the other disturbances specific to the initiating disorder.

Symptomatic jealousy is characterized by the following:

1. An underlying process, usually in the form of a mental disorder such as schizophrenia or an organic psychosis, that developed prior to or simultaneously with the jealousy.
2. A course and evolution that can reasonably be related, in large part, to the progress of the underlying disorder.
3. The presence of the clinical features of the underlying process that occur alongside the jealousy.
4. The absence of any provocation that could reasonably be related to fears of infidelity.

The jealousy may reflect characterological traits in the sufferer that predated the onset of the mental disorder, and equally may give expression to very real and often long-standing vulnerabilities and tensions in the patient's relationships. When symptomatic, the jealousy does not emerge as a reaction but is triggered by the underlying mental disorder, and its course is linked to this pathogenesis. The personality and developmental history may account for why the mental disorder has focused on fears of infidelity rather than persecutory or grandiose ideas, but it is the underlying process that accounts for the disorders of mental state of which the jealousy is a part.

There is considerable overlap between symptomatic and reactive jealousies. In the reactive jealousy model, primacy is given to the jealousy complex, with, for example, the pre-existing personality disorder providing the framework for the emergence of the jealousy, and the relationship and external events determining the progress and resolution. In the symptomatic conceptualization, the mental disorder has primacy, providing the causal explanation and determining the course of the jealousy. In symptomatic jealousy the relationship and the environment provide a coloring rather than a critical influence. The focus of attention is shifted between the jealousy and the mental disorder, according to which ideology is applied.

The symptomatic model, though nearly always a simplification, does have utility. The practicing clinician may find this approach both familiar and helpful in formulating the patient's case and in organizing treatment. The following sections examine jealousy as it is manifested in some of a number of psychiatric syndromes.

Organic Psychosyndromes

Organic brain disorder, in which the orderly nature of cerebral functioning is disrupted, may give rise to any and all of the abnormalities of mental function found in psychiatric disorders. There is no symptom in psychiatry that cannot be reproduced by lesions of the central nervous system (CNS). When, for example, cerebral syphilis was still sufficiently common to account for a significant proportion of those in mental hospitals, it was frequently associated with delusions, including those of infidelity (Kraepelin, 1896/1974). Delusions of infidelity are reported to accompany a wide variety of CNS disorders (Cummings, 1985). In a recent series of cases of pathological jealousy, 20 cases out of 138 had organic disorders of the brain (including multiple sclerosis, Huntington chorea, and Alzheimer disease) as the basic pathology underlying the mental disorder of which the delusions of infidelity formed a part (Mullen & Maack, 1985). Shepherd (1961) noted that elderly patients may display morbid jealousy as a prominent and incongruous symptom in association with dementia and other organic conditions, and he quotes Gruhle as noting that jealousy may emerge as an isolated symptom of degenerative cerebral conditions.

Jealousy may be the first indication of an emerging cerebral disorder. One of our cases, who came to attention for the first time following a furious attack on his fiancée for supposed infidelity, was developing a rare presenile dementia, Friedreich's ataxia. This young man had shown no evidence of jealousy traits until a short time previously, when he rapidly developed bizarre beliefs about his girlfriend's sexual activities. It was only while he was in prison awaiting trial that this man's progressive neurological deficits became apparent.

Head injury with cerebral damage may have a wide variety of psychological consequences, among which are personality change and the emergence of psychiatric disorders including morbid jealousy. Johnson's (1969) study of ex-boxers who had had repeated head trauma found that pathological jealousy with delusions of infidelity was present in 5 out of the 17 cases. A young patient of ours was first troubled by jealousy following an accident on a motorcycle in which he sustained brain damage, particularly to the frontal lobes. Previously he had been an extroverted if belligerent man, who had treated his wife with cavalier but cheerful indifference. Following his recovery from the accident, he was unable to let his wife out of his sight because he was terrified she would leave him. He was plagued by vivid images of her having intercourse with other men, and he misinterpreted her every word and action as indicative of past or future infidelity. The jealousy totally disrupted both their lives, and his rehabilitation was prevented by his unwillingness to leave his wife's side to attend any rehabilitation workshops. Fortunately, it was possible to treat this man's jealousy and eventually to return him to work. The cerebral damage itself and the patient's recognition of his loss of capacities, both physical and intellectual, probably all combined to evoke the jealousy.

In another patient with advanced multiple sclerosis, the morbid jealousy emerged gradually as the disorder progressed. This man became increasingly dependent on his wife because of his physical deterioration. When the disorder affected his sexual and bladder functions, he became convinced that he would no longer be able to retain his wife, who would find herself a "real man." Grotesque delusions of infidelity emerged, and he was left fluctuating between clinging dependence and furious accusations directed at his wife for the supposed infidelities. Here the delusional state could most convincingly be attributed to the cerebral damage consequent on the sclerosis, whereas the jealous content of the morbid beliefs probably reflected the patient's real-life situation of increasing vulnerability and dependence.

Endocrine and other metabolic disorders may also present with pathological jealousy as a clinical feature (Cummings, 1985; Shepherd, 1961). A patient of ours presented with delusions of infidelity emerging in the context of thyrotoxicosis. Treatment of the thyroid disorder needed to be supplemented with antipsychotic medication to terminate the paranoid state. Three years later this lady stopped taking her prescribed medication; the thyrotoxicosis returned, and with it the delusional jealousy.

The relationship of the jealousy complex to the organic disorder is complex. In some instances, the premorbid personality or relationship is characterized by features that could be viewed as predisposing to jealousy; in others, no prodromata are obvious. In one of our cases, delusions of infidelity emerged in a man afflicted with progressive dementia associated with Jacob–Creutzfeld disease. This particular individual had been treated 10 years previously for pathological jealousy, which had at that time been part of a schizophrenic syndrome. Here two entirely unrelated conditions, one a functional psychosis and the other an organic psychosis, had both been characterized by prominent delusions of infidelity. There were no obvious premorbid abnormalities of personality and no known propensities to jealous reactions in this man. Whether the appearance of jealousy during both disorders reflected some underlying predisposition, or whether, having once developed delusions of infidelity, he was left vulnerable to recurrence or recapitulation can only be guessed at.

Mood Disorders

Jealousy may emerge in the context of a depressive illness. In these cases the jealousy complex, which may or may not include delusions of infidelity, is present alongside the other features of depression.

In the case of the elderly man who began accusing his wife of gross and flagrant adultery (described at the beginning of this chapter), there was an underlying depressive disorder. This man showed both florid delusions of infidelity and a characteristic picture of agitated depression, with sleep disorder, weight loss, restlessness, ruminations of guilt and worthlessness, hypochondriacal preoccupations, and suicidal ideation. Treatment of this man's depression with antidepressant medication terminated both the mood disorder and the jealousy. In this case, we discovered from relatives that the wife had been given to philandering in her youth 40 or 50 years previously. There had been very real reason for jealousy in the early years of their marriage, but apparently the husband either had remained in ignorance or had chosen not to indicate his knowledge of the wife's infidelities. It is interesting, even if futile, to speculate on whether the emergence of the jealousy over 40 years later may have reflected long-suppressed fears and resentments.

In this case the temporal relationship between the depression and the jealousy was clear, in that the change in mood preceded the emergence of jealousy and the remission of depression corresponded with a disappearance of the jealousy complex. In our experience, when jealousy coexists with significant depressive symptomatology, the relationship is usually unclear; in particular, it is often difficult to sort out which came first. Jealousy creates enormous distress and often brings with it significant disruption of an individual's social networks and support. It is to be expected that such stresses should lead to a lowered mood and in some cases should precipitate or exacerbate a depressive illness. In one study of patients with morbid jealousy, over 50% had received a diagnosis of depression as the primary or an associated diagnosis (Mullen & Maack, 1985). The implications of the relationship between depressive syndromes and the jealousy complex for treatment are discussed in Chapter 9.

The jealousy complex is an unusual accompaniment of manic states. It is, however, well recognized and has been accounted for in terms of the patient's interpretation of the sexual partner's failure to respond to the increased libido of the manic, as well as on occasion forming part of the persecutory delusions that may accompany this disorder (Shepherd, 1961).

The Schizophrenias

The schizophrenias are the commonest disorders in which delusions may be prominent. The clinical subtype of paranoid schizophrenia, in which delusions predominate over other abnormalities of mental state, and in which there is reasonable preservation of personality and emotional responsiveness, is where delusional jealousy is usually encountered.

The jealousy complex may emerge in the progress of a schizophrenic disorder, either as a central theme or as one element among a number of disturbances of mental function. In some cases jealousy may be the presenting problem, and the other features of the schizophrenic process may not become apparent until much later. In the study by Mullen and Maack (1985), 15 cases out of 138 received a diagnosis of schizophrenia. Five of Shepherd's (1961) 81 cases and 5 of Langfeldt's (1961) 66 cases had a specific diagnosis of schizophrenia. Shepherd (1961) reported that 14% of patients admitted over a 3-year period to the Maudsley Hospital in London with a diagnosis of paranoid schizophrenia, paranoia, or paranoid illness had jealousy as a prominent clinical feature.

Todd (1978) described the case of a middle-aged woman with a long history of schizophrenic disorders who claimed that her husband was having sexual relations with a number of other women, including her own mother, then aged 67 years. She knew of his infidelities because of "voices"; these hallucinations informed the patient of her husband's infidelities. A young homosexual patient of ours had his lover's infidelity revealed to him by the evening news. He said that the newscaster's reference to the bombing of a refugee camp in Lebanon was a thinly disguised message about his boyfriend's infidelities. In the first of these two examples, the lady had had a long history of mental illness prior to this relapse in which the jealousy complex was the central feature. In the second case, the young man developed delusions of infidelity as part of his first schizophrenic breakdown. Occasionally jealousy can be the harbinger of a schizophrenic illness. Retterstol (1967) reported on two patients who presented initially with a jealousy complex, which progressed to definite schizophrenic disorders over the subsequent few years. These cases showed the progression from well-organized jealous notions to unsystematized delusions of persecution and influence, with hallucinations in one patient and grotesque delusions (involving gangs using power lines, gas, and magnets to spy on her and influence her) in the other.

Schizophrenic disorders are relatively common; the lifetime risk of suffering such a condition is in the region of 1%. Those who have or have had an episode of schizophrenic disorder are not exempt from also exhibiting jealousy. The jealousy may emerge on the basis of understandable suspicions and may not be morbid in any degree. On the other hand, the jealous reaction may become entwined in the disturbances of the patient's mental state. In one case the patient's suspicions about his wife were manifested, in part, in the remarks and comments of hallucinatory voices. No other features of the jealousy itself were pathological; on the contrary, the unfortunate man's suspicions seemed well grounded and his responses circumspect and appropriate. Here an understandable jealousy appeared to be expressing itself in part through the content of the auditory hallucinations. In the more severe and persistent forms of the schizophrenias, there may be considerable disruption of the integrity of the sufferer's normal personality. These changes can put considerable strains on marital and other relationships. On occasion, this produces a morbid sensitivity in the patient that creates a greatly increased propensity to jealous reactions. Jealousy in those with a schizophrenic disorder may be based on delusions of infidelity, but can also be reactive with or without delusional development. In some cases the jealousy complex, though colored by the patient's condition, is otherwise normal.

Delusional (Paranoid) Disorders

The delusional disorders are of critical importance in pathological jealousy, for here the jealousy complex may constitute the core of the disorder; systematized delusions of infidelity may be present without other accompanying psychotic symptoms. The so-called "jealousy–paranoic disorders," including "conjugal paranoia" (Revitch, 1954), are customarily treated under the concept of paranoia;

DSM-III-R specifies both Jealousy and Erotomania as specific types of Paranoid Disorders.

Kraepelin (1915/1921) provided the classic description of paranoia. He limited the condition to disorders with a systematized delusional system, without true hallucinations, disorders of language, or primary mood changes that could account for the genesis of the delusions. He noted that the patients remain sensible, clear, and reasonable, both in expression of their morbid ideas and in their lives outside of the delusional concerns. The delusions become a component part of their very being and personality, "passing into the flesh and blood of the patients" (1915/1921). The delusions are always structured and show a coherence and interconnectedness indicative of thoughtful elaboration. They are not characterized by the bizarre contradictions, absurd non sequiturs, and confused relationships so often found in the delusions of schizophrenia. Obscure points and contradictions are carefully eliminated or rationalized by the patients to produce superficially plausible accounts which, except for the frequently improbable foundations, do not contain any absolute impossibilities. The patients will listen to objections and counterarguments and will at least attempt to substantiate their claims, albeit often with an air of disdainful superiority. Though the patients may admit that they cannot absolutely prove their assertions, any attempt to reason with them inevitably ends in frustration for the therapist without any appreciable dents in the delusional system.

The reality of paranoia or the delusional disorders as a distinct group of disorders has been challenged (Lewis, 1970; Post, 1982), but the clinical utility of a term that catches the essence of a group of uncommon but striking conditions insures its survival.

When the jealousy complex is central to paranoia, the patient is usually gradually overwhelmed by the convictions that the partner is deceiving him or her. Systematization and elaboration inevitably follow. Pseudomemories often abound; the patient "remembers" incidents that clearly point to infidelity, and reinterprets past actions and previous comments as incontrovertible proof. Misinterpretations abound: The way the husband walks indicates recent intercourse; the color of the wife's dress is an obvious message to the lover; a light left on in the bathroom is a sign to the paramour hidden in the garden; the discarded empty packet of condoms glimpsed in a public park was certainly left by the wife's lover after their tryst in the rhododendrons. The examples that can be provided by any clinician who has dealt with patients in the grips of paranoia are inexhaustible.

In paranoia the delusions of infidelity and associated jealousy complex may form the sole features of mental disorder. To term the

jealousy "symptomatic" in such a situation raises theoretical problems. To add to this difficulty, paranoia is considered by some authorities to consist primarily of a reaction. Bleuler (1916/1924) believed that the delusions in paranoia are a reaction to certain internal
and external situations, and he denied that paranoia is a direct result
of any process in the brain. He considered that at the root of the
disease is a situation to which the patient is not equal, and to which
the patient reacts by means of the disease. If this formulation is
accepted, it creates a significant overlap between the paranoia group
of morbid jealousies and the pathologically reactive jealousies emerging on the basis of the so-called "paranoid" or "sensitive" personality
disorders.

Alcohol Abuse

Marcel (1847; cited by Lagache, 1947) is credited with first describing
an association between alcoholism and pathological jealousy. This
connection was given prominence by Krafft-Ebing (1905), who reported that about 80% of the male alcoholics he studied who still had
sexual relations were afflicted by delusions of jealousy. He said that
the jealousy arises in the later stages of alcoholism and usually
consists of organized but isolated delusions of infidelity. He noted
that once jealousy has arisen in the chronic alcohol abuser, it is
"extremely fixed." Krafft-Ebing viewed the delusion as a product of
the effects of alcohol on the brain in combination with the influence
of chronic drunkenness on the individual's interpersonal and sexual
relationships.

Alcohol abuse may lead to increased desire and decreased performance. Krafft-Ebing (1905) suggested that sexual coldness develops in the alcoholic's wife because of an "aversion to the rough,
brutal husband, often drunk at the time of intercourse, . . . whose
pathologically tardy ejaculation causes pain through persistent and
frequent attempts." He continued, "The brutal, irritable, mentally
enfeebled husband, who otherwise lives in a state of quarrel with his
wife seeks and finds the cause of his sexual dissatisfaction in the
infidelity of the wife." Thereafter, "The delusion becomes fixed and
elaborated purely by means of false combinations. . . . [For example,]
in the household there is privation because the husband spends
everything on drink; therefore the unfaithful wife gives money and
food to her lovers" (p. 514).

Krafft-Ebing took the view that the social and biological results
of alcohol abuse are what generated pathological jealousy, and that
pre-existing character traits and inclinations are irrelevant. This

view was challenged by a number of subsequent authorities, who felt that the complex interaction between alcohol abuse and jealousy cannot be reduced to such a simple causal relationship (Kolle, 1932; Lagache, 1947; Shepherd, 1961). Vauhkonen (1968) concluded from his studies that alcohol plays a role in giving content and structure to the ideas of jealousy, but that the genesis of both alcohol abuse and pathological jealousy is to be found in more deep-rooted, though unspecified, factors. Kolle (1932) pointed out that jealousy may take various forms in alcoholics, and though the jealousy complex is common, the phenomenology and subsequent progress is far more variable than suggested by Krafft-Ebing.

In some alcohol abusers, intoxication exaggerates pre-existing character traits of distrust and increases the tendency to misinterpret events as evidence of infidelity. These periodic jealousy reactions may only be manifested during intoxication, or the ideas may become more persistent between bouts of drinking. In either case, the jealousy when present can remain similar to normal jealousy or can take on the appearance of pathological jealousy (Langfeldt, 1961). In other alcohol abusers, the jealousy complex may gradually extend over months or years, until the alcoholics have extensive delusions of infidelity that are present even during sober periods but become more insistent and flamboyant during periods of intoxication. In some of these individuals, a return to sobriety is followed by the resolution of the pathological jealousy, but in others it persists despite abstinence. Finally, in some alcoholics, the pathological jealousy merges into a wider and often poorly organized persecutory delusional system that may be accompanied by hallucinations. These latter states may be indistinguishable from schizophrenia and often follow a similar course even if sobriety returns.

Freud (1911/1955) considered that the role of alcohol in the genesis of pathological jealousy is "intelligible in every way." He stated that alcohol, "that source of pleasure," removes inhibitions and undoes sublimations. Men who resort to the public house and to the company of other men for drinking are provided with emotional satisfaction and gratifications that they have often failed to obtain with their wives at home. Their fellow drinkers may now become the objects of the men's affections, which consciously may be expressed in general bonhomie and friendliness, but unconsciously reflect repressed or sublimated homosexual urges. The libidinous attachment (cathexis) to these men may threaten to become conscious under the disinhibiting influence of alcohol. The drunkards' defenses against their own latent homosexuality recruit projective mechanisms. The realization of the homosexual desires are warded off by the formula "It is not I who love this man, she loves him." The men then suspect their wives in relation to all the men they themselves are tempted to love.

Glatt (1961) reported that over 20% of his alcoholic subjects admitted to jealousy as a problem. In the only systematic study to date of sexual jealousy in alcoholics, Shrestha, Rees, Ris, Hore, and Faragjer (1985) found an overall incidence of 35% in men and 31% in women, and considered that in 27% of the men and 15% of the women the jealousy was pathological.

In the more recent series of cases of pathological jealousy, the contribution of alcoholism has been modest. Langfeldt (1961) had only 3 cases out of 66, Shepherd (1961) 6 out of 81, Vauhkonen (1968) 10 out of 55, and Mullen and Maack (1985) 15 out of 138.

Drug Abuse

The jealousy complex may emerge in the context of drug abuse. Kraepelin (1915/1921) regarded cocaine abuse as peculiarly likely to produce pathological jealousy; if he was correct, the renewed interest in this drug for recreation may produce a spate of new cases. In the more recent literature, amphetamines have been linked to pathological jealousy (Shepherd, 1961; Todd, 1978). Amphetamine and cocaine abuse can produce a state indistinguishable from paranoid schizophrenia, in which delusions of infidelity may be prominent. In one case described elegantly by Todd (1978), a chronic amphetamine user accused his wife of regularly introducing men into their home between 5 A.M. and 6 A.M. so she could have intercourse with them on the bathroom floor. As convincing evidence of this infidelity, he offered that he had found fluff on her coat identical to that on the bathroom pipes and had discovered stains on bath towels he believed to have been left by lubricants that he "knew" his wife used to facilitate sexual intercourse with her various partners. He conceded that he had never actually seen any men in the house, but explained that his failure to interrupt his wife's regimen of infidelity was due to his being a heavy sleeper; he always slept through the critical hour.

Obsessive–Compulsive Disorders

Jealousy in normal individuals has a number of qualities that bear a superficial resemblance to the obsessional disorders. True obsessional phenomena are usually centered around a basic fear (phobia), which is often connected to the general areas of death, dirt, and sexuality (Straus, 1966). The obsessional person becomes intensely concerned with checking on all aspects that touch on this fear. In obsessional states the fear is connected to a subjective compulsion to do, think, or say something. This compulsion is resisted, at least to some degree, because the sufferer recognizes it as senseless or at the very least senselessly insistent. A vacillating quality is often introduced by the conflict between the compulsion and the resistance. The attempt to resist the compulsion creates escalating anxiety, which culminates in the patient's carrying out the compulsion or some other replacement activity. The performance of the compulsion or its surrogate often becomes ritualized, and the sufferer is then plagued first by the compulsion, then by the anxiety generated by resistance, and finally by the fear that the ritualized act has been performed incorrectly.

An example involving a fear of infidelity is provided by a motor mechanic who reported becoming increasingly fearful that his young wife would leave him for another man. He rejected this fear as ungrounded, but nevertheless the image of his wife with other men began to intrude increasingly into his consciousness, together with an overwhelming anxiety about being deserted. Initially he spent considerable time checking up on his wife, but though he found no evidence to support his fears, he could equally find no relief or lasting reassurance. He then attempted to push the thoughts out of his mind, with some success when he was at home with his wife, but with little success when he was away from her, particularly at work. To cope with the intrusive fears and images, he began to distract himself by concentrating intensely on his work—in particular, by carefully checking each stage of disassembling and reassembling motors. Some relief resulted, but he became increasingly concerned with the precise details of the work; he focused special attention on how many turns it required to tighten up certain bolts on engine casings. He found himself playing a mind game: He would estimate the number of turns that would drive a bolt home and then, if he was correct, would be reassured that in some way his suspicions of his wife were false. If he guessed wrong, however, then his anxieties would redouble and he would remove all the bolts and start again. The manner of tightening the bolts became increasingly structured and ritualized, to the point that he was rendered virtually incapable of completing any job. Throughout this whole progression, he retained insight into the falsity of his suspicions and absurdity of his activities.

In Chapter 2 we discussed primary and secondary appraisal processes involved in monitoring and judging the behavior of the beloved. Jealous individuals often experience a need to check and recheck any aspect of life that could relate to evidence of infidelity; they are certainly obsessed with this question in the everyday meaning of the word. Their concern becomes increasingly focused on the supposed infidelity, and they experience a sense of compulsion to accuse or trap their partners. The subjective resistance to both the idea of infidelity and the compulsion to check may well also be present in jealousy, as is the ruminative quality of going over and over in the mind every detail of the supposed evidence. Jealousy does not usually have the release mechanism for the escalating anxiety that is available to obsessional individuals in the performance of the compulsion or its equivalent. There are therefore a number of formal resemblances between the phenomenology of jealousy and that of the obsession; in most cases, however, the resemblances are partial and superficial. The jealous are obsessed with the possibility of infidelity in the everyday use of that term, rather than afflicted with an obsessional illness.

Lagache (1947) was of the opinion that true obsessional disorder is incompatible with a focus on jealousy. In some cases, however, the jealousy may in our opinion form the focus of a true obsession, and a sufferer with an obsessional disorder may also be jealous. Another of our cases was plagued by the intrusive thought that his wife was at that moment committing adultery. Since his marriage, the man had had an intense fear that his wife would leave him. The thoughts of actual infidelity in progress began some years into the relationship and would occur whenever he was separated from his wife. He would reject the thoughts as ungrounded and unfair and attempt to drive them from his mind. The patient was an accountant with a considerable talent for mental arithmetic. He tried to combat the intrusive thoughts by occupying himself with extensive mental calculations. This was initially helpful, but then a new problem arose: He began to be troubled by the thought that if he miscalculated, then his wife would indeed be unfaithful. This unfortunate man spent much of his day performing complex calculations in his head and checking them with his computer, in a state of high tension for fear a failure in his accuracy would presage a slip in his spouse's fidelity. The poor man was quite aware of the patent absurdity of the compulsion but was helpless to combat it.

Primary obsessional disorders are uncommon, and the unusual variant focusing on fear of infidelity is a true rarity. Obsessional phenomena are more commonly encountered as part of the symptomatology of depression, and it is in this far more common secondary obsessional disorder that jealousy, when it occurs in the form of an obsession, is likely to be found. In the first example in this section, the case of the motor mechanic, the man's obsessional problems were connected to the gradual onset of a depressive disorder; the second case, that of the accountant, was an example of the far rarer condition of a primary obsessional illness.

CONCLUSIONS

Pathological jealousy presents a problem and a challenge to the conceptual framework of current psychiatry, dominated as it is by the notion of discrete disease entities. The difficulties have tended to produce a situation in which pathological jealousy is either relegated to the status of a rare psychiatric syndrome (despite the frequency with which it occurs), or incorporated into our classificatory systems as a clinical feature or symptom with no independent existence. Pathological jealousy is an embarrassment because it breaks the rules by turning up in association with a wide variety of psychiatric syndromes, but it can also constitute an apparently independent syndrome. The difficulty of separating pathological from normal reactions only adds to the disrepute of the former.

The marginal and ambiguous position of pathological jealousy in contemporary psychiatry is clear from this chapter. Equally clear, we hope, is its importance in clinical practice. The solution for most clinicians is to approach jealousy and its pathological extensions with a pragmatic eclecticism.

8

Jealousy and Violence

Has anyone counted the victims of jealousy? Daily a revolver
cracks somewhere or other because of jealousy; daily a knife
finds entrance into a warm body; daily some unhappy ones,
racked by jealousy and life weary, sink into fathomless depths.
What are all the hideous battles, narrated by history, when
compared to this frightful passion jealousy.

Stekel (1921, p. 65)

Intrinsic to the jealousy complex is a state of mind in which pain and
anger predispose the jealous person to acts of aggression. The 17th-
century divine Robert Burton wrote in *The Anatomy of Melancholy* that
"those which are jealous proceed from suspicion to hatred; from
hatred to frenzie; from frenzie to injurie, murder and despair" (1621/
1827, p. 428). Fortunately, not everyone who falls under the sway of
jealousy proceeds all the way down this path from suspicion to
murder. The impulse to hurt or harm is intimately linked to the
experience of jealousy, but it does not necessarily find expression in
the battering of the loved one or the rival. This chapter focuses on
those exceptions who fail to restrain their impulses and give vent to
jealousy in overtly destructive acts. We hope to highlight the complex issues of the relationship between the jealousy complex and acts
of aggression.

THE DIRECTION OF THE VIOLENCE
IN JEALOUSY

Spinoza placed anger and aggression at the very center of his definition of jealousy when he stated that "the hatred towards an object

loved, together with the envy of another is called jealousy" (1948, p. 62). The rage stirred up by jealousy has as its object both the loved one and the supposed rival, but it is on the loved one that the aggression usually spends itself. Othello, in the grips of the "bloody passion of jealousy," smothers Desdemona, not Cassio, the supposed rival. As in literature, so in life, the object of love often becomes the object of violence. The romantic myth of the jealous rivals dueling for the hand of the beloved is far removed from the harsh reality of the domestic violence that so often accompanies this grim passion.

The doubts about who falls victim to jealousy are dispelled by the studies of the violence engendered by jealousy. Ruin (1933) reported on 17 cases of homicidal jealousy, in 14 of which the victim was the partner. The cases of pathological jealousy reported by Lagache (1947) included 18 subjects who killed; in 14 of these, the loved one fell victim to the violence. Psarska (1970) reported on a series of 38 jealous homicides and attempted homicides. Here again the victims were the partners, with a single exception where the jealous person attacked and killed the rival. A detailed and extensive study in this area was performed by Mowat (1966). He reported on 71 individuals who had killed and 39 who had attempted murder while in the grips of pathological jealousy. The victims of these jealous attacks were the loved ones in 94 instances, with the actual or supposed rivals being the object of violent attention in only 7 cases. In a study of homicide in Detroit, 58 examples of jealousy conflict leading to murder were identified, but here almost as many rivals were slain as partners (Daly et al., 1982). This sample was community-based and may have included many cases of normal jealousy, whereas other studies have relied predominantly on psychiatric cases. Mullen and Maack (1985) have provided a detailed analysis of the pattern of aggression in 138 jealous subjects. Assaults of one type or another were carried out by 71 of the subjects on their partners. Only 7 out of the 138 actually attacked their rivals, with 4 others issuing threats in the direction of their partners' supposed lovers. The majority of available studies indicate clearly that the aggression in jealousy is directed at the partner, the presumed loved one.

DOMESTIC VIOLENCE AND JEALOUSY

The violence of jealousy is predominantly domestic violence. Jealous passions can afflict both men and women, but whether they stimulate both to physical violence is less clear. The studies on jealous individuals who have killed reveal a preponderance of male killers and female victims (Lagache, 1947; Mowat, 1966; Psarska, 1970). The killing associated with jealousy is usually genocidal rather than homicidal. In the study of Daly et al. (1982), this trend is less obvious, for though 47 killings were precipitated by male jealousy in contrast to 11 by female jealousy, there were 9 females who killed their jealous accusers and 2 cases in which jealous males were murdered by their partners' relatives. In a study of 36 consecutive spousal homicides from Baltimore, 25 were attributed to jealousy, and in 24 of these cases wives were the victims (Guttmacher, 1955). Mullen and Maack (1985) reported that serious violence was more often used by males. However a number of women did launch attacks against their loved ones; some improved the odds against their larger and presumably stronger partners by striking while the partners slept. In this context, Burton (1621/1827) quotes the story of a jealous wife from Narbone who crept up on her sleeping husband in the night "and cut off his privities because she thought he plaid false with her" (p. 442). It has been suggested that jealousy moves men more frequently to violence and even murder of their partners, whereas women are more likely to turn their violence on themselves in self-mutilation (Bianchi, 1906). The violence of jealousy may be to some degree less clearly sexually specific than other types of spousal abuse, but is still more often associated with the battering of women.

The level of domestic violence is difficult to estimate, given the problems both of definition and of ascertainment. Violence is claimed to occur on at least one occasion in half of American families; Hilberman (1980) has referred to the marriage license as a hitting license. Conservative estimates report that a third of marriages are marred by violence involving the battering of the woman by her male partner (Straus, 1978). Serious and repeated violence is reported to be inflicted on women in between 4% and 10% of marriages (Gelles, 1979; Mullen, Romans-Clarkson, Walton, & Herbison, 1988; Steinmetz, 1986). According to the statistics of the Federal Bureau of Investigation, 13% of all homicides in the United States are accounted for by husbands' slaying their wives (Rosenbaum & O'Leary, 1981). In a British study of 300 men charged with homicide, the victims were either wives, lovers, or girlfriends in over 40% of the cases (Mowat, 1966).

Jealousy is only one of the potential motives for men who slay their sexual partners. Gibbens (1958), however, in his study of 195 homicide cases, reported that jealousy itself was the prime motivation in 43 (22%) of these cases. In Wolfgang's (1958) study of 588

Philadelphia homicides, jealousy was the third most common motivation, and in West's (1968) study in Manhattan, sexual jealousy also
ranked third after domestic quarrels and crime-related murders. In
their excellent review of male sexual jealousy, Daly et al. (1982)
suggest that male sexual jealousy may be the source of conflict in an
overwhelming majority of spousal homicides in North America.
They cite the studies of Guttmacher (1955) and Chimbos (1978),
who intensively studied those coming before the courts for killing
their spouses and who both found jealousy to be by far the most
important source of conflict leading up to the killing. Hafner and
Boker (1982), in their study of violent offenders, reported jealousy to
be the motivation for over 13% of all violent assaults. Taylor (1985)
also noted that frequency of jealousy as a motivation to violence in
her series of violent offenders and stated that jealousy is "a very
dangerous thing."

Murderers who kill again after release from prison or hospital
frequently suffer from morbid jealousy (Scott, 1977). The case of
Terence John Iliffe is illustrative. He was committed to a hospital for
the criminally insane following the killing of his wife. Following his
release from Broadmore Hospital in England, he remarried, suffered
a return of his jealousy, and killed yet another unfortunate woman
(Butler, 1975).

Violence in close relationships can rarely be attributed to a
single factor, but emerges from the complexities of those relationships. Jealousy contributes to creating the context in which violence
emerges and to precipating individual assaults. In a number of
studies of abused and battered wives, the husbands have been noted
to exhibit jealousy and possessiveness in an extreme form (Church,
1984; Dobash & Dobash, 1980; Gayford, 1975; Hilberman & Manson, 1977; Rounsaville, 1978; Whitehurst, 1971a). Two-thirds of the
women at a refuge for battered wives reported that their husbands
were excessively jealous—without any grounds, in the vast majority
of cases—and that this was the motivation for the repeated assaults
(Gayford, 1975, 1979). Extreme jealousy was reported to be manifested by 57 of the husbands of 60 battered women studied by
Hilberman and Manson (1977). These husbands, in addition to assaulting their wives and accusing them of infidelity, attempted to
isolate them from any social contacts on the grounds of preventing
the opportunity for adulterous relationships. In some cases they
opposed contact with women friends for fear of lesbian liaisons.
Church (1984) noted that 87 of the 101 battered women in his series
rated their husbands as very or extremely jealous and possessive.
Those husbands who were rated highest on possessiveness were

most likely to make unreasonable demands and to have become physically abusive earlier in the relationship. Church also reported that the most common unreasonable demands on these battered women related to jealousy. The batterers insisted that their wives not go out alone, not even to work or shop. Whitehurst (1971a) reported on 100 cases of spousal violence. In nearly every case, the husband was responding out of frustration at his inability to control the wife, but the overt justification and accusation was that the wife was having an affair. The jealousy was usually unfounded, but acted as the focus for the resentment and a legitimation of the violence.

These statistics are the superficial expression of human misery and degradation. Behind the cold figures lie a multitude of individual relationships and lives damaged and even destroyed by the ravages of the violence unleashed or legitimated by jealousy. Mullen and Maack (1985) attempted to detail the forms and intensity of aggression engendered by jealousy. Only 27 (19.4%) of the cohort of 138 jealousy patients had not acted aggressively toward their partners. Thirty-three (24%) had confined themselves to threats to kill or maim, but this group included six men and two women who accompanied their threats by brandishing knives; a further nine men underlined their words by waving blunt instruments, such as pokers; and one man held a gun to his wife's head while he issued threats on her life. This study group was collected from a series of referrals for psychiatric assessment; none came from the courts, and only two had ever been charged with crimes of violence. Nevertheless, in 78 patients (56.5%), there was a history of committing acts of some form of violence. Assaults were inflicted on their partners by 48 of the 85 men and 28 of the 53 women. The seriousness of the attacks varied widely. Ten men gave clear histories of throttling their wives with homicidal intent. One man tried to kill his wife by poisoning her with coal gas as she slept. Twelve subjects stabbed or slashed their partners with knives. Nine men and two women struck their partners with clubs or other blunt instruments on one or more occasions, causing multiple fractures in four instances. The commonest pattern of violence to emerge in this study was that of repeated attacks involving hitting, punching, and kicking the partner. This catalogue of violence and abuse had never come to the notice of the police, despite a number of the partners' receiving hospital treatment for the injuries they had received.

Jealousy and possessiveness emerge from a number of studies as central elements in the interactions that lead to domestic violence. Jealousy is not the only explanation for domestic violence, but it is an important contributor to the system that generates it.

THE COUPLE'S INTERACTION
AND JEALOUS VIOLENCE

Jealous aggression, like so many other forms of human behavior, is overdetermined in the sense of representing the endpoint of a number of intentions, acts, and themes. Jealousy involves the outrage at an act of infidelity, of disloyalty; it threatens loss of the central relationship; it involves humiliation; it raises an intensely ambivalent eroticism; it escalates interpersonal conflict within the relationship; and it is accompanied by uncertainty, frustration, and helplessness. Any or all of these may predispose an individual to acts of aggression. Furthermore, the social and individual ethical and moral imperatives against the use of force are often attenuated in situations that presuppose sexual infidelity.

One important feature of the couple's interactions concerns the jealous person's desire for confirmation of his or her fears. Jealousy has little interest in refutation and searches only after positive proof. In some relationships it is possible for the partner to dispel the fears of betrayal, but for this to occur there has to be sufficient mutual trust for the reassurance to be meaningful. Sadly, trust is often abandoned when jealousy takes root. The past actions and future intentions of the partner are exactly what jealousy puts in question; the fidelity of the partner is at issue, and therefore he or she cannot be trusted. Those consumed by jealousy seek evidence that will confirm their worst fears. They may reject all reassurance, seeing it as dissembling. Accusations that are denied generate further and more vehement accusations. Accusations that induce admissions, however partial or fabricated, lead to distress, rage, and yet further and more vehement accusations. Jealousy all too often involves an escalating conflict between the partners that may culminate in physical violence. Gesell (1906) cites the case of a young Russian, naturally genial and generous, who goaded his wife to confess and reconfess a former faithlessness, and finally beat her to death with a whip.

The jealous may need to extract a confession and hence may be unable to accept denial. This dilemma is depicted with dreadful vividness by Emile Zola (1890/1956) in his novel of jealousy and murder, *The Beast in Man*. Rouband, the stationmaster, suspects a past liaison on the part of his young wife. After accusing her and battering her furiously when she denies his accusations, he continues:

> "Confess!" he repeated, "You did sleep with him." By going quite limp, she escaped from him and tried to run for the door. Leaping after her with a single infuriated blow, he knocked her down,

grabbed her hair and by it held her head to the floor. . . . "Confess!
You slept with him!" She no longer dared say no, so she said
nothing. "Confess you slept with him, God damn you," he cried,
"or I'll knife you!"

She could see murder plain on his face. . . . Fear overcame
her; she capitulated just to end it all. "All right, then, yes, it's true.
Now let me go." After that, it was frightful. The admission which
he had so savagely extracted was a direct body blow. . . . He seized
her head and banged it against the table leg. . . . he dragged her
across the room by her hair. (p. 18)

The violence continues and escalates, and the questioning of Rouband begins again, demanding sexually specific details of the wife's
past infidelity. This extract captures the all too familiar pattern of
the violence of jealousy played out in a relationship: the need to
extract a confession, even if it is beaten out of the loved one, and
then the horror and rage if a confession is forthcoming. The insati-
able need to know that is inherent in jealousy cannot be satisfied by
confession. The jealous person may demand the repeated revelation
of every detail of the actual or supposed infidelities.

The way in which jealousy is dealt with in the relationship will
influence whether the conflict escalates to violence. Studies and
observations on those situations in which jealousy has led to serious
assault and even murder give additional information on the release
of physical aggression.

Overt disdain or rejection expressed by the partner toward the
jealous spouse during an argument about the actual or supposed
infidelity was identified by Psarska (1970) as an important precipitant of serious violence in his series. The victim of jealousy, out of
frustration and anger or from contempt for the partner, may give
voice to dismissive, belittling remarks in response to the continuing
accusations. In one of our cases, the wife, confronted with yet
another round of accusations and cross-questioning about a boyfriend she had had before marriage and with whom she had had a
child, responded that at least her previous lover had been man
enough to get her pregnant. This touched on the husband's fears
about his potency and fertility, and triggered a furious assault.
Another woman was confronted in the street by her husband while
she was talking quite innocently with a male colleague from work,
and was subjected to vehement accusations and imprecations. She,
overwhelmed by embarrassment, first tried to laugh it off and then,
angered beyond caution, chose to point out there and then the
husband's intellectual, social, and physical shortcomings and
rounded it off by telling him they were through. This was followed

by a violent assault upon her. In Bizet's opera *Carmen*, it is Don José's final rejection by his ex-lover, who tells him that she loves him no more and that his declarations of love are a waste of time, that provokes him to kill her. She throws her love for the toreador in his face and challenges him by saying, "Strike me now or let me pass." Don José takes up her challenge and stabs Carmen to death. In one of our own cases, a wife threatened by her jealous husband with a knife was unwise enough to follow Carmen's example and challenge him either to stab her or to let her leave; he chose the former, fortunately without fatal result.

Jealousy raises the passion, but the response of the loved one may create the context for the violent outcome. This is not to excuse the violence; Don José remains the rather pathetic cast-off lover unable to accept his rejection, and Carmen the courageous, if inconsiderate, free spirit. The violence of the rejected lover is as unforgiveable as any other assault, but equally it often requires only the slightest exercise of empathy to understand how it has come about.

One of the paradoxes of jealousy is that the accuser insists that the partner is incapable of fidelity and therefore unworthy, but at the same time seeks promises of the partner's continuing commitment to the relationship. The jealous person insists that the relationship is soiled and in ruins, but is terrified of hearing these strident claims confirmed. Violence may not emerge in relationships until the partner, harassed beyond endurance, finally makes it clear to the jealous lover that they are through and the relationship is at an end. This, in a number of reports in the literature and among our own case material, has triggered violence, sometimes with fatal results. In one case, the accused stabbed his wife to death when she finally convinced him she was leaving. This man, though he had driven his wife from the marital home by his accusations, forced her to seek police protection because of his threats, and compelled her to take legal action by preventing her access to their joint money and property, nevertheless believed that his wife would be reconciled and return to him. He finally realized that she was indeed intending to divorce him when she arranged a meeting on neutral ground in an attempt to say her goodbyes to him away from the courts and the confusion of their legal wrangles. He throttled her when he realized that his fantasy of the realtionship's continuing could not be sustained. He said later that her calmness and sadness convinced him it was over, so he killed her. Killers of their wives and lovers will sometimes say that they carried out the murders so that nobody else could have their partners.

The apprehension of loss is part of being jealous. The confrontation with actual loss or separation produces in most subjects an initial exacerbation in their jealousy. Prolonged separation, particularly if an individual can come to accept it as permanent and begin to disengage, usually results in the amelioration or even the disappearance of jealousy. This is the basis for advising separation in cases of morbid jealousy and in cases where violence has been a feature. The initial separation, particularly with the morbidly jealous subject, is, however, fraught with danger when violence is present or threatened. The emotional turmoil and associated fear of loss are increased with the prospect of separation. In morbidly jealous subjects with delusions, enforced separation brought about by the partners' leaving or the jealous individuals' being hospitalized have been noted to intensify the jealousy (Hafner & Boker, 1982). In one tragic case we came across, a young man who exhibited delusions of jealousy agreed to accept voluntary admission to a hospital for treatment, but, prior to coming into the ward, was given permission to return home to collect some clothes and toilet articles. His wife returned unexpectedly while he was in the house, and he made an impulsive and lethal assault upon her. Later, he said that he was overwhelmed by the thought that she would leave him and run off with another man while he was in the hospital.

The jealous individual is likely to misinterpret innocent or trivial acts or statements on the part of the suspected partner as evidence of gross infidelity. The symbolic meaning attributed by the jealous individual to some apparently unrelated act or occurrence has been reported to be the precipitant of violence in some cases (Psarska, 1970). The world of the jealous is one in which every chance event and casual remark becomes invested with a particular and personal meaning associated with the pervasive fear of infidelity. This oppressive world of the jealous is caught vividly by Alain Robbe-Grillet in his novel *Jealousy*.

Given the jealous individual's exquisite sensitivity to every nuance in his or her environment that may hint at unfaithfulness, and the tendency to divine hidden and sinister meaning in the loved one's every action, it is not to be wondered at that violence may be triggered by events whose significance is not apparent to the outside observer. In one of our cases, a woman launched an attack on her husband as he lay reclining in the sun because he had expressed a desire for a beer. She had interpreted the apparent relish in his voice at the prospect of this beverage as associated with a woman who served in a local bar and who (so the wife believed) had had a liaison with him. The connection between desiring a beer and desiring this particular barmaid was so clear to the wife that she could not understand why the husband and others were surprised she was provoked.

A particularly vivid example of violence triggered by symbolic association was provided by a colleague. A lady saw a woman in the street whom she believed (probably correctly) was having an affair with her husband. She attempted to walk on by, ignoring the other woman; however, as she passed her, she noticed what she took to be a look of self-satisfaction on her face. This provoked a sudden surge of anger, and she turned and grabbed the women's coat. Holding her firmly by the collar, she warned the woman to keep away from her husband. In gripping hold of the woman's clothing, she somehow caused a degree of constriction around the woman's throat, who began to make choking noises, presumably in an attempt to breathe against the constriction. The sound of the other woman's attempts to breathe triggered in the jealous assailant an association with the heavy breathing and cries of orgasm. For her, the grasping for breath became the sounds of this woman's orgasm with her husband. At this point, she lost control and in truth throttled her unfortunate rival.

Violence usually emerges with relationships against the background of deep-seated conflicts. In one study of the psychodynamics of homicide within a series of eight marriages (Cormier, 1962), it was suggested that the relationships were characterized by close and intense dependence permeated by distrust and jealousy. Verbal and physical abuse often develop gradually in the context of the ongoing conflict. In those relationships where jealousy becomes the focus for violence, there is often a long history of conflict and distrust, quite apart from the issue of sexual fidelity. Sometimes jealousy emerges as part of a major mental disorder or when a partner is suddenly confronted with incontrovertible evidence of infidelity (e.g., the partner is caught in the act). In most situations, however, violence is the endpoint of an escalating conflict against a background of long-lasting discontents and difficulties. Jealousy disrupts relationships, but also emerges in the context of disordered and disrupted relationships. Jealousy may contribute to and trigger aggression in a relationship; however, in many cases it is but one factor among a number that determine the emergence of violence out of the conflicted relationship.

THE INDIVIDUAL CHARACTERISTICS OF THE VIOLENTLY JEALOUS

Jealousy is a drama played out within a relationship, but whether violence flares will reflect, at least to some degree, the specific characteristics of the individual who threatens violence. Some people are more likely than others to behave aggressively in response to provocations, which include infidelity. The question of how potentially dangerous a particular jealous person is must always be addressed when individuals or couples present for treatment or counseling (see chapter 9).

Dangerousness is not a quality of an individual but of that individual's actions. There are no violent people, only violent deeds. The prediction of the likelihood that a particular individual will commit future violence depends on the association of specific characteristics with a general increase in the likelihood of assaults' being perpetrated.

Violent offenses in most advanced industrialized communities are most likely to be committed by young males, with a preponderance of those from lower socioeconomic classes (Hurwitz & Christiansen, 1983; Shaw & McKay, 1969; Short, 1976). This is particularly true if they are also members of minority ethnic and racial groups subject to economic and social deprivation (Mulvihill & Tumin, 1969; Silberman, 1978). The single most powerful predictor of future violent behavior is a previous record of violent offending (Monahan, 1981). Substance abuse, including alcohol, also increases the risk of such behaviors. The presence of mental disorder in general has no predictive value in the assessment of dangerousness, though specific psychiatric syndromes (including the schizophrenias and certain delusional disorders, among which is morbid jealousy) carry an increased risk of committing violent offenses (Hafner & Boker, 1982; Mullen, 1984b, 1988b; Taylor & Gunn, 1984).

The general rules that govern the prediction of dangerousness have some utility in the situation of jealousy. Past behavior predicts future behavior, and a history of overt violence should always alert the clinician to the risk of repetition. An escalating pattern of aggression is often encountered in jealousy; once established, this pattern may be difficult to stop without separating the partners. Those who resorted to assault in the group studied by Mullen and Maack (1985) did not have a previous record of violent offending. In Mowat's (1966) series of mentally abnormal murderers, however, over 15% had previous convictions for assault, though it was not clear whether these were also motivated by jealousy or reflected a more general tendency to act violently. This rate compares with a history of previous convictions for violence of 8.5% for insane killers and 11% for killers not deemed mentally abnormal. The case studies of jealousy that ends in tragedy leave little doubt that many jealous persons give ample evidence of resorting to physical assaults prior to the final lethal attack. These warnings should be taken seriously. Threats of violence, on the other hand, are so common in jealousy that their predictive value is inevitably low, but common sense dictates that the more emphatic the threat and the closer it comes to actual violence, the more weight it should be given. Bursten (1980), in his study of violence toward the loved one, acknowledged the importance of a history of violence; however, he noted that "those who idealize their partners despite obvious rejection, who constantly and rather desperately attempt to repair a relationship and who exhibit no signs of anger in the process, may also pose a danger which can erupt into tragic violence" (p. 121). This is useful to remember in situations of jealousy and infidelity in which imminent or recent separation is a factor.

Whitehurst (1971a), on the basis of his study of marital violence predominantly associated with accusations of infidelity, noted that middle-class males probably interpret jealousy more readily in terms of the threat to social and economic position, and see the use of violence as less congruent with their self-concept, than do lower-class males. He concludes, "it is possible that the tendencies to act aggressively are similar, but the middle-class male puts the brakes on sooner" (p. 38). The past history of violence and social class of jealous individuals, though of some value, are probably less predictive of violence than in other areas of assaultive behavior.

Violent offending in general is a behavior of young men, with those in their late teens and 20s having the highest incidence of such acts, and a rapid decline in this style of offending occurring after the age of 40 (Glazer, 1975). In studies of homicide, the vast majority of the perpetrators are under 40, though insane offenders tend to be somewhat older. In the over-60s, who comprise 15% of the population, crime becomes a relative rarity, with only 2% of acquisitive and 4% of violent crimes being committed by this age group (East, 1936, 1949; Epstein, Mills, & Simon, 1970; Schichor & Kobris, 1978). Violent offenses are usually the result of powerful emotional reactions that are attenuated with age and may even come under the moderating influences of wisdom and experience.

Jealousy is an exception to this general rule, for it continues to promote violence into advanced age. In Mowat's (1966) series, the jealous murderers were on the average in their mid-40s, with nearly all being over 30 years of age and a number in their 60s and 70s. East (1949) described the case of a 68-year-old man who accused his wife of an incestuous relationship with their grown-up son and believed that she was pregnant as a result of it. She was a sober and respectable woman; in response to these accusations, she arranged for both a nurse and a doctor to examine her and reassure her husband that she was not pregnant. Despite both their and her efforts, the husband could not be persuaded that his beliefs were false, and the sad affair ended in his shooting and killing his wife.

Alcohol deserves particular mention as a factor in the violence of jealousy. The relationship of alcohol abuse to the development of jealousy and delusions of infidelity has been discussed in detail in Chapter 7. Alcohol in our society is frequently implicated in the release of aggressive behavior (Brain, 1986; Collins, 1982). Its disinhibiting effects are obvious in the accounts of both major and minor bouts of aggression in jealousy. Alcohol abuse itself may both predispose individuals to and influence jealousy.

Ideas and delusions of infidelity commonly occur among the mentally disordered. The presence of a major mental disorder is a factor in the prediction of dangerousness in jealousy. The risk of violence occurring in those with psychotic illnesses has been subjected to extensive study and even more extensive debate. The current state of knowledge can be broadly summarized by saying that though there is no reason to assume that those who have a mental disorder or have had one in the past are any more likely to offend in a violent manner than their fellow citizens, there are subgroups within the total population of the mentally disordered who do appear to show an increased level of violent behavior (Mullen, 1988b; Taylor & Gunn, 1984). Prominent among those at higher risk of violence are psychotic subjects with delusions of infidelity.

Though males are more destructive, jealous women can also be assaultive to a degree unusual in other situations. In jealousy, though previously violent behavior retains its predictive value, the other correlates of dangerousness are probably less reliable; in particular, reassurance cannot be drawn from the factors that are negatively correlated with assaultiveness in other situations, such as being female, elderly, and upperclass. In one case, a lady in late middle age with an impeccable background shot and killed her doctor husband's receptionist, because she suspected that the two were having an affair (Sokoloff, 1947). The woman's social, economic, and personality profile would predict her to be one of the least likely individuals to commit a crime of violence. Jealous violence appears to break the rules.

Predicting the risk of violence in a relationship troubled by jealousy is important if preventive action is to be instituted. Though jealousy does break the rules and deprive us of the few guidelines available in estimating dangerousness, it is still possible with a full history to recognize some potentially violent situations (see Chapter 9).

PASSION AND PROVOCATION:
JEALOUSY AND THE CRIMINAL LAW

Frankie and Johnny were lovers,
Oh God how they would love.
Swore to be true to each other.
He was her man but he done her wrong. . . .

Now it wasn't murder in the first degree,
It wasn't murder in the third.
Frankie she simply dropped her man,
Like a hunter drops a bird.
She killed that man 'cos he done her wrong.

Traditional American song,
arr. Josh White

The criminal law in Western societies has traditionally racognized that certain states of affairs may provoke such a passionate response as to produce in the ordinary citizen a sudden and temporary loss of self-control. If in the grips of this passion the individual attacks and kills the provoker, then the killer has a defense to the charge of murder if the provocation is judged sufficient. The illustration most commonly put forth is that of a man who finds his wife in the act of adultery and kills her or her paramour. The law has always regarded this as an act that amounts not to murder but only to manslaughter, even though there is no doubt the accused intended to cause death (Morris & Howard, 1964).

The so-called "crime of passion" has always aroused both fascination and considerable sympathy for the offender. Nineteenth-century criminologists believed that the crime of passion constituted an entirely separate category both of offense and offenders. The "criminal by passion" was considered to be "a man of wholesome birth and of honest life possessed of keen, even exaggerated sensibilities who under the stress of some great, unmerited wrong, has wrought justice for himself" (H. Ellis, 1890, p. 24). The origins of this attitude lay in what were considered the traditional rights of the male to defend his and his family's honor, and to exact retribution for insults and infringements of his rights. A variety of insults and injuries have been viewed as likely to provoke the ordinary man to such passion that he might lose control and attack.

The nature of what is considered sufficiently provoking by the general population and the courts varies from society to society and from one historical period to another. Confrontation with evidence of a spouse's infidelity has remained the most consistent example of a provocation across both national boundaries and time. The 18th-century English jurist Blackstone commented that killing in a situation where a spouse is found in the act of adultery "is of the lowest degree of manslaughter; . . . for there could not be a greater provocation" (quoted in Smith & Hogan, 1983, p. 288). The law in the United States currently holds that an act of blatant adultery is sufficient provocation that when the spouse intentionally kills either the partner, the lover, or both, the crime is voluntary manslaughter rather than murder (La Fave & Scott, 1972). Some jurisdictions, such as New Mexico and Utah, go even further; they hold that it is a complete defense to murder when a husband kills on discovering another in the act of intercourse with his wife, and therefore that the killing is no crime (Perkins, 1969). The law in the United States and most other industrialized countries has in relatively recent times extended this privilege to betrayed wives, though the situation for homosexual couples remains in some doubt.

The crime of passion is associated in the popular imagination with France and the French—with good reason, for it was there that it reached its most developed form. In the 19th century, the influence of romanticism on French culture and values was profound. The crime of passion became a subject of intense public interest, and the courts were greatly influenced by the prevailing attitudes. Zeldin (1977) reports that Alexander Dumas, the author of such romantic classics as *The Three Musketeers* and *The Man in the Iron Mask*, would appear at assize courts in Paris standing behind the presiding judge as though to assert the rights of passion, so that even killing in the name of passion should be recognized. Murder when committed in the name of love became an object more for admiration than for condemnation. The attitudes of this time and place were typified by the case of Marie Biere, who in 1879 shot and killed her unfaithful lover. She immediately gave herself up to the police, tearfully confessed her crime, and invoked uncontrollable emotions as responsible for the slaying, which she now regretted. The court acquitted her after only a few minutes' deliberation.

The sympathy of juries and the courts to the enraged cuckold has in practice extended far beyond the situation of being exposed to the sight of a spouse caught *in flagrante delicto*. It has been held by the courts both in the United States and the United Kingdom that suddenly being told of infidelity, or even a reasonable though erroneous belief that a spouse is committing adultery, may form sufficient provocation to establish a defense to murder. The courts have also given recognition to jealousy that has developed over weeks, months, or even years before it erupts into fatal violence. In a British case, a plea of not guilty to murder on the grounds of provocation was accepted in a case where the defendant had battered his wife to death with a hammer as she lay asleep in bed one morning. The trial judge accepted that the wife's repeated infidelities and "Saturday night and Sunday morning activities with boyfriends" over many years had finally provoked the husband to such an extent that he had lost control of himself and killed her (Wasik, 1982). In an American case, the accused contended that he had throttled his wife because he had been provoked into an uncontrollable jealous rage by her repeated infidelities. A psychiatrist testified in this case that the defendant, who had been made aware of his wife's infidelities on a number of occasions, had by these cumulative provocations been reduced to a state of uncontrollable rage and had killed under the sway of this passion. The defense was sustained on appeal, and he was sentenced for manslaughter (La Fave, 1978).

The defendant, who kills as a result of jealousy induced by real or supposed infidelities only benefits from a defense of provocation, at least in theory, if he or she can convince a judge and jury that the situation at the time of the killing was such that it would induce a sudden loss of control in a normal individual. Devlin, a prominent English jurist, made it clear in one of his decisions that circumstances that induce a desire for revenge are inconsistent with provocation. He argued that the conscious formulation of a desire for revenge means that the person has had time to think and reflect, and this would be inconsistent with a sudden loss of self-control, which is the essence of provocation (cited in Smith & Hogan, 1983). Ruth Ellis, the last woman to be hanged in the British Isles, was subjected to a strict interpretation of this doctrine. She was a 28-year-old model who lived with a racing driver named David Blakely. She became increasingly jealous of him as a result of his infidelities, and when he failed to return home one night, she armed herself with a revolver and traveled several miles to where she correctly assumed him to be. Without more ado, she shot him dead. The court clearly viewed her actions as calculated revenge, rather than passionate loss of control, and sentenced her to death. Had she been tried in Paris rather than London, her fate would undoubtedly have been different. Ruth Ellis also had the disadvantage of not being a lawful wife, and the courts have shown some reluctance to equate the provocation of adultery with that of the infidelity of a lover. In Illinois as recently as 1965, a court ruled that it would not apply the exculpatory features of *crime passionel* to the killing of a mistress or lover, regardless of the duration of the relationship; as a result, a Mr. McDonald was convicted of murdering his cohabitee of some 25 years' standing (La Fave & Scott, 1972).

The courts are far from consistent in dealing with crimes involving jealousy, where passions may be stirred not only in the accused by in the judge and jury. A Londoner by the name of Fantle, jealous at his wife's relationship with one Linsey, purchased a revolver and shot him. At his trial, Fantle claimed that when he confronted Linsey he was insulted and treated with contempt, and this was the final straw that provoked his loss of control. His plea was accepted and he was sentenced to 3 years' imprisonment for manslaughter (Eddy, 1958). The leniency in interpretation of the law can be considerable in cases where jealousy and infidelity are involved. In Britain after World War II, there was a spate of killings of wives who had not been sufficiently patient and constant in awaiting the warriors' return. The courts became so lenient in dealing with these cases that the House of Lords found it necessary to reaffirm the traditional definition of murder (Eisler, 1949).

One of our own cases illustrates the courts' potential for leniency. The accused was a young man from Italy who had become increasingly jealous of his American wife. He determined to trap his spouse in the act of adultery. This man pretended to leave for Italy to see his mother, but stole back to the marital home and secreted himself in the loft. He remained in hiding for several days, and then emerged one evening armed with a butcher's knife. He flung open the bedroom door to discover an empty bed. The sound of voices attracted him to the kitchen, where he discovered his wife having a cup of coffee with a male friend from work. The husband then stabbed his wife to death. At his trial, a defense of provocation was rejected because of the obvious planning involved in the crime. Two psychiatrists gave an opinion for the defense that the accused was suffering from depression. The doctors engaged for the prosecution gave as their view that the man was unhappy and distressed at his wife's behavior, but did not have anything that could remotely be called a mental illness. Despite the contested evidence, the judge gave an unequivocal direction to the jury to find the accused not guilty of murder. He then sentenced him to 2 years' imprisonment for manslaughter. It was difficult not to come to the conclusion that the court in this case was as concerned with establishing the dead wife's guilt on the moral offense of adultery as they were with the husband's guilt on the charge of murder. The judge, having satisfied himself as to the wife's culpability, clearly took a generous view of the husband's peccadillo in killing her. The overt sympathy accorded the accused in this case could doubtless act as a warning and deterrent to unfaithful wives, though not, one might think, to murderous husbands.

The generosity often accorded the jealous killer has provoked the occasional protest from both the public and the courts. Glanville Williams (1978), a prominent English legal academic, has stated,

> Killing upon provocation is very unusual. This is particularly true of killing in jealousy which is one of the best established instances of provocation. In 1976 adultery was alleged in 39,231 petitions for divorce (in England) and doubtless there were many spouses who discovered this conduct without taking divorce proceedings. We lack figures of voluntary killings for adultery but in comparison with the instances of adultery they must be insignificant. To say that the ordinary man or woman kills for adultery is a grotesque untruth.

This view hits at the very heart of the use of provocation as a defense for those who kill from jealousy, and exposes the absurdity of the attitudes and assumptions that underlie it.

The law, at least in its everyday workings, reflects prevailing social attitudes. The way in which the violence of jealousy is dealt with in the courts is a barometer of our attitudes toward sexual infidelity, marital rights, and the claim that passion can excuse an individual's actions. Given that most of the violence of this type appearing before the courts is the result of husbands' attacking their wives for actual or supposed infidelity, it also tells us a great deal about society's attitude toward women.

REVENGE AND THE RIVAL

The type of violence discussed so far has been predominantly explosive aggression released in the heat of the moment. The assaults associated with jealousy are typically those that occur when the passion is at its height. The jealousy and interpersonal tension may well have been long-standing, but the attack is usually triggered by a particularly disturbing event or an argument that escalates out of control. The essence of revenge, by contrast, is the exacting of punishment or retribution for a harm or injury. It is a calculated act in which the anger of the moment is translated into a more lasting and purposeful vindictiveness. Surprisingly, calculated revenge is a relatively rare motivation for violence in our society. In a study that examined in detail the motivation for violent offenses among 212 men, only 3 were found to fit the criteria for a crime of calculated revenge (Taylor, 1985). An earlier study on 200 murderers, deemed sane, reported 31 cases motivated by revenge (East, 1936). In our own case material, calculated acts of revenge are remarkably rare. Jealous individuals often ruminate at length on what they would like to do to their unfaithful partners and their paramours, but these fantasies, colorful though they often are, seem rarely to be put into action. The violence of jealousy is usually the violence of the moment, unplanned and unexpected, rather than the culmination of a conscious vendetta.

Those instances in which jealousy translates into a plan for violent revenge that is carried through to completion seem more often to involve attacks upon the actual or supposed rival. This should occasion no surprise, for the opportunities for heated interchanges and escalating conflicts that culminate in violence are usually far greater between the partners than between the rival and the jealous. When calculated vengeance is inflicted on a loved one, it appears in our experience to occur more commonly when the partners have been separated for a time and are no longer in immediate day-to-day contact.

A number of examples of calculated revenge by jealous individuals on their actual or supposed rivals are provided by Sokoloff (1947). Among those is the case of Harry K. Thaw, which attracted intense media attention at the turn of the century. Thaw was a millionaire from Pittsburgh who discovered following his marriage that his wife had had a previous affair with the prominent architect Stanford White. Though his wife had no contact with White after the marriage, Thaw became obsessed with his jealousy and ruminated on vengeance for many months. He learned that White was to attend a society party in New York. Thaw went to this gathering and shot his victim three times, leaving him dying in the center of the crowded room. He then calmly left, saying that White would never go out with another woman. This was a calculated and cold-blooded killing. At his trial Thaw expressed no regret, and his counsel pleaded that his act was committed for "the purity of American homes; struck for the purity of American maidens; struck for the purity of American wives" (quoted in Sokoloff, 1947, p. 175). In the event he was found not guilty for murder, but spent some 9 years at Matthewson State Hospital for the Criminal Insane before his final release.

Poison is the instrument of the calculating murderer *par excellence*, which may account for the fascination of such crimes. The case of a jealous poisoner is reported by Savage (1892). The would-be killer was a mentally deranged spinster who fell in love with the local doctor and came to believe, quite without grounds, that he reciprocated her feelings and that only his wife stood between her and the desired union. She decided to remove this impediment to her happiness and take revenge for what she believed was keeping her would-be lover from her. The deluded lady, finding that the doctor's wife was fond of chocolate creams, managed with considerable ingenuity to introduce poisoned creams into the stock from which the doctor's wife bought her sweets. Tragically, though the intended victim escaped, the poisoned sweets were taken by several children. One of our cases attempted to poison her unfaithful husband. This was a typical act of revenge, in that it was contemplated over a long period and then put into practice with foresight and cunning. The woman had not given the husband any indication of her jealousy or any opportunity to defend himself from the accusation. The woman's suspicions and rage had been kept hidden until they reached fruition in the poisoning, which, fortunately for the husband, was unsuccessful.

Revenge often involves not just calculated violence, but violence at a distance—the poison, the flames, and the gun. It is different from the violence of uncontrolled passion, which often inflicts its damage with fists, feet, and any instrument that comes to hand. The violence of revenge relies less on brute force and is determined more by the dictates of reason (albeit perverted) than by loss of control. The impression that emerges from reading the literature, and from one's own inevitably limited experience, is that women figure relatively more frequently among those whose violence can be labeled as calculated revenge. This may, of course, reflect nothing more than the fears and fantasies of the men who write up such cases and remember them with such vividness.

JEALOUSY AND SADOMASOCHISM

Krafft-Ebing (1937) described sadism as the experience of pleasurable sexual sensations (including orgasm) produced by cruelty, which might involve humiliation, hurting, wounding, or even destruction. He considered masochism the opposite of sadism, in that it is sexual excitement derived from experiencing pain or subjugation. Sadism, he believed, involves the desire to control and subdue, whereas in masochism the pleasure derives from being completely and unconditionally subject to the will of the other. The often interchangeable relationship of the sadistic and masochistic attitudes has frequently been noted. Though some writers on this subject seem to have been dazzled by the more extreme and gross examples of physical abuse that may be inflicted or accepted in pursuit of this perverse pleasure, a number have noted the frequency with which minor degrees of this form of sexual excitement can be observed and how commonly it is part of sexual fantasy (Bloch, 1922; Krafft-Ebing, 1937; Reik, 1941, 1957, 1958).

The sexualization of anxiety and aggression is claimed to be involved in sadomasochism. Boss (1949) suggested that the desire for close human contact and love is the generating force behind these sexual anomalies. He believed that they may be the only way love can express itself in those developmentally limited in their capacity for forming close relationships. Taking pleasure from hurting and humiliating is often loosely referred to as sadomasochism. This is an unwarranted extension of a concept that is better restricted to the obtaining of sexual excitement and satisfaction from the actual or imagined distress of others.

Gottschalk (1936) claimed in his studies of jealousy that sadism and masochism play a prominent role in normal jealousy. He believed that sexual jealousy contains an element of direct lust and may itself be sexually exciting. Sadistic impulses may be combined with the jealousy, and this can give rise to fantasies that identify the infidelity with a rape situation. Ankles (1939) interviewed 30 normal volunteers who admitted to problems with jealousy, and he also came to the conclusion that sadism and masochism form an integral part of the jealousy complex. He suggested that "the pleasure-loving unscrupulous person usually localizes his sadism to the jealous field thinking this least harmful to him on account of the privacy enjoyed by this emotion as also the social sanction" (p. 112). His case reports make it clear that emotional cruelty and self-abasement combined with sexual fantasies, rather than actual physical abuse, are what form the basis for these individuals' excursions into sadomasochism.

"Sadomasochism" is a term with considerable elasticity. It can encompass the hideous cruelties and sexual excesses of a monster like the 15th-century French nobleman Gilles de Rays, said to have tortured some 800 children to death in pursuit of his sexual delight. At the other extreme, it can be used to describe the pleasure to be extracted from the little defeats and minor embarrassments inflicted upon one's sexual partner. In the latter context, Krafft-Ebing (1937) described as "sadistic" men who are sexually excited by demanding the sexual act in unusual places (i.e., outside of the marital bed), because this offers an opportunity to show their superiority over women and to provoke their defenses, only to delight in their subsequent confusion and abashment. In jealousy, the sadomasochism can be manifested unequivocally in the fantasy life of the jealous and in the eroticization of humiliations and hurts both inflicted and received, which appear at some level to induce a perverse sexual pleasure.

A number of our jealous male patients described vivid fantasies of the supposed infidelities of their partners, which involved their rape and humiliation by the supposed or actual rivals. Some of these men recounted having vivid mental images of their partners' being sexually abused by the rivals. They often expressed the belief that the partners really enjoyed these fantasized sexual attacks. Even those who readily accepted that there could be no basis for their imaginings described intense emotional arousal in association with these daydreams, and some admitted masturbating to them or conjuring them up during intercourse with their partners to augment their excitement. A number who believed that there was some actual basis to these ideas would try to induce their partners to describe the rapes and sexual humiliations in detail. Masochistic gratification resulted from their own sense of being betrayed or excluded, and from intense identification with the partners in the fantasy. The sadistic gratification came from imagining the hurt and humiliation of the partners.

The use of fantasies about a partner's infidelity for sexual excitement and masturbation is not confined to men. Seeman (1979), in her detailed account of five women with excessive jealousy, noted the identification with the supposed rival in fantasies that cast the rival in the role of a resisting virgin deceived and cajoled into submission by the unfaithful husband. These women all gave some variant of the raped-virgin fantasy as their most common masturbatory fantasy in adolescence; this suggested that pre-existing masochistic traits were finding expression through the jealousy. The infamous Sachar Masoch employed jealousy to satisfy his needs for the perverse pleasures that now bear his name. His wife, in her memoirs, described her distress and surprise when he made it clear to her soon after their marriage that she was expected to take a lover and to flaunt her infidelities in his face, so as to expose him to the tortures of jealousy and the exquisite pain of betrayal (cited in Eisler, 1949).

The sadomasochism of fantasy and that of the acts of harming or being hurt may well have their roots in the same desires and impulses, but are entirely different in their effects. The sadomasochism that confines itself to violent imagining is quite a different animal from that which attacks and destroys. Bloch (1908) believed that sadomasochistic inclinations are normally concerned with the idea of suffering and humiliation rather than the inflicting of actual pain. Indeed, he stated that, for all but the rare exception, actual pain does not arouse lust; only the fantasy of it does. The danger of the passion of jealousy is that it provides an ideal excuse and cover for those closet sadomasochists who are willing to act upon their perverse desires. Moreover, the violence released by jealousy may all too easily become sexualized, fostering both sadistic and masochistic tendencies that might otherwise have remained latent or confined to the realm of ideas.

The frequency of overtly sadomasochistic fantasies in our case material contrasts with the rarity of obviously sadomasochistic actions. That the aggression shown by the jealous brought them satisfaction was clear in many cases, but the sexual element, if any, in this pleasure was rarely apparent to either perpetrators or victims. Anger, rage, the desire for revenge, the wish to extract confessions, the urge to punish—these were the conscious motives most frequently articulated by the jealous for their aggression. It is, of course, possible that beneath the admitted intentions lay the denied and repressed drives of sadomasochism. In practice, even when sexual excitement is admitted to, it is often difficult to clarify the erotic element that emerges in the jealousy. A number of factors are acting to increase sexual arousal; these include the identification of the accuser with either the rival or the beloved, the desire to win back the wandering partner, the enhancement of the sexual attractiveness of the beloved because of his or her being desired by another, and misattribution of emotions.

A relatively common scenario recounted by jealous couples consists of outbursts of aggression that may even involve some physical abuse and that culminate in sexual intercourse. Guilt and puzzlement are occasionally expressed both by the jealous and by the accused because of the heightened sexual arousal they experience during these scenes. When questioned, such individuals usually vehemently reject the suggestion that either inflicting pain or being subjugated and distressed has contributed to the eroticization of the situation. Though some skepticism about the denials may be justified, it is rarely productive to pursue the topic. Even those who are prepared to describe sadomasochistic fantasies are usually unwilling to accept that any aggressive actions they have indulged in were sexually gratifying, or that they obtained sexual pleasure from any actual humiliations to which they have been subjected. The barriers between the satisfactions of the idea of pain and the distress of actual pain were maintained by most of our jealous subjects.

One young woman plagued by jealousy did give an account of sexual excitement derived from being physically abused and humiliated. She had had a number of relationships usually lasting for a year or so, in each of which she had become jealous of her partner and become increasingly accusatory and intrusive. She had evoked anger, rejection, and (from two of her lovers) violent physical retaliation. She was painfully aware of the erotic satisfaction she obtained, both from the fantasies of sexual betrayal and from the rage and attacks both verbal and physical that her accusations brought down upon her. It emerged in psychotherapy that she had been sexually and physically abused as a child by a stepfather who, though violent on occasion, had also been one of the few consistent and (at some level) caring figures in her development. The masochistic pleasure this young woman received from the jealousy and its associated conflict was rooted at least in part in these early experiences. The abusive relationships of her adult life repeated her experience of childhood, but with a difference. As an adult she was able first to arouse her partner to be abusive and then eventually to reject and humiliate him. She could thus extract both a masochistic erotic pleasure and ultimately the satisfaction of control and revenge.

One couple's case illustrates how sadomasochistic jealous behavior may develop. The wife was the designated patient, as she had received psychiatric treatment in the past for a depressive disorder and had mood swings between mild elation and marked despondency. The marriage had been troubled by the wife's suspiciousness and accusations of infidelity against the husband. This jealousy was exacerbated when the wife's mood was either unusually high or low. The husband found his wife's unjustified accusations distressing, particularly as her far greater verbal facility left him quite unable to defend himself. The injustice of the situation was for him heightened by his suspicions that she might be less innocent of infidelity than he. This marital situation continued for some years with intermittent flareups, until on one occasion the wife launched into accusations when the husband was particularly anxious and irritable for other reasons. For the first time, he delivered several blows to his wife. This battering, once commenced, rapidly escalated. The violence in terms of both physical violence and overt sexual humiliation became a new feature of their relationship. The couple came jointly for help because of a justified fear that if the situation continued, either serious injury or separation was inevitable. The husband, once he had overcome his shame and embarrassment, was able to discuss the sexual excitement and gratification that he had discovered in physically and sexually abusing his wife. Fortunately, in this case the clear exposure of the sadomasochism was sufficient to bring the behavior to an abrupt end.

The accuser in jealousy plays a dominant and dominating role.

The very accusation of infidelity implies the assertion of rights and the demand for an accounting. It places the partner in a subservient role, for he or she must either confess or otherwise respond to the accusations. The fantasies of the jealous, and the righteous indignation and rage of the betrayed or the sense of humiliation and utter defeat of the abandoned, offer ample scope for gratifying sadomasochistic tendencies. The most sinister aspect is, however, that jealousy may provide a cloak of respectability and acceptability to the violence of this perverse pleasure.

CHILDREN AND THE
VIOLENCE OF JEALOUSY

In families bedeviled by jealousy, the children can become drawn into the conflict, and where violence flares, they may be among its victims. Children in these situations may be subjected to physical and emotional abuse as a by-product of the conflict raging between their parents. Alternatively, they may be drawn into the preoccupations or even delusions of the jealous partner and become a direct object of suspicion and aggression.

The male's ruminations on the supposed infidelities, both present and past, of his female partner can lead him to question the paternity of the children of their union (paternity confidence has been proposed as a sociobiological cause of jealousy; see Chapter 3). The themes of jealousy and fears about paternity are present in Strindberg's (1887/1964) play The Father, which itself portrays (or at least draws on) Strindberg's own experiences of the jealousy that marred all his three marriages (Anderson, 1971). These fears that the children are the living embodiment of the infidelity may draw onto the children the rage and aggression of the jealous parent.

A case of ours illustrates a bizarre variant on the relationship between jealousy and fears regarding paternity. The husband, an insecure young man, had always been easily roused to jealousy of his wife. When she became pregnant, he was delighted, partly at the prospect of paternity and partly because he believed the child would bind his wife permanently to him. She was far less pleased about this unplanned conception and made moves to seek an abortion. This led to considerable disagreement between the couple, which only ceased when the wife agreed to continue with the pregnancy. Fearful of a last-minute change of heart, the husband insisted on accompanying his wife to her initial antenatal appointment. At the doctor's office, he insisted on being present at his wife's examination. He found the procedure extremely disturbing and interpreted it as a form of sexual assault. Subsequently, he began to ruminate at length on his wife's fidelity. He started cross-questioning her on why she had chosen this particular obstetrician and whether she had known him previously. Over the following weeks, he became increasingly concerned that his wife was having an affair with the obstetrician. The wife considered these accusations so extraordinary that she refused even to discuss them. The jealousy escalated, with threats to the doctor and complaints to the Medical Council over his supposed professional misconduct. The husband insisted on a change of obstetrician, and the wife entered hospital for delivery under the care of a different doctor. By chance, as the husband was waiting outside the delivery room suite following the birth of his child, the original obstetrician exited, having been involved in another case. This triggered an outburst in which the enraged husband accused the doctor and his wife of having sexual relations while she lay recovering after having given birth. He also accused the nursing staff of having abetted this adultery. Following this curious scene, the husband's jealousy seemed to recede; his wife was reassured sufficiently to return home with the baby. In the following weeks, however, he was troubled by fears that the child was not his but the obstetrician's. He finally resolved these doubts by coming to believe that though the child was fathered by him, it was now under the control of the wife's supposed lover, the obstetrician, who had carried out some mysterious process during the pregnancy to bring this baby under his direct control. The husband's suspicions and jealousy were focused on the infant. This deluded young man came to believe that his child was the embodiment and instrument of the supposed rival's attempt to steal his wife. This situation culminated in a tragic and fatal assault on the child.

Jealousy may focus directly on the child of a relationship. Jealousy, particularly in its pathological extensions, can conceive of and become convinced by the most unlikely of associations, and gives credence to the most extraordinary types of supposed intercourse. Children can in this context become the direct object of jealousy. In the study of Mullen and Maack (1985), 6 of their 138 jealous subjects attacked their children; in Mowat's (1966) series, 9 of the 71 jealous murderers killed one or more of their children. In a number of cases, the children became the object of suspicion and accusations of an incestuous relationship, which culminated in the assaults. One father made a determined effort to set fire to his teenage son, whom he believed to be involved in an incestuous relationship with his mother. In another of our cases, a morbidly jealous woman attacked and injured her son, whom she accused of an incestuous homosexual intercourse with the father. Teenage children can become entangled in the delusions of a morbidly jealous parent and can be viewed as competing for the affection of the other parent. The assaults on children in our case material were usually on teenagers in contrast to the findings in other areas of child abuse, where assault is virtually confined to the younger age groups. The response in a situation of actual incest by the uninvolved (though not infrequently colluding) parent has not, to our knowledge, been systematically studied. In our experience of such situations, overt jealousy has not been a factor in the response of the uninvolved parent to the incest. In some cases of father-daughter incest, the mothers do reject the involved daughters; some families actually unite against the abused daughters, blaming them and driving them out.

Children may become direct victims of a jealous aggressor when they are attacked or even killed as a means of revenge against the supposedly unfaithful spouse. There are no examples in our case material; however, in classical Greek mythology, Medea, the wife of Jason (of Golden Fleece fame), was so enraged by her husband's infidelity that in revenge she attacked and killed their three sons (Hope Moncrieff, 1912).

The violence that explodes in relationships plagued by jealousy may involve others in the immediate environment, particularly children. In relationships where physical abuse and battering are continuing problems, children may become the victims of attacks, either when they try to intervene or apparently without rhyme or reason. The association between wife battering and coincidental child abuse has been noted by several authors. Gayford (1975) reported that over half of the battering men in his study also physically abused their children. He also found that over a third of the abused wives in their turn physically assaulted their children. Hilberman (1980) concluded that in domestic violence, children are deeply affected and at high risk of emotional neglect as well as physical and sexual abuse. Psarska (1970) described incidents in which children fell victim to their jealous parents when they tried to intervene to protect the parents who were under attack. Children in homes marred by the violence of jealousy are forced to be onlookers to parental assaults and may be attacked both by the jealous parents and on occasion by the battered parents, who turn their rage and hurt on the most available and vulnerable targets.

JEALOUSY AND AGGRESSION
AGAINST THE SELF

The violence of jealousy may turn against the self. The despair at the feared loss, the sense of humiliation, the frustrated rage, even the desire for revenge—all these may precipitate the jealous toward self-destructive acts. Nietzsche (1880/1966) described jealousy as like the trapped scorpion, which in its rage and frustration turns its sting against itself. Lagache (1947) reported that 12% of his jealous subjects made clear attempts at suicide and a further 6% indulged in self-destructive or self-mutilating acts. In Mowat's (1966) series, 9.5% attempted to kill themselves prior to turning their violence on their partners, and nearly a third attempted suicide after the event. Mullen and Maack (1985) reported that 28% of their 138 subjects were self-destructive, with 7 indulging in self-mutilation (largely by cutting and slashing themselves), 18 taking overdoses, 7 making other types of suicide attempts, and 1 killing himself during the period of the study.

In one of our cases, the jealous ruminations culminated in a near-fatal suicide attempt. The jealousy had developed after some 10 years of marriage in the context of a deteriorating sexual relationship and increasing alcohol abuse in the husband. He had become plagued by suspicions that his wife had been unfaithful and was continuing to indulge in affairs. He retained a degree of insight into how unjustified these suspicions were and how absurd his reasons for entertaining them were, but nevertheless the thoughts continued to intrude. He began torturing himself with notions that his children were not in fact his, but had been fathered by a neighbor with whom he feared his wife had had relations. This particular man, who was of a rather shy and oversensitive nature, could not bring himself to confront his wife with his suspicions for fear of their being confirmed. Early one morning, after lying awake in his bed for several hours in an agony of doubt, he went into his garage and in desperation drank battery acid. Another depressed patient in his 60s was overwhelmed by ideas of his elderly wife's imagined sexual infidelities and took an overdose of aspirin, fortunately without a fatal outcome. One young woman who had overdosed gave her reasons as the wish to punish her boyfriend, who, she believed, had become involved with one of her friends. This last type of situation is not uncommon among young self-poisoners; disturbed romantic attachments, which may include jealousy, sometimes precipitate impulsively self-destructive acts.

The violence engendered by jealousy may turn upon its author, producing self-destructive and suicidal acts. The relative frequency of self-directed violence as opposed to other-directed violence in jealousy is unknown, but clinical experience highlights the importance of both. It is an important and practical clinical point that those individuals who appear to be at high risk for violence against their partners will nearly always also be at high risk for suicide.

CONCLUSION

Jealousy is a common, if not ubiquitous, human experience that is only occasionally accompanied by overt violence. This chapter has concentrated on the exceptional and often extreme instances of aggression in the jealousy complex. The justification for the prominence accorded to violence in this book is that it accounts for considerable damage and destruction among those affected and makes a significant contribution to the criminal violence that afflicts our society.

This chapter has relied heavily on studies of subjects with pathological jealousy. This not only reflects the more extensive documentation available on this group, but may also point to a real increase in their propensity to resort to violence. The combination of a psychotic state with jealousy is a particularly explosive one. In generalizing from the extreme instance and the pathological case, considerable caution is required. However, these extraordinary instances are often just what can illuminate and highlight the mechanisms that lie behind more mundane examples. The hope is that as we come to understand more about the essential elements that predispose jealous individuals to violence and provoke it in them, our capacity to act preventively will increase.

9

The Clinical Management of Jealousy

This book sets out to present jealousy for clinicians and clinical researchers. The justification of the clinical enterprise is action that will relieve distress. It is not enough for clinicians to know more about jealousy; they must also bring about beneficial changes in those sufferers who seek their help. In this chapter, the information and approaches set out in the previous chapters are applied to the critical issues of management and treatment.

A thorough clinical assessment is the first phase in developing a plan of management. Its objectives are to characterize the nature of this particular individual's jealousy and to determine how it interacts with his or her present relationship, life situation, and past history. The issue of actual or potential violence must always be addressed.

The approach to assessment of a patient or client varies according to the training and experience of the health professional involved. A psychiatrist will encounter jealousy most frequently in its pathological forms, and by training will be predisposed to regard the jealousy as a symptom of an underlying process rather than as a disorder in and of itself. In contrast, a marriage guidance counselor will rarely see the pathological jealousies, but will be all too aware of the destructive potential of so-called normal jealousy. The counselor's gaze will inevitably be drawn to relationship factors and away from individual psychopathology. The clinical psychologist will approach jealousy through the mediation of his or her training and experience, usually with a central concern for individual behavior and cognitive processes, but eschewing the psychiatrist's propensity to resort to conceptual models dependent on process and disease.

Constantine (1986), in an excellent review of marital therapy in jealousy, comments that the extreme of "pathological" jealousy is a manifestation of chronic, seriously disturbed relationship patterns. He implies that it would be an error to see jealousy as reflecting primarily the individual psychopathology of the jealous person. This insight undoubtedly reflects the experience of a marital therapist, but would run counter to that of a psychiatrist who sees many symptomatic jealousies. The differences in approach reflect differences in training and differences in the types and range of those who consult us. It is even possible that if we exchanged our patients, or exchanged patients for clients, we would find our models being exchanged with them.

The attitudes and (let it be admitted) prejudices that guide assessment will also color the choice and execution of therapeutic options. We cannot escape our own established frames of reference and action, but we can be aware of their existence and limitations. It is destructive for a psychiatrist to treat a woman struggling with the realities of an oppressive and failing marriage as if she were simply a depressed patient whose jealousy can be relegated to a mere symptom. It is equally destructive for a marital therapist to blithely interpret a jealousy that is indeed symptomatic of a depressive illness exclusively in terms of family dynamics.

ASSESSMENT

The Context

The framework usually employed in assessment involves both individual and joint interviews with the partners. The initial interview is determined by the context of the referral. When the jealous individual presents himself or herself for help, the person will be seen alone and only later interviewed jointly with the partner. The partner is seen alone whenever possible following the joint interview. This structure acknowledges that the jealous person who has presented for help is indeed the focus of attention, but provides ample opportunity to explore the situation with the partner. When the partners present together, then a joint interview precedes the individual sessions. Referrals from the courts are dealt with in the same way whenever possible, though on occasion the tensions or fears present in such relationships preclude seeing the partners jointly or even having them in the same building. The time required for assessment varies not only with the individual case, but with the professional affiliations of the therapist. The suggestion from some more radical or playful therapists that the rival be included rarely seems relevant in our own experience.

There are advantages in employing two therapists in both assessment and treatment. Our own preference has been for a male and a female therapist, even in cases involving homosexual couples. On occasion, the presence of two interrogators has clearly had an inhibiting influence on the interview. The solution of having each therapist interview one partner and then having them come together for the joint interviews has been explored. This model, so useful in sexual and other relationship problems, has limitations in the jealousy complex, where shared goals and congruent perceptions cannot be assumed. The therapists too easily slide into advocacy roles that are not necessarily helpful in work with jealousy.

The structure and purpose of the assessment procedure should be explained to the couple at the outset. It is important that each partner know what is behind both the joint interview and the interviews that occur with the other partner in his or her absence. Jealousy involves suspicion and is often sustained in an atmosphere of obfuscation and ambiguity. For therapists to reproduce the very conditions in which jealousy thrives is not particularly smart. The assessment procedures should be negotiated at each stage, and resistance should be dealt with by respecting rather than interpreting or ignoring its roots.

On occasion, an independent informant outside of the couple in conflict may be useful.

The Assessment Interviews

The approach to assessment draws on the knowledge base outlined earlier in this book. The assessment gathers the information necessary to plan a therapeutic strategy. Differing therapeutic modalities will emphasize different aspects of the history. In general, however, the data base for effective therapeutic intervention will involve obtaining a history of the present jealousy and the relationship in which it has arisen. Past experiences of jealousy and the relationship contexts in which they have emerged need to be explored. A family history and some account of the individual's personal development are useful, as is an assessment, however tentative, of the personality structures of each partner. A mental status examination will form a central feature of a psychiatrist's interview, but will figure less prominently, if at all, in the assessments of other health professionals. These elements in the assessment are now discussed in more detail.

A History of the Present Jealousy

A history of the present jealousy should include the following: (1) the chronology of the development and progress of the jealousy, and (2) the ways in which the jealousy is experienced by both partners.

An account of the origins and progress of the jealousy should be obtained from each partner. In most cases, accounts of the progress of the jealousy and the claimed vindications are provided with alacrity. Problems arise in stemming the flow of accusations and self-justifications rather than in encouraging disclosure. The spontaneously provided history usually consists of reported actions and their interpretation, countered by denials or alternative explanations. Even when actual infidelity is acknowledged, the extent and type are usually in contention.

The events surrounding the emergence of the jealousy are of central importance—not just those obviously related to the jealousy's development, but also anything that may have stressed or undermined the self-esteem of the jealous individual or altered the dynamics of the relationship. Why did the jealousy emerge then? This is a critical question. Equally critical is another question: Why present for help with jealousy now? Both these questions should be shared with the partners and explored directly with them.

A chronological account of the development of suspicions and attempts to deal with them should be obtained from the jealous person. A similar account should be obtained from the partner of the jealousy's effects and the partner's responses to these.

An adequate history often needs to extend beyond the bare bones of the story to experiences and behaviors that are less readily admitted or acknowledged. In inquiring into these areas, the clinician enters a realm about which the jealous individual may be reluctant or unable to speak. The formulation of questions is critical. Ask most jealous subjects whether they spy on their partners or check their clothes for the telltale signs of illicit sexual activity, and they will deny it. It is far more effective to offer them the opportunity to talk about such behavior by noting the frequency with which those in the grips of jealousy find themselves drawn to checking up on their partners and even find themselves searching through pockets or in piles of discarded clothes for incriminating evidence. With the deluded or vehemently self-righteous, no such delicacy is necessary. With the highly suggestible, however, caution in the use of leading questions needs to be emphasized.

The areas requiring elucidation are described below.

Judgments. The overt judgment or appraisal offered in jealousy is usually that sexual infidelity has occurred. This judgment needs to be explored further. The perceived extent of the threat or damage to self-esteem or to the relationship needs to be determined. It is illuminating to encourage the jealous person to discuss what he or she believes his or her rights in the relationship should be and how the partner should behave. One man, when offered this opening, expressed his helplessness in the face of a wife who, having returned to the workforce after child rearing, now earned more than he and also expected him to undertake tasks at home that contradicted his firmly held but unacknowledged canons of manhood. In this case, jealousy was an element in a power struggle by a man deprived of the supports for his fragile masculinity; he felt that his wife had rendered him useless and robbed him of his self-esteem. He wanted her at home and dependent, but because he was a self-declared liberal progressive, it was easier to accuse her of adultery than to voice what he acknowledged to be blatantly sexist demands.

Feelings. Anger and fear are usually offered without prompting. The sadness and nascent despair can be revealed through gentle inquiry. Guilt, shame, humiliation, and envy, though frequently present, are often expressed only on direct questioning. Some report heightened sexual attraction (see below).

Desires. The jealous person desires to know; like a scientist, he or she claims to be searching for the truth and nothing but the truth. It is important to discover whether the truth the person speaks of is a confirmation of his or her suspicions or a vindication of the partner. Where actual sexual infidelity is acknowledged, the jealous individual's contradictory desires often shift to divining whether the partner still truly loves him or her or prefers the rival; again, it is important to determine whether the person's investment is in exposing the partner's total betrayal or in gaining reassurance of his or her true contrition. Jealousy often stimulates sexual desire, though occasionally the suspicions of infidelity introduce disgust into the sexual interaction. Exploring the impact of jealousy on the individual's sexuality is a delicate and tension-charged process. It is rarely wise to enter this area until the therapeutic relationship is firmly established.

Fantasy and Imagination. The confusion and shame evoked by the sexual fantasies that so often accompany the jealous passion makes their open disclosure difficult. We usually approach this area by exploring the mental images that intrude on and trouble the jealous individual. Jealousy is imagistic, and the vivid fantasies of the partner's activities are often at the forefront of a jealous person's mind. The response to these fantasies and the impact on the person's own sexual interests and desires can then be explored.

The more sophisticated of our patients are aware that jealousy is supposed to carry homosexual undertones and that their fantasies are said by some psychodynamically oriented therapists to express homoeroticism. In these individuals, either an overready acceptance or a horrified rejection of such a supposed interpretation can disrupt the chances of obtaining an adequate account of what desires and fantasies have actually been evoked by the jealousy. It is always worth remembering that in any attempt to explore the mental life of another, the preconceptions and prejudices of both the client and the therapist lie between what is actually experienced and what is finally recorded as having occurred.

Behavior. The clinician needs to know what has been done about those predispositions to act that the jealous person has controlled or rejected. It is not only what the person has done, but what he or she has thought about and wished to do, that needs exploring. How has the jealous individual acted? Has he or she watched, cross-questioned, checked on, or attempted to entrap the partner? As already noted, it is far more difficult to elicit a candid account of this area than might appear. Most jealous individuals who are otherwise normal are ashamed of the actions prompted by jealousy, let alone the impulses that they have managed to control. Those with delusions of infidelity may be secretive and distrustful; though willing to accuse, they are reluctant to disclose their own activities.

The account of the present episode of jealousy then needs to be augmented by an account of previous eruptions of jealousy that have marred this relationship. In practice, the history of the jealousy problems in the relationship is usually given as a single account of interrelated episodes, but occasionally there is a clear separation between the current problems and past experiences of jealousy. This is particularly so in pathological jealousy, where a break is recognized between how the individual used to respond and how he or she is responding on this occasion.

Relationship History

The relationship history is central to the assessment of jealousy. An account of the natural history of the relationship should be obtained. This includes how the couple met, what the initial attractions were, how the relationship progressed, and what the patterns of intimacy and conflict were. Such an autobiography of the relationship will often differ markedly for each partner. It is also necessary to question the couple about specific aspects of relationships that research suggests are important in the development of jealousy. As we have indicated in Chapter 5, the clinician will often have considerable difficulty separating aspects of the relationship per se from the individual characteristics of the parties that are manifested in the context of the relationship. For example, a strong desire for sexual exclusivity may emerge from the relationship or may be a direct result of the pre-existing character traits of one or both partners. The following aspects of the relationship are useful to explore:

Power, Dependence, and Decision Making. The perception of who has the greatest power and influence in particular domains will often be consistent with asymmetries of influence in decision making. The partner who perceives himself or herself as less powerful will usually also regard himself or herself as relatively more dependent on the relationship. There is a greater frequency of jealousy in the more dependent partner. One partner can be vulnerable to external threats to the relationship because of a disproportionate investment combined with a sense of lack of control. A person low in power is likely to perceive himself or herself as having fewer and less attractive alternatives to the relationship (Thibaut & Kelley, 1959). In addition, inducing jealousy can be a power tactic to force the partner to behave in a desired way, or to punish the partner for past inequities (White, 1980a).

Equity. The partner who has put greater effort into developing and maintaining the relationship is more likely to demonstrate increased sensitivity to threats to the relationship. The perception of the justness of outcome in the relationship is at issue here. Does one partner feel that he or she is putting relatively more into the relationship but failing to obtain the desired rewards for these efforts? A partner who assumes that he or she is not receiving "just deserts" is more likely to react with jealousy.

Benefits. It is useful to obtain an account of how each partner has become dependent on the other for valued outcomes, including self-esteem. Remember that these may be quite idiosyncratic (e.g., status at a sports club, entrée into a social circle, participation in an extended family). Fear of the potential loss of valued outcomes may increase the sensitivity to, and force of, jealous reactions.

Exclusivity Norms. Here the focus is on the overt and covert manner in which the couple have negotiated norms concerning exclusivity, especially (but not limited to) sexual exclusivity. The process by which such norms have been reached is often as important as their content. An effort should be made to explore both the cultural and relationship-specific norms that are operating. Both partners may be encouraged to describe the norms that have developed in the relationship in such areas as dating, extramarital friendships, and the limits of what is acceptable with regard to other sexual involvements. Their own norms about disclosing relationship problems to others, and their expectations about how they should acknowledge their sexual feelings about others, can be explored. In particular, attention needs to be directed at each partner's ideas about the importance of loyalty and how the partner regards particular behaviors as revealing disloyalty or confirming loyalty.

Perceived Adequacy as a Partner. It is important, though often difficult, to elucidate the adequacy or inadequacy each partner feels—that is, the degree to which each partner characterizes himself or herself as a good or poor match for the other. Those with a tendency to perceive themselves as inadequate and powerless to change this status are susceptible to jealousy.

Sex-Role Stereotypes. The partners' views on gender roles and activities should be explored. The degree to which the partners acknowledge or positively assent to cultural norms needs exposing in such areas as the division of labor (men do the heavy work, the man's career provides the basis for the relationship's economic stability, women are the homemakers), emotional stereotypes (women express feelings, men keep their own counsel), and sexual stereotypes (men are promiscuous by nature). The hope is that making such expectations explicit will allow them to be directly examined, and that if this can be done the focus of the jealous conflict may be shifted from the personality characteristics of the couple to the somewhat more malleable area of role and norm definitions. This increases the range of strategies available in managing the jealousy.

Previous Solutions. Finally, the couple should be encouraged to identify previous solutions and their effects. The specific behaviors each partner has employed to cope with jealousy problems, and their usefulness in reducing the threat both to self and to the relationship, should be assessed by each partner. Attempted solutions that have misfired, creating more problems rather than ameliorating the difficulties, should be identified, and the likely reasons for the failure of the attempted solutions should be explored. It is worth remembering that though the partners are likely to agree on the general goal of lessening and, if possible, extirpating the jealousy, they may have very different ideas on how this goal can be reached.

Past History of Jealousy and Relationships

A detailed account of past relationships, with particular emphasis on problems of infidelity and desertion, is required. If jealousy has marred past relationships, the similarities between those and the present episode are often revealing. Conversely, if jealousy was not a feature of past relationships, the clinician has the opportunity to explore what it is about this particular relationship that has promoted the jealousy. The obvious answer is actual or suspected infidelity, but this line of questioning may also reveal the critical differences between this relationship and past liaisons.

Previous Mental and Physical Health

A previous history of psychiatric disorder, such as a depressive episode or schizophrenic illness, is of obvious relevance. When such a history is forthcoming, every effort should be made to obtain all the available information, including reports and notes from those who previously looked after the patient. The past medical history is of importance, both in general terms and with regard to any possible interaction with such functions as sexual or work capacity that might have increased vulnerability or lowered self-esteem. A history, for example, of long-standing diabetes mellitus in men should alert the clinician to the possibility of potency problems and painful intercourse.

Family History

The family history appropriate to any assessment needs to be augmented by some specific inquiries. The presence of mental disorders in close relatives may be relevant, particularly if the diagnosis falls within either the schizophrenic or major affective disorders, which have a significant genetic component. Jealousy is found to run in some families. We have encountered a number of cases where there is a family tradition of excessive (and, in some instances, violent) jealousy. In one dramatic example, a middle-aged man of Asian extraction was referred from the courts, where he was facing a charge of attempting to murder his wife. He reported that his own mother had been killed by his father in a jealous rage. The household he grew up in contained his parents, whose relationship even before the fatal assault was marred by jealousy and violence, and his grandparents, whose relationship was similarly troubled. The grandfather had, in fact, been removed from the family at one stage because of his persistent accusations against his wife. The patient had grown to adulthood in an environment where accusations of infidelity were constantly being leveled at both women in the household. Whether the emergence of his jealousy reflected environmental or genetic endowment is impossible to know for certain, but it would have been unwise to ignore the family influence, however it was mediated.

Personal and Developmental History

Problems with rivalry and envy during childhood are useful to explore. The level of actual and perceived success with peers and in terms of achievement may give useful insight into an individual's self-esteem. In many ways, the objective capacities are of less relevance than the persons's perception of success and degree of contentment with his or her performance.

Alcohol and Substance Abuse

A thorough account of alcohol usage is mandatory, given its relationship to jealousy and its importance in assessing dangerousness. Drug usage (particularly of amphetamines or cocaine) should also be assessed, specifically for the time course of use and the development of jealousy.

Assessment of the Personality

The most common group of personality variables encountered in the jealous center around lowered self-esteem and increased sensitivity to loss or threat in the area of the romantic relationship. The jealous person's self-esteem may of course be reduced as a *result* of the threats implied by the rival relationship, instead of the jealousy's being a *manifestation* of poor self-esteem. The individual's judgment of his or her own jealousy may well be that it implies a personality flaw and indicates insecurity or other deficiency. This self-denigration may well be reinforced by the partner or friends, who may also identify the jealousy as a product of personality defects. Thus, when lowered self-esteem is encountered in a jealous individual, it is important to explore whether this is an enduring aspect of the individual's personality and self-image, or whether the lowered self-esteem has followed the threat to the relationship and the jealousy.

The subjective meaning of events and their implications for self-esteem need to be assessed. The task is to address the subjective meaning of the events triggering jealousy, with a particular focus on how such meanings affect and are affected by self-esteem. These factors should be explored with both partners. The subjective import of particular events can be explored by questions that focus on the experiences generated by specific behaviors of the partner or the rival—for example, "How does it make you feel about yourself when your partner does X?" or "What do you think other people would think about you if they knew about X?"

Mental Status Examination

In a formal psychiatric assessment, mental status will be the central focus of the examination. This reflects a training and orientation determined by the needs of managing individuals with mental disorders in which major abnormalities of mental state are frequent and often critical to diagnosis and treatment. Other mental health professionals do not accord primacy to this aspect of assessment for equally compelling reasons, based on their own disciplines' clinical realities. In pathological jealousy, particularly when a symptomatic conceptualization may be appropriate, an adequate assessment of the person's mental status will be required to clarify the issue. This will require input from a psychiatrist or other clinician competent in examining mental status. The specific disturbances of mental state that may accompany jealousy have been discussed in Chapter 7. It is not possible to pursue this issue further here; the reader who wishes for more information should consult one of the available accounts of descriptive psychopathology and the examination of the mental state (Fish, 1967; Kraupl Taylor, 1979; Mullen, 1985; Scharfetter, 1980; Taylor, 1981).

Assessment of the Potential for Violence

The issue of violence in the jealousy complex has been reviewed in Chapter 8. The violence of jealousy poses the greatest threat to the partner, though the supposed rival and even children of the relationship may be caught up in the aggression. Self-destructive and suicidal behavior also poses a risk that requires consideration.

Pathological jealousies may reasonably be presumed to pose a greater risk of violence, but normal jealousy also presents a potential threat that must be assessed. It cannot be emphasized too strongly that the assessment of dangerousness is a necessary step in all cases of jealousy.

The inquiry into aggression involves eliciting information about violent impulses, desires, and fantasies, as well as aggressive actions, both direct and indirect. This information is largely obtained through asking questions. Occasionally, past medical or court records may be available to supplement the data base; if such records exist, they should be consulted whenever possible. Those who are inexperienced in assessing dangerousness may underestimate the value of asking direct questions. It is useful to be open with the client—to state that an assessment of the likelihood of serious aggression's arising from the jealousy is necessary, and that the clinician requires the client's full cooperation. It never ceases to amaze us how candid and trusting most of our patients are in revealing violent impulses and actions, both past and present. This very candor can create profound ethical dilemmas, which are discussed later.

It is usually productive to put questions in a hierarchical manner, beginning with the anger and irritation that are virtually universal, and working up through violent impulses and fantasies to aggressive acts.

Threats are common. The situation in which they were uttered and how they were emphasized should be ascertained. A threat to kill that is yelled at the height of a stormy argument in which recriminations and abuse are being freely exchanged is less chilling than a similar threat delivered in measured tones over the breakfast table. One of our patients woke his wife in the early hours of the morning and threatened her life while standing over her, apparently calm and grimly serious. The wife did not reveal this event until some months later, after a serious and potentially lethal assault had in fact occurred. How frightened the partner is by the threat is not an infallible guide to seriousness, but it is relevant. A threat that is underscored by violent gesture or brandishing a weapon evokes greater apprehension. The implications of threatening words and gestures must be judged against the norms for that individual and that relationship. Men and women who are given to loud altercations and frequent imprecations over the trivia of family life, but who have not previously resorted to physical violence, provoke less anxiety by their threats than those who have never before raised their voices in anger.

Sudden urges to violence and fantasies of retribution should be explored. Increasing frequency and power of either the impulses or the daydreams should alert the interviewer to possible danger. The more detailed a fantasy, particularly when it involves actual planning, the more apprehension it should create. When a fantasy gives way to actions in the terms of collecting weapons or preparing alibis, then the danger must be regarded as considerable. We have had patients who, following long periods of fantasizing about avenging themselves, have begun to make concrete preparations for attack. In one case the man actually began practicing by knifing sheep as surrogates for his wife.

A catalogue of acts of violence must be obtained from both the jealous subject and the partner. Inquiries can be made into whether the jealous person has done the following:

1. Destroyed the partner's property or broken and smashed objects during an argument.
2. Pushed, shoved, or shaken the partner in anger.
3. Struck the partner, and if so, whether with open hand or fist. If the jealous individual has kicked the partner, then the details are important, as there is a world of difference between kicking a standing person on the shin and booting a person as he or she lies helpless on the ground.
4. Thrown objects at the partner with the intention of hurting him or her.
5. Attempted to throttle the partner, or put hands around his or her throat in anger.
6. Attacked the partner with (a) a club-like object,
   (b) a knife, or
   (c) a gun.
7. Taken any other action that could have injured or harmed the partner (e.g., poisoning, driving at the partner, pushing him or her in front of traffic, etc.).

The context of each such act should be explored with both partners, as well as what initiated it and what terminated the action. The damage inflicted must be ascertained. It should be remembered that domestic violence not infrequently comes to involve mutual abuse (Straus, 1978). This is particularly important when the female partner is the jealous subject who may be initiating the violence, but it is the male who presents the threat of serious damage.

The more detailed questioning about violent acts can be completed rapidly in most cases where the aggression is safely controlled, but even in apparently straightforward cases surprises can occur. One middle-aged lady appeared amazed at the inquiries about threats and violence, dismissing them with detached humor, until the interviewer asked whether she had ever done anything else aimed to hurt or harm her husband. After a brief pause, she quietly confessed to having attempted to poison him some weeks previously. A husband and wife who were in treatment some years ago were not asked directly about aggression; the issue was explored only in generalities. There appeared no obvious reasons to be anxious in their case about violence. It was only after the police brought to the clinician's attention that the armed offenders' squad had been called to the marital home on two occasions that direct questions were asked. It emerged that a number of violent incidents had occurred that the couple had not told the clinician about; the husband was ashamed, and the wife wanted to protect him.

Once the pattern of aggression in the present episode of jealousy has been determined, it is necessary to establish whether the individual's previous behavior, both in the domestic situation and more generally, has been marked by outbursts of aggression or violence. Past behavior predicts future behavior. Those who have previously resorted to violence constitute a high-risk group. The greater the similarities between the context that generated the previous violence and the present situation, the more concerned the clinician should be.

In assessing an individual's violence potential, the general factors of age, sex, and socioeconomic background should be given some weight, but less so than in situations not involving jealousy. Alcohol and substance abuse are of considerable importance. Jealousy frequently involves violent impulses that are controlled; the disinhibition of intoxication may make it all too easy to translate such impulses into actions. The irritability and overarousal that characterize the withdrawal phase following alcohol consumption may also predispose an individual to aggressive outbursts. The morning after can be just as dangerous.

The final judgment as to whether there is a high or low risk of violence against the partner remains subjective. The more clearly a pattern of escalating aggression and overt violence can be established, the more certain it is that violence will follow. It is our practice to share our apprehensions with both partners about past and possible future dangerousness. When there is clearly a high risk of injury, separation must be encouraged in the interests of both partners. It is no benefit to a jealous individual to maintain him or her in a situation that could culminate in a jail sentence for harming the partner.

In normal jealousy, all the clinician can do is to share his or her opinion and to insure that the potential victim is informed about legal rights and the services available to him or her. If the partners decide to remain together despite the warnings, then the clinician can only accept this and work to minimize the risk. In pathological jealousy, the issue of whether the combination of mental disorder and threat to others is strong enough to justify hospitalization, either voluntary or compulsory has to be faced. In pathological jealousy with a significant risk of violence, our own policy is to opt for admission earlier rather than later. The involvement of the courts in our cases has usually come at too late a stage to offer any preventive or remedial role for the justice system. It is theoretically possible to employ the provisions of the justice system to enforce separation and reduce the risk of further molestation in cases where violence has already led to successful prosecution.

The specific mental disorders associated with or underlying the jealousy may affect the risk of violence. With delusions of infidelity, particularly those emerging in the context of a schizophrenic syndrome, there may be coexisting delusions of persecution. The subject not only may have a delusional jealousy, but may also believe that the partner is poisoning or otherwise plotting against him or her. In such a situation, the deluded individual may believe that the loved one not only is unfaithful, but presents a real threat to his or her survival. When proximity and an intense relationship coexist with delusions of infidelity and persecution, then the risk of violence is increased (Hafner & Boher, 1982; Taylor & Gunn, 1984). One of our patients with a schizophrenic disorder was convinced that his wife was flagrantly unfaithful; in addition, he believed that at night she withdrew the "vital essence" from his backbone, and that this rendered him impotent and was slowly destroying him. He planned to save himself by killing his "witch wife"—a course of action fortunately forestalled by hospital admission. Major depressions may also increase the likelihood of serious violence by inducing a state in which subjects feel that their own lives are rendered useless and that they might as well kill the lovers they hold responsible as well as themselves. The murder–suicide combinations that occur on occasion can have a basis in morbid jealousy.

The management of violence within relationships lies outside the scope of this book. Rosenbaum and O'Leary (1986), in their excellent review, emphasize the responsibility of the therapist to make it clear to couples that physical abuse is both unacceptable and illegal. When violence has been manifested, it is part of our role as therapists to insure that the victims are aware of the legal and community resources available to them for protection, redress, and assistance. Familiarity with such facilities as shelters, women's refuges, support agencies, legal advice bureaus, and police liaison services available in one's own area is essential. If children are placed at risk by the violence, then the involvement of the child protection team is, we believe, a necessity, and in many jurisdictions is mandatory. In practice, it is often necessary to manage the marital violence as a problem in its own right while simultaneously addressing the issues raised by the jealousy. A number of approaches to the management of violence in relationships are available, including self-help strategies, groups, and conjoint marital therapy (Margolin, 1979; Purdy & Nickle, 1981; Sonkin & Durphy, 1983). The priority when violence is present is safety. The responsibility for the violence belongs to the aggressor, however provocative the partner may be.

Suicidal and self-destructive behavior poses a significant threat in persistent jealousy. The risk is highest where significant depression coexists with the jealousy. The clinician should inquire routinely into suicidal ruminations, plans, and possible actions. Hopelessness about the future should raise suspicion, particularly when combined with guilt-ridden and self-derogatory preoccupations. It is our clinical impression that those who present a profile suggestive of a high risk of violence toward others are also at high risk of harming themselves.

Classification of Jealousy
Based on Assessment Information

In Chapter 7 we suggested that jealousies can be usefully classified as normal, pathologically reactive, or symptomatic (see Figure 9.1). In symptomatic jealousies the underlying disorder(s) becomes the major focus of therapy. In reactive jealousies the management of jealousy is central, although, occasionally, associated conditions (e.g. depression or sexual dysfunction) may need treatment in their own right. In normal reactive jealousy the relationship is usually the focus of therapy whereas in pathologically reactive jealousy the jealous individual is the focus. When diagnosing pathologically reactive jealousy the assumption is made that the jealous individual has responded in an inappropriate and deviant manner, which reflects disordered functioning. The relationship and the wider social context remain relevant, but secondary. With all of the jealousies, the evaluation of the potential for violence is critical as such potential will markedly affect the choice of management strategies.

It is often impossible on initial assessment to identify the role that more subtle or denied characterological features may play. Displacement of feeling, perverse sexuality, or sadistic gratification, for example, may surface only after some time in counseling. Often the therapist suspects that a lack of progress on the resolution of normal jealousy reflects individual pathology. It is then that a reassessment of the primary and secondary gains to both partners may reveal

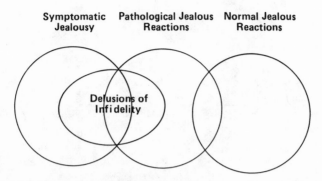

FIGURE 9.1. Diagram of the overlapping nature of symptomatic jealous reactions, pathological jealous reactions, and normal jealous reactions. In practice, the largest group by far is that of the normal jealous reactions. Delusions of infidelity are to be found in both the symptomatic and the pathological categories.

deviant and displaced forces that sustain the jealous feelings and behaviors. Hence, the initial classification of jealousy as normal, pathologically reactive, or symptomatic needs to be reviewed as therapy progresses.

MANAGEMENT AND TREATMENT

Figure 9.2 presents a schematic approach to the management of symptomatic, pathologically reactive, and normal jealousies. After initial assessment of the presenting jealousy as symptomatic, pathologically reactive, or normal; it is important to assess dangerousness. A high risk of violence should lead to an initial focus on safety, including a decision to separate the couple or not. Assessment of low risk of violence should lead to different treatment depending on the type of jealousy. In symptomatic jealousy the underlying disorder is treated, management of jealousy within the relationship if necessary is directed at containment. In pathologically reactive jealousy the treatment focus will be on the jealous individual, not on the relationship. Couples therapy if conducted should be directed at containment of jealousy and consolidation of treatment gains in individual therapy. With normal jealousy, treatment focuses on the relationship with individual work taking secondary importance. Specific suggestions about the treatment of different jealousies are presented in the sections that follow.

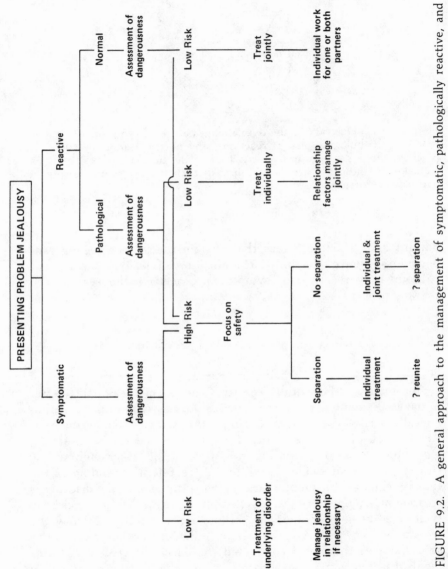

FIGURE 9.2. A general approach to the management of symptomatic, pathologically reactive, and normal jealousies.

In approaching treatment issues in jealousy, the division into normal, pathologically reactive, and symptomatic categories has continuing utility. Delusions of infidelity are found in some jealousies in both the symptomatic and pathologically reactive categories; because they raise treatment issues of their own, these are discussed separately. The treatment approaches can be conceptualized within a hierarchical model. The management strategies applicable to normal jealousy may well have a part to play in the treatment of the pathological jealousies. The therapeutic maneuvers used in pathological reactions may also be found useful for symptomatic jealousies, but a number of treatments employed for symptomatic jealousies are specific for particular disorders producing jealousy as a symptom. The treatment of normal jealousy is discussed first, because it is by far the most common and because the approaches can be generalized for use in the pathological jealousies.

Management of the Normal Jealousies

This section begins by outlining the therapeutic goals applicable to the management of normal jealousy. Since there is no comparative literature on the efficacy of the various treatment methods advocated for attaining such goals, it is difficult to advance any authoritative statement on which of the many available therapeutic techniques should be employed. However, we attempt a brief review of some of the treatment approaches detailed in the literature. Finally, a discussion of jealousy workshops is included, as these are a novel and potentially important development in jealousy management.

White and Devine (in press) surveyed therapists about their experience of treating jealousy. They randomly surveyed counselors from members of the American Association of Marriage and Family Therapy. The 60 counselors who responded were heterogeneous as regards professional training and theoretical orientation; they included (among others) clinical psychologists, social workers, and those whose practice depended on psychodynamic, behavioral, and systems approaches. This sample reported that jealousy was a major factor in one-third of all clients seeking relationship therapy and was the primary presenting problem in about 10%. An even larger number of those seeking such help reported jealousy as a minor or secondary difficulty. Highest rates were reported in clients under 30, with a gradual decline in the older groups.

The therapists were asked to rate the importance of a number of factors in contributing to jealousy. Chronic feelings of low self-esteem and excessive dependence on the partner were consistently rated as the most important for both men and women. These two factors were followed by feelings of inadequacy as a partner and excessive demands for attention and sexual exclusivity. These four factors were rated to play a part in well over half of the cases of jealousy. Being in a position of low power in the relationship was considered of importance in women, but not in men (but then women may have been more likely to have been deprived of power). Contrary to psychodynamic formulations, Oedipal problems were not rated as particularly important, even by those therapists who described themselves as having a psychodynamic orientation. The length of marriage and number of children were not found to affect the frequency of jealousy problems. An important observation was that couples were more likely to present in the context of an actual and acknowledged rival relationship than with jealousy that was groundless or obviously inappropriate.

White and Helbick (1988) reviewed the clinical literature available on treatment of normal jealousy and reported seven therapeutic goals commonly cited in the clinical reports:

1. To challenge irrational beliefs and assumptions.
2. To improve communication skills.
3. To facilitate explicit negotiations over acceptable and nonacceptable behaviors with others.
4. To build the self-esteem of the jealous partner.
5. To resolve personal or relationship issues that have led to the jealousy.
6. To reformulate the meaning of jealousy, in order to provide more benign and less negative interpretations of this passion.
7. To develop new coping behaviors.

On the basis of our own clinical experience, we would like to suggest the following additional goals, if indicated by the assessment of the relationship and personal history:

8. To increase the symmetry of power and decision making—that is, to help the less powerful partner to gain power, and the more powerful partner to gracefully surrender the advantage. This will also tend to promote equity in the relationship.
9. To increase mutual control over the rate and extent to which the partners are becoming dependent upon each

other. Violated expectations about how fast or slow the relationship should be progressing may have consequences for jealousy. Anxieties over dependency should be addressed. A partner who is overly dependent on the other for his or her own self-esteem may be helped in couples or individual therapy to develop more autonomy of self-evaluation.

10. To specify actions that signal to each partner that the other is "committed" to a particular stage of the relationship (e.g., serious dating, cohabitation with exclusivity) or to a particular degree of intimacy. This allows the couple to explore the issue of present and future commitment to their relationship, and provides specific markers other than relationships with others that the partner is committed. The overarching goal is to help the partners attend to the qualities of their own relationship and the implications for commitment, rather than to monitoring the qualities of real or potential rival relationships.

The goals listed above can be seen as predominantly directed at reducing the forces that initially generate primary appraisal of threat or loss. The last recommendation, however, concerns the coping behaviors that the jealous adopt to reduce threats and losses. The goals of altering the circumstances of the relationship and altering the ongoing coping behaviors should generally proceed in tandem.

To move now from goals to therapeutic strategies, the management of normal jealousy can be regarded as involving three levels:

1. The situation that has provoked the jealousy.
2. The relationship and those elements in it that are maintaining the jealousy.
3. The individual characteristics of the jealous subject and the partner that have fostered the arousal and continuance of jealousy.

Clanton and Smith (1977) emphasize such a multilayered approach to the therapy of jealousy. They suggest that at the personal level the focus should be on the feelings, behaviors, and assumptions of the jealous individual. At the relationship level they advocate a discussion of the rules of the relationship, and at the situation level they emphasize the responsibility of the partner and rival to minimize the threat to the jealous subject. Teismann (1979) employs a similar tripartite approach to jealousy, addressing problems of the individual's awareness and insight, the couple's interpersonal awareness skills, and techniques to enhance their systematic problem solving.

Situational Approaches

The situation that has provoked the jealousy is usually connected to an actual or supposed infidelity. Whether or not infidelity is acknowledged is critical. In clinical practice with normal jealousy, another relationship is often admitted, though the extent of the threat presented by this extradyadic involvement is frequently in contention. Even when the infidelity is admitted, the accused partner may deny that the jealousy is justified or reasonable. Constantine (1986) notes that people are more likely to see their own jealousy as situational and that of their partners as being the result of the partners' personality defects: "She is jealous because that's the way she is, whereas I'm jealous because of what she is up to with her new boyfriend."

The process of clarification of the jealousy is necessary. When no actual threat to the relationship exists, the issues that have generated the unnecessary fears need to be identified; in so doing, an effective reassurance that the jealousy is groundless may be attained (Im, Wilner, & Breit, 1983).

A reframing and relabeling of the jealousy may often assist by casting the problem, jealousy, in a new and less problematic light. Teismann (1979) emphasizes that the pejorative language used to describe jealousy often prolongs the problem. Jealousy may be relabeled as an expression of love and concern and may be described in such terms as "passionate," "involved," and "sensitive," whereas the deceit of the accused partner (if deceit is involved) can be restated in terms of being ashamed and not wishing to hurt (Constantine, 1986; Teismann, 1979). Even infidelity may be conceptualized as an attempt to save the marriage by highlighting the difficulties and bringing them to treatment (Im et al., 1983). The focus can on occasion be shifted by such changes of language away from questions of the infidelity to issues in the relationship.

The meanings that the jealous partner attaches to particular behaviors he or she finds threatening, and the behavioral consequences of such meanings, should be explored and charted (Watzlawick et al., 1967). Though this involves an exploration of the perceptions of the jealous partner, it generates information that can be employed to modify the behavior of the suspected partner and the behavioral responses of the jealous. This, if initiated early, can interrupt the progress of those interactions leading to jealousy.

The realistic deprivations and fears associated with actual infidelity need to be acknowledged, but the false or exaggerated beliefs require confrontation and challenge. All too often, the jealous individuals descend into their own visions of what provoked the jealousy and become hopelessly entangled in their own half-truths and misconceptions. Such individuals characterize their partners as ungrateful and unconcerned, themselves as helplessly incompetent in comparison to the rival, and the situation as irredeemably awful. Therapy cannot progress until these self-defeating assumptions are effectively removed. Hawkins (1976) has also stressed the importance of challenging unspoken assumptions about the meaning of the rival relationship and, in particular, the separation of love from jealousy.

This process of clarification and reassurance, combined with relabeling that aims at changing the jealous person's assumptions, expectations, and behavior with regard to the actual or supposed infidelity, may in some cases be sufficient. Frequently, however, though the situation that provoked the jealousy has been effectively demystified and the jealous partner accepts intellectually that continuing fear for the relationship is unwarranted, the jealousy persists. At this point, the focus of therapy changes to the primary relationship and to the system that is sustaining the jealousy.

Relationship Approaches

The relationship is central to normal jealousy, and therapeutic strategies that ignore this dimension rarely succeed. Teismann (1979) emphasizes this by referring to a "jealous system" as opposed to a "jealous individual." Initially, the boundaries of the relationship need to be explored and defined, for "jealousy in systemic terms represents a threat to, or violation of, the boundary of the relationship" (Constantine, 1976, p. 384). Once jealousy is established, it becomes a part of the relationship system, and its perpetuation often depends on the reactions and attempted solutions of both partners. For example, a jealous system can be perpetuated not by the demands and accusations, but by both partners' attempts to seek resolution of the conflict (Watzlawick, Weakland, & Fisch, 1974). The accused partner may, for instance, become increasingly careful not to give any occasion for suspicion or doubt. In attempting to prevent jealous outbursts, the accused may carefully censor what he or she tells the jealous partner about events that could be misconstrued, such as a chance meeting with an old flame. As a result, the jealous partner either may become increasingly aware that he or she is not being told everything and assume that what is withheld is incriminating, or may discover that the innocent encounter was not revealed and invest the event with a sinister import simply because it was not mentioned. Another sequence of a failing system is as follows: The accused partner begins to absent himself or herself from the joint home to avoid conflict and allow tensions to settle, but the increasing absence stimulates greater suspicion and more intense conflict, which in turn encourage more frequent absences.

Systemic conceptualizations, although not precluding consideration of intrapsychic mechanisms or denying the importance of external provocations, do focus attention on the relationship and its vicissitudes. A wide variety of approaches and strategies have been proposed to modify the jealousy system; some of these are described below.

Systematic Problem Solving. Systematic problem solving (Teismann, 1979, 1982) is a short-term therapeutic strategy for working with couples, with or without actually including the rival in treatment. Individual insight is played down in favor of systems-oriented interventions. The therapist attempts to alter the dyadic or triadic system with behavioral prescriptions. The therapist, for example, may phone or write to the rival in the presence of the couple and urge him or her to join in the therapy sessions. The almost inevitable refusal by the rival is followed by the therapist's earnestly urging the rival to see the accused partner so that the therapist will know how to treat the couple. This interaction is intended to establish therapeutic control of the dynamics of the jealous triangle; it also places the rival in the role of an adjunct to therapy—someone peripheral to the real issues, whose only reason for being is to strengthen the couple's relationship.

Direct behavioral prescriptions are also provided, such as responding to jealous accusations by walking around scratching one's head until the partner calms down, and then expressing verbal and physical affection. The objective of such prescriptions is to disrupt the habitual pattern of the jealous interaction and to begin to introduce a new organization of the systems process. Interrupting the escalating and unresolvable conflict situations so characteristic of jealousy by prescribing paradoxical or closed nonescalating responses seems the central element in this approach. The apparent playfulness of many of Teismann's suggestions is intentional, for he believes that play interjected into the pain-filled jealous system offers not only temporary relief, but a new perspective and creative alternative for the couple's problem-solving attempts.

Role Playing and Role Reversal. Role playing and role reversal have been exploited by some therapists in managing jealousy. The partners are instructed to act out an actual or typical jealous conflict in front of the therapist. This not only exposes elements of the jealousy to the therapist's direct gaze; it can also be a useful form of desensitization and a forum for learning and trying out new coping strategies (Ard, 1977; Constantine, 1986). Role playing may be used to train the jealous person to control the jealous behavior and act in a nonjealous manner, in which case the jealous feelings may dissipate with time (Im et al., 1983). The accused partner also learns to behave more reasonably and positively. The eventual result, if the role playing is successful, is that the downward interactional spiral of conflict is interrupted and the opportunity emerges for genuine reassurance and resolution.

The couple may also be encouraged to play out role reversal scenarios in an attempt to disrupt the destructive interaction pattern further and encourage increased understanding of each other's dilemmas. Role reversal need not be bilateral, for coaching the jealous partner in nonjealous behavior may be all that is necessary. "Turning the tables" (Im et al., 1983) and "symptom transfer" (Teismann, 1979) are related approaches in which, for example, the accused is asked to role-play the part of being jealous, or the jealous partner is told that in fact his or her task is to reassure the suspicious and enraged partner.

Exaggerating the Conflict. Exaggerating the conflict to the point of absurdity has been advocated to expose the unreasonable quality of the couple's interactions. Im et al. (1983) have applied Whitaker's (1975) "psychotherapy of the absurd" to jealousy. The example provided was of a middle-aged couple who sought consultation because the husband was spending excessive time caring for three cats he had inherited from his late wife. His new wife was intensely jealous of these cats. The therapist, ignoring the issue of the cats' representing the husband's continued attachment to his late wife, offered the suggestion that the new wife could not be expected to tolerate such selfish and narrow-minded behavior and should seek an immediate divorce. The husband was offered almost identical advice. The couple resolved their conflict by compromise once the absurdity of the interaction was exposed. Such an approach, of course, needs to be used with caution in couples with well-established and severe problems of jealousy.

Conjoint Marital Therapy. Conjoint marital therapy, though less novel, is nevertheless the mainstay of most therapists' approaches to jealousy management. Its aims are to clarify the issues and conflicts in the marriage, making overt the mechanisms by which the jealousy is sustained and the secondary gains that accrue to both partners from the jealousy. In the case of jealousy, many of these conflicts can be resolved into the five categories of relationship issues discussed in Chapter 5: degree of investment/rewards; degree of self-esteem defined by the relationship; vulnerability of investment; vulnerability of self; and potential for a rival relationship. One feature of jealousy, as with many other relationship problems, is the capacity of the partners not to hear what is being said to them. The jealous individual will clearly articulate his or her insecurity and need for reassurance, and the partner will respond by rejecting the jealous person's accusation. The accused will offer assurances of continuing commitment, and the jealous will respond by emphasizing the accused's past untrustworthiness, thus rendering the proffered reassurance useless. The work of translation and arbitration often needs to be augmented by the various techniques of family therapy aimed at producing change in the system.

The continuance of the jealousy conflict may in part reflect a marked imbalance of power in the relationship; in our culture, such inequalities are endemic. To overcome the jealousy, it may be necessary to negotiate changes in the relationship that overcome or ameliorate the inequities. For example, giving the woman greater access and say in the use and distribution of income may contribute to overcoming her need to control and limit the male by jealousy. Helping the couple develop more open and effective decision-making processes may overcome inequalities and take some of the heat out of the jealousy. Low power status can fuel jealousy; its modification can produce changes that decrease the need for, and secondary gains from, the jealousy.

Individual Approaches

Psychoanalytic approaches in particular, and psychodynamic ones in general, emphasize the treatment of jealousy through work with the individual. The theoretical and practical aspects of these treatment modalities have been discussed in Chapter 4 and are not reiterated here.

The role of lowered self-esteem in rendering the individual vulnerable to a jealous reaction and in sustaining that state has been repeatedly emphasized. Building a more robust sense of self-worth in the jealous partner can help to reduce the sense of helplessness. This in turn enables the jealous person to regain the confidence and resourcefulness needed to cope with the situation, and to begin to negotiate more as an equal with the partner about resolving the dilemma. The focus of esteem building may be on aspects of the individual's functioning outside the relationship (e.g., in job-related or social roles) or in areas in which the person does satisfy the partner. The therapeutic relationship is itself a forum in which the individual's self-worth may be acknowledged and bolstered. Ellis (1977) and Hibbard (1975) suggest the use of rational–emotive therapy to challenge beliefs, including those rooted in the jealous individual's lowered self-esteem (e.g., the belief that he or she is incompetent compared to the rival, that he or she would be devastated by the partner's departure, or that he or she cannot stand or cope with the mate's involvement with others). Hawkins (1976) has noted the importance of exploring feelings of low self-worth related to psychological and economic dependency.

The self-esteem of the accused partner may also have been seriously damaged by the jealousy. This may on occasion contribute to the continuance of the jealousy. Some individuals with a poor self-image may stimulate and prolong their partners' jealousy to enhance their own feelings of self-worth. In such situations, if the individuals can be helped to find less destructive sources of self-esteem, then the need to provoke and maintain their partners' jealousy will be reduced.

Baute (1978), in his account of jealousy from the point of view of transactional analysis, emphasizes the powerless and reactive role into which the jealous individual is thrust. Baute's objectives in therapy are to enhance the jealous individual's ego strength and self-esteem, and to diminish the "hypnotic" power of the drama between the partner and the rival. This is attempted in the context of a treatment approach that intentionally brings comic relief to this stressed and depressed situation. In a so-called "love is war, anything goes" strategy, Baute suggests that the jealous individual be encouraged to playfully engage in unpredictable behavior that outdramatizes the other two actors. Examples suggested are suddenly leaving home, creating domestic uproars, going on shopping binges, and seeming to alternate between divorce counseling and loving approaches. Baute believes that making the melodrama more overt weakens its power to influence behavior. The problem with this approach is that many of the jealous individuals we see are already enacting such melodramas and that this is the problem, not the solution.

The fear of losing the relationship when an actual rival exists may prevent the jealous from making effective use of therapy. The jealous person may be so overwhelmed by the desire to please and retain the partner that he or she may be quite unable to assess his or her own needs or respond to attempts to modify the jealous system. One way of attempting to produce a respite in the jealous individual's blinding anxieties is to negotiate a time-limited commitment from the nonjealous partner not to leave the relationship or to see the rival. Such a negotiation, if managed well, produces important reassurance; however, if the partner obviously has to be pressed hard to offer such a commitment, then the element of reassurance is probably minimal.

Morgan (1975) has emphasized jealous individuals' attempts to arbitrarily impose rules on their partners, in order to reduce their opportunities for becoming involved with potential rivals. Such rules include prohibitions against makeup or attractive clothes, opposition to work outside of the home, and daily reports on activities. The partners may accept such prohibitions out of concern, fear, or frustration, but in so doing they increase their own dissatisfaction with the relationship and restlessness within it. Morgan attempts to encourage a renegotiation of such rules, which have been developed to control the jealousy in the context of enhancing the low self-esteem of the jealous partner.

The jealous individual's need to control the partner may be expressed in terms of his or her rights and prerogatives, usually as a husband. The culturally sanctioned rules that reflect male dominance may be advanced both as explanations and as justifications of the controls and sanctions imposed by the jealous husband. This can present real problems for the therapist when the couple, or at least the man, comes from a culture in which these norms are still unambiguously accepted. In practice, it is usually possible to clarify how these imperatives are being used to cover the jealous individual's own lack of confidence and failure to trust.

Sexual problems in the relationship are often encountered in jealousy. These frequently predate the emergence of jealousy, but may have been initiated or enhanced by the jealous conflict. It is important to deal with such difficulties as a problem in their own right. A referral to a practitioner specializing in sexual counseling is often beneficial. Conversely, there may be an increased libido associated with jealousy, with enhanced desire and greater frequency of orgasm (Mooney, 1965; Seeman, 1979). Seeman (1979) has suggested that the increased sexual desire may reflect such elements as an evolutionary mechanism to prevent either separation or homoerotic fascination with the rival. It is also possible that the arousal is due to jealous anxiety relabeled as passion (White et al., 1981). If it appears that the secondary gain from increased sexual activity tends to sustain rather than diminish the jealousy, it needs to be discussed and clarified with the couple and the jealous individual in particular.

Beecher and Beecher (1971) propose a treatment approach based on individual therapy with the jealous subject. They suggest the following methods for managing the jealous individual:

- Confronting the person with the jealousy and demonstrating how it influences his or her world view.
- Revealing how the person is diverting his or her own energies and creativity into the jealousy.
- Pointing out how jealousy infantilizes the person and makes him or her dependent on the opinion of others.
- Challenging the person to be more cooperative, mature, and constructive.

The aims of therapy are to enhance independence, to increase the ability to live by one's own values, and to build up self-sufficiency and security.

Jealousy Workshops

A recent innovation in the management of normal jealousy is the jealousy workshop. There are three published accounts of short-term jealousy workshops. Blood and Blood (1977) conduct a 2-day workshop for couples, individuals, and triads. Each partner starts by describing his or her feelings about the mate. Triangles are then assembled, usually involving the couple and a stand-in for the rival (or missing partner). Each member of the triangle then forms a static sculpture of the three actors, which is then put into movement and discussed for relevance to the actual situation. Actors then draw pictures of the jealousy and of the jealous person in the triangle, and take turns describing how parts of the picture represent parts of themselves.

After a break, each couple identifies a specific problem that is threatening the relationship and contributing to the jealousy. Behavioral resolutions of this problem are negotiated with the aid of the group and facilitators. Each triangle performs a free-form dance in front of the group, followed by a triangle massage where two members rotate massage of the third. Finally, the workshop is reviewed.

Blood and Blood report a variety of outcomes of this diverse program, though no structured assessment is used and no follow-up is reported. Reported outcomes include discovery that the relationship is too weak to withstand external involvements; the establishment of more realistic norms concerning the handling of alternative attractions and relationships; the development of jealousy by the partner originally presenting as nonjealous; and the decision to seek further counseling. However, it seems to us that the use of the triangle and some of the nonverbal exercises have the potential to create fairly intense and explosive confrontation, which may be inappropriate to a short-term workshop setting. Blood and Blood provide little information about the ways in which they monitor and incorporate the emotional crises that may well develop in their format.

Constantine (1976) conducts 1- and 2-day workshops for couples and triangles. The avowed purpose is to promote "resolutional" behaviors, such as joint problem solving, exploration of feelings, and negotiation around the jealousy situation, and to discourage isolational, antagonistic, or intellectualizing coping behaviors. Constantine stresses the usefulness of jealousy in limiting the complexity of relationships by setting boundaries, and suggests the need to look at self- and relationship dissatisfaction.

The workshop focuses first on specifying the actual behaviors, feelings, and interpersonal events of the jealousy situation. The real relationship between the nonjealous partner and the rival is examined, in order to reduce unwarranted and threatening fantasies and to diagnose the possibility that the nonjealous partner may be playing rival and mate off against each other. The nonjealous person also discusses ways in which the rival relationship is beneficial (as well as harmful) to himself or herself. Each individual's and couple's boundaries are then explored and negotiated, with a strong focus on the unique needs of each partner that would be most threatened if a rival relationship were to progress in specific ways. Nonverbal "boundary sculptures" supplement discussion, and other semistructured exercises are given to increase positive feelings about the relationship. Constantine routinely gives training in negotiation skills as well. Unfortunately, Constantine has not reported on outcomes of this workshop format.

White and Helbick (1988) have developed a 2-day workshop for couples only. They have five goals for this workshop:

1. Educating each couple about the causes and consequences of jealousy.

2. Training the partners in communication and negotiation skills, so that the couple has a structure with which to communicate during and after the workshop.
3. Helping the couple to identify and assess the utility of current coping strategies.
4. Designing new coping strategies.
5. Promoting discussion of the possibility of seeking relationship counseling.

Each person is interviewed separately to screen for pathological jealousy or psychological disorder that would contraindicate a workshop approach.

Evidence is first presented to the group for the universality of jealousy, and stress is placed on its potential usefulness in helping a couple develop a more satisfying relationship. The self-protective and relationship-protective intents of coping behavior are emphasized. This leads to exploring negative self-evaluations about being jealous in the first place; this is important, since a strong social desirability bias has been found against being jealous (Lobsenz, 1977).

After this introduction, each individual is asked to list specific situations that trigger his or her own or the partner's jealousy. This list is then presented to the partner. Each person describes how he or she would feel in such a situation. The partner is advised merely to listen to the mate and then to paraphrase back to him or her the eliciting situation and attendant feelings. These lists are then shared with the group, and their commonalities are discussed.

At this point, some of the common correlates of jealousy are presented and illustrated by the specific situations mentioned in the participants' own lists. Sex-role and cultural influences are also presented, in part to take some of the focus off the "flaws" of the jealous partners. Some of the power implications that may be present in jealousy are highlighted. Basic communication skills training is introduced (Stuart, 1980); this focuses on differentiating thoughts from feelings, making "I" statements, and negotiating behavioral contracts. Participants are given structured individual homework to list their own and their partners' most common behaviors when jealous and the effects these behaviors seem to have.

On the second day of the workshop, participants share their behaviors–consequences list and engage in a guided fantasy reenacting two or three of the least and most successful of their own coping behaviors. Partners then discuss with each other how each is affected by the coping behavior of the other, and they assess whether the coping behavior is useful for reducing the threat to the jealous person's self-esteem, reducing the threat to the relationship, or both. The group is then reassembled, and new coping behaviors are designed with the help of the group and facilitators. These new solutions focus largely on the following:

1. More explicit communication and negotiation in regard to jealousy-provoking behaviors and coping behaviors.
2. Examination of the positive benefits of the jealousy situation, to help uncover how each partner may have played a (perhaps unwitting) role in maintaining jealousy.
3. Helping the partners identify how they could reduce the threat posed by real or potential rivals by improving the primary relationship or developing nonthreatening sources of satisfaction for needs not being met in the relationship.

The last step of the workshop is for couples to role-play situations they have previously identified as actually or potentially threatening. New coping strategies are explicitly practiced with the aid of group participation and feedback. Finally, the workshop is evaluated, and couples are asked to discuss how they might go about continuing to reduce the unwanted aspects of jealousy. Though the sample size is small, early experience with this format is favorable enough to encourage its creators to continue (White & Helbick, 1988).

Treatment of Pathologically Reactive Jealousies

In pathologically reactive jealousy, there is an exaggerated response to the provocation of an actual or supposed infidelity. The factors that may render the jealous individual unusually sensitive to threats to the relationship include the following:

- Current mental state
- Personality
- Past experiences of loss and desertion
- Nature of the current relationship

Management can be directed at any or all of these elements.

Regardless of whether jealous reactions are within or outside of normal limits, the provoking events should be addressed directly by clarifying the actual situation and reassuring the jealous individual where possible. Im et al. (1983) point out that where there is no actual threat to the relationship, the simplest and most straightforward approach entails identifying the issues and reassuring the jealous partner that his or her fears are groundless. In pathological reactions, the intensity of the emotions and the degree of involvement of the jealous individual in this passion usually make such clarification difficult, if not impossible. The person usually has too much invested in the jealousy to be able to abandon it when confronted with mere reality. This being said, a firm and persistent return to the concrete realities of the situation does form a background to the ongoing therapy in those cases where the suspicions are probably groundless or grossly exaggerated. Moving the jealous individual from recounting suspicions and defending interpretations back to the actual events can assist in modifying the irrational beliefs and assumptions.

Mental State

A number of our own patients and clients recognize their jealousy either as without foundation or as exaggerated and out of proportion to the realities of the situation. The intrusive thoughts and compulsion to question and check that afflict such individuals have been formulated in terms of an obsessive–compulsive disorder. Both the jealous ruminations and activities have been subjected to treatment with behavioral psychotherapy (Cobb & Marks, 1979). Self-regulated exposure in fantasy and *in vivo* to situations that provoke jealous behavior (rituals), with response prevention and thought-stopping techniques to control the jealous ruminations, have been advocated (Marks, 1976; Marks, Hodgson, & Rachman, 1975; Rosen & Schnapp, 1974). Cobb and Marks (1979) reported that the behavioral techniques contributed to lessening the jealous behavior in three of their four patients, but that ruminations were only modified in one subject. This study is of particular interest, in that it offers a strategy aimed at directly modifying the individual's experience of jealousy using well-established behavioral methods of treatment.

The patient may have been predisposed to the pathological reaction by an abnormality in his or her state of mind; most frequently, in practice, this is a depressive disorder. The relationship between jealousy and depressed mood is complex. In planning management, a high priority should be given to effective and vigorous treatment of any depression that is present. Continuing depression reduces the efficacy of other treatment approaches, and in our opinion its presence significantly increases the danger of jealous violence to the partner and of self-destructive behavior in the jealous subject. In reactive jealousy, the resolution of the depression will not of itself necessarily bring the jealousy to an end, but it will make it more amenable to other therapeutic endeavors. The importance of the early recognition and treatment of depression in jealousy cannot be emphasized too strongly.

Alcohol abuse may be contributing to the initiation and prolongation of the jealous reaction through its effects, both acute and chronic, on the individual's state of mind. The effective management of alcohol or other substance abuse is essential. Occasionally there is very considerable resistance in the jealous individual, not just to accepting that he or she has an abuse problem, but to recognizing its connection to the jealousy. One of our patients was horrified when informed that he should forego his thrice-daily joints of marijuana, for he insisted that they were the only thing that made his tortured life tolerable, and without them he would probably lose his self-control and assault his unfaithful spouse. In fact, a careful history indicated that though he did become calmer and more detached immediately following smoking the drug, 2 or 3 hours later he showed hypersensitivity and hypervigilance associated with frequent misinterpretations and persecutory self-referential experiences. Stopping the drug did improve the jealousy and made him amenable to therapy for the first time.

Personality

The approaches employed in normal jealousy to enhance the diminished self-esteem of the jealous individual also have equal utility in many cases of pathological reactions. Psychoanalytically oriented approaches also aim to modify the long-standing personality traits that predispose individuals to jealousy, and they have been claimed to be of efficacy in patients with pathological reactions, including those with frank delusions of infidelity (Fenichel, 1935; Jones, 1937; Riviere, 1932).

Individuals with Paranoid Personality Disorders, as defined by DSM-III-R, are said to be particularly vulnerable to pathological jealousy. Though such individuals are difficult to work with, let alone help, a prerequisite for effective therapy is to gain their trust—no small task with persons who are hypersensitive to offense and of rather restricted and cold affectivity. Persistence, time, and recognition of the limits of one's effectiveness as a therapist are the only remedies we know of. Once a therapeutic relationship is established, it is sometimes possible to directly confront such a person's sensitive self-reference and misinterpretations. It is even possible that the person may begin to realize that the world does not revolve exclusively and maliciously around him or her. If judicious use of medication can be negotiated with the patient, it will decrease the arousal and hypervigilance so characteristic of this condition. Benzodiazepines (e.g., Valium) should, we believe, be avoided in this group because of problems with disinhibition and paradoxical reactions. Antipsychotics in small doses may, however, be beneficial.

Past Experiences

Pathological reactions may have their roots in previous experiences of desertion and betrayal. A number of our patients had been sensitized in this manner and found it difficult, if not impossible, to trust their new partners. The lives of some unfortunates seem to have been constructed out of losses and desertions, and their expectations are for more of the same. These individuals are often unaware of the extent to which they are influenced by their own expectations of infidelity and the extent to which their behavior contributes to a self-fulfilling prophecy. Similarly, their partners may be unaware that they are being made to pay the price of the jealous individuals' past losses. Exposing these assumptions, and clarifying the differences between the current and past relationships, are often the only interventions required.

The Relationship

The relationship is often as critical to sustaining the jealousy in pathological reactions as in the normal jealousies. The approaches to managing the relationship discussed in connection with normal jealousy are often applicable; however, the clinician must always take into consideration the increased risk of violence and the often greater volatility of the situation.

Specific Treatment of Delusions of Infidelity

In symptomatic jealousy and in some pathologically reactive jealousies that are characterized by delusions of infidelity, it is often necessary to attempt to treat the delusions in their own right.

Some authors have considered delusions of infidelity to be peculiarly resistant to treatment. Todd and Dewhurst (1955) have stated that in their experience treatment usually fails to influence delusions unless there is an underlying depression that may respond to treatment. The prognosis has been considered "very doubtful,"

and though treatment of the underlying psychosis may lead to resolution, on occasion the delusions of infidelity may become more
obvious as the other symptoms clear (Enoch & Trethowen, 1979).
The morbid jealousy that constitutes one symptom of affective,
schizophrenic, or even alcoholic disorders is, however, considered by
Shepherd (1961) to abate if the illness remits spontaneously or is
treated successfully. Langfeldt (1961) has expressed a similar opinion
in those cases where the jealousy seems to be coordinated with other
psychotic symptoms of the basic disorder, but has emphasized the
premorbid personality as influencing the outcome of individual
cases.

Mooney (1965) claimed that the use of antipsychotic medica-
tions of the phenothiazine (e.g., chlorpromazine) group produced an
initial improvement in all eight of his cases with delusions of infidelity. This improvement, however, only sustained in five patients; the
other three relapsed, in part due to failure to continue the prescribed
medication. It was Mooney's opinion that antipsychotic medication
often needed to be continued to suppress a return of the jealousy.
Dominik (1970) reported far less favorable results in deluded patients, with fewer than half responding well, despite the use of high
dosage schedules and the augmentation of antipsychotic medication
with electroconvulsive therapy (ECT) in some cases.

The problem with comparing the various reports on the treatment of delusions of infidelity is that the patient populations are
disparate; though the physical methods of treatment are detailed,
the all-important factors of the patients' personality, their relationships, their social circumstances, and their disabilities and abilities
are often not mentioned. The reports based on the treatment of
substantial numbers of cases tend to be less sanguine about outcome
than the smaller samples, but in the latter a more consistent therapeutic approach may have been employed.

Our own experience supports the effectiveness of antipsychotic
medication in assisting the resolution of delusions of infidelity. This
is true even in cases where the underlying pathology is not amenable
to treatment. In one case of an individual with Huntington chorea,
for example, the delusions of infidelity completely disappeared on a
modest dose of antipsychotic medication, though the basic disorder
was beyond our power to change. In other cases, where the delusions of infidelity have emerged in the context of an organic or
psychiatric disorder and have persisted following resolution of the
underlying condition, it has been possible to terminate the delusions
with antipsychotic medication. Patients whose delusions of infidelity
have emerged in the context of a major depressive disorder have not

infrequently required antipsychotic medication in addition to antidepressant treatment to produce an effective therapeutic response. In one of our cases, where the delusions emerged in association with thyrotoxicosis, it was not sufficient to treat the thyroid condition, and antipsychotics were required to bring the patient's morbid jealousy to an end.

Claims for the specific advantages of one antipsychotic over another in morbid jealousy have been advanced (Hoaken, 1976), but there is no firm evidence of the superiority of any particular product. Phenothiazines such as chlorpromazine and trifluoperazine; thioxanthenes, including flupenthixol; and the butyrophenone haloperidol have all been used with success. Clinicians are advised to employ the antipsychotics with which they are the most familiar and in which they place the greatest faith.

Persuading pathologically jealous patients to take medication for their jealousy is a formidable task. They often point out that the problem is not their jealousy, but their partners' behavior. Even in those who have insight into the morbid nature of their beliefs, this insight tends to fluctuate, and with it their willingness to take medication. The antipsychotic drugs produce a number of unpleasant side effects, which are often sufficient to translate the patients' reluctant compliance into blunt refusal. In practice, we find that therapists often expend considerable time and effort in negotiating the taking of medication, and even more in maintaining the patients' commitment to this aspect of treatment. Attempts to short-cut such negotiations by compulsion or overbearing insistence can produce short-term compliance, but at the risk of compromising the long-term cooperation that is so essential.

Temporary or permanent separation can have the effect of quieting the turbulent emotions of morbid jealousy (Shepherd, 1961) and may be of assistance in the management of symptomatic and reactive forms. Nonpharmacological approaches to encouraging the resolution of delusions in general and delusions of infidelity in particular have been advocated. Psychoanalytic approaches to jealousy include models of delusions of infidelity, which in theory would make such delusions amenable to dynamically oriented psychotherapy. A number of individual case studies have reported successful analytic treatment of delusions of infidelity. The psychoanalytic formulations of delusions of infidelity correspond more closely to the reactive model than to the symptomatic, though they often include paranoia and even what most psychiatrists would view as schizophrenia within these conceptualizations.

It has been suggested that there is therapeutic value in confronting patients with reality and challenging their false beliefs (Rudden, Gilmore, & Frances, 1982). Cognitive–behavioral approaches have been attempted, and a mixture of questioning and reality testing is said to facilitate change (Hole, Rush, & Beck, 1979). These reports and other studies on cognitive approaches to modifying delusions (Shapiro & Ravenette, 1959; Watts, Powell, & Austin, 1973) have not been specifically concerned with delusions of infidelity, but their general approach can usefully be incorporated into management strategies. In some patients, gently confronting them with the ambiguity of much of the claimed evidence and the inherent unlikeliness of many of their accusations does appear to reduce the intensity of their convictions; in others, such confrontational tactics breed suspicion and withdrawal.

Delusions may be resolved with effective therapy in a number of ways. Hole et al. (1979) reported that resolution may involve a waning in the strength of the conviction, a decrease in the pervasiveness of the delusion (as evidenced by the time spent ruminating on the ideas and looking for confirmatory evidence), and a gradual modification of the delusional ideas to fit with the realities of the patient's situation. Delusions can also become encapsulated: The beliefs retain their original force, but become walled off in the individual's private internal world and cease to intrude into his or her interactions with others. To these mechanisms can be added a process of denial, in which the patient increasingly refuses to acknowledge his or her previous beliefs and statements and claims never to have thought or said any such things; and a process of rationalization, whereby the delusional beliefs are gradually modified to make them appear less extreme and closer to acceptable convictions. In this latter process, firm convictions and absolute certainties are metamorphosed into slight suspicions and passing thoughts.

Treatment of Symptomatic Jealousies

The symptomatic jealousies should, in theory, be resolved with the successful treatment of the underlying disorder of which they are one of the outward manifestations or symptoms. In practice, this gratifying simplicity is not always apparent. The underlying disorder may be difficult or impossible to treat successfully. The jealousy may persist when the process that initiated it is resolved, and even when the belief in the partner's infidelity dissipates. Considerable assistance may be required in such situations if the relationship is to be restored.

Among the commonest disorders in which delusions of infidelity appear as a symptom are the schizophrenias. In the schizophrenias, delusional beliefs usually can be successfully treated with antipsychotic medication. The jealousy tends to wane along with the other active symptoms of the disorder. The residual effects of the jealousy may be overshadowed in these disorders by the devastating effects of the other aspects of the condition on the personal and social functioning of the individual. The schizophrenias have a tendency to relapse; if this occurs, the morbid jealousy is likely to return with the other positive symptoms, particularly if the jealousy was a prominent feature of the disorder. When violence has accompanied the jealousy, this may also recur with the schizophrenic disorder. Where the threat of such future dangerousness is significant, it always justifies careful and continuing follow-up and may indicate the long-term use of antipsychotic medication to reduce the frequency of relapse.

Major depressive disorders may on occasion be accompanied by morbid jealousy. The successful treatment of the mood disturbance may be all that is necessary to terminate the jealousy. In some cases, however, particularly when delusions of infidelity are prominent, it is necessary to use antipsychotic medication in addition to antidepressants to produce a rapid resolution of symptoms. The jealousy that emerges as part of a depressive disorder is, in our experience, more likely to reflect pre-existing tension in the relationship or personality vulnerabilities than is the morbid jealousy accompanying schizophrenic disorders. The partners are also less likely to accept that the patients' jealousy is entirely a manifestation of illness than in the schizophrenias, where the madness is often painfully obvious to all. It is for these reasons that some continuing individual and couples therapy is necessary to assist the final resolution of the jealousy and the reintegration of the relationship.

A wide variety of disorders that disrupt brain function can produce pathological jealousy as part of the clinical picture. Many of these disorders, such as the dementias, are not presently amenable to treatment. Even when the underlying organic process can be modified or corrected, the morbid jealousy once set in train may continue, despite the resolution of the disorder from which it arose. In both these situations, the problem becomes one of effective treatment of the jealousy independent of the initiating disorder. Management in such situations is directed at the symptom—that is, the jealousy—rather than the disorder itself. Delusions of infidelity are usually prominent in the organic syndromes, and therapy is primarily directed at these.

In summary, the therapeutic approach in symptomatic jealousy consists of the following:

1. Vigorous treatment of the underlying disorder, where such treatment is possible.
2. Antipsychotic medication directed specifically at the delusions of infidelity.
3. Clarification and, in suitable cases, confrontation of the misinterpretations and convictions that form the delusional state.

Not infrequently, the relationship issues that either are created by the jealousy or precede its emergence require to be addressed in their own right. Equally, personality factors and past experience may be playing a major role in maintaining the jealousy and must also receive attention from the therapist. In practice, the approaches and techniques described for managing normal and reactive jealousies often need to be added to the treatment of the symptomatic jealousies.

Ethical Issues

Jealousy management regularly presents the therapist with ethical dilemmas. These usually revolve around issues of confidentiality and courses of action in the face of potential or actual violence.

In exploring jealousy issues, one or the other partner may confess in an individual session to present or past infidelities. Not infrequently, the individual may try to extract an assurance that what he or she says will be treated in strict confidence and in particular will not be revealed to the partner. Alternatively, the therapist may feel constrained, not by the partner's demands for confidentiality, but by his or her own fears of the impact on the jealous subject of the revelation of actual infidelities. It is all too easy to take on the apprehensions of patients, and there may be good reasons to do so. If the therapist has given a guarantee of confidentiality or feels such a constraint, he or she may wind up working in an untenable situation in which the jealous subject is accusing, the partner is denying and reassuring, and the therapist is in receipt of information that the accusations are substantially or to some degree correct.

Such a dilemma can be circumvented by only seeing the partners as a couple, or by making explicit at the outset that any material touching on the central concerns about fidelity will be shared. This can be built into the therapy without difficulty with the majority of couples, but problems may arise in pathological jealousy, particularly if the risk of violence is considered to be substantial. Even in such cases, however, it is usually our practice to insist on a straight-forward sharing of relevant information.

The occasional case of pathological jealousy is so fraught with tension, because of the patient's disturbed mental state and behavior, that any attempt at clarification (let alone open disclosure) is rendered foolhardy if not impossible. In such a case, attention is invariably focused on individual management rather than on the relationship; rightly or wrongly, this can lead to a less than rigorous adherence to the principles of openness and sharing of information. If necessary, the jealous person can be treated individually while the couple is seen, with another therapist, for crisis therapy.

Such practical difficulties in managing delusions of infidelity do not justify a return to paternalism, for it is just as important to work where possible in an atmosphere of openness. It is absurd to place oneself in the position of colluding in denying the essential truth of a deluded patient's accusations, for in so doing one justifies the patient's claims of being denied the truth and being conspired against. It may be that an explicit policy of openness may discourage partners from being entirely frank, but we believe that this is a price that must be accepted. In managing jealousy, the modeling of an open approach and the negotiation of options can be an adjunct to therapy, for therapists are often dealing with couples for whom dissembling and manipulation have become the dominant modes of communication.

The sharing of information with regard to dangerousness is more complex. This is not just a matter of disclosing information revealed by one partner to another, but of sharing the therapist's own anxieties and assessment of the risks of serious aggression. On occasion, the jealous individual may admit to violent impulses or ruminations about harming the partner and may attempt to insist on the confidentiality of these disclosures. If the therapist believes that there is any risk of the jealous individual's acting in a violent manner, this belief must be conveyed to the partner. Whether or not the details of the information on which such a judgment is based should also be disclosed is a matter for the therapist's discretion in the specific situation. A not infrequent scenario is one in which the partners give a history of physical abuse in the context of the jealousy, but both minimize the seriousness of the risk of future recurrence or escalation. The therapist may take a far more serious view of the situation, based on the assessment. Again, we believe that the ethically correct procedure is to share this apprehension with the couple. In some jurisdictions, this may also constitute a legal obligation.

Those whose clinical practice includes forensic work may find themselves involved in the long-term management of individuals who have committed serious violence in the context of jealousy. Such individuals may establish new relationships. In those individuals who have exhibited violence in the context of jealousy in one relationship, there is a substantial risk of the jealousy's recurring with its associated violence in a new relationship. Pathological jealousy has a particularly sinister reputation in this regard and has been associated with a number of repeat homicides (Scott, 1977).

If a sound therapeutic relationship has been established, it is often possible to persuade such a patient to attend a session with the new partner to discuss how best to respond if jealousy becomes an issue. On occasion the patient will adamantly refuse to involve the new partner, for fear that he or she will be scared off by the revelations about the previous relationship. In the face of such a refusal, the therapist's response is often dictated by the concrete exigencies of the situation. If there has been serious violence previously, the patient may be on parole or subject to some continuing court order, in which case the parole office or court may have to be informed. Alternatively, the individual, being a free agent, may effectively absent himself or herself and evade further contact with the therapist. The therapist, we believe, has an ethical responsibility to inform the partner wherever possible of the potential risks—not only in the partner's interests, but in those of the patient or client.

Appendix: Assessing Jealousy

Much of the research we have reviewed in this book used one or more jealousy scales. Most of these are not well reported in the literature. This appendix presents these scales and discusses some of their psychometric properties. One purpose of presenting the exact scales is to avoid the problem of reification of the concept of jealousy. Readers can see for themselves the concrete questions with which each scale assesses jealousy.

Just because researchers label their scales as "jealousy scales" does not mean that the scales actually measure something that other observers would also call "jealousy." As in any developing field of research, it is important to understand how researchers are assessing constructs of interest. What one "jealousy scale" measures may be quite different from what another "jealousy scale" measures. Inconsistencies and contradictions in research data often result from the use of scales that supposedly measure the same construct but actually measure different constructs. And part of the reason why different scales are used is that different researchers have different ideas about how to conceptualize jealousy.

Because of this, understanding the results of research using these scales requires understanding differences in the concepts that have guided scale development. We discuss such differences, and also briefly present some issues of methodological concern in the construction of jealousy research scales. After these preliminaries, the scales themselves are presented.

DIFFERENCES IN CONCEPTUAL APPROACHES

White (1984) has classified existing jealousy scales as reflecting three different underlying approaches to conceptualizing jealousy. These are termed the "dispositional," the "rational," and the "phenomeno-logical." To these we add a fourth, the "theoretical" approach.

Those taking the dispositional approach have an interest in jealousy as a property of personality. Jealous predispositions or traits should generalize across situations, or at least should interact predictably with specific situations. Given this assumption, items assessing dispositional jealousy attempt to sample "jealousy," whatever that is, in different domains, not just the romantic context that is the focus of this book. A problem of this approach is in deciding which words to use for the reactions that people have in greatly differing situations. Should subjects be asked whether they are "jealous" at work, at play, in romances, with siblings, and so forth? Or should some other word be used, such as "upset" or "bothered"? Would these words mean the same thing in different situations? For example, does "upset" mean anxious, angry, sad, envious, and so on, or does it stand for all or some combination of these reactions?

The rational approach, which has been taken by most constructors of jealousy scales, rests on the assumption that jealousy is a "thing" that exists independently of theory or context. This thing may be construed as a simple or complex emotion, as a particular frame of mind, or as behavior. The task is then to find the best way to measure this thing that exists independently of the act of measurement, much as one might assess qualities of a rock, fish, or table.

To develop such measures, researchers have used factor analysis. Typically, subjects are presented with lists of emotions, behaviors, or thoughts and are asked to indicate whether these items characterize themselves or whether they would be characteristic of them in specified jealousy-inducing situations. These items are usually selected because they appear to be face-valid to the researchers as measures of "jealousy" or because other subjects have spontaneously reported that these are emotions, behaviors, or thoughts that they have had in the past when jealous. We could find no instances of rational scale items that were selected because of a theoretical definition of jealousy.

The correlations among these ratings are then factor-analyzed, and the resulting factors are labeled according to items that statistically define them. These factors are then held out as dimensions of a thing called "jealousy." Different methods of factor analysis may yield different dimensions. For example, some researchers have used principal-components analysis, which assumes no error of measurement (an unlikely assumption); others have used the principal-axis method, which assumes that the multiple correlation of each item with all other items defines item variability free of error. If substantial error does exist, principal-components analysis is more likely to yield factors that are hard to replicate in other samples.

The phenomenological approach, with which we have greater sympathy, is interested in what it is that people label as "jealousy"; it also includes as labelers not only the "jealous" person, but also other actors and observers. The assumption is that certain behaviors, thoughts, emotions, or patterns among these are more likely than others to be labeled as jealousy. The interest is ultimately in understanding the conditions that give rise to the invocation of the label, the particular patterns that are so labeled, and the consequences of such labeling. Subjects are asked to identify the extent to which they (or others) are or would be jealous, with specific inclusion of the words "jealousy" and "jealous." Care is taken to distinguish romantic jealousy from envy, as the word "jealousy" is often used as a synonym for "envy" (Smith et al., 1988).

In a theoretical approach, a theory defines what jealousy is, and then items are written to capture the essence of the definition. In great part, we have written this book to offer a theory that can guide future measurement. But we should point out that our definition and model of jealousy point to a number of cognitive, behavioral, and affective elements of a jealousy complex. We think that future jealousy research will advance by measuring these elements. These elements are not to be considered dimensions of jealousy, for that would reify jealousy as a thing rather than a complex of interrelated elements.

More specifically, we think it will prove useful to assess perceived threat or loss to self-esteem and perceived threat or loss of relationship qualities. These perceptions should be related to estimates of the potential for a rival relationship and belief in the existence of an actual rival relationship. Perceived threats/ losses should also be related to elements and patterns of elements of the jealousy complex (secondary appraisal, emotion, and coping efforts).

We expect that other researchers will define jealousy differently and accordingly will develop very different scales. Several theorists, for example, consider jealousy an emotion and attempt either to measure presumed component emotions or to assess the intensity of jealousy as emotion. We have discussed throughout this book several conceptual problems involved in defining jealousy as an emotion.

METHODOLOGICAL AND CONCEPTUAL
PROBLEMS IN ASSESSING JEALOUSY

We do not attempt to discuss general problems of assessment here; instead, we merely highlight those problems that are of particular interest in the development of jealousy measures.

Problems with Accuracy of Self-Reports

People may not accurately respond to self-report measures, particularly those that use the term "jealousy," because (1) they are denying or repressing this self-knowledge in order to manage affect or (2) they do not want to appear to be socially undesirable, because jealousy may be commonly perceived as a flaw of personality. Sommers (1984), for example, found that Americans think that jealousy should be suppressed or disguised from others. Jealousy measures that are not highly correlated with these processes may well be preferred. The problem is that such "uncontaminated" measures may not capture some essential features of jealousy, as jealousy situations may be inherently anxiety-provoking and productive of socially undesirable behavior.

Use of Different Question and Response Formats

A variety of question and response formats have been used by researchers. Some items ask subjects to predict what they would be like in hypothetical situations; some ask subjects to recall what they were actually like in past situations; and some ask subjects to indicate their current state. Rational scales are especially likely to mix items assessing behaviors, feelings, attitudes, desires, or thoughts together. Items may or may not employ the word "jealousy," and even if they do not, they may or may not be transparent in their intention to assess jealousy. Some items ask for self-perceptions; others ask for perceptions of others who may (actually or hypothetically) be jealous. A variety of different response formats have been used to indicate presence–absence of a quality, frequency, likelihood, agreement, or intensity.

This state of affairs is not unusual in a newly developing field. However, since items with similar types of questions and similar response formats are likely to be more highly correlated because of shared method variance, this diversity makes it difficult to interpret either within-scale correlations among items or correlations between scales.

Further, anticipated jealousy measures are a form of role play-ing. Even with the use of imagery-provoking instructions, role-playing one's reaction to a jealousy-provoking situation may be more likely to assess one's self-concept as a jealousy-prone person. In any event, research on role-playing methodologies generally finds that they are not very useful in uncovering subtle or interactional effects (Greenberg & Folger, 1988). Since we argue that jealousy is a compli-cated interpersonal process likely to be influenced by a number of interacting factors, we are wary of measures of anticipated jealousy as substitutes for reports of past or current jealousy situations.

Disagreements between Actors and Observers

It may or may not be the case that the self-report of a "jealous" person is correlated with reports of others who observe him or her, such as the romantic partner, the rival, or friends. Such discrepan-cies may be the result of the person's impression management of his or her jealousy, differential access to personal history and subjective state, the press of role in the situation, or a variety of other pro-cesses. Such discrepancies are a particular problem for rational scales, since their underlying assumption is that jealousy "exists" and that reports by different observers should be highly correlated, as for any object. By contrast, discrepancies are not much of a problem for the phenomenological approach, which is interested in the cul-tural, relationship, and personal factors that may account for the degree of congruence of such reports.

Cultural Bias in Scales

"Cultural bias" refers not only to the problem of adequate transla-tion of scales, but also to the problem that the meaning of jealousy varies from culture to culture. The behaviors expected of the jealous may differ markedly, or the linkages between and among behaviors and emotions may be different. White (1984), for example, presents some evidence that the meaning of jealousy is generally different for women than for men within a Western college sample.

One of the strengths of the phenomenological approach is that this problem is minimized, because the subject is merely asked to indicate the presence of jealousy, whatever its cultural meaning. Rational scales with specific behaviors, thoughts, emotions, atti-tudes, and so on that are based on face validity to constructors or on surveys of subjects within one culture are most risky in this regard. Dispositional scales have the problem of the equivalence of situational domains across which the jealous disposition should have its effect. Theoretical scales have the problem of underlying constructs' being potentially inapplicable to other cultures.

With these problems in mind, we now present scales that have been used in published and unpublished jealousy research.

THE JEALOUSY SCALES

The scales are presented below in alphabetical order. Items for each scale are presented. If the scale has been factor-analyzed, the factors are indicated by the factor labels given by scale developers, or by Roman numerals. Items that are reverse-scored in creating factor scores are followed by a minus (−).

Test–retest and internal-consistency reliabilities are also given where they have been made available. Some scales have had more than one reliability reported. In such cases we have reported the reliability of the larger sample or have indicated the general range in which reported reliabilities fall. The published or unpublished source of the scale is also indicated, as are some of the studies that have employed the scale.

Bryson's Jealousy Factors

Bryson (1976, 1977; Shettel-Neuber et al., 1978) had college students list feelings and behaviors they had had when jealous. The 24 most frequent feelings and 24 most frequent behaviors were then selected. Another sample of college students indicated how well each of these 48 items described themselves when jealous (actual response scale was never specified). Eight factors resulted from a principal-components factor analysis. Factor loadings and reliabilities are unreported. The factors and items reported to define them are as follows:

Emotional Devastation. Feel helpless; like I'm in a daze; insecure; less able to cope with other aspects of my life; physically ill; inadequate; fearful; depressed; uncomfortable around other people; anxious; confused; exploited; cry when I'm alone.

Reactive Retribution. Start going out with other people; do something to get my partner jealous; become more sexually aggressive with other people; try to make my partner think I don't care; make critical comments about my partner in front of other people; get a friend to go talk to my partner.

Arousal. Pay more attention to my partner than before; become more sexually aggressive with my partner; try to monopolize my partner's time; feel more sexually aroused by my partner; resign myself to the situation (−).

Need for Social Support. Talk to close friends about my feelings; refuse to talk about my feelings with others (−); cry when I'm alone; check with others who might confirm or disconfirm my feelings; get away from the situation.

Intropunitiveness. Feel guilty about being jealous; get involved in other nondating activities; feel angry toward myself; feel like getting even (−); hope that my partner ends up being hurt (−).

Confrontation. Ask my partner to explain the situation; confront the other person directly; try to make other people think I don't care (−); try to make my partner think I don't care (−); feel inadequate (−).

Anger. Feel angry toward my partner; feel angry toward the other person; feel that my partner has made a mistake; feel betrayed; feel disappointed in my partner; feel like getting even.

VIII. Try to make other people think I don't care; try to make my partner think I don't care; feel more irritable toward other people; get drunk or get high (−). (Factor unlabeled but highly correlated with gender.)

Chronic Jealousy and Relationship Jealousy Scales

The Chronic Jealousy and Relationship Jealousy Scales are both six-item scales that attempt to assess the degree to which the respondent (or any person being rated) can be described as jealous. The Chronic Jealousy Scale attempts to assess the extent to which a person has a history of romantic jealousy. The Relationship Jealousy Scale attempts to assess jealousy in a current romantic relationship. These scales were developed by White and have been used in a number of studies (White, 1981b, 1984, 1985b, 1985c) and were differentiated out of an earlier Jealousy Scale (White, 1976, 1977, 1981a, 1981b). Bush et al. (1988) have used a two-item version of the Relationship Jealousy Scale.

Coefficient alphas for both scales are in the .80s; test-retest reliabilities over a month are in the .75–.85 range. Correlations between the two scales have ranged from the .50s to the .70s, which is high, although the scales have been associated with different predictors (White, 1981b, 1984). White (1984) reports that the self-reports of jealous persons and partner reports of the persons on the Chronic Jealousy and Relationship Jealousy Scales are moderately correlated.

Principal-axis factor analyses with varimax rotation on several samples have consistently yielded two well-defined factors corresponding to the Chronic Jealousy and Relationship Jealousy Scales.

Items use a 5-point response scale with endpoints and midpoints labeled appropriately. White has preceded his research surveys (which includes these two scales) with a note differentiating romantic jealousy from envy in general terms. For each of the items below, the endpoints and midpoints are given; item reversal is obvious.

Chronic Jealousy. How jealous a person are you generally (not at all jealous, moderately jealous, fairly jealous)? How often have you experienced jealousy in your romantic relationships (fairly often, sometimes, very rarely)? When you get jealous, how intense is that feeling usually (very strong, somewhat strong, very weak)? Do those who know you well tend to think of you as (not usually jealous, sometimes jealous, often jealous)? How much have your jealous feelings been a problem in your romantic relationships (no problem at all, sometimes a problem, often a problem)? Do you think of yourself as a person who can get jealous easily (definitely yes, sometimes, definitely no)?

Relationship Jealousy. Compared to your other romantic relationships, are you more or less jealous in your relationship with your partner (more jealous, equally jealous, less jealous)? How much is your jealousy a problem in your relationship with your partner (no problem at all, sometimes a problem, often a problem)? How jealous do you get of your partner's relationships with those of the opposite sex (not at all jealous, somewhat jealous, fairly jealous)? Do those who know your relationship with your partner tend to think of you as (not usually jealous, somewhat jealous, often jealous)? How intense are your feelings of jealousy in your relationship with your partner (very strong, somewhat strong, very weak)? How often do you get jealous of your partner's relationships with those of the opposite sex (fairly often, sometimes, very rarely)?

Interpersonal Jealousy Scale

Mathes and his colleagues developed the Interpersonal Jealousy Scale (IJS) and have used it in a number of studies (Mathes, 1984; Mathes, Phillips, Skowran, & Dirk, 1982; Mathes, Roter, & Joerger, 1982; Mathes & Severa, 1981). There are 27 items; each is rated for the extent to which it is currently true on a 9-point scale ranging from -4 to 0 to $+4$, with each point labeled ("absolutely false," "definitely false," "false," "slightly false," "neither true nor false," "slightly true," "true," "definitely true," "absolutely true").

Internal consistency has been reported at .92 for the total scale. Factor analyses have not been reported. Each respondent is typically asked to fill in the current romantic partner's name in a blank space, but we have used the word "partner" in place of a blank. The items are as follows:

+2 1. If partner were to see an old friend of the opposite sex and respond with a great deal of happiness, I would be annoyed.
2. If partner went out with same-sex friends, I would feel compelled to know what he/she did.
3. If partner admired someone of the opposite sex, I would feel irritated.
4. If partner were to help someone of the opposite sex with his/her homework, I would feel suspicious.
5. When partner likes one of my friends I am pleased (−).
6. If partner were to go away for the weekend without me, my only concern would be with whether he/she had a good time (−).
7. If partner were helpful to someone of the opposite sex, I would feel jealous.
8. When partner talks of happy experiences of his/her past, I feel sad that I wasn't part of them.
9. If partner were to become displeased about the time I spend with others, I would be flattered.
10. If partner and I went to a party and I lost sight of him/her, I would become uncomfortable.
11. I want partner to remain good friends with the people he/she used to date (−).
12. If partner were to date others, I would feel unhappy.
13. If I noted that partner and person of the opposite sex have something in common, I would become envious.
14. If partner were to become very close to someone of the opposite sex, I would feel very unhappy and/or angry.
15. I would like partner to be faithful to me.
16. I don't think it would bother me if partner flirted with someone of the opposite sex (−).
17. If someone of the opposite sex were to compliment partner, I would feel that the person was trying to take partner away from me.
18. I feel good when partner makes a new friend (−).
19. If partner were to spend the night comforting a friend of the opposite sex who had just had a tragic experience, partner's compassion would please me (−).

20. If someone of the opposite sex were to pay attention to partner, I would become possessive of him/her.
21. If partner were to become exuberant and hug someone of the opposite sex, it would make me feel good that he/she was expressing his/her feelings openly (−).
22. The thought of partner kissing someone else drives me up the wall.
23. If someone of the opposite sex lit up at the sight of partner, I would become uneasy.
24. I like to find fault with partner's old dates.
25. I feel possessive toward partner.
26. If I saw a picture of partner and an old date I would feel unhappy.
27. If partner were to accidentally call me by the wrong name, I would become furious.

Interpersonal Relationship Scale

The Interpersonal Relationship Scale (IRS) was developed by Hupka and his colleagues and has been used in a few studies (Hupka & Bachelor, 1979; Hupka & Rusch, 1977). The scale has 27 items that were developed through factor-analytic refinement of a large pool of initial, face-valid items. Split-half reliability is .85. Test–retest reliability over 7–10 days is .86. The scale correlates .54 with simple self-report of jealousy.

Principal-axis factor analysis with varimax rotation identified six factors, one termed an "envy" factor and the others termed "jealousy" factors. Factor reliabilities and loadings are unreported.

Respondents use a 6-point scale to indicate the extent of agreement with each item (the points are labeled "strongly agree," "moderately agree," "slightly agree," "slightly disagree," "moderately disagree," and "strongly disagree"). Respondents are told that words such as "partner," and so on refer to someone they love very much. The factors and items are as follows:

Threat to Exclusive Relationship. When I see my lover kissing someone else, my stomach knots up; when somebody hugs my lover, I get sick inside; I feel bad inside when I see my partner kissing someone else at a New Year's party; I feel depressed when my partner speaks favorably about someone of the opposite sex; when my partner is at a party having fun and I'm not there, I feel depressed; when my partner pays attention to other people, I feel lonely and left out.

Dependency. I often feel I couldn't exist without him/her; life wouldn't have much meaning without him/her; losing my lover would prevent me from being the person I want to be.

Sexual Possessiveness. It would bother me if my lover frequently had satisfying sexual relations with someone else; when my lover goes out with another wo/man, I become physically upset; I want my lover to enjoy sex only with me.

Competition and Vindictiveness. Jealousy is a sign of true love; I always try to "even the score"; I like to flirt now and then in front of my date to keep his/her interest.

Trust. I have confidence that my lover is not cheating behind my back; when I am away from my mate for any length of time, I do not become suspicious of my mate's whereabouts; I see my mate as a faithful person.

Self-Deprecation/Envy. It is somewhat annoying to see others have all the luck in getting the best dating partners; I don't imagine I'll ever have a romantic relationship as good as some I've seen; When I see an attractive person, I feel inadequate; I often find myself idealizing persons or objects; I don't know why, but I usually seem to be the underdog; I feel empty inside when I see a successful relationship; most of my friends have a more exciting love life than I do.

Multidimensional Jealousy Scale

The Multidimensional Jealousy Scale (MJS) was recently developed by Pfeiffer and Wong (1987) and has three subscales of Cognitive, Emotional, and Behavioral Jealousy. The scale was developed through factor-analytic refinement of face-valid items. Internal consistency is high for each subscale (alphas in the .80–.90 range), and interscale correlations are generally in the .30s. Responses to the Cognitive and Behavioral Jealousy subscales are made on a 1–7 scale with endpoints labeled "never" and "all the time"; Emotional Jealousy items use a 1–7 scale with endpoints labeled "pleased" and "upset." Each subscale is moderately to highly correlated with White's Relationship Jealousy Scale and with the Sexual Jealousy subscale of Bringle's Self-Report Jealousy Scale (SRJS; see below). The subscales and items are as follows:

Cognitive Jealousy. I suspect that X is secretly seeing someone of the opposite sex; I am worried that some member of the opposite sex may be chasing after X; I suspect that X may be attracted to someone else; I suspect that X may be physically intimate with another member of the opposite sex behind my back; I think that some members of the opposite sex may be romantically interested in X; I am worried that someone of the opposite sex is trying to seduce X; I think that X is secretly developing an intimate relationship with someone of the opposite sex; I suspect that X is crazy about members of the opposite sex.

Emotional Jealousy. X comments to you on how great-looking a particular member of the opposite sex is; X shows a great deal of interest or excitement in talking to someone of the opposite sex; X smiles in a very friendly manner to someone of the opposite sex; a member of the opposite sex is trying to get close to X all the time; X is flirting with someone of the opposite sex; someone of the opposite sex is dating X; X hugs and kisses someone of the opposite sex; X works very closely with a member of the opposite sex.

Behavioral Jealousy. I look through X's drawers, handbag, or pockets; I call X unexpectedly, just to see if s/he is there; I question X about previous or present romantic relationships; I say something nasty about someone of the opposite sex if X shows an interest in that person; I question X about his/her telephone calls; I question X about his/her whereabouts; I join in whenever I see X talking to a member of the opposite sex; I pay X a surprise visit just to see who is with him or her.

Self-Report Jealousy Scale

The SRJS was developed by Bringle and his colleagues and has been used as a measure in a number of studies (Bringle, 1981; Bringle et al., 1983; Bringle, Roach, et al., 1977; Bringle et al., 1979; Bringle & Williams, 1979; Salovey & Rodin, 1988). Its purpose is to measure dispositional jealousy. Development was based on refinement of earlier items assessing intended domains. There are 20 items assessing the domains of social, sexual, family, and work situations. Coefficient alpha is over .90; 2-week test–retest reliability is .73.

Factor analysis (type unreported) with varimax rotation yielded a four-factor solution, but with an oblique rotation the factors correlated on an average of .42 with each other.

The subject is asked to indicate how jealous he or she has been, or might be, in each of the 20 situations. A 9-point response format with endpoints labeled "not very jealous" and "jealous" is used. Jealousy is not distinguished from envy in the instructions. The unlabeled factors and items are as follows:

I. Your find your spouse is having an affair: a spouse or steady looks at another; a spouse or steady spends increasingly more time with others; you are stood up, and then learn that your date was out with another person; your steady date expresses a desire to date others; another person is flirting with your date or spouse; a spouse or steady spends increasingly more time in outside activities.

II. A close friend obtains goals which you value; a friend is smarter and gets higher grades; an outsider becomes too close to your children; a group of people who would not include you in their activities; friends who have more money and are able to buy clothes, etc.; a classmate has superior athletic abilities; a classmate gets more attention from a teacher.

III. Another person gets the promotion for which you were qualified; someone else gets the praise or credit for something you did.

IV. A brother or sister excels in school; a brother or sister is receiving presents, and you don't get any; your brother or sister is given more freedom, such as staying up later, or driving the car; your brother or sister seems to be receiving more affection and/or attention from your parents.

Survey of Interpersonal Reactions

The Survey of Interpersonal Reactions (SIR) was developed by Rosmarin and her colleagues (Bush et al., 1988; Rosmarin et al., 1979; Rosmarin & LaPointe, 1978). They report a number of psychometric analyses that generally show the SIR to be superior psychometrically to the IRS of Hupka and Bachelor (1979). The SIR was developed through a series of item analyses of larger sets of items, which resulted in 36 items defining five relatively pure factors. Coefficient alpha for the total scale is .88; 1-month test-retest reliability is .57. The total scale correlates .60 with a simple self-descriptive rating of oneself as jealous.

The respondent uses a 5-point scale to indicate the extent to which a behavior, thought, or feeling is characteristic of himself or herself; points are labeled "very uncharacteristic of me," "uncharacteristic of me," "neutral," "characteristic of me," and "very characteristic of me." Principal-axis factor analysis with varimax rotation yielded five factors. Factors were defined by items loading >.30; factor reliabilities are not reported. The factors and items are as follows:

Individuation in Relationship. Happiness is not exclusively dependent on one person or event; it is good for partner to feel like s/he is free to enjoy other people and interests; if I can't have a good time,

partner shouldn't either (−); I feel annoyed with partner when he/
she gets recognition for his/her work and I don't (−); I accept partner
as a person unique from our relationship; I let partner spend his/her
time the way s/he wants to; I encourage partner to engage in activities without me; I give my support to partner in his/her career or
friendship choices; when partner and I are together in a social situation, I spend my time freely interacting with others rather than
monitoring what partner is doing; partner and I communicate openly
about our other relationships.

Exclusivity—Feelings and Behaviors. Partner can love someone else
and still love me; when partner expresses interest in someone else, I
feel uncomfortable (−); if partner becomes close to someone else, I
feel happy for him/her; I don't worry or become suspicious when
someone of the opposite sex calls; I don't become defensive when
partner starts showing interest in another wo/man.

Exclusivity—Beliefs. If two people truly love each other, they will
feel no need for other relationships; becoming interested in another
person does not mean you have grown tired of or dissatisfied with
your current relationship; partner's wanting to become close to
someone else doesn't mean s/he is less interested in me; if partner
really loved me, s/he wouldn't want to be with anyone else (−); if
partner wants to go out with other people, s/he must not care for me
anymore (−).

Egoistic Suspicion. If partner had the chance, s/he'd cheat on me; I
wonder who that wo/man is whom partner is showing so much
interest in; I worry a lot about our relationship; I often worry that
partner will find being with someone else more fun than being with
me; I'm really an inadequate person, no wonder partner wants to see
others; that wo/man is trying to take partner away from me; I feel
left out, neglected, or resentful when partner has a good time and
I'm not there; when partner has spent the night talking to everyone
but me, I give him/her the silent treatment; I often accuse partner of
not caring about me; I often browse through partner's personal
belongings to see if there is something about which partner hasn't
told me; I often accuse partner of being unfaithful.

Anxious Attachment. Worrying about what your lover is doing is a
waste of time (−); it would be a terrible thing if we broke up; I feel
miserable or neglected when partner and I are separated; if I think
that partner is interested in someone else, I can't sleep at night;
when partner and I are separated, I participate fully in what I'm
doing rather than spend part of my energy wondering what partner
is doing (−).

LESS FREQUENTLY USED JEALOUSY SCALES

A few other jealousy scales have been reported, but we do not describe them at length here, either because they have been used in only one original report or because scale items and reliabilities are not provided in enough detail. We mention them here for reference, however.

Tipton, Benedictson, Mahony, and Hartnett (1978) reported development of a 31-item jealousy scale with five factors: Need for Loyalty, Need for Intimacy, Moodiness, Self-Confidence, and Envy. These factors correlated with some variables thought to be related to jealousy.

Thissen, Steinberg, Pyszczynski, and Greenberg (1983) presented the Romantic Jealousy Assessment Scale in the context of a methodological article on scale item analysis. It consists of six scenarios followed by a 9-point response scale for rating degree of anticipated jealousy (endpoints are labeled "not at all jealous" and "extremely jealous"). Coefficient alpha is .87. This scale was used in one study reported by Greenberg and Pyszczynski (1985) as an individual-difference variable.

Hupka et al. (1985) reported a 69-item Romantic Jealousy–Romantic Envy "instrument," which was given to respondents in seven different nations. They report the results of principal-axis factor analyses done for each national sample's data, including factor loadings for items that defined a factor in at least one sample. (The factors are presented and discussed in Chapter 6.)

Pines and Aronson (1983) used a single self-report question to assess jealousy. However, they also present a great many items that may be informative for future scale development.

CONCLUDING COMMENTS

We think that scales derived via factor analysis share an underlying conceptual flaw, in that they regard jealousy as a thing with various "dimensions" that can be measured. Many of the factors reported above can be seen as aspects of what we have called the jealousy complex. We think that advances in the field will come from measuring discrete elements of the jealousy complex, such as various emotions, coping strategies, and beliefs about the nature of the threat posed by the rival (primary and secondary appraisal), and then from linking these variables (or patterns of these variables) to antecedent events or theoretical variables. Otherwise, "jealousy scales" run the risk of being rather scattered collections of behaviors, thoughts, and feelings that happen to drop out of a factor analysis.

We have some sympathy with the intention of the SRJS to measure dispositional aspects of jealousy. However, White (1984) has reported that the SRJS (and the SIR) are so highly correlated with simple self-reports of jealousy that it is doubtful that the elaborate scale is worth the effort. The problem is again conceptual—what is it that is meant as a jealous disposition? We suggest that a fruitful area for developing dispositional measures is to assess people's *beliefs* that they have "jealous" personalities or that "jealousy" is something central to their self-concept. The extent to which such self-knowledge is related to consistency of behavior over time within certain domains (family, work, romantic, etc.) or across different domains can then be a matter of empirical interest.

Finally, it is difficult to know just what to make of previous research using multidimensional scales that correlate highly with simple self-reports of how jealous the respondents currently are. Phenomenological scales that directly assess such self-report, we think, are useful in understanding the process of labeling oneself as jealous. Correlates of direct self-reports can be understood as correlates or predictors of the use of a label. This suggests that previous research using multidimensional scales that are highly correlated with direct self-reports may also be conceptualized as research on variables that are related to the tendency to label oneself as jealous.

References

Aberle, D. F. (1961). Navaho. In D. M. Schneider & K. Gough (Eds.), *Matrilineal kinship* (pp. 96–201). Berkeley: University of California Press.

Abramovitch, R., Pepler, D., & Corter, C. (1982). Patterns of sibling interaction among preschool-age children. In M. Lamb & B. Sutton-Smith (Eds.), *Sibling relationships: Their nature and significance across the lifespan*. Hillsdale, NJ: Erlbaum.

Adler, A. (1928). Characteristics of the 1st, 2nd and 3rd child. *Children, 3* (Whole No. 5).

Ainsworth, M. D. S., Blehar, M. C., Waters, E., & Wall, S. C. (1978). *Patterns of attachment: A psychological study of the strange situation*. Hillsdale, NJ: Erlbaum.

Alexander, R. D., & Noonan, K. M. (1979). Concealment of ovulation, parental care, and human social evolution. In N. A. Chagnow & W. Irons (Eds.), *Evolutionary biology and human social behavior* (pp. 436–453). North Scituate, MA: Duxbury Press.

Altman, I., & Taylor, D. A. (1973). *Social penetration*. New York: Holt, Rinehart & Winston.

American Psychiatric Association. (1974). *Clinical aspects of the violent individual*. Washington, DC: Author.

Amstutz, D. (1982). *Androgyny and jealousy*. Unpublished doctoral dissertation, Northern Illinois University.

Anderson, C. R. (1977). Locus of control, coping behaviors and performance in a stress setting: A longitudinal study. *Journal of Applied Psychology, 62,* 446–451.

Anderson, E. W. (1971). Strindberg's illness. *Psychological Medicine, 1,* 104–117.

Ankles, T. M. (1939). *A study of jealousy as differentiated from envy*. London: Stockwell.

Ard, B. N., Jr. (1977). Avoiding destructive jealousy. In G. Clanton & L. G. Smith (Eds.), *Jealousy* (pp. 166–169). Englewood Cliffs, NJ: Prentice-Hall.

Arnold, M. B. (1960). *Emotion and personality* (Vols. 1 & 2). New York: Columbia University Press.

Ashmore, R. D., & Del Boca, F. K. (Eds.). (1986). *The social psychology of female-male relations*. New York: Academic Press.

Ashmore, R. D., Del Boca, F. K., & Wohlers, A. J. (1986). Gender stereotypes. In R. D. Ashmore & F. K. Del Boca (Eds.), *The social psychology of female-male relations* (pp. 69–120). New York: Academic Press.

Ausubel, D. P., Sullivan, E. V., & Ives, S. W. (1980). *Theory and problems of child development*. New York: Grune & Stratton.

Averill, J. R. (1979). The functions of grief. In C. E. Izard (Ed.), *Emotions in personality and psychopathology* (pp. 339–368). New York: Plenum.

Averill, J. R. (1982). *Anger and aggression: An essay on emotions*. New York: Springer.

Backman, C. W. (1981). Attraction in interpersonal relationships. In M. Rosenberg & R. H. Turner (Eds.), *Social psychology: Social perspectives* (pp. 181–214). New York: Basic Books.

Bandura, A. (1976). Self-reinforcement: Theoretical and methodological considerations. *Behaviorism, 4*, 135–155.

Bandura, A. (1978). The self-system in reciprocal determinism. *American Psychologist, 33*, 344–358.

Bandura, A. (1986). *Social foundations of thought and action*. Englewood Cliffs, NJ: Prentice-Hall.

Banks, S. P., & Kahn, M. D. (1982). *The sibling bond*. New York: Basic Books.

Barag, G. (1949). A case of pathological jealousy. *Psychoanalytic Quarterly, 18*, 1–18.

Barash, D. (1976). Male response to apparent female adultery in the mountain bluebird (Sialia currucoides): An evolutionary interpretation. *American Naturalist, 110*, 1097–1101.

Barash, D. (1977). *Sociobiology and behavior*. Amsterdam: Elsevier.

Barlow, G. W., & Silverberg, J. (Eds.). (1980). *Sociobiology: Beyond nature/nurture?* Boulder, CO: Westview Press.

Barr, C. E., & Hupka, R. B. (1988). *Attribution and intent on determination of emotions in a jealousy situation*. Unpublished manuscript, California State University, Long Beach.

Barry, H., III. (1980). Description and uses of the Human Relations Area Files. In H. C. Triandis & J. W. Berry (Eds.), *Handbook of cross-cultural psychology: Vol. 2. Methodology* (pp. 445–478). Boston: Allyn & Bacon.

Bartell, G. D. (1970). Group sex among mid-Americans. *Journal of Sex Research, 6*, 113–130.

Baute, P. (1978). The love is war: Anything goes ploy in triangles. *Psychotherapy Bulletin, 13*, 13–24.

Beecher, M., & Beecher, W. (1971). *An anatomy of jealousy*. New York: Harper & Row.

Bell, A. P., & Weinberg, M. S. (1978). *Homosexuality*. New York: Simon & Schuster.

Bem, D. J. (1972). Self-perception theory. In L. Berkowitz (Ed.), *Advances in experimental social psychology* (Vol. 6, pp. 2–62). New York: Academic Press.

Bem, S. (1974). The measurement of psychological androgyny. *Journal of Consulting and Clinical Psychology, 42*, 155–162.

Benedict, R. (1961). *Patterns of culture.* Boston: Houghton Mifflin.

Benjamin, L. S. (1974). Structural analysis of social behavior. *Psychological Review, 81*, 392–425.

Berger, P. L., & Luckmann, J. (1966). *The social construction of reality.* New York: Doubleday.

Bergler, E. (1956). Unconscious reasons for husbands' confessions to their jealous wives. *Psychiatric Quarterly, 30*, 73–76.

Bernard, J. (1971). Jealousy in marriage. *Human Sexuality, 5*, 200–215.

Bers, S. A., & Rodin, J. (1984). Social comparison jealousy: A developmental and motivational study. *Journal of Personality and Social Psychology, 47*, 766–769.

Berscheid, E. (1983). Emotion. In H. H. Kelley, E. Berscheid, A. Christensen, J. H. Harvey, T. L. Huston, G. Levinger, E. McClintock, L. A. Peplau, & D. R. Peterson, *Close relationships* (pp. 110–168). San Francisco: W. H. Freeman.

Berscheid, E., & Fei, J. (1977). Romantic love and sexual jealousy. In G. Clanton & L. G. Smith (Eds.), *Jealousy* (pp. 101–109). Englewood Cliffs, NJ: Prentice-Hall.

Berscheid, E., & Walster, E. (1974). Physical attractiveness. In L. Berkowitz (Ed.), *Advances in experimental social psychology* (Vol. 7, pp. 158–216). New York: Academic Press.

Berscheid, E., & Walster, E. H. (1978). *Interpersonal attraction* (2nd ed). Reading, MA: Addison-Wesley.

Bertalanffy, L. von. (1968). *General systems theory.* New York: Braziller.

Bianchi, L. (1906). *Psychiatry* (J. H. MacDonald, Trans.). London: Balliere, Tindall & Cox.

Blasband, D., & Peplau, L. A. (1985). Sexual exclusivity versus openness in gay male couples. *Archives of Sexual Behaviour, 14*, 395–412.

Blau, P. M. (1964). *Exchange and power in social life.* New York: Wiley.

Bleuler, E. (1924). *Textbook of psychiatry* (A. A. Brill, Trans.). New York: Macmillan. (Original work published 1916)

Bloch, I. (1908). *The sexual life of our time* (E. Paul, Trans.). London: Heinemann.

Blood, R., & Blood, M. (1977). Jealousy workshops. In G. Clanton & L. G. Smith (Eds.), *Jealousy* (pp. 199–207). Englewood Cliffs, NJ: Prentice-Hall.

Bohm, E. (1961). Jealousy. In A. Ellis & A. Abarbanel (Eds.), *The encyclopedia of sexual behavior* (Vol. 1, pp. 567–574). New York: Hawthorn Books.

Boranga, G. (1981). *On the psychogenesis of jealousy–paranoic psychosis.* Unpublished M.D. thesis, Royal Australian and New Zealand College of Psychiatrists.

Boss, M. (1949). *Meaning and content of sexual perversions* (L. L. Abell, Trans.). New York: Grune & Stratton.

Boucher, J. D. (1979). Culture and emotions. In A. J. Marsella, R. Tharp, & T. Ciborowski (Eds.), *Perspective on cross-cultural psychology* (pp. 159–178). New York: Academic Press.

Bowlby, J. (1969). *Attachment and loss: Vol. 1. Attachment.* New York: Basic Books.

Braiker, H. B., & Kelley, H. H. (1979). Conflict in the development of close relationships. In R. L. Burgess & T. L. Huston (Eds.), *Social exchange in developing relationships* (pp. 135–168). New York: Academic Press.

Braiker-Stambul, H. B. (1975). *Stages of courtship: The development of premarital relationships.* Unpublished doctoral dissertation, University of California at Los Angeles.

Brain, P. F. (1986). *Alcohol and aggression.* London: Croom Helm.

Brehm, J. W. (1972). *Responses to loss of freedom: A theory of psychological reactance.* Morristown, NJ: General Learning Press.

Brehm, S. S. (1985). *Intimate relationships.* New York: Random House.

Brickman, P., & Bulman, R. J. (1977). Pleasure and pain in social comparison. In J. M. Suls & R. K. Miller (Eds.), *Social comparison processes: Theoretical and empirical perspectives* (pp. 149–186). Washington, DC: Hemisphere.

Bringle, R. G. (1981). Conceptualizing jealousy as a disposition. *Alternative Lifestyles, 4,* 274–290.

Bringle, R. G. (1986). *Effects of dispositional jealousy on marital quality.* Unpublished manuscript, Indiana University at Indianapolis.

Bringle, R. G., & Buunk, B. (1985). Jealousy and social behavior. *Review of Personality and Social Psychology, 6,* 241–264.

Bringle, R. G., & Buunk, B. (1986). Examining the causes and consequences of jealousy: Some recent findings and issues. In R. Gilmour & S. Duck (Eds.), *The emerging field of personal relationships* (pp. 225–240). Hillsdale, NJ: Erlbaum.

Bringle, R. G., Evenbeck, S. E., & Schmedel, K. (1977). *The role of jealousy in marriage.* Paper presented at the annual meeting of the American Psychological Association, San Francisco.

Bringle, R. G., & Gray, K. (1986). *Jealousy and the third person in the love triangle.* Unpublished manuscript, Indiana University at Indianapolis.

Bringle, R. G., Renner, P., Terry, R. L., & Davis, S. (1983). An analysis of situation and person componants of jealousy. *Journal of Research in Personality, 17,* 354–368.

Bringle, R. G., Roach, S., Andler, C., & Evenbeck, S. (1977). *Correlates of jealousy.* Paper presented at the annual meeting of the Midwestern Psychological Association, Chicago.

Bringle, R. G., Roach, S., Andler, C., & Evenbeck, S. (1979). Measuring the intensity of jealous reactions. *Catalog of Selected Documents in Psychology, 9,* 23–24.

Bringle, R. G., & Williams, L. J. (1979). Parental–offspring similarity on jealousy and related personality dimensions. *Motivation and Motion, 3,* 265–286.

Brunswick, R. M. (1929). The analysis of a case of paranoia (delusions of jealousy). *Journal of Nervous and Mental Disease, 70,* 5–21, 155–178.

Bryant, B., & Crockenberg, S. (1980). Correlates and discussion of prosocial behavior: A study of female siblings with their mothers. *Child Development, 51,* 529–544.

Bryson, J. B. (1976). *The nature of sexual jealousy: An exploratory paper.* Paper presented at the annual meeting of the American Psychological Association, Washington, DC.

Bryson, J. B. (1977). *Situational determinants of the expression of the jealousy.* Paper presented at the annual meeting of the American Psychological Association, San Francisco.

Burgess, R. L., & Huston, T. L. (Eds.). (1979). *Social exchange in developing relationships.* New York: Academic Press.

Bush, C. R., Bush, J. P., & Jennings, J. (1988). Effects of jealousy threat on relationship perception and emotions. *Journal of Social and Personal Relationships, 5,* 285–303.

Buss, A. H. (1980). *Self-consciousness.* San Francisco: W. H. Freeman.

Bursten, E. (1980). Isolated violence to the loved one. *Bulletin of the American Academy of Psychiatry and the Law, 9,* 116–127.

Burton, R. (1827). *The anatomy of melancholy.* London: Longman. (Original work published 1621)

Butler, R. A. (1975). *Report of the Committee on Mentally Abnormal Offenders.* London: Her Majesty's Stationery Office.

Buunk, B. (1978). Jaloezie/Ervaringen van 250 Nederlanders. *Intermediair, 14,* 43–51.

Buunk, B. (1980). Sexually open marriages: Ground rules for countering potential threats to marriage. *Alternative Lifestyles, 3,* 312–328.

Buunk, B. (1981). Jealousy in sexually open marriages. *Alternative Lifestyles, 4,* 357–372.

Buunk, B. (1982a). Anticipated sexual jealousy: Its relationship to self-esteem, dependence and reciprocity. *Personality and Social Psychology Bulletin, 8,* 310–316.

Buunk, B. (1982b). Strategies of jealousy: Styles of coping with extramarital involvement of the spouse. *Family Relations, 31,* 13–18.

Buunk, B. (1984). Jealousy as related to attributions for the partner's behavior. *Social Psychology Quarterly, 47,* 107–112.

Buunk, B. (1986). Husband's jealousy. In R. A. Lewis & R. E. Salt (Eds.), *Men in families* (pp. 97–114). Beverly Hills, CA: Sage.

Buunk, B. (1987). Conditions that promote breakups as a consequence of extradyadic involvements. *Journal of Social and Clinical Psychology, 5,* 271–284.

Buunk, B., & Bringle, R. G. (1987). Jealousy in love relationships. In D. Perlman & S. Duck (Eds.), *Intimate relationships: Development, dynamics, and deterioration* (pp. 123–147). Beverly Hills, CA: Sage.

Buunk, B., Bringle, R. G., & Arends, H. (1984). *Jealousy—a response to threatened self-concept?* Paper presented at the International Conference on Self and Identity, Cardiff, Wales.

Buunk, B., & Hupka R. B. (1987). Cross-cultural differences in the elicitation of sexual jealousy. *Journal of Sex Research, 23,* 12–22.

Caplan, A. C. (Ed.). (1978). *The sociobiology debate.* New York: Harper & Row.

Carson, R. C. (1969). *Interaction concepts of personality.* Chicago: Aldine.

Chimbos, P. D. (1978). *Marital violence: A study of interspousal homicide.* San Francisco: R. & E. Research Associates.

Christensen, H. T. (1963). A cross-cultural comparison of attitudes towards marital infidelity. In J. Mogey (Ed.), *Family and marriage* (pp. 124–137). Leiden, The Netherlands: E. J. Bill.

Church, J. (1984). *Violence against wives: Its causes and effects.* Christchurch, New Zealand: Author.

Churchland, P. S. (1986). *Neurophilosophy.* Cambridge, MA: MIT Press.

Clanton, G. (1981). Frontiers of jealousy research. *Alternative Lifestyles, 4,* 259–273.

Clanton, G., & Smith, L. G. (Eds.). (1977). *Jealousy.* Englewood Cliffs, NJ: Prentice-Hall.

Clark, M. S. (1985). Implications of relationship type for understanding compatibility. In W. Ickes (Ed.), *Compatible and incompatible relationships* (pp. 119–140). New York: Springer-Verlag.

Clark, M. S., & Mills, J. (1979). Interpersonal attraction in exchange and communal relationships. *Journal of Personality and Social Psychology, 37,* 12–24.

Cobb, J. P. (1979). Morbid jealousy. *British Journal of Hospital Medicine, 21,* 511–518.

Cobb, J. P., & Marks, I. M. (1979). Morbid jealousy featuring as obsessive compulsive neurosis: Treatment by behavioural psychotherapy. *British Journal of Psychiatry, 134,* 301–305.

Collins, J. J. (1982). *Drinking and crime.* London: Tavistock.

Constantine, L. L. (1976). Jealousy: From theory to intervention. In D. H. Olson (Ed.), *Treating relationships* (pp. 383–398). Lake Mills, IA: Graphic.

Constantine, L. L. (1986). Jealousy and extramarital sexual relations. In N. S. Jacobson & A. S. Gurman (Eds.), *Clinical handbook of marital therapy* (pp. 407–427). New York: Guilford Press.

Constantine, L. L., & Constantine, J. M. (1974). Sexual aspects of multilateral relations. In J. R. Smith & L. G. Smith (Eds.), *Beyond monogamy* (pp. 268–290). Baltimore: Johns Hopkins University Press.

Coopersmith, S. (1967). *The antecedents of self-esteem.* San Francisco: W. H. Freeman.

Copeland, J. R. M., Kelleher, M. J., & Smith, A. M. R. (with Gourlay A. J.). (1975). Influence of psychiatric training, medical qualification and paramedical training on the rating of abnormal behaviour. *Psychological Medicine, 5,* 89–95.

Cormier, B. (1962). Psychodynamics of homicide committed in a marital relationship. *Journal of Corrective Psychiatry, 8,* 185–194.

Cowper Powys, J. (1934). *Autobiography.* London: MacDonald.

Cox, C. R., & Le Boeuf, B. J. (1977). Female incitation of male competition: A mechanism for sexual selection. *American Naturalist, 111,* 317–335.

Cummings, J. L. (1985). Organic delusions: Phenomenology, anatomical correlations and review. *British Journal of Psychiatry, 146,* 184–197.

Daly, M., Wilson, M., & Weghorst, S. J. (1982). Male sexual jealousy. *Ethology and Sociobiology, 3,* 11–27.

D'Andrade, R. G. (1984). Cultural meaning systems. In R. A. Shweder & R. A. LeVine (Eds.), *Culture theory* (pp. 88–119). Cambridge, England: Cambridge University Press.

Darwin, C. (1871). *The descent of man and selection in relation to sex.* London: John Murray.

D'Augelli, J. F., & D'Augelli, A. R. (1979). Sexual involvement and relationship development: A cognitive development approach. In R. L. Burgess & T. L. Huston (Eds.), *Social exchange in developing relationships* (pp. 307–350). New York: Academic Press.

Davis, K. (1936). Jealousy and sexual property. *Social Forces, 14,* 395–405.

Davitz, J. R. (1969). *The language of emotions.* New York: Acadmic Press.

de Clerambeault, C. G. (1942). *Les psychoses passionelles.* Paris: Presses Universitaires.

De Moja, C. A. (1986). Anxiety, self-confidence, jealousy, and romantic attitudes toward love in Italian undergraduates. *Psychological Reports, 58,* 138.

Denfeld, D. (1974). Dropouts from swinging: The marriage counselor or informant. In J. R. Smith & L. G. Smith (Eds.), *Beyond monogamy* (pp. 260–267). Baltimore: Johns Hopkins University Press.

Dion, K. L., & Dion, K. K. (1973). Correlates of romantic love. *Journal of Consulting and Clinical Psychology, 41,* 51–56.

Dion, K. K., & Dion, K. L. (1975). Self-esteem and romantic love. *Journal of Personality, 43,* 39–57.

Dobash, R. E., & Dobash, R. P. (1980). *Violence against wives: A case against the patriarchy.* London: Open Books.

Dobzhansky, T. (1951). Human diversity and adaptation. *Cold Spring Harbor Symposia on Quantitative Biology, 15,* 385–400.

Docherty, J. P., & Ellis, J. (1976). A new concept and finding in morbid jealousy. *American Journal of Psychiatry, 133,* 679–683.

Dominik, M. (1970). Pathological jealousy in delusional syndromes. *Acta Medica Poland, 11,* 267–280.

Downing, C. (1977). Jealousy: A depth-psychological perspective. In G. Clanton & L. G. Smith (Eds.), *Jealousy* (pp. 72–79). Englewood Cliffs, NJ: Prentice-Hall.

Duck, S. (1984). A perspective on the repair of personal relationships: Repair of what, when? In S. Duck (Ed.), *Personal relationships: Vol. 5. Repairing personal relationships* (pp. 113–184). New York: Academic Press.

Dunn, J. (1983). Sibling relationships in early childhood. *Child Development, 54,* 787–811.

Dunn, J. (1984). *Sisters and brothers.* London: Fontana.

Dunn, J., & Kendrick, C. (1981). Interaction between young siblings: Association with the interaction between mother and first-born. *Developmental Psychology, 17,* 336–343.

Dunn, J., & Kendrick, C. (1982). *Siblings: Love, envy and understanding.* Cambridge, MA: Harvard University Press.

Dunn, J., Kendrick, C., & MacNamee, R. (1981). The reactions of first-born children to the birth of a sibling: Mothers' reports. *Journal of Child Psychology and Psychiatry, 22,* 1–18.

Durham, W. H. (1979). Toward a coevolutionary theory of human biology and culture. In N. A. Chagnon & W. Irons (Eds.), *Evolutionary biology and human social behavior* (pp. 39–58). North Scituate, MA: Duxbury Press.

East, N. W. (1936). *Medical aspects of crime.* London: Churchill.

East, N. W. (1949). Crime, senescence and senility. In *Society and the criminal* (pp. 48–69). London: His Majesty's Stationery Office.

Eddy, J. P. (1958). The new law of provocation. *Criminal Law Review,* 778–785.

Eisler, R. (1949). *Man into wolf.* London: Spring Books.

Ekman, P. (1984). Expression and the nature of emotion. In K. S. Scherer & P. Ekman (Eds.), *Approaches to emotion* (pp. 319–343). Hillsdale, NJ: Erlbaum.

Ellis, A. (1977). Rational and irrational jealousy. In G. Clanton & L. G. Smith (Eds.), *Jealousy* (pp. 170–179). Englewood Cliffs, NJ: Prentice-Hall.

Ellis, A. B. (1890). *The Ewe-speaking peoples of the slave coast of West Africa.* London: Chapman & Hall.

Ellis, C., & Weinstein, E. (1986). Jealousy and the social psychology of emotional experience. *Journal of Social and Personal Relationships, 3,* 337–357.

Ellis, H. (1890). *The criminal.* London: Walter Scott.

Enoch, D. M., & Trethowen, W. J. (1979). *Uncommon psychiatric syndromes* (pp. 36–49). Bristol, England: John Wright & Sons.

Epstein, L. J., Mills, C., & Simon, A. (1970). Antisocial behavior of the elderly. *Comprehensive Psychiatry, 11,* 36–42.

Esquirol, E. (1976). *Des maladies mentales.* New York: Arno Press Classics in Psychiatry. (Original work published 1838)

Ey, H. (1950). Jalousie morbide. In *Études psychiatriques* (Vol. 2). Paris: Desclee de Brouwer et Cie.

Faergemann, P. M. (1963). *Psychogenic psychoses.* London: Butterworths.

Farber, L. H. (1973). On jealousy. *Commentary, 55,* 180–202.

Fenichel, O. (1935). A contribution to the psychology of jealousy. *Imago, 21,* 143–157.

Fenichel, S. (1945). *The psychoanalytic theory of neurosis.* New York: Norton.

Ferenczi, S. (1952). On the part played by homosexuality in the pathogenesis of paranoia. In *First contributions to psychoanalysis.* London: Hogarth Press.

Fetzer, J. H. (1985). *Sociobiology and epistemology.* Boston: D. Reidel.

Field, T., & Reite, M. (1984). Children's responses to separation from mother during the birth of another child. *Child Development, 55,* 1308–1316.

Firth, R. (1936). *We, the Tikopin.* New York: American Book.

Fish, F. (1967). *Clinical psychopathology.* Bristol, England: John Wright & Sons.

Fiske, S. T., & Taylor, S. E. (1984). *Social cognition.* Menlo Park, CA: Addison-Wesley.

Foa, E. B., & Foa, U. G. (1980). Resource theory: Interpersonal behavior as exchange. In K. J. Gergen, M. S. Greenberg, & R. H. Willis (Eds.), *Social exchange* (pp. 77–102). New York: Plenum.

Foa, U. G. (1961). Convergences in the analyses of the structure of interpersonal behavior. *Psychological Review, 68*, 341–353.

Folkman, S., & Lazarus, R. S. (1980). An analysis of coping in a middle-aged community sample. *Journal of Health and Social Behavior, 21*, 219–239.

Ford, C. S., & Beach, F. A. (1951). *Patterns of sexual behavior.* New York: Harper & Row.

Foster, S. (1927). A study of the personality make-up and social settings of fifty jealous children. *Mental Hygiene, 11*, 53–77.

Francis, J. L. (1977). Toward the management of heterosexual jealousy. *Journal of Marriage and Family Counseling, 10*, 61–69.

Freud, S. (1955). Psychoanalytic notes on an autobiographical account of a case of paranoia. In J. Strachey (Ed. and Trans.), *The standard edition of the complete psychological works of Sigmund Freud* (Vol. 12, pp. 9–82). London: Hogarth Press. (Original work published 1911)

Freud, S. (1955). Some neurotic mechanisms in jealousy, paranoia and homosexuality. In J. Strachey (Ed. and Trans.), *The standard edition of the complete psychological works of Sigmund Freud* (Vol. 18, pp. 221–232). London: Hogarth Press. (Original work published 1922)

Freud, S. (1959). Group psychology and the analysis of the ego. In J. Strachey (Ed. and Trans.), *The standard edition of the complete psychological works of Sigmund Freud* (Vol. 18, pp. 65–143). New York: Norton. (Original work published 1922)

Freud, S. (1959). Inhibitions, symptoms and anxiety. In J. Strachey (Ed. and Trans.), *The standard edition of the complete psychological works of Sigmund Freud* (Vol. 20, pp. 73–174). London: Hogarth Press. (Original work published 1926)

Freud, S. (1963). Introductory lectures on psychoanalysis. In J. Strachey (Ed. and Trans.), *The standard edition of the complete psychological works of Sigmund Freud* (Vol. 25). London: Hogarth Press. (Original work published 1917)

Freud, S. (1964). New introductory lectures on psychoanalysis. In J. Strachey (Ed. and Trans.), *The standard edition of the complete psychological works of Sigmund Freud* (Vol. 22, pp. 3–158). London: Hogarth Press. (Original work published 1933)

Friday, N. (1985). *Jealousy.* London: William Collins.

Frieze, I. H., Parsons, J. E., Johnson, P. B., Ruble, D. N., & Zellman, G. L. (1978). *Women and sex roles.* New York: Norton.

Fromkin, R. M. (1957). Authoritarian sexual jealousy and American ideology. *Journal of Family Welfare, 4*, 1–7.

Garfinkel, H., & Sacks, H. (1970). On formal structures of practical actions. In J. M. McKinney & E. A. Tiryakian (Eds.), *Theoretical sociology: Perspectives and development.* New York: Appleton-Century-Crofts.

Gayford, J. J. (1975). Wife battering: A preliminary survey of 100 cases. *British Medical Journal, i*, 194–197.

Gayford, J. J. (1979). Battered wives. *British Journal of Hospital Medicine, 22*, 496–503.

Gelles, R. J. (Ed.). (1979). *Family violence.* Beverly Hills, CA: Sage.

Gergen, K. J., & Davis, K. E. (1985). *The social construction of the person.* New York: Springer.

Gergen, K. J., Greenberg, M. S., & Willis, R. H. (Eds.). (1980). *Social exchange.* New York: Plenum.

Gesell, A. (1906). Jealousy. *American Journal of Psychology, 17,* 437–496.

Gibbard, G. S., Hartman, J. J., & Mann, R. D. (1978). *Analysis of groups.* San Francisco: Jossey-Bass.

Gibbens, T. C. N. (1958). Sane and insane homicide. *Journal of Criminal Law, Criminology and Police Science, 49,* 110–115.

Gillespie, D. L. (1971). Who has the power? The marital struggle. *Journal of Marriage and Family Living, 33,* 445–458.

Gilmartin, B. G. (1977). Jealousy among the swingers. In G. Clanton & L. G. Smith (Eds.), *Jealousy* (pp. 152–158). Englewood Cliffs, NJ: Prentice-Hall.

Glazer, D. (1975). *Crime and delinquency issues: A monograph series. Strategic criminal justice planning* (DHEW Publication No. ADM 76-195). Washinton, DC: U.S. Government Printing Office.

Glatt, M. M. (1961). Drinking habits of English (middle class) alcoholics. *Acta Psychiatrica Scandinavica, 37,* 88–113.

Goodwin, G. (1942). *The social organization of the Western Apache.* Chicago: University of Chicago Press.

Gottschalk, H. (1936). *Skinsygens problemer* [Problems of jealousy]. Copenhagen: Fremad.

Gough, K. (1961). Nayar: Central Kerala. In D. M. Schneider & K. Gough (Eds.), *Matrilineal kinship* (pp. 298–384). Berkeley: University of California Press.

Gould, S. J. (1978). Biological potential vs. biological determinism. In A. L. Caplan (Ed.), *The sociobiology debate* (pp. 343–351). New York: Harper & Row.

Gould, S. J. (1980). Sociobiology and natural selection. In G. W. Barlow & J. Silverberg (Eds.), *Sociobiology: Beyond nature/nurture?* (pp. 257–269). Boulder, CO: Westview Press.

Gould, S. J. (1981). *The mismeasure of man.* New York: Norton.

Gouldsbury, C., & Sheane, H. (1911). *The Great Plateau of Northern Rhodesia.* London: Edward Arnold.

Graziano, W. G., & Musser, L. M. (1982). The joining and the parting of the ways. In S. Duck (Ed.), *Personal relationships: Vol. 4: Dissolving relationships* (pp. 75–106). New York: Academic Press.

Green, A. H. (1984). Child abuse by siblings. *Child Abuse and Neglect, 8,* 311–317.

Greenberg, J., & Folger, R. (1988). *Controversial issues in social research methods.* New York: Springer-Verlag.

Greenberg, J., & Pyszczynski, T. (1985). Proneness to romantic jealousy as a determinant of response to jealousy in others. *Journal of Personality, 53,* 468–479.

Greenwald, A. G., & Breckler, S. J. (1985). To whom is the self presented? In B. R. Schlenker (Ed.), *The self and social life* (pp. 126–145). New York: McGraw-Hill.

Griffin, E. W., & De La Torre, C. (1983). Sibling jealousy: The family with a new baby. *American Family Practice, 28,* 143–146.

Grold, L. J. (1972). Patterns of jealousy. *Medical Aspects of Human Sexuality, 6,* 118–126.

Gross, A. E. (1978). The male role and heterosexual behavior. *Journal of Social Issues, 34,* 362–367.

Guthrie, G. M., & Tanco, P. P. (1980). Alienation. In H. C. Triandis & J. G. Draguns (Eds.), *Handbook of cross-cultural psychology: Vol. 6. Psychopathology* (pp. 9–60). Boston: Allyn & Bacon.

Guttmacher, M. S. (1955). Criminal responsibility in certain homicide cases involving family members. In P. H. Hoch & J. Zubin (Eds.), *Psychiatry and the law.* New York: Grune & Stratton.

Haan, N. (1977). *Coping and defending: Processes of self-environment organization.* New York: Academic Press.

Hafner, R. J. (1979). Agoraphobic women married to abnormally jealous men. *British Journal of Medical Psychology, 52,* 99–104.

Hafner, H., & Boker, W. (1982). *Crimes of violence by mentally abnormal offenders* (H. Marshall, Trans.). Cambridge, England: Cambridge University Press.

Hahn, B. (1933). Eifersucht als neurose. *Fortschritte der Medizin, 51,* 336–344.

Hansen, G. L. (1982). Reactions to hypothetical jealousy producing events. *Family Relations, 31,* 513–518.

Hansen, G. L. (1983). Marital satisfaction and jealousy among men. *Psychological Reports, 52,* 363–366.

Harris, M. (1974). *Cars, pigs, wars and witches.* New York: Random House.

Harrison, R. (1977). Defenses and the need to know. In R. T. Golembiewski & A. Blumberg (Eds.), *Sensitivity training and the laboratory approach* (pp. 78–83). Itasca, IL: F. E. Peacock.

Hartmann, H. (1958). *Ego psychology and the problem of adaptation.* New York: International Universities Press.

Hartnett, J., Mahoney, J., & Bernstein, A. (1977). The errant spouse: A study in person perception. *Perceptual and Motor Skills, 45,* 747–750.

Hatfield, E., Traupmann, J., Sprecher, S., Utne, M., & Hay, J. (1985). Equity and intimate relations: Recent research. In W. Ickes (Ed.), *Compatible and incompatible relationships* (pp. 91–118). New York: Springer.

Hawkins, R. O. (1976). Jealousy: A solvable problem. *Journal of Sex Education and Therapy, 1,* 39–42.

Hazan, C., & Shaver, P. (1987). Romantic love conceptualized as an attachment process. *Journal of Personality and Social Psychology, 52,* 511–524.

Hendrick, C., & Hendrick, S. (1983). *Liking, loving, and relating.* Monterey, CA: Brooks/Cole.

Hibbard, R. W. (1975). A rational approach to treating jealousy. *Rational Living, 10,* 25–27.

Hilberman, E. (1980). The wife beater's wife reconsidered. *American Journal of Psychiatry, 137,* 1336–1346.

Hilberman, E., & Manson, M. (1977). Sixty battered women. *Victimology, 2,* 460–471.

Hill, C. T., Rubin, Z., & Peplau, L. A. (1976). Breakups before marriage: The end of 103 affairs. *Journal of Social Issues, 32,* 147–168.

Hindy, C. G., & Schwarz, J. C. (1986). *Lovesickness in dating relationships: An attachment perspective.* Unpublished manuscript, University of North Florida.

Hindy, C. G., Schwarz, J. C., & Brodsky, A. (1989). *If this is love, why do I feel so insecure?* New York: Atlantic Monthly Press.

Hoaken, P. C. A. (1976). Jealousy as a symptom of psychiatric disorder. *Australian and New Zealand Journal of Psychiatry, 10,* 47–51.

Hoffman, L. (1981). *Foundations of family therapy.* New York: Basic.

Holdstock, T. L., & Rogers, C. R. (1983). Person-centered theory. In R. J. Corsini & A. J. Marsella (Eds.), *Personality theories, research and assessment* (pp. 189–228). Itasca, IL: F. E. Peacock.

Hole, R. W., Rush, A. J., & Beck, A. T. (1979). A cognitive investigation of schizophrenic delusions. *Psychiatry, 42,* 312–319.

Holroyd, B. A. (1985). *Coping with romantic jealousy: Predictors and consequences of coping behavior.* Unpublished master's thesis, University of Auckland, Auckland, New Zealand.

Hope Moncrieff, A. E. (1912). *Classic myth and legend.* London: Gresham.

Horney, K. (1937). *The neurotic personality of our time.* New York: Norton.

Howard, J. A., Blumstein, P., & Schwartz, P. (1986). Sex, power and influence tactics in intimate relationships. *Journal of Personality and Social Psychology, 51,* 102–109.

Hrdy, S. B., & Williams, G. (1983). Behavioral biology and the double standard. In S. K. Wasser (Ed.), *The social behavior of female vertebrates* (pp. 3–18). New York: Academic Press.

Hupka, R. B. (1981). Cultural determinants of jealousy. *Alternative Lifestyles, 4,* 310–356.

Hupka, R. B. (1984). Jealousy: Compound emotion or label for a particular situation? *Motivation and Emotion, 8,* 141–155.

Hupka, R. B. (1987). *The schema-driven attribution of jealousy.* Paper presented at the annual meeting of the Western Psychological Association, Anaheim, California.

Hupka, R. B., & Bachelor, B. (1979). *Validation of a scale to measure romantic jealousy.* Paper presented at the annual meeting of the Western Psychological Association, San Diego, California.

Hupka, R. B., Buunk, B., Falus, G., Fulgosi, A., Ortega, E., Swain, R., & Tarabrina, N. V. (1985). Romantic jealousy and romantic envy: A seven nation study. *Journal of Cross-Cultural Psychology, 16,* 423–446.

Hupka, R. B., & Eshett, C. (1984). *Cognitive organization of emotion: Differences between labels and descriptors of emotion in jealousy situations.* Paper presented at the annual meeting of the Western Psychological Association, Los Angeles.

Hupka, R. B., & Eshett, C. (1988). Cognitive organization of emotion: Differences between labels and descriptions of emotion in jealousy situations. *Perceptual and Motor Skills, 66,* 935–949.

Hupka, R. B., Jung, R., & Porteous, R. L. (1981). *Strategies for impression management in romantic jealousy situations.* Paper presented at the annual meeting of the American Psychological Association, Los Angeles.

Hupka, R. B., Jung, J., & Silverthorn, K. (1987). Perceived acceptability of apologies, excuses and justifications in jealousy predicaments. *Journal of Social Behaviour and Personality, 2,* 303–313.

Hupka, R. B., & Rusch, P. A. (1977). *The Interpersonal Relationship Scale.* Paper presented at the annual meeting of the Western Psychological Association, Seattle, Washington.

Hupka, R. B., & Ryan, J. M. (1981). *The cultural contribution to emotions: Cross-cultural aggression in sexual jealousy situations.* Paper presented at the annual meeting of the Western Psychological Association, Los Angeles.

Hurwitz, S., & Christiansen, K. O. (1983). *Criminology.* London: George Allen & Unwin.

Huston, T. L. (1983). Power. In H. H. Kelley, E. Berscheid, A. Christensen, J. H. Harvey, T. L. Huston, G. Levinger, E. McClintock, L. A. Peplau, & D. R. Peterson, *Close relationships* (pp. 169–219). San Francisco: W. H. Freeman.

Huston, T. L., & Ashmore, R. D. (1986). Women and men in personal relationships. In R. D. Ashmore & F. K. Del Boca (Eds.), *The social psychology of female–male relations* (pp. 167–210). New York: Academic Press.

Huston, T. L., Surra, C. A., Fitzgerald, N. M., & Cate, R. M. (1981). From courtship to marriage: Mate selection as an interpersonal process. In S. Duck & R. Gilmour (Eds.), *Personal relationships: Vol. 2. Developing personal relationships* (pp. 53–88). New York: Academic Press.

Ickes, W. (Ed.). (1985a). *Compatible and incompatible relationships.* New York: Springer.

Ickes, W. (1985b). Sex-role influences on compatibility in relationships. In W. Ickes (Ed.), *Compatible and incompatible relationships* (pp. 187–208). New York: Springer.

Ilfeld, F. W. (1977). Current social stressors and symptoms of depression. *American Journal of Psychiatry, 134,* 161–166.

Im, W., Wilner, R. S., & Breit, M. (1983). Jealousy: Interventions in couples therapy. *Family Process, 22,* 211–219.

Irons, W. (1979). Investment and primary social dyads. In N. A. Chagnon & W. Irons (Eds.), *Evolutionary biology and human social behavior* (pp. 181–213). North Scituate, MA: Duxbury Press.

Izard, C. E. (1977). *Human emotions.* New York: Plenum.

Jahoda, G. (1980). Theoretical and systematic approaches in cross-cultural psychology. In H. C. Triandis & W. W. Lambert (Eds.), *Handbook of cross-cultural psychology: Vol. 1. Perspectives* (pp. 69–141). Boston: Allyn & Bacon.

James, W. (1890). *Principles of psychology.* New York: Henry Holt.

Jaremko, M. E., & Lindsey, R. (1979). Stress coping abilities of individuals high and low in jealousy. *Psychological Reports, 44,* 547–553.

Jaspers, K. (1910). Eifersuchswahn: Zeitschrift fur die gesamte. *Neurologie und Psychiatrie, 1,* 567–637.

Jaspers, K. (1963). *General psychopathology* (7th ed., J. Hoenig & M. W. Hamilton, Eds. and Trans.). Manchester, England: Manchester University Press. (Original work published 1946)

Jenks, R. J. (1985). Swinging: A test of two theories and a proposed new model. *Archives of Sexual Behavior, 14,* 517–527.

Johnson, J. (1969). Organic psychosyndromes due to boxing. *British Journal of Psychiatry, 115,* 45–53.

Johnson, P. (1976). Women and power: Toward a theory of effectiveness. *Journal of Social Issues, 32,* 147–168.

Jones, E. (1937). Jealousy. In E. Jones, *Papers on psychoanalysis* (pp. 469–485). London: Balliere, Tindall.

Jones, E. E., & Davis, K. E. (1965). From acts to dispositions: The attribution process in person perception. In L. Berkowitz (Ed.), *Advances in experimental social psychology* (Vol. 2, pp. 219–267). New York: Academic Press.

Jones, S. C. (1973). Self- and interpersonal evaluations: Esteem theories versus consistency theories. *Psychological Bulletin, 79,* 185–199.

Jung, C. G. (1961). *Memories, dreams, and reflections.* New York: Random House.

Kahn, R. L., Wolfe, D. M., Quinn, R. P., Snoek, J. D., & Rosenthal, R. A. (1964). *Organizational stress: Studies in role conflict and ambiguity.* New York: Wiley.

Kanin, E. J., Davidson, K. D., & Scheck, S. R. (1970). A research note on male–female differentials in the experience of heterosexual love. *The Journal of Sex Research, 6,* 64–72.

Kanter, R. M. (1972). *Commitment and community: Communes and utopias in sociological perspective.* Cambridge, MA: Harvard University Press.

Kaplan, A. (1964). *The conduct of inquiry.* Scranton, PA: Chandler.

Kaplan, H. I., & Sadock, B. J. (1985). *Modern synopsis of comprehensive textbook of psychiatry* (4th ed.). Baltimore: Williams & Wilkins.

Karsten, R. (1925). The Toba Indians of the Bolivian Gran Chaco. *Acta Academiae Aboensis, 4,* 1–126.

Katz, D., & Kahn, R. L. (1978). *The social psychology of organizations.* New York: Wiley.

Kelley, H. H. (1979). *Personal relationships: Their structure and processes.* Hillsdale, NJ: Erlbaum.

Kelley, H. H. (1983). Love and commitment. In H. H. Kelley, E. Berscheid, A. Christensen, J. H. Harvey, T. L. Huston, G. Levinger, E. McClintock, L. A. Peplau, & D. R. Peterson, *Close relationships* (pp. 265–314). San Francisco: W. H. Freeman.

Kelley, H. H. (1984). Affect in interpersonal relations. In P. Shaver (Ed.), *Review of personality and social psychology* (Vol. 5, pp. 89–115). Beverly Hills, CA: Sage.

Kelley, H. H., Berscheid, E., Christensen, A., Harvey, J. H., Huston, T. L., Levinger, G., McClintock, E., Peplau, L. A., & Peterson, D. R. (1983). *Close relationships.* San Francisco: W. H. Freeman.

Kelley, H. H., & Thibaut, J. W. (1978). *Interpersonal relations: A theory of interdependence.* New York: Wiley.

Kemper, T. D. (1978). *A social interactional theory of emotions.* New York: Wiley.

Kendler, K. S., Glazer, W. M., & Morgenstern, H. (1983). Dimensions of delusional experience. *American Journal of Psychiatry, 140,* 466–469.

Kendrick, C., & Dunn, J. (1983). Quarrels between young siblings and their mother's reactions. *Developmental Psychology, 19,* 62–70.

Kernberg, O. (1975). *Borderline conditions of pathological narcissism.* New York: Jason Aronson.

Kinsey, A. C., Pomeroy, W. B., Martin, C. E., & Gebhard, P. H. (1953). *Sexual behavior in the human female.* Philadelphia: W. B. Saunders.

Klein, M., & Riviere, J. (1964). *Love, hate, and reparation.* New York: Norton.

Knox, D. H., & Sporakowski, M. J. (1968). Attitude of college students toward love. *Journal of Marriage and the Family, 30,* 638–642.

Knudson, R. M. (1985). Marital incompatibility and mutual identity confirmation. In W. Ickes (Ed.), *Compatible and incompatible relationships* (pp. 233–252). New York: Springer.

Koch, H. L. (1960). The relation of certain formal attributes of siblings to attitudes held toward each other and toward their parents. *Monographs of the Society for Research in Child Development, 25* (Whole No. 4).

Kohut, H. (1968). The psychoanalytic treatment of narcissistic personality disorders. *Psychoanalytic Study of the Child, 23,* 86–113.

Kolle, K. (1932). Paraphrenie and paranoia. *Fortschritte der Neurologie und Psychiatrie, 3,* 319–334.

Kosins, D. J. (1983). Developmental correlates of sexual jealousy. *Dissertation Abstracts International, 44,* 1242B. (Order No. DA8319169)

Kraepelin, E. (1921). *Manic depressive insanity and paranoia* (R. M. Barclay & G. M. Robertson, Trans.). Edinburgh: Livingston. (Original work published 1915)

Kraepelin, R. (1974). *Psychiatrie: Ein lerhbuch fur stadirende und aerzt.* New York: Arno. (Original work published 1896)

Krafft-Ebing, R. von. (1905). *Textbook of insanity* (C. G. Chaddock, Trans.). Philadelphia: S. A. Davis.

Krafft-Ebing, R. von. (1937). *Psychopathia sexualis* (F. J. Rebman, Trans). New York: Physicians and Surgeons.

Kraupl Taylor, F. (1979). *Psychopathology: Its causes and symptoms.* Sunbury on Thames: Quartermaine House.

Kretschmer, E. (1952). *A textbook of medical psychology* (10th German ed., E. B. Strauss, Trans.). London: Hogarth Press. (Original work published 1918)

Kretschmer, W. (1974). The sensitive delusions of reference. In S. R. Hirsch & M. Shepherd (Eds.), *Themes and variations in European psychiatry* (pp. 153–196). Bristol, England: John Wright & Sons.

Kroeber, A. L., & Kluckhohn, C. (1952). Culture: A critical review of concepts. *Papers of the Peabody Museum of American Archaeology and Ethnology* (Harvard University), *47*(1).

Krupinski, J., Marshall, E., & Yule, V. (1970). Patterns of marital problems in marriage guidance clients. *Journal of Marriage and the Family, 32,* 138–143.

Kuhn, A. (1974). *The logic of social systems.* San Francisco: Jossey-Bass.

Kuiper, N. A., & Derry, P. A. (1981). The self as a cognitive prototype: An application to person perception and depression. In N. Cantor & J. F. Kihlstrom (Eds.), *Personality, cognition, and social interaction* (pp. 215–232). Hillsdale, NJ: Erlbaum.

Kurland, J. A. (1979). Paternity, mother's brothers, and human sociality. In N. A. Chagnon & W. Irons (Eds.), *Evolutionary biology and human social behavior* (pp. 145–180). North Scituate, MA: Duxbury Press.

Lacan, J. (1977). *Écrits: A selection* (A. Sheridan, Trans.). London: Tavistock.

La Fave, W. R. (1978). *Principles of criminal law.* New York: West.

La Fave, W. R., & Scott, A. W. (1972). *Handbook on criminal law.* New York: West.

Lagache, D. (1947). *La jalousie amoureuse.* Paris: Presses Universitaires de France.

Lagache, D. (1949). Homosexuality and jealousy. *International Journal of Psycho-Analysis, 30,* 24–32.

Lamb, M. E. (1978). The development of sibling relationships in infancy: A short-term longitudinal study. *Child Development, 49,* 1189–1196.

Lamb, M. E., & Sutton-Smith, B. (Eds.). (1982). *Sibling relationships: Their nature and significance across the lifespan.* Hillsdale, NJ: Erlbaum.

Lancaster, J. B. (1985). Evolutionary perspectives on sex differences in the higher primates. In A. S. Rossi (Ed.), *Gender and the life course* (pp. 3–27). Chicago: Aldine.

Langfeldt, G. (1961). The erotic jealousy syndrome: A clinical study. *Acta Psychiatrica Scandinavica, 36* (Suppl. 151), 7–68.

Larson, P. C. (1982). Gay male relationships. In W. Paul, J. D. Weinrich, J. C. Gonziorek, & M. E. Hotveldt (Eds.), *Homosexuality as a social issue.* Beverly Hills, CA: Sage Publications.

Lazarus, A. A. (1977). Has behavior therapy outlived its usefulness? *American Psychologist, 32,* 550–554.

Lazarus, R. S., & Folkman, S. (1984). *Stress, appraisal and coping.* New York: Springer.

Lazarus, R. S., & Launier, R. (1978). Stress-related transactions between person and environment. In L. A. Pervin & M. Lewis (Eds.), *Perspectives in interactional psychology.* New York: Plenum.

Leacock, E. (1980). Social behavior, biology, and the double standard. In G. W. Barlow & J. Silverberg (Eds.), *Sociobiology: Beyond nature/nurture?* (pp. 465–488). Boulder, CO: Westview Press.

Leary, M. R., Barnes, B. D., & Griebel, C. (1986). Cognitive, affective, and attributional effects of potential threats to self-esteem. *Journal of Social and Clinical Psychology, 4,* 461–474.

Leary, T. (1957). *Interpersonal diagnosis of personality.* New York: Ronald Press.

Lee, J. A. (1977). A typology of styles of loving. *Personality and Social Psychology Bulletin, 3,* 173–182.

Lester, D., Deluca, G., Hellinghausen, W., & Scribner, D. (1985). Jealousy and irrationality in love. *Psychological Reports, 56,* 210.

Levenson, H., & Harris, C. N. (1980). Love and the search for identity. In K. S. Pope (Ed.), *On love and loving* (pp. 266–281). San Francisco: Jossey-Bass.

Leventhal, H. (1980). Toward a comprehensive theory of emotion. In L. Berkowitz (Ed.), *Advances in experimental social psychology* (Vol. 13, pp. 139–207). New York: Academic Press.

Levinger, G. (1965). Marital cohesiveness and dissolution: An integrative review. *Journal of Marriage and the Family, 27,* 19–28.

Levinger, G. (1966). Source of marital dissatisfaction among applicants for divorce. *American Journal of Orthopsychiatry, 36,* 803–807.

Levinger, G. (1979). A social exchange view on the dissolution of pair relationships. In R. L. Burgess & T. L. Huston (Eds.), *Social exchange in developing relationships* (pp. 169–196). New York: Academic Press.

Levinger, G., & Huesmann, L. R. (1980). An "incremental exchange" perspective on the pair relationship: Interpersonal reward and level of involvement. In K. J. Gergen, M. S. Greenberg, & R. H. Willis (Eds.), *Social exchange* (pp. 165–196). New York: Plenum.

Levy, D. M. (1934). Rivalry between children of the same family. *Child Study, 11,* 233–261.

Levy, R. I. (1984). Emotion, knowing, and culture. In R. A. Shweder & R. A. LeVine (Eds.), *Culture theory* (pp. 214–237). Cambridge, England: Cambridge University Press.

Lewicki, P. (in press). Self-schema and social information processing. *Journal of Personality and Social Psychology.*

Lewin, K. A. (1936). *Principles of topological psychology* (F. Heider & G. Heider, Trans.). New York: McGraw-Hill.

Lewin, K. A. (1948). The background of conflict in marriage. In K. A. Lewin, *Resolving social conflicts: Selected papers on group dynamics* (pp. 84–102). New York: Harper & Row.

Lewis, A. (1934). Melancholia, a clinical survey of depressive states. *Journal of Mental Science, 80,* 277–378.

Lewis, A. (1970). Paranoia and paranoid: A historical perspective. *Psychological Medicine, 1,* 2–12.

Lewis, R., & Spanier, G. (1979). Theorizing about the quality and stability of marriage. In W. R. Burr, R. Hill, F. I. Nye, & I. L. Reiss (Eds.), *Contemporary theories about the family* (Vol. 1). New York: Free Press.

Lewontin, R. C., Rose, S., & Kamin, L. J. (1984). *Not in our genes.* New York: Pantheon.

Livingstone, K. R. (1980). Love as a process of reducing uncertainty—cognitive theory. In K. S. Pope (Ed.), *On love and loving* (pp. 133–151). San Francisco: Jossey-Bass.

Lobsenz, N. M. (1977). Taming the green eyed monster. In G. Clanton and L. G. Smith (Eds.), *Jealousy* (pp. 26–35). Englewood Cliffs, NJ: Prentice-Hall.

Loevinger, J. (1976). *Ego development.* San Francisco: Jossey-Bass.

Luborsky, L. (1977). Measuring a pervasive psychic structure in psychotherapy. The core conflictual relationships theme. In N. Freedman & S. Grand (Eds.), *Communicative structures and psychic structures*. New York: Plenum.

Luft, J. (1969). *Of human interaction*. Palo Alto, CA: National Books Press.

Lumsden, C. J., & Wilson, E. O. (1981). *Genes, mind, and culture*. Cambridge, MA: Harvard University Press.

Lutz, C. (1983). Parental goals, enthnopsychology, and the development of emotional meaning. *Ethos, 11*, 246–262.

Lutz, C., & White, G. M. (1986). The anthropology of emotions. *Annual Review of Anthropology, 15*, 405–436.

Maccoby, E. E. (1980). *Social development*. New York: Harcourt Brace Jovanovich.

Maccoby, E. E., & Jacklin, C. N. (1974). *The psychology of sex differences*. Stanford, CA: Stanford University Press.

Macklin, E. D. (1972). Heterosexual cohabitation among unmarried college students. *The Family Coordinator, 21*, 463–472.

Mahoney, J., & Heretick, D. M. (1979). Factor-specific dimensions in person perception for same- and opposite-sex dyads. *Journal of Social Psychology, 107*, 219–225.

Maire, L. P. (1953). African marriage and social change. In A. Phillips (Ed.), *Survey of African marriage and family life*. New York: Oxford University Press.

Mairet, A. (1908). *La jalousie: Étude psycho-physiologique, clinique et médico-légale*. Paris: Montpellier.

Malinowski, B. (1929). *The sexual life of savages*. New York: Harcourt, Brace.

Mandler, G. (1984). *Mind and body*. New York: Norton.

Margolin, G. (1979). Conjoint marital therapy to enhance anger management and reduce spouse abuse. *American Journal of Family Therapy, 7*, 13–23.

Marks, I. M. (1976). The current status of behavioral psychotherapy, theory and practice. *American Journal of Psychiatry, 133*, 253–261.

Marks, I. M., Hodgson, R., & Rachman, S. (1975). Treatment of chronic obsessive compulsive neurosis by *in vivo* exposure. *British Journal of Psychiatry, 127*, 349–364.

Markus, H. (1977). Self-schemata and processing information about the self. *Journal of Personality and Social Psychology, 35*, 63–78.

Markus, H., Smith, J., & Moreland, R. L. (1985). Role of the self-concept in the perception of others. *Journal of Personality and Social Psychology, 49*, 1494–1512.

Mathes, E. W. (1984). Convergence among measures of attraction. *Motivation and Emotion, 8*, 77–84.

Mathes, E. W. (1986). Jealousy and romantic love: A longitudinal study. *Psychological Reports, 58*, 885–886.

Mathes, E. W., Adams, H. E., & Davies, R. M. (1985). Jealousy: Loss of relationship rewards, loss of self-esteem, depression, anxiety, and anger. *Journal of Personality and Social Psychology, 48*, 1552–1561.

Mathes, E. W., Phillips, J. T., Skowran, J., & Dick, W. E. (1982). Behavioral correlates of the Interpersonal Jealousy Scale. *Educational and Psychological Measurement, 42*, 1227–1230.

Mathes, E. W., Roter, P. M., & Joerger, S. M. (1982). A convergent validity study of six jealousy scales. *Psychological Reports, 50*, 1143–1147.

Mathes, E. W., & Severa, N. (1981). Jealousy, romantic love, and liking: Theoretical considerations and preliminary scale development. *Psychological Reports, 49*, 23–31.

Matthews, W. (1877). *Ethnography and philology of the Hidatsa Indians.* Washington, DC: U.S. Goverment Printing Office.

Maudsley, H. (1867). *The physiology and pathology of mind.* London: Macmillan.

Mazur, R. (1977). Beyond jealousy and possessiveness. In G. Clanton & L. G. Smith (Eds.), *Jealousy* (pp. 181–187). Englewood Cliffs, NJ: Prentice-Hall.

McCall, G. J. (1974). A symbolic interactionist approach to attraction. In T. L. Huston (Ed.), *Foundations of interpersonal attraction* (pp. 217–235). New York: Academic Press.

McClintock, C. G. (1972). Game behavior and social motivation in interpersonal settings. In C. G. McClintock (Ed.), *Experimental social psychology* (pp. 126–168). New York: Holt, Rinehart, & Winston.

McFarland, M. B. (1937–1938). Relationships between young sisters as revealed in their overt responses. *Journal of Experimental Education, 6*, 173–179.

McGuire, W. J. (1984). Search for the self: Going beyond self-esteem and the reactive self. In R. A. Zucker, J. Aronoff, & A. I. Rabin (Eds.), *Personality and the prediction of behavior* (pp. 73–120). New York: Academic Press.

McGuire, W. J., & McGuire, C. V. (1982). Significant others on self-space: Sex differences and developmental trends in the social self. In J. Suls (Ed.), *Psychological perspectives on the self* (Vol. 1, pp. 211–237). Hillsdale, NJ: Erlbaum.

McKenna, P. J. (1984). Disorders with overvalued ideas. *British Journal of Psychiatry, 145*, 579–585.

Mead, M. (1931). Jealousy: Primitive and civilized. In S. D. Schmalhauser & V. F. Calverton (Eds.), *Woman's coming of age* (pp. 35–48). New York: Horace Liveright.

Miller, J. G. (1978). *Living systems.* New York: McGraw-Hill.

Millett, K. (1970). *Sexual politics.* New York: Doubleday.

Millon, T. (1981). *Disorders of personality.* New York: Wiley.

Mirsky, J. (1937a). The Dakota. In M. Mead (Ed.), *Cooperation and competition among primitive peoples.* New York: McGraw-Hill.

Mirsky, J. (1937b). The Eskimo of Greenland. In M. Mead (Ed.), *Cooperation and competition among primitive peoples.* New York: McGraw-Hill.

Mishkin, B. (1937). The Maori of New Zealand. In M. Mead (Ed.), *Cooperation and competition among primitive peoples.* New York: McGraw-Hill.

Monahan, J. (1981). *The clinical prediction of violent behavior.* Rockville, MD: U.S. Department of Health and Human Services.

Mooney, H. (1965). Pathologic jealousy and psychochemotherapy. *British Journal of Psychiatry, 111*, 1023–1042.

Moore, T. (1969). Stress in normal childhood. *Human Relations, 22*, 235–250.

Moos, R. H., & Billings, A. G. (1982). Conceptualizing and measuring coping resources and processes. In L. Goldberger & S. Breznitz (Eds.), *Handbook of stress* (pp. 212–230). New York: Free Press.

Morgan, D. H. (1975). The psychotherapy of jealousy. *Psychotherapy and Psychosomatics, 25,* 43–47.

Morris, D. (1967). *The naked ape: A zoologists' study of the human animal.* New York: McGraw-Hill.

Morris, N., & Howard, C. (1964). *Studies in criminal law.* London: Oxford University Press.

Morris, V. (1982). Helping lesbian couples cope with jealousy. *Women-in-Therapy, 1,* 27–34.

Mowat, R. R. (1966). *Morbid jealousy and murder.* London: Tavistock.

Mullen, P. E. (1984a). Introduction to descriptive psychopathology. In P. McGuffin, M. F. Shanks, & R. J. Hodgson (Eds.), *The scientific principles of psychopathology* (pp. 608–621). London: Academic Press.

Mullen, P. E. (1984b). Mental disorder and dangerousness. *Australian and New Zealand Journal of Psychiatry,* 188–197.

Mullen, P. E. (1985). The mental state and states of mind. In P. Hill, R. Murray, & A. Thorley (Eds.), *Essentials of postgraduate psychiatry* (2nd ed., pp. 3–35). London: Grune & Stratton.

Mullen, P. E. (1988b). Violence and mental disorder. *British Journal of Hospital Medicine, 40,* 460–463.

Mullen, P. E. (in press-a). The phenomenology of jealousy. *Australian and New Zealand Journal of Psychiatry.*

Mullen, P. E. (in press-b). Disorders of passion. In J. Gunn & P. Taylor (Eds.), *Forensic psychiatry: Clinical, legal and ethical issues.* London: Heinemann.

Mullen, P. E., & Maack, L. H. (1985). Jealousy, pathological jealousy, and aggression. In D. P. Farrington & J. Gunn (Eds.), *Aggression and dangerousness* (pp. 103–126). New York: Wiley.

Mullen, P. E., Romans-Clarkson, S. E., Walton, V., & Herbison, G. P. (1988). Impact of sexual and physical abuse on women's mental health. *Lancet, i,* 841–846.

Mulvihill, D. J., & Tumin, M. M. (1969). *Crimes of violence* (Vol. 12). Washington, DC: U.S. Government Printing Office.

Murray, H. A. (1938). *Explorations in personality.* New York: Oxford University Press.

Murstein, B. I. (1974). *Love, sex, and marriage through the ages.* New York: Springer.

Nadelman, L., & Begun, A. (1982). The effect of the newborn on the older sibling: Mothers' questionnaires. In M. Lamb & B. Sutton-Smith (Eds.), *Sibling relationships: Their nature and significance across the lifespan* (pp. 13–38). Hillsdale, NJ: Erlbaum.

Neu, J. (1980). Jealous thoughts. In A. O. Rorty (Ed.), *Explaining emotions* (pp. 425–463). Berkeley: University of California Press.

Neubeck, G. (Ed.). (1969a). *Extramarital relations.* Englewood Cliffs, NJ: Prentice-Hall.

Neubeck, G. (1969b). Other societies: An anthropological review of extramarital relations. In G. Neubeck (Ed.), *Extramarital relations* (pp. 27–69). Englewood Cliffs, NJ: Prentice-Hall.

Nietzsche, F. (1966). The wanderer and his shadow. In W. Kaufman (Trans.), *Basic writings of Nietzsche*. New York: Modern Library. (Original work published 1880)

Obendorf, C. P. (1929). Psychoanalysis of siblings. *American Journal of Psychiatry, 8,* 1007.

Odegaard, J. (1968). Interaksjonen mellom partnerne ved de patologiske sjalusireaksjoner. *Nordisk Psykiatrisk Tidsskrift, 22,* 314–319.

Oppenheim, H. (1912). Zur frage der genese des eifersuchtswahnes *Zentralblatt fur Psychoanalyse und Psychotherapie und Psychotherapie, 2,* 67–77.

Ortega y Gasset, J. (1957). *On love* (T. Talbot, Trans.). New York: Meridian.

Orvis, B. R., Kelley, H. H., & Butler, D. (1976). Attributional conflict in young couples. In J. H. Harvey, W. J. Ickes, & R. F. Kidd (Eds.), *New directions in attribution research* (Vol. 1, pp. 353–386). Hillsdale, NJ: Erlbaum.

Otto, H. A. (Ed.). (1972). *Love today: A new exploration*. New York: Delta.

Ovesey, L. (1955). Pseudo homosexuality, the paranoid mechanism and paranoia. *Psychiatry, 18,* 163–173.

Panskepp, J. (1982). Towards a general psychobiological theory of emotions. *Behavioural and Brain Sciences, 5,* 407–467.

Parsons, T. (1951). *The social system*. New York: Free Press.

Paykel, E. S. (1982). Social and psychological causes of affective disorders. In J. K. Wing & L. Wing (Eds.), *Handbook of psychiatry* (Vol. 3, pp. 141–146). Cambridge, England: Cambridge University Press.

Pearlin, L. I., & Schooler, C. (1978). The structure of coping. *Journal of Health and Social Behavior, 19,* 2–21.

Peplau, L. A. (1979). Power in dating relationships. In J. Freeman (Ed.), *Women: A feminist perspective* (pp. 107–121). Palo Alto, CA: Mayfield.

Peplau, L. A. (1983). Roles and gender. In H. H. Kelley, E. Berscheid, A. Christiansen, J. H. Harvey, T. L. Huston, G. Levinger, E. McClintock, L. A. Peplau, & D. R. Peterson, *Close relationships* (pp. 220–264). San Francisco: W. H. Freeman.

Peplau, L. A., Cochran, S. D., Rook, K., & Padesky, C. (1978). Loving women: Attachment and autonomy in lesbians' relationships. *Journal of Social Issues, 35,* 7–27.

Peplau, L. A., & Gordon, S. L. (1983). The intimate relationships of lesbians and gay men. In E. R. Allgeier & N. B. McCormick (Eds.), *Changing boundaries: Gender roles and sexual behavior*. Palo Alto, CA: Mayfield.

Peplau, L. A., & Gordon, S. (1985). Women and men in love: Sex differences in close heterosexual relationships. In V. E. O'Leary, R. K. Unger, & S. B. Wallston (Eds.), *Women, gender, and social psychology* (pp. 118–137). Hillsdale, NJ: Erlbaum.

Perkins, R. M. (1969). *Criminal law*. New York: Foundation Press.

Peterson, D. (1988). *Personality*. New York: Harcourt Brace Jovanovich.

Pfeiffer, S. M., & Wong, P. T. P. (1987). *Multidimensional jealousy and unrequited love*. Unpublished manuscript, Trent University, Peterborough, Ontario.

Pines, A., & Aronson, E. (1981). Polyfidelity: An alternative lifestyle without jealousy? *Alternative Lifestyles, 4*, 373–392.

Pines, A., & Aronson, E. (1983). Antecedents, correlates, and consequences of sexual jealousy. *Journal of Personality, 51*, 108–136.

Plutchik, R. (1980). *Emotion*. New York: Harper & Row.

Pope, K. S. (Ed.). (1980). *On love and loving*. San Francisco: Jossey-Bass.

Popper, K. R. (1965). *Conjectures and refutations*. New York: Harper & Row.

Post, F. (1982). Paranoid disorders. In J. K. Wing & L. Wing (Eds.), *Handbook of psychiatry* (Vol. 3, pp. 22–27). Cambridge, England: Cambridge University Press.

Powers, S. (1877). *Tribes of California*. Washington, DC: U.S. Government Printing Office.

Psarska, A. D. (1970). Jealousy factor in homicide in forensic material. *Polish Medical Journal, 9*, 1504–1510.

Purdy, F., & Nickle, N. (1981). Practice principles for working with groups of men who batter. *Social Work and Groups, 4*, 111–122.

Quine, W. V. O. (1960). *Word and object*. Cambridge, MA: MIT Press.

Ramey, J. W. (1974). Communes, group marriage, and the upper middle class. In J. R. Smith & L. G. Smith (Eds.), *Beyond monogamy* (pp. 214–229). Baltimore: Johns Hopkins University Press.

Read, S. J. (1987). Constructing causal scenarios: A knowledge structure approach to causal reasoning. *Journal of Personality and Social Psychology, 52*, 288–302.

Reik, T. (1941). *Masochism in modern man*. New York: Grove Press.

Reik, T. (1957). *Of love and lust*. New York: Grove Press.

Reik, T. (1958). *Myth and guilt*. London: Hutchinson.

Reis, H. T. (1985). The role of the self in the initiation and course of social interaction. In W. Ickes (Ed.), *Compatible and incompatible relationships* (pp. 209–232). New York: Springer.

Retterstol, N. (1967). Jealousy-paranoic psychosis: A personal follow-up study. *Acta Psychiatrica Scandinavica, 43*, 75–107.

Revitch, E. (1954). The problem of conjugal paranoia. *Diseases of the Nervous System, 15*, 271–277.

Reyburn, W. (1962). Kaka kinship, sex and adultery. *Practical Anthropology, 9*, 223–234.

Rivers, W. H. R. (1906). *The Melanesians of British New Guinea*. Cambridge, England: Cambridge University Press.

Riviere, J. (1932). Jealousy as a mechanism of defence. *International Journal of Psycho-Analysis, 13*, 414–424.

Rose, S. (Ed). (1982). *Against biological determinism*. New York: Schocken.

Rosen, R. C., & Schnapp, B. J. (1974). The use of a specific behavioral technique (thought stopping) in the context of conjoint couples therapy: A case report. *Behavior Therapy, 5*, 261–264.

Rosenbaum, A., & O'Leary, D. (1981). Marital violence—characteristics of abusive couples. *Journal of Consulting and Clinical Psychology, 49,* 63–71.

Rosenbaum, A., & O'Leary, D. (1986). The treatment of marital violence. In N. S. Jacobson & A. S. Gurman (Eds.), *Clinical handbook of marital therapy* (pp. 407–427). New York: Guilford Press.

Rosenberg, M. (1979). *Conceiving the self.* New York: Basic Books.

Rosmarin, D. M., Chambless, D. L., & LaPointe, K. (1979). *The Survey of Interpersonal Reactions: An inventory for the measurement of jealousy.* Unpublished manuscript, University of Georgia.

Rosmarin, D., & LaPointe, K. A. (1978). *Construction of an empirical scale to measure jealousy.* Paper presented at the annual meeting of the Western Psychological Association, San Francisco.

Ross, B. M. (1931). Some traits associated with sibling jealousy in problem children. *Smith College Studies in Social Work, 1,* 364–376.

Rossi, A. S. (1985). Gender and parenthood. In A. S. Rossi (Ed.), *Gender and the life course* (pp. 161–191). Chicago: Aldine.

Rothgeb, C. L., & Clemens, S. M. (1978). *Abstracts of the collected works of C. G. Jung* (DHEW Publication No. ADM 78-743). Washington, DC: U.S. Government Printing Office.

Rounsaville, B. J. (1978). Theories in marital violence: Evidence from a study of battered women. *Victimology, 3,* 11–21.

Roy, M. (1977). A current survey of 150 cases. In M. Roy (Ed.), *Battered women: A psychological study of domestic violence* (pp. 98–109). New York: Van Nostrand Reinhold.

Rubin, Z. (1970). Measurement of romantic love. *Journal of Personality and Social Psychology, 16,* 265–273.

Rudden, M., Gilmore, M., & Frances, A. (1982). Delusions: When to confront the facts of life. *American Journal of Psychiatry, 139,* 929–932.

Ruin, R. (1933). *La jalousie homicide.* Paris: Universite de Paris.

Rusbult, C. E. (1980). Commitment and satisfaction in romantic associations: A test of the investment model. *Journal of Experimental Social Psychology, 16,* 172–186.

Rusbult, C. E. (1983). A longitudinal test of the investment model: The development (and deterioration) of satisfaction and commitment in heterosexual involvements. *Journal of Personality and Social Psychology, 45,* 101–117.

Safilios-Rothschild, C. (1969). Attitudes of Greek spouses toward marital infidelity. In G. Neubeck (Ed.), *Extramarital relations* (pp. 77–93). Englewood Cliffs, NJ: Prentice-Hall.

Sahlins, M. D. (1976). *The use and abuse of biology.* Ann Arbor: University of Michigan Press.

Salovey, P., & Rodin, J. (1984). Some antecedents and consequences of social-comparison jealousy. *Journal of Personality and Social Psychology, 47,* 780–792.

Salovey, P., & Rodin, J. (1985, September). The heart of jealousy. *Psychology Today,* pp. 22–29.

Salovey, P., & Rodin, J. (1986). The differentiation of social-comparison jealousy and romantic jealousy. *Journal of Personality and Social Psychology, 50,* 1100–1112.

Salovey, P., & Rodin, J. (1988). Coping with envy and jealousy. *Journal of Social and Clinical Psychology, 7,* 15–33.

Savage, G. H. (1892). Jealousy as a symptom of insanity. In D. Hack Tuke (Ed.), *A dictionary of psychological medicine* (pp. 721–723). London: Churchill.

Scarr, S., & Grajek, S. (1982). Similarities and differences among siblings. In M. E. Lamb & B. Sutton-Smith (Eds.), *Sibling relationships: Their nature and significance across the lifespan.* Hillsdale, NJ: Erlbaum.

Schaefer, E. S. (1971). From circular to spherical conceptual models for parent behavior and child behavior. In J. P. Hill (Ed.), *Minnesota Symposium on child psychology* (Vol. 4). Minneapolis: University of Minnesota Press.

Schank, R. C., & Abelson, R. P. (1977). *Scripts, plans, goals and understanding.* Hillsdale, NJ: Erlbaum.

Schapera, I. (1941). *Married life in an African tribe.* New York: Sheridan House.

Scharfetter, C. (1980). *General psychopathology* (H. Marshall, Trans.) Cambridge, England: Cambridge University Press.

Scheier, M. F., & Carver, C. S. (1980). Individual differences in self-concept and self-process. In D. M. Wegner & R. R. Vallacher (Eds.), *The self in social psychology* (pp. 229–251). New York: Oxford University Press.

Schichor, D., & Kobris, L. (1978). Criminal behavior among the elderly. *Gerontologist, 18,* 213–218.

Schlenker, B. R. (1980). *Impression management.* Monterey, CA: Brooks/Cole.

Schmiedeberg, M. (1953). Some aspects of jealousy and of feeling hurt. *Psychoanalytic Review, 15,* 1–16.

Schmitt, B. H. (1988). Social comparison in romantic jealousy. *Personality and Social Psychology Bulletin, 14,* 374–387.

Schneider, K. (1959). *Clinical psychopathology* (M. Hamilton, Trans.) New York: Grune & Stratton.

Schutz, A. (1967). *The phenomenology of the social world* (G. Walsh & F. Lehnert, Trans.). Evanston, IL: Northwestern University Press. (Original work published 1932)

Schwartz, D. A. (1963). A review of the paranoid concept. *Archives of General Psychiatry, 8,* 349–361.

Scott, P. D. (1977). Assessing dangerousness in criminals. *British Journal of Psychiatry, 131,* 127–142.

Seeman, M. V. (1979). Pathological jealousy. *Psychiatry, 42,* 351–361.

Seidenberg, R. (1967). Fidelity and jealousy: Socio-cultural considerations. *Psychoanalytic Review, 54,* 27–52.

Selye, H. (1976). *The stress of life.* New York: McGraw-Hill.

Sewall, M. (1930). Some causes of jealousy in young children. *Smith College Studies in Social Work, 1,* 6–22.

Shapiro, M. B., & Ravenette, A. T. (1959). A preliminary experiment on paranoid delusions. *Journal of Mental Science, 105,* 295–312.

Sharpsteen, D. J., & Schmalz, C. M. (1988). *Romantic jealousy as a blended emotion.* Unpublished manuscript, University of Denver.

Shaver, P., Schwartz, J., Kirson, D., & O'Connor, C. (1987). Emotion knowledge: Further exploration of a prototype approach. *Journal of Personality and Social Psychology, 52,* 1061–1086.

Shaw, C. R., & McKay, H. D. (1969). *Juvenile delinquency and urban areas.* Chicago: University of Chicago Press.

Shepherd, M. (1961). Morbid jealousy: Some clinical and social aspects of a psychiatric symptom. *Journal of Mental Science, 107,* 607–753.

Sherman, R., & Fredman, N. (1986). *Handbook of structured techniques in marriage and family therapy.* New York: Brunner/Mazel.

Shettel-Neuber, J., Bryson, J. B., & Young, C. E. (1978). Physical attractiveness of the "other person" and jealousy. *Personality and Social Psychology Bulletin, 4,* 612–615.

Short, J. F. (1976). *Delinquency, crime and society.* Chicago: University of Chicago Press.

Shrestha, K., Rees, D. W., Ris, K. J. B., Hore, B. D., & Faragjer, E. B. (1985). Sexual jealousy in alcoholics. *Acta Psychiatrica Scandinavica, 72,* 283–290.

Shweder, R. A. (1985). Menstrual pollution, soul loss, and the comparative study of emotions. In A. Kleinman & B. Good (Eds.), *Culture and depression* (pp. 182–215). Berkeley: University of California Press.

Silberman, C. E. (1978). *Criminal violence, criminal justice.* New York: Random House.

Silverberg, J. (1980). Sociobiology, the new synthesis? An anthropologist's perspective. In G. W. Barlow & J. Silverberg (Eds.), *Sociobiology: Beyond nature/nurture?* (pp. 25–74). Boulder, CO: Westview Press.

Silverstein, C. (1981). *Man to man: Gay couples in America.* New York: Morrow.

Simmel, G. (1950). *The sociology of Georg Simmel* (K. Wolf, Ed.). New York: Free Press.

Skinner, B. F. (1938). *The behavior of organisms: An experimental analysis.* New York: Appleton-Century.

Smith, J. C., & Hogan, B. (1983). *Criminal law* (5th ed.). London: Butterworths.

Smith, J. R., & Smith, L. G. (1970). Co-marital sex and the sexual freedom movement. *Journal of Sex Research, 6,* 131–142.

Smith, L. G., & Smith, J. R. (1973). Co-marital sex: The incorporation of extra-marital sex into the marriage relationship. In J. Money & J. Zubin (Eds.), *Critical issues in contemporary sexual behavior* (pp. 391–408). Baltimore: Johns Hopkins University Press.

Smith, R. H., Kim, S. H., & Parrott, W. G. (1988). Envy and jealousy: Semantic problems and experiential distinctions. *Personality and Social Psychology Bulletin, 14,* 401–409.

Sokoloff, B. (1947). *Jealousy: A psychiatric study.* New York: Howell, Soskin.

Solomon, R. C. (1976). *The passions.* Garden City, NY: Doubleday/Anchor.

Sonkin, D., & Durphy, M. (1983). *Learning to live without violence: A book for men.* San Francisco: Volcano Press.

Sommers, S. (1984). Adults evaluating their emotions: A cross-cultural perspective. In C. Malatesta & C. Izard (Eds.), *Emotion in adult development* (pp. 161–185). Beverly Hills, CA: Sage.

Spielman, P. M. (1971). Envy and jealousy: An attempt at clarification. *Psychoanalytic Quarterly, 40*, 59–82.

Spinoza, B. (1948). *Ethics.* London: Dent. (Original work published 1677)

Staines, G. C., & Libby, P. L. (1986). Men and women in role relationships. In R. D. Ashmore & F. K. Del Boca (Eds.), *The social psychology of female-male relations* (pp. 211–258). New York: Academic Press.

Steinmetz, S. K. (1986). The violent family. In M. Lystad (Ed.), *Violence in the home: Interdisciplinary perspectives.* New York: Brunner/Mazel.

Stekel, W. (1921). *The depths of the soul* (S. A. Tannenbaum, Trans.). London: Kegan Paul.

Sternberg, R. J. (1986). A triangular theory of love. *Psychological Review, 93*, 119–135.

Stets, J., & Pirog-Good, M. A. (1987). Violence in dating relationships. *Social Psychology Quarterly, 50*, 237–246.

Stewart, R. B., & Beatty, M. J. (1985). Jealousy and self-esteem. *Perceptual and Motor Skills, 60*, 153–154.

Stewart, R. B., Mobley, L. A., Van Tuyl, S. S., & Salvador, M. A. (1987). The firstborn's adjustment to the birth of a sibling: A longitudinal assessment. *Child Development, 58*, 341–355.

Straus, E. W. (1966). Shame as a historiological problem. In E. W. Straus, *Phenomenological psychology: Selected papers of Erwin W. Straus.* London: Tavistock.

Straus, M. A. (1978). Wife beating: How common and why. *Victimology, 4*, 52–65.

Strindberg, A. (1964). In M. Meyer (Trans.), *The father.* London: Secker & Warburg. (Original work published 1887)

Stuart, R. B. (1980). *Helping couples change: A social learning approach to marital therapy.* New York: Guilford Press.

Sullivan, H. S. (1953). *The interpersonal theory of psychiatry.* New York: Norton.

Suls, J. M., & Miller, R. L. (1978). Ability comparison and its effect on affiliation preferences. *Human Relations, 31*, 267–282.

Sutton-Smith, B., & Rosenberg, B. G. (1970). *The sibling.* New York: Holt, Rinehart & Winston.

Swartz, M. J., & Jordan, D. K. (1980). *Culture: The anthropological perspective.* New York: Wiley.

Swensen, C. H. (1972). The behavior of love. In H. A. Otto (Ed.), *Love today* (pp. 86–101). New York: Dell.

Symons, D. (1979). *The evolution of human sexuality.* Oxford: Oxford University Press.

Szasz, T. (1960). The myth of mental illness. *American Psychologist, 15*, 113–118.

Taplin, G. (1879). *The folklore, manners, customs, and language of the South Australian Aborigines.* Adelaide: Spiller.

Taylor, M. A. (1981). *The neuropsychiatric mental status examination.* New York: SP Medical & Scientific Books.

Taylor, P. J. (1985). Motives for offending among violent and psychotic men. *British Journal of Psychiatry, 147,* 491–498.

Taylor, P. J., & Gunn, J. (1984). Psychosis and violence. *British Medical Journal, 288,* 1945–1949.

Taylor, P. J., Mahendra, B., & Gunn, J. (1983). Erotomania in males. *Psychological Medicine, 13,* 645–650.

Teismann, M. W. (1979). Jealousy: Systematic, problem-solving therapy with couples. *Family Process, 18,* 151–160.

Teismann, M. W. (1982). Persistent jealousy following the termination of an affair: A strategic approach. In A. S. Gurman (Ed.), *Questions and answers in the practice of family therapy* (Vol. 2). New York: Brunner/Mazel.

Teismann, M. W., & Mosher, D. L. (1978). Jealous conflict in dating couples. *Psychological Reports, 42,* 1211–1216.

Tellenbach, H. (1974). On the nature of jealousy. *Journal of Phenomenological Psychology, 4,* 461–468.

Tennov, D. (1979). *Love and limerance: The experience of being in love.* New York: Stein & Day.

Tesser, A., & Campbell, J. (1982). Self-evaluation maintenance and the perception of friends and strangers. *Journal of Personality, 50,* 261–279.

Tesser, A., & Paulus, D. (1983). The definition of self: Private and public self-evaluation management strategies. *Journal of Personality and Social Psychology, 44,* 672–682.

Tetlock, P. E., & Manstead, A. S. R. (1985). Impression management versus intrapsychic explorations in social psychology: A useful dichotomy? *Psychological Review, 92,* 59–77.

Thibaut, J. W., & Kelley, H. H. (1959). *The social psychology of groups.* New York: Wiley.

Thissen, D., Steinberg, L., Pyszczynski, T., & Greenberg, J. (1983). An item response theory for personality and attitude scales: Item analysis using restricted factor analysis. *Applied Psychological Measurement, 7,* 211–226.

Thomson, A. S. (1859). *The story of New Zealand* (Vol. 1). London: John Murray.

Thornes, B., & Collard, J. (1979). *Who divorces?* London: Routledge & Kegan Paul.

Tiggelaar, J. (1956). Pathological jealousy and jealousy delusions. *Folia Psychiatrica, Neurologica et Neurochirurgica Netherlandia, 59,* 522–541.

Tipton, R. M., Benedictson, C. S., Mahoney, J., & Hartnett, J. (1978). Development of a scale for assessment of jealousy. *Psychological Reports, 42,* 1217–1218.

Todd, J. (1978). The jealous patient. *The Practitioner, 220,* 229–233.

Todd, J., & Dewhurst, K. (1955). The Othello syndrome: A study of the psychopathology of sexual jealousy. *Journal of Nervous and Mental Disease, 122,* 367–374.

Tolstoy, L. (1985). *The Kreutzer sonata and other stories* (D. McDuff, Trans.). Harmondsworth, England: Penguin Books. (Original work published 1889)

Trivers, R. L. (1972). Parental investment and sexual selection. In B. Campbell (Ed.), *Sexual selection and the descent of man, 1871–1971* (pp. 136–179). Chicago: Aldine.

Turbott, J. (1981). Morbid jealousy: An unusual presentation with the reciprocal appearance of psychopathology in either spouse. *Australian and New Zealand Journal of Psychiatry, 15,* 164–167.

Turner, F. (1884). *Samoa.* London: Macmillan.

Turner, R. H. (1970). *Family interaction.* New York: Wiley.

Vaillant, G. E. (1977). *Adaptation to life.* Boston: Little, Brown.

Varni, C. A. (1974). An exploratory study of spouse swapping. In J. R. Smith & L. G. Smith (Eds.), *Beyond monogamy* (pp. 214–229). Baltimore: Johns Hopkins University Press.

Vauhkonen, K. (1968). On the pathogenesis of morbid jealousy. *Acta Psychiatrica Scandinavica,* (Suppl. 202).

Vollmer, H. (1946). Jealousy in children. *American Journal of Orthopsychiatry, 16,* 660–671.

Vuyk, R. (1959). *The child in the two-child family.* Bern, Switzerland: Hans Huber.

Wade, N. (1976). Sociobiology: Troubled birth for a new discipline. *Science, 191,* 1151–1155.

Waelder, R. (1951). The structure of paranoid ideas: A critical survey of various theories. *International Journal of Psycho-Analysis, 32,* 167–177.

Waletzky, L. R. (1979). Husband's problems with breast-feeding. *American Journal of Orthopsychiatry, 49,* 349–352.

Waller, W., & Hill, R. (1951). *The family.* New York: Dryden Press.

Walster, E., & Walster, G. W. (1977). Sexual jealousy. In G. Clanton & L. G. Smith (Eds.), *Jealousy* (pp. 91–99). Englewood Cliffs, NJ: Prentice-Hall.

Walster, E., & Walster, G. W. (1978). *A new look at love.* Reading, MA: Addison-Wesley.

Walster, E., Walster, G. W., & Berscheid, E. (1978). *Equity: Theory and research.* Boston: Allyn & Bacon.

Warner, W. L. (1937). *Black civilization.* New York: Harper & Row.

Wasik, M. (1982). Cumulative provocation and domestic killings. *Criminal Law Review,* 29–38.

Watson, J. W., Switzer, R. E., & Hirschberg, J. C. (1972). *Sometimes I'm jealous.* New York: Golden Press.

Watts, F. N., Powell, G. E., & Austin, S. V. (1973). The modification of abnormal beliefs. *British Journal of Medical Psychology, 46,* 359–363.

Watzlawick, P., Beavin, J., & Jackson, D. (1967). *Pragmatics of human communication.* New York: Norton.

Watzlawick, P., Weakland, J., & Fisch, R. (1974). *Change: Principles of problem formulation and problem resolution.* New York: Norton.

Weeks, J. H. (1914). *Among the primitive Bakango.* London: Seeley, Service.

Weghorst, S. J. (1980, June). *Behavioral correlates of self-reported jealousy in a field experiment.* Paper presented at the meeting of the Animal Behavior Society, Ft. Collins, CO.

Weltfish, G. (1965). *The lost universe.* New York: Basic Books.

West, D. J. (1968). A note on murders in Manhattan. *Medicine, Science and the Law, 8,* 249–255.

West, M. M., & Konner, M. L. (1976). The role of the father: An anthropological perspective. In M. E. Lamb (Ed.), *The role of the father in child development* (pp. 185–218). New York: Wiley.

Westermarck, E. (1936). *The future of marriage in Western civilization.* New York: Macmillan.

Whitaker, C. A. (1975). Psychotherapy of the absurd: With a special emphasis on the psychotherapy of aggression. *Family Process, 14,* 1–16.

White, G. L. (1976). The social psychology of romantic jealousy. *Dissertation Abstracts International, 37,* 5449B–5450B (University Microfilms No. 77-7700).

White, G. L. (1977). *Jealousy and attitudes toward love.* Unpublished manuscript.

White, G. L. (1980a). Inducing jealousy: A power perspective. *Personality and Social Psychology Bulletin, 6,* 222–227.

White, G. L. (1980b). Physical attractiveness and courtship progress. *Journal of Personality and Social Psychology, 39,* 660–668.

White, G. L. (1981a). Jealousy and partner's perceived motives for attraction to a rival. *Social Psychology Quarterly, 44,* 24–30.

White, G. L. (1981b). A model of romantic jealousy. *Motivation and Emotion, 5,* 295–310.

White, G. L. (1981c). Relative involvement, inadequacy, and jealousy: A test of a causal model. *Alternative Lifestyles, 4,* 291–309.

White, G. L. (1981d). *Social comparison, motive attribution, alternatives assessment and coping with jealousy.* Paper presented at the annual meeting of the American Psychological Association, Anaheim, CA.

White, G. L. (1981e). Some correlates of romantic jealousy. *Journal of Personality, 49,* 129–147.

White, G. L. (1984). Comparison of four jealousy scales. *Journal of Research in Personality, 18,* 115–130.

White, G. L. (1985a). *Portrayals of romantic jealousy in television programs.* Unpublished manuscript, University of Auckland.

White, G. L. (1988). *The role of jealousy in premarital relationship conflict, dissolution, and aggression.* Unpublished manuscript, University of California, Santa Cruz.

White, G. L. (1985c). *Gender, power, and romantic jealousy.* Unpublished manuscript, University of Auckland, Auckland, New Zealand.

White, G. L. (1986a). *Romantic jealousy: Secondary appraisal and coping processes.* Manuscript submitted for publication.

White, G. L. (1986b). *Effects of appraisal and coping in romantic jealousy: A longitudinal study.* Unpublished manuscript, University of Auckland, Auckland, New Zealand.

White, G. L., & Devine, K. (in press). Romantic jealousy: Therapists' perception of causes, consequences, and treatment. *Family Relations.*

White, G. L., Fishbein, S., & Rutstein, J. (1981). Passionate love and the misattribution of arousal. *Journal of Personality and Social Psychology, 41,* 56–62.

White, G. L., & Helbick, T. M. (1988). Understanding and treating jealousy. In R. A. Brown & J. R. Field (Eds.), *Treatment of sexual problems in individual and couples therapy*. Boston: PMA Publishing.

Whitehurst, R. N. (1971a). Violently jealous husbands. *Sexual Behaviour, 1*, 32–47.

Whitehurst, R. N. (1971b). Violence potential in extramarital sexual responses. *Journal of Marriage and the Family, 33*, 683–691.

Whitehurst, R. N. (1977). Jealousy and American values. In G. Clanton & L. G. Smith (Eds.), *Jealousy* (pp. 136–139). Englewood Cliffs, NJ: Prentice-Hall.

Wicklund, R. A. (1980). Group contact and self-focused attention. In P. B. Paulus (Ed.), *Psychology of group influence* (pp. 189–208). Hillsdale, NJ: Erlbaum.

Wilson, E. O. (1975). *Sociobiology*. Cambridge, MA: Harvard University Press.

Williams, G. (1978). *Textbook of criminal law*. London: Stevens & Sons.

Wills, T. A. (1985). Supportive functions of interpersonal relationships. In S. Cohen & S. L. Syme (Eds.), *Social support and health* (pp. 61–82). New York: Academic.

Winnicott, D. W. (1977). *The piggle*. London: Hogarth Press.

Wish, M., Deutsch, M., & Kaplan, S. J. (1976). Perceived dimensions of interpersonal relations. *Journal of Personality and Social Psychology, 33*, 409–420.

Wittgenstein, L. (1963). *Philosophical investigations* (G. Anscombe, Trans.) New York: Macmillan.

Wolfgang, M. E. (1958). *Patterns in criminal homicide*. Philadelphia: University of Pennsylvania Press.

Wollheim, R. (1971). *Freud*. London: Fontana.

Wylie, R. C. (1974). *The self-concept: A review of methodological considerations and measuring instruments*. Lincoln: University of Nebraska Press.

Xenophon. (1923). *Memorabilia* (E.G. Marchant, Trans.). London: Heinemann. (Original work written ca. 380 B.C.)

Yate, W. (1835). *An account of New Zealand*. London: Seeley & Burnside.

Zeldin, T. (1977). *France 1848–1945* (Vol. 2). London: Oxford University Press.

Zetterberg, H. L. (1966). The secret ranking. *Journal of Marriage and the Family, 28*, 134–142.

Zillmann, D. (1983). Transfer of excitation in emotional behavior. In J. T. Petty & R. Cacioppo (Eds.), *Social psychophysiology: A sourcebook* (pp. 215–240). New York: Guilford Press.

Zola, E. (1956). *The beast in man* (A. Brown, Trans.). London: Elek Books. (Original work published 1890)

Index